The Hole

Another look at the sinking of the *Estonia* ferry on September 28, 1994

Drew Wilson

Drew Wilson © Copyright 2006, 2013

All rights reserved

No parts of this publication may be reproduced, stored in aretrieval system, or transmitted in any form or by anymeans, electronic, mechanical, photocopying, recording orotherwise without the prior permission of the copyrightowner.

British Library Cataloguing In Publication Data
A Record of this Publication is available
from the British Library

ISBN 1492778362
978-1-49277-836-3

First Published by Exposure Publishing in 2006
Second edition published by Drew Wilson in 2013

Cover design: Giedre Karsokiene

Contents

Notes to the second edition / 7
Foreword / 11

PART ONE: Escape
    1 . The Labyrinth / 27

PART TWO: Explanations
    2 . Government Version of the Disaster / 47
    3 . The Logic of the Hole / 53

PART THREE: Three Events that Shaped the Investigation
    4 . Cult of the Visor / 65
    5 . The Dive to the Shipwreck / 71
    6 . Concrete Blanket / 81

PART FOUR: The Backdrop
    7 . 1994: Chaos Unleashed / 91

PART FIVE: Alternative Scenarios

    7. Alternative Scenarios / 111

    8. Hit and Run / 113

    9. Dark Signature / 153

    10. Baltic Drainpipe / 189

    11. The Consignment / 199

    12. Cocktail Effect / 211

PART SIX: Hidden Agendas

    13. Detours / 223

    14. Strategic Compassion / 239

    15. Conclusion: A Work in Progress / 261

POSTSCRIPTS

    A. The Struggle to Explain the Swift Sinking / 275

    B. The Historical Spotlight / 293

APPENDICES

    I. Recovery Charts / 298

    II. Kalmar Chart / 300

    III. Felix Report Excerpts / 301

    IV. The Submarine Fax / 308

    V. FOIA Responses / 313

    VI. Classified request for cargo / 316

    VII. Undersea tracks / 317

    VIII. Timeline of Key Events / 318

    IX. Glossary / 322

List of Illustrations / 324
Sources / 325
Notes / 335

The Hole

Motor Vessel *Estonia*

Flag: Republic of Estonia
Builder: Jos L. Meyer Shipyard, Papenburg, Germany
Date built: 1980
Type: Passenger ferry, roll on-roll off (ro-ro)
Length (meters): 155,40 Breadth 24.20 Maximum draft 5.60
Gross Tonnage: 15,598
Maximum Capacity: Passengers and crew 2000; trucks 47; cars 460.
Owner: Estline, a 50/50 joint venture between Estonian
Shipping Co Ltd (Estonia) and Nordström & Thulin AB (Sweden).
Captain: Arvo Andresson, Estonian, 40
Relief Captain: Avo Piht, Estonian, 40
Route: Tallinn, Estonia to Stockholm, Sweden
First sailing: February 1993
Final sailing: September 27, 1994
(Photo: Courtesy of Pär-Henrik Sjöström)

Notes to the second edition

This version of *The Hole* is not an update but a reprint of the first edition, published in 2006. Although three new items have been added to the appendix and a few minor text changes related to spelling, grammar and clarity have been made, the versions are exactly the same.

Since 2006, no news has been revealed about the cause of the disaster, though a few events are worth summarizing.

In 2005, public pressure in Estonia resulted in the formation of an Estonian government group to investigate the official Joint Accident Investigation Commission (JAIC) report, which was concluded in 1997. Led by Margus Kurm, the Estonian group did not organize a dive to examine the wreck, but rather looked over evidence made available and asked questions. They concluded that the ship could have went down the way the JAIC described only if one looks at "the hitherto collected evidence." But the way in which the ferry sank ("sinking mechanics") does not "exclude scenarios that presume a hole in the bottom of the hull or entry of water to the vehicle deck other than through the bow ramp."

The report continued: "If it is desirable to prove that the hull is intact, the exterior of the wreck must be systematically studied and the study activities must be duly recorded. As we know, this has never been done."

Kurm's group essentially said that with the available evidence, several conclusions are likely, including the official one. It's a political answer. Even though the report doesn't satisfy all parties, it doesn't take sides. And of course, key questions are left unanswered.

The second event involves a Freedom of Information Act request to the US National Security Agency about information concerning the *Estonia* ferry sinking. In the first edition of *The Hole*, I reprinted the NSA's response to an initial request in 2002, which says documents exist but the request is denied because their release would severely damage US national security.

In 2009, I resubmitted my FOIA request for documents, hoping that the new presidential administration would bring in a refreshing policy of openness.

The NSA's response repeated that *Estonia* ferry documents remain classified as "secret" because if released, they could severely damage national security. The NSA did provide a bit more detail: "…the CIA has asked that we protect non-substantive information" the letter read. In other words, nothing could be released, even if the sensitive text was blacked out (the letter is one of the new items in the appendix).

Neither the Kurm investigation nor the 2009 FOIA response prove anything. But they do support the suspicions of many who would like to know why information about a Scandinavian sea accident due to a supposed technical flaw would, 15 years later, be reexamined by Estonian authorities and kept classified by the US government.

On one level the *Estonia* disaster is a tragic passenger ship accident in which nearly 1000 people died in some 35 minutes. On another level, the catastrophe is about geopolitics after the fall of the Soviet Union – an incredible rearrangement of the global political system when advantage and power was the reward for those who acted outside the law. *The Hole* is not just a report on the details of the sinking, but a reminder that even the most democratic and transparent governments will disregard the public interest, even in an civilian accident, whenever politically expedient.

In 2013, the *Estonia* still rests just 38 kilometers off the coast of Finland on a slope only 50-80 meters depth. The fact that Sweden still prevents the ferry from being scientifically examined is astonishing.

Drew Wilson
October 2013
Estoniaferry@gmail.com

Foreward

Caught in the periscope crosshairs, the ship was a colossal target. German built, crammed with passengers, it plowed through the Baltic Sea like a moving mountain.

The Soviet submarine fired three torpedoes, pitchfork style. The underwater missiles tore through the liner's hull in the bow, center and engine room, sending the ship into a sharp starboard list. Thousands of tons of seawater rushed inside. People were thrown against walls or into the sea. Lights went out. Emergency measures had no time to unfold. Lifeboats couldn't be launched. Confused passengers fought to get off the sinking ship.

The sub had scored a triple hit. Despite the liner's superb German engineering and construction that held a justified reputation for withstanding extraordinary forces, its hull was torn open.

That was January 1945. More than 7000 people died as the *Wilhelm Gustloff*, with holes in the hull bigger than houses, sank to the bottom of the Baltic Sea in about 50 minutes.[1]

Almost 50 years later, in a different part of the Baltic Sea, another German-built vessel plied the waterway, this time on a cruise from Tallinn, Estonia to Stockholm, Sweden. With about one thousand passengers, the *M/V Estonia* ferry sailed its thrice-weekly tourist route, never straying too far from the southern coast of Finland.

In the early morning hours of September 28, 1994, high waves from an autumn storm reportedly wrenched loose the *Estonia's* visor door at the front of the ship. As the visor popped off, it tugged open the cardeck ramp, a second barrier to the sea. Seawater flooded onto the middle deck, the ship listed to starboard and never flipped back upright. In 35 minutes the *Estonia* had dropped to the bottom of the Baltic Sea, taking some 850 people to their death.

The 16,000-ton ferry with an intact hull, deemed seaworthy by the highest maritime authorities in Northern Europe, had sunk faster than the thrice-torpedoed *Wilhelm Gustloff* with the demolished hull.

How could that be possible?

Seawater takes time to fill up seven decks of a 150-meter long ship. Closed cabin doors and watertight areas of the ferry's intricate interior serve as barriers that slow water intake. The hull itself, which the ship normally floats on, is remarkably buoyant. Anybody who has tried to push an air mattress or inflated tire underwater can attest to the resisting force of trapped air. The *Estonia* ferry should have floated on its side for hours, if not for days.

But the Joint Accident Investigation Commission's Final Report on the sinking, which took three years to complete and involved Sweden, Estonia and Finland, gave no explanation of how the *Estonia* could go under in 35 minutes without a hole in the hull. No explanation at all, leaving the phenomenon open to interpretation.

The premise of this book is simple: The hull of the *Estonia* had a breach of integrity below the waterline that facilitated the rapid fall to the bottom of the Baltic Sea. The *Estonia* had a hole.

Challenging the government's Final Report, this book highlights the ignored issues and inconsistencies of the official findings. It puts the disaster back into its historical context--the cynical world that unfolded as the U.S.S.R. collapsed, when state priorities shifted and law became elastic or was thrown aside.

I speculate on alternative causes for the sinking, but I draw no conclusions. A scenario may have a curious degree of plausibility, but that does not make it true. In fact, no definitive explanation for the disaster exists--including the Final Report. The answer is about 60 meters deep in the Baltic Sea, the spot where the ferry rests, a spot militarily guarded by Sweden. An impartial examination is forbidden.

The broader aim of this book is to fan the embers of public debate over the 20th century's worst peacetime disaster in European waters, which Sweden has worked hard to smother.

The *Estonia* catastrophe has dozens of detours and side issues, many with more than one interpretation that fall outside the scope of this book. I did not explore technical or regulatory issues such as ferry stability or ferry safety, topics that have been exhaustively analyzed in other books and reports by highly-qualified authorities.

In writing about the *Estonia* disaster, I am boarding a moving train. Other researchers who had already uncovered useful information offered me a seat. I am particularly grateful to Knut Carlqvist, journalist and historian in Sweden; Werner Hummel, the marine claims detective who investigated the *Estonia* case and Jutta Rabe, investigative journalist, both in Germany. Thanks also go to U.S. Col. Ret. Alexander Einseln, former head of the Estonian Armed Forces, for help with sources and information, the Finnish Accident Investigation Board for willingness to answer questions, to the International Transport Workers Federation in London for the use of their maritime library and to all others who gave up their time to talk to me.

This book took nearly three years to research and write, mainly because it involved hunting down information in several countries with different languages and divergent ideas about openness. I have tried hard to avoid inaccuracies and anonymous sources. The complexity of the disaster and its unresolved status mean there will be changes and amendments to the official record that will very likely affect this text.

Drew Wilson
March 2006

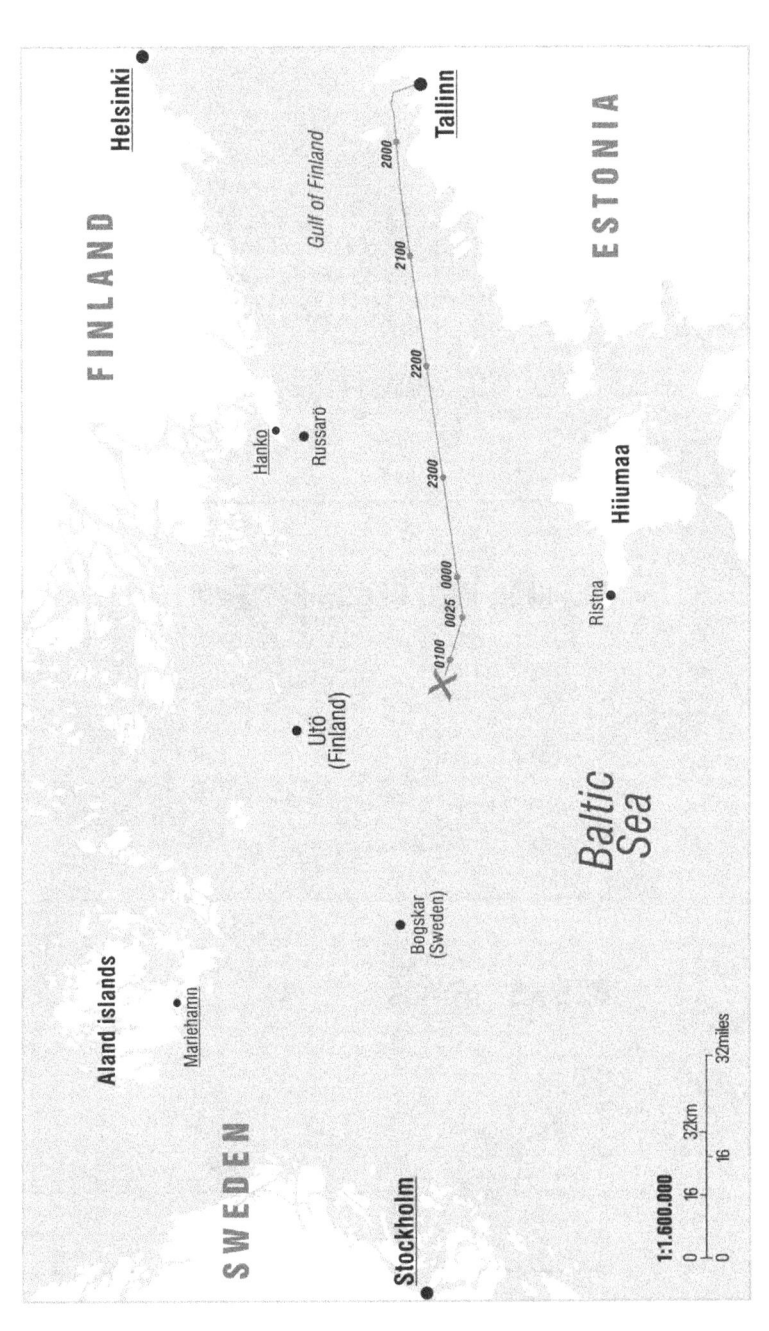

Accident site. The *Estonia* left Tallinn around 19:15 on September 27, 1994 en route to Stockholm. It encountered trouble somewhere around 01:00 and went down halfway through the journey, not far from the Finnish island of Utö. The shipwreck containing most of the 757 missing victims remains there today, in about 60 meters of water.

16 THE HOLE

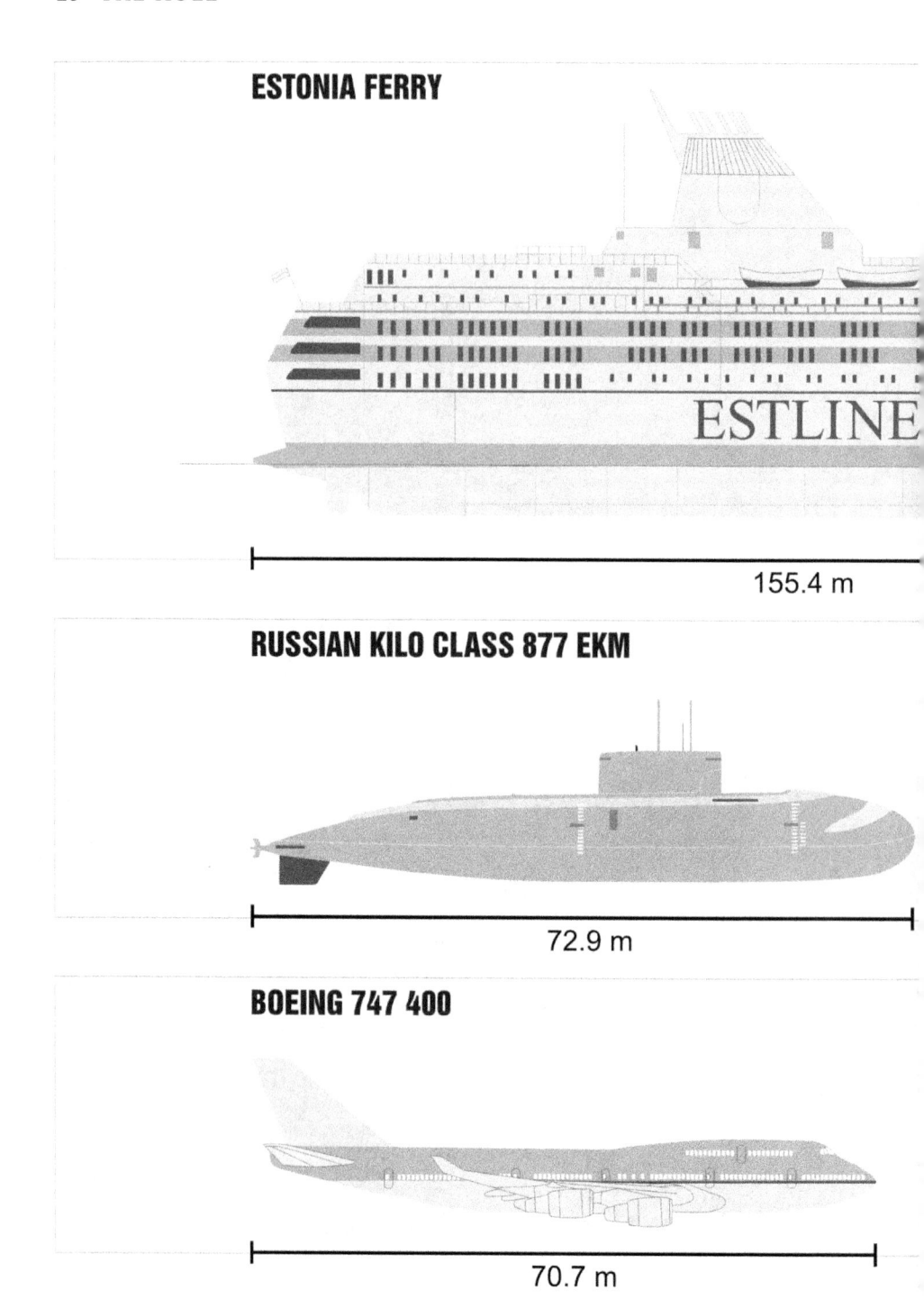

ESTONIA FERRY

|———————————————————————————|
155.4 m

RUSSIAN KILO CLASS 877 EKM

|———————————————|
72.9 m

BOEING 747 400

|———————————————|
70.7 m

1:80
0   8   16m

PART ONE

Escape

20 THE HOLE

DECK ONE

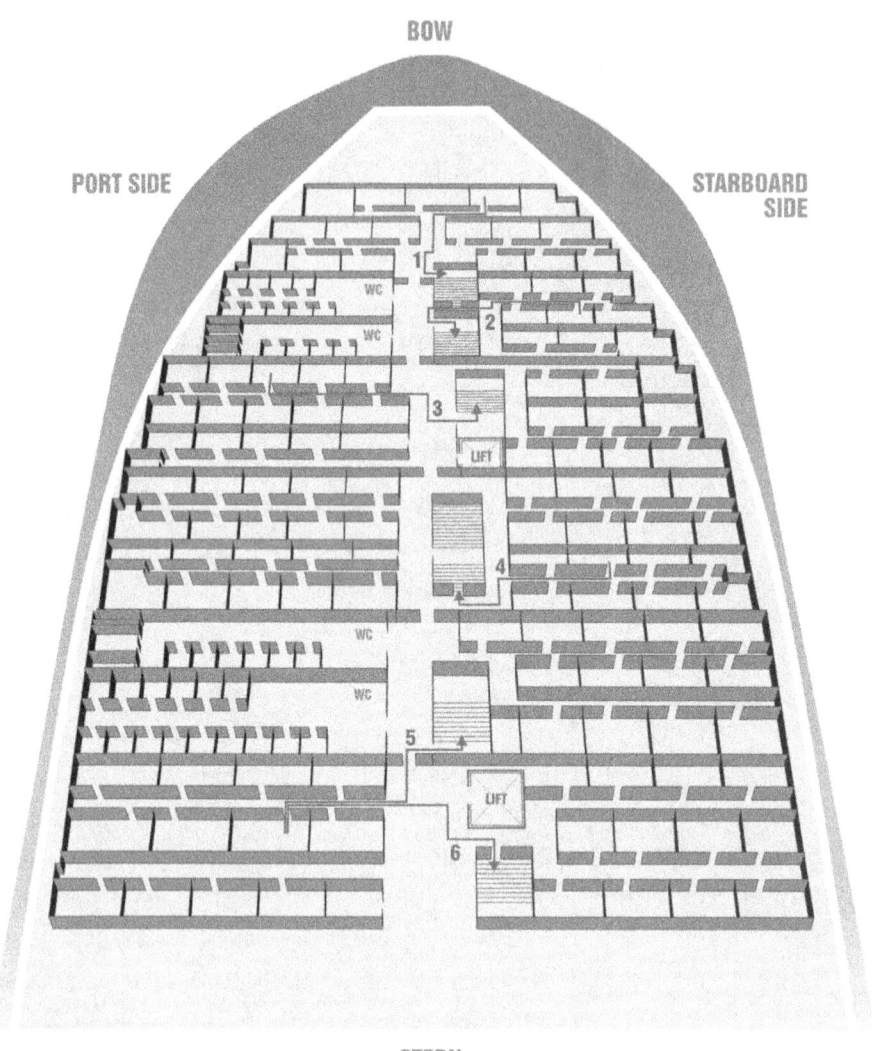

BOW

PORT SIDE

STARBOARD SIDE

STERN

The *Estonia* was as high as a ten-story building, the interior a labyrinth. For the fresh passenger, finding the way from the first deck to the exit several decks above, in calm seas, requires a knack for direction. Stairways don't go straight to the top decks. Long corridors could lead to dead ends and locked doors.

Estonia passengers had to get to the Deck 7 exit at the top of the ferry and move outside. As the list exceeded 30 degrees, escape demanded fast decisions, agility and raw strength. The lights would go out. A directional mistake probably meant dying.

#1 and #2 These stairwells stop at the cardeck one floor above. A passenger would have to come back down and start over.
#3 Stairwell goes up to Deck 7, but opens to wide foyer that becomes treacherous when the ship tilts. Elevators aren't safe; they could stop during a list.
#4 Stairs lead to the fourth deck and stop. A passenger must then step outside, walk about five meters to another door and re-enter the ferry in order to continue to higher decks.
#5 Leads to Deck 4 and opens to another foyer that must be negotiated to find the continuing stairwell.
#6 Stairwell stops at Deck 5, requiring a desperate search for the continuing stairwell.

01:00-01:15

The *Estonia* ferry bounces at high speed through stormy seas. Most passengers are in their cabins sleeping.

Around 1:00, two loud, unnatural banging sounds are heard in various parts of the ship.

The Labyrinth

Deck 4

The ship's accountant woke up on the carpeted floor of her cabin. Her shoulder hurt. She'd been flung out of bed.

Her name was Siiri Same (Sah-may). Among other things, Siiri's job was to ensure the money from the ferry's shops, restaurants, bars and currency exchange was counted and secured.

She grabbed the chrome wall railing and managed to turn on the light. Her cabin mate, another Estonian girl, lay sprawled in front of her, talking as people do when they dream. Siiri shook her and they both dressed.

The floor tilted in the direction of the door. She knew the ferry would soon swing back to a level position--that's the way ships normally behave in rough seas.

But over the ship's loudspeaker, a woman's strained voice repeatedly said *"Haire,"* the word for "alarm" in Estonian. The alarm required crewmembers to go to specific stations on the ferry. Siiri put on extra warm clothes. Her station was the top deck at the back of the ship--outside.

The cabin door was blocked. A wardrobe closet had fallen over. A table, cassettes, books, dresser drawers and clothes had piled up and the two girls flung them away. The cabin door opened inward and faced starboard side. Due to the ship's starboard tilt, the door would have to be almost lifted open like a hatch. Siiri pulled the door handle and her friend hefted the door edge, opening it. The corridor was empty.

There were two ways to run. Left, to the closest stairway and right to the farthest. As crewmembers, both girls knew the ship's layout well. The plan was to get upstairs. But with a starboard list, was one way safer than the other?

Some instinct urged them to the right. They dashed down the corridor to the far stairwell in the rear of the ferry, a simple decision that kept them alive. Moving left, they would have emerged into a wide-open foyer. Because of the ship's tilt, the two could have tumbled several meters and smashed into the wall.

The ferry's structure groaned. Siiri hurried toward the rear, her steps both careful and clumsy like someone running across a fence top. Then she stumbled, and disappeared.

Deck 1

Four men reclined in two sets of bunk beds in the cabin. The four worked together in the municipal government of the Estonian region called Katrina Wald. One was Jaan Stern, age 53.

The group was headed to Stockholm where they would board a train to Norway. A Norwegian regional government had invited them as part of a program extending technical help to post-Soviet Estonia.

The cabins were austere and noisy, with bunk beds that made them look like military barracks. Estonians had little spending money. If Estonians took the ferry, they opted for the $25 budget cabins below the waterline on the first deck. When a wave struck, the hull reverberated and creaked as the cabin rose and fell, until the next impact.

The ferry pounded through the rough sea at high speed. Motion-sensitive car alarms blared on the cardeck above, barely audible due to the constant rumbling from the hull. Some of Jaan Stern's friends were nervous.

In earlier years, Stern had served as part of a tank crew in the Soviet army. He'd also worked in a shipbuilding factory, knew something about how vessels were built, and reassured his friends that all was well with the ferry. Wave collisions were like turbulence on an airline.

Then the impact noises abruptly changed. Suddenly the loud bangs didn't sound like waves. They were unnatural sounds, Stern thought.

The cabin fell momentarily silent and the ferry started to tilt starboard. Swedish words, confused and loud, came from the corridor. What was happening? Stern couldn't open the door to find out because luggage had slid in front of it.

The men cleared the doorway, but the increasingly slanted floor made them stumble. When Stern pulled away the final and bulkiest suitcase, he saw ankle-high water along the wall. Sterns' cabin was on the lowest passenger deck of the ship and located under the sea. If water was down here, then upstairs must be flooded.

"Guys, let's get off quick!" Stern yelled. As the others dressed, Stern bolted out the door in his underwear. The instinct to flee was not rational, but he felt like a passenger in a car that someone else was driving. He had to get upstairs and out of the ferry.

The angled stairwell slowed his climb. He steadied himself by grasping the wobbly railing, fastened to the wall by a few screws. Three other passengers also gripped it. One was a crying child. Stern was forced to move around them. Stopping to help meant sacrificing himself.

01:15-01:30

Siiri lay inside a cabin. Her ribs burned. While running down the corridor, she'd stepped on one of the cabin doors, which had become part of the floor due to the tilt. But cabin doors weren't designed to be jumped on. Her drop into the cabin was not much different than falling off a roof.

She crawled toward the door and wrestled her way out, holding the doorjamb. Her shoulder was numb. One shoe was gone. She slid the other off her foot to keep balance and moved on, now mindful to step over the cabin doors. Her roommate was gone. The two would never meet again.

She arrived at the rear stairwell. In an upright ferry, the stairwell was little more than a meter wide. With the tilt, going upstairs was something like crawling on hands and knees through a shaft. Both hands held the railing tightly to help her pivot each time the stairway turned to the next deck.

On Deck 5, the top half of the duty-free shop's glass door had broken. The shards on the bottom half became a potential guillotine, as slanted floors were slippery. Luckily, Deck 5 was not her goal.

Siiri maneuvered past people who had fallen or frozen in place; the choice was cruel and plain: stop to help and share their fate or keep moving.

She emerged on Deck 7, the top floor that held the nightclub--and the door to the outside. With the ship askew, the big dancefloor was now a steep incline with no rope to climb it.

A mess accumulated at the bottom starboard side: broken bar glasses and bottles of liquor, loose chairs, coffee cups, ash trays, chairs, purses, shoes and people. One man with a bloody face sat against the wall as if he had just awakened. Some people appeared to be unconscious. Anything that wasn't bolted down when the ferry listed had piled up at the wall.

Siiri knew she had to step outside and stand on portside of the hull, which by now was nearly a level plane. According to crew training, the portside rear was her rendezvous point in an emergency and she had to be there. The door leading outside was her target. But getting there meant running up a steep incline. In fact, it meant leaping up some three meters to the door that led to the outside deck. It was a stupid challenge. Almost like asking someone to jump up to a second-floor balcony.

Tables were floor mounted. Theoretically she could climb up from table to table, like someone at an indoor mountain climbing gym, until she reached the door that was becoming the ceiling. But if she fell, her body would bash against the bolted tables on the way down like the ball in a pinball game.

There were no ropes, nothing to hold onto to pull herself toward the door. As she looked for an escape, the enormous ferry suddenly rolled back to portside. Moving with the momentum, Siiri ran toward the door and grabbed the doorjamb before the *Estonia* rocked back to starboard. As she held on, a man emerged from outside and pulled her through.

Outside in the wind and rain, she stood on the side of the ship. Because of the storm, a person had to yell to be heard. Other crewmembers were there in life jackets. Someone had managed to open a lifejacket storage box. She grabbed an orange vest and threw them to other passengers.

The storm was severe. Like a breathing organism, the sea rushed up to within a few meters, then receded so fast it looked she stood on a rooftop. Siiri was in jeans and a t-shirt. Maybe 20 minutes had passed since waking on the cabin floor.

34 THE HOLE

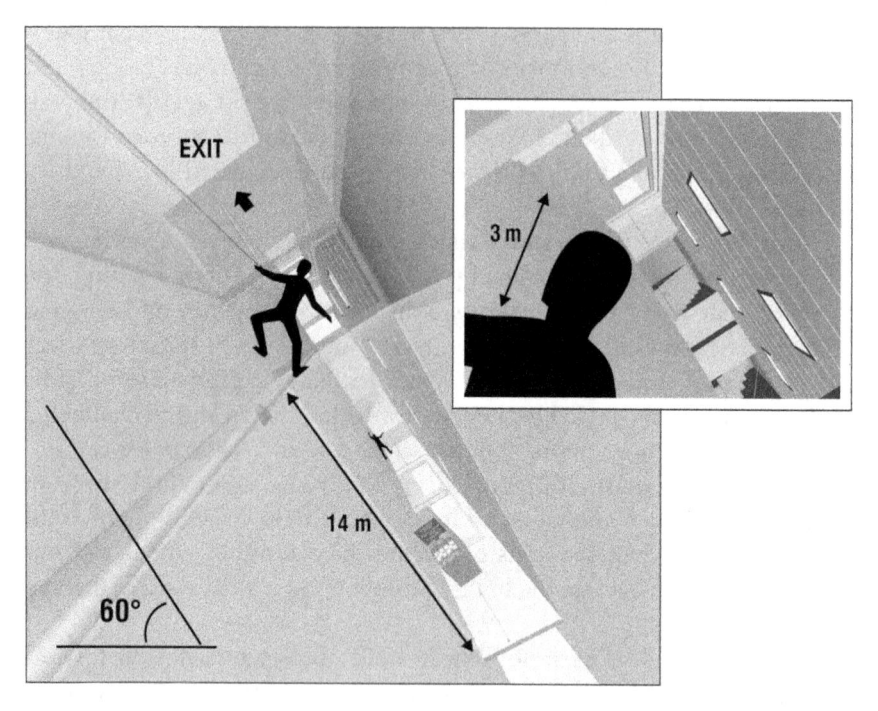

The end of a corridor opened to a foyer. A passenger had to run uphill about three meters and grab the exit door. Doors to the outside opened outward, requiring a surge of strength. Failing to grab and hold the door meant falling downhill and tumbling into a wall. Choices had to be made fast. The ship continued to rotate starboard, increasing the angle.

* * *

Stern arrived at the last deck. The narrow stairway shaft had ended. Now he faced a foyer as big as any hotel lobby. The problem was, the lobby was angled. To reach temporary safety outside the ship, he had to seize the railing on the opposite wall, the portside wall, and pull himself up and out the exit door. How can a person walk up a steep ramp with nothing to hold onto?

Someone half his age would have trouble attempting it; most men couldn't even do a couple pull-ups.

The ferry abruptly rocked back toward port, just for a moment, before resettling on its starboard side. The motion was enough to fling Stern across the open foyer, as if jerked by a leash. Instinctively, he grabbed the railing and muscled his way out the door.

On the outside deck, rain pelted his face. Someone shoved a lifejacket into his hands and instructed him to follow. Stern carried the lifejacket with him.

On normal voyages, passengers liked to lean on the ferry's long deck rail and stare at the sea. The rail was a favorite spot for photographs. Now people shuffled across the rail like on a balance beam, some passengers hunched over to hold it more securely. It was slippery and Stern was barefoot. No one wanted to tumble into the sea.

He moved toward the bow, ending at the bulbous bow--a steel protrusion normally under the hull that's useful in punching through ice. A couple of dozen people in lifejackets were also there, flinching from wave spray. He couldn't make out what they were shouting over the wind or why they had chosen to stand here.

The ferry's lights flickered, then went out. Had Stern still been in the ferry, the darkness would have stopped his escape. Adrenalin kept his naked body from freezing in the autumn storm. He thrust an arm through the life vest, but the wind snatched it away.

01:30-01:50

Stern crawled on all fours toward the bulbous bow. Decision time had arrived. He knew he had to jump some 15 meters into the dark sea, but did not want to do it. He reasoned that if he held on and waited, the ship would float and he'd eventually be rescued. But he didn't really believe it. Still, no way he would jump. But as the ferry filled with seawater and rotated further, he fell into the sea.

The Baltic felt surprisingly warm, though it was actually 11 degrees (52 F). Stern tasted saltwater, surfaced and saw the crippled 155-meter *Estonia*. He'd fallen on the starboard side--the best side because the ferry helped block the house-size waves coming from port.

He saw an upside down life raft--basically a pup tent on a circular platform, inverted--swam to it and grabbed a dangling rope. But he couldn't pull himself in.

"Give me your hand, I'll help you!" someone shouted in Estonian.

A man pulled Stern onto the raft, where he collapsed and caught his breath. Another man sprawled out beside him had a rope line double-wrapped around his hand. Below the three, inside the inverted pup tent was an air pocket that contained another survivor.

Storm conditions worsened. The first thing Stern did was wrap one of the raft's dangling ropes around his arm. If waves upended the raft, he would tumble with it.

* * *

Siiri stood on the port side of the ferry. Her duty in an emergency was to cut the rope lines holding cylinders that contained inflatable rafts and ensure they opened. She and other crewmembers worked at the task.

It seemed to happen all at once: A wave's threatening roar, intuitively grasped as the buildup and imminent release of tremendous energy, followed by a wash of seawater that blinded Siiri, turned her head, slid her feet, raised her body and thrust it forward. For a moment she felt herself twirling, feet first. As the wave spent its energy, it spun her around a deck railing in a propeller motion before she was dislodged and flung into the sea.

Then she sank. Siiri had been a competitive swimmer in high school and at Tartu University in Estonia. She was not afraid of the sea. But the fast downward momentum continued, and the deeper she went the more she feared not coming back up.

Underwater, it was quiet. No storm, no screaming, no crashing waves. The water even started to feel warm. She saw herself, her own body, sinking into the water and felt a comfortable sensation. When thoughts fixed on her six-year-old son, she understood it was not time to give up. Thrashing upwards, she broke the surface in a burst of breath.

Moving clouds revealed moonlight and the storm erupted in intervals. She shivered violently. Something was wrong with her shoulder and her chest. Ten meters away was the *Estonia* ferry, its roof and mast spotlights now level with the sea. A wave shoved her underwater, and again she swam to the surface.

The *Estonia's* life rafts were scattered around the sea. The wind blew one toward Siiri and she grabbed it. Inching around the raft with her hands, she found the door flap but had no energy to pull herself in. Getting inside required the same exertion as a swimmer trying to get into a boat. From the door flap, a man emerged and tried to yank her inside, but couldn't. A knife-like pain stabbed her shoulder and ribs.

Siiri knew the rafts had rope ladders, but through the rain and waves she couldn't find one. Gripping the edge of the raft, she lifted her legs inside the opening and tried wriggle inside feet first, but her legs cramped and she had to drop them. Then, underwater, one leg brushed against the ladder. As the raft bobbed, she put her knee in the rung and worked her torso toward the door flap until the man inside grabbed the belt loops of her jeans and tugged. She flew into the raft.

Inside was a pile of half-naked passengers, shivering and crying. One man prayed in a strange language. Water sprayed in continuously and a survivor bailed out what he could with a cup. The door flap had to stay open however. If the flap was closed and a wave overturned the raft, they would die trying to fight their way out underwater.

Life rafts such as this one were blown around the sea and rolled over by waves. Few were lucky enough to get inside. Many life rafts floated upside down. Survivors clung to the sides or lay on the upturned bottom. Life boats, by comparison, could not be launched and went down with the ferry.

Life rafts such as this one were blown around the sea and rolled over by waves. Few were lucky enough to get inside. Many life rafts floated upside down. Survivors clung to the sides or lay on the upturned bottom. Life boats, by comparison, could not be launched and went down with the ferry.

*   *   *

The moon emerged occasionally to illuminate the sea. The *Estonia* ferry lay on its side, sitting so low the emergency lights were barely visible. For some moments, the sea was still. Then, in a fast, continuous motion, the ferry's stern disappeared underwater as the bow rose in the air. Someone still on the bridge sounded the claxon horn, the final warning that the ship was lost. Was it the captain? The *Estonia* towered above the small rafts briefly, then slid forward into the sea.

Every 10 meters the ferry sank, another 15 pounds of water pressure exerted force on the superstructure. Increasing pressure caused some walls to buckle and the larger windows to pop out. Huge air bubbles drifted up in the darkness. The ship struck the bottom, bounced and rolled in slow motion, creating thin clouds of silt. The *Estonia* came to rest almost upside down at a depth of about 60 meters.

02:00-07:30

Cold water pulls heat from the body 25 times faster than cold air does. The body shakes violently in the beginning stages of hypothermia. The blood flows out of the arms and legs to protect the vital organs and the skin starts to turn blue. A person loses mental and physical control. In their final throes, some survivors in rafts would begin rolling their eyes and thrashing arms and legs before losing consciousness and dying.

Sitting in the raft, Siiri fought the pull of sleep. She glanced at her arms and in the dark her skin looked purple.

The sky suddenly lit up. Somebody in another raft had fired a flare gun. Other ferries were only a short distance away. In fact, the ferries seemed to be surrounding them, enclosing them in a circle to block the rough seas.

She drifted in and out of consciousnesses. Something told her not to sleep. When the body's temperature is low, sleep meant death. Instead she thought about her son. Hours passed.

The coast of Finland was some 38 kilometers (24 miles) away. Moreover, just a little more than an hour's flying time, near the Denmark Straits, a flotilla of ships, jets and helicopters from at least a dozen countries had gathered for a NATO training exercise including emergency sea rescue techniques. They did not assist.

In Jaan Stern's upturned and slowly deflating raft, the men held tightly to the ropes. They constantly shifted their weight so it wouldn't tip over when struck by waves.

After a few hours, as night turned to dawn, they heard helicopters. A sea rescue helicopter from Finland hovered over Stern's raft. A man on a cable descended and attached a sling to Stern and lifted him. It was 7 a.m.

About the same time, a man from another rescue helicopter was lowered on a line to Siiri's raft. When he put a lifting belt around her, she screamed. Doctors would later tell her she'd broken her ribs close to her lungs, broken her shoulder in three places, and cut her leg muscles to the bone. Days passed before she could stand.

Some 750 people went down with the *Estonia* ferry. Death was not instantaneous. Medical and technical experts estimated that any passenger trapped in air pockets inside the *Estonia* could survive a maximum of 30 minutes.

Any survivor inside the wreck 60 meters below would be shivering, forcing the body's metabolic rate up to help raise body temperature, which in turn would mean rapid breathing and an increase in the poisonous carbon monoxide that people exhale. Suffocation from soaring carbon dioxide levels would cause death for many of the trapped victims.

Pressure at that depth and the cold temperature also create disorientation and lethargy. If conscious passengers were among those that sank with the ship, perhaps they didn't comprehend how close to death they were and that lack of knowledge had provided some mercy.

PART TWO

Explanations

Government Version of the Disaster

To investigate the catastrophe, the Joint Accident Investigation Commission (JAIC), with members from Sweden, Estonia and Finland, was set up shortly after the ferry sank. In December 1997, the JAIC delivered its Final Report, representing the government's official explanation for the disaster.

In summary . . .

The Estonian-flagged ro-ro passenger ferry *Estonia* departed from Tallinn, the capital of Estonia, on 27 September 1994 at 1915 hrs [Estonian time] for a scheduled voyage to Stockholm, the capital of Sweden. She carried 989 people, 803 of whom were passengers.

The voyage proceeded normally. Sea conditions along the Estonian coast were moderate, but became more rough when the ship left the sheltered waters. The ship had a slight starboard list due to a combination of athwartships weight disposition, cargo disposition and wind pressure on the port side.

As the voyage continued, the wind velocity increased gradually and the wind veered to south-west. Visibility was generally more than 10 nautical miles. At midnight the wind was south-westerly 15-20 m/ps with a significant wave height of 3-4 meters. The rolling and pitching of the vessel increased gradually, and some passengers became seasick.

At about 0025 hrs the *Estonia* reached a midpoint in its journey and headed on course 287° toward Stockholm. The speed was about 14 knots and the vessel encountered the seas on her port bow.

Due to increasing rolling, the fin stabilizers were extended.

On the cardeck, the seaman of the watch heard shortly before 0100 hrs a metallic bang from the bow area as the vessel hit a heavy wave. He reported the noise, checked the visor locking system and told the bridge that everything seemed to be normal.

At 0100 hrs a crew shift change took place on the bridge.

Further observations of unusual noise, starting at about 0105 hrs, were made during the following 10 minutes by many passengers and some crew members who were off duty in their cabins.

When the seaman of the watch returned from his round, soon after the change of watches, he caught up with the captain and entered the bridge just behind him. Shortly afterwards he was sent back down to the cardeck to find out the cause of the sounds. He did not, however, manage to reach the cardeck.

At about 0115 hrs the visor separated from the bow and tilted over the stem. The ramp was pulled fully open, allowing large amounts of water to enter the cardeck. Very rapidly the ship took on a heavy starboard list. She was turned to port and slowed down.

Passengers started to rush up the staircases and panic developed at many places. Many passengers were trapped in their cabins and had no chance of getting out in time.

Lifejackets were distributed to those passengers who managed to reach the boat deck. They jumped or were washed into the sea.

At about 0120 hrs a weak female voice called *"Haire, haire, laeval on haire"* the Estonian words for "Alarm, alarm, there is alarm on the ship," over the public address system.

A first Mayday call from the *Estonia* was received at 0122 hrs. A second Mayday call was transmitted shortly afterwards and by 0124 hrs 14 ship-and-shore-based radio stations had received the Mayday calls.

At about this time all four main engines had stopped. The main generators stopped somewhat later and the emergency generator started automatically, supplying power to essential equipment and to limited lights in public areas and on deck. The ship was now drifting, lying across the seas.

The list to starboard increased and water had started to enter the accommodation decks. Flooding of the accommodation continued with considerable speed and the starboard side of the ship was submerged at about 0130 hrs. During the final stage of flooding the list was more than 90 degrees. The ship sank rapidly, stern first, and disappeared from the radar screens of ships in the area at about 0150 hrs.

Rescue efforts were initiated. About one hour after the *Estonia* had sunk, four passenger ferries in the vicinity arrived on the scene of the accident. Rescue helicopters were summoned and the first one arrived at 0305 hrs.

During the night and early morning, helicopters and assisting ships rescued 138 people, of whom one later died in hospital. During the day and on the two following days 92 bodies were recovered. Most of the missing persons accompanied the vessel to the seabed.1

The JAIC's Final Report concluded the *Estonia* had been seaworthy and properly manned. The cargo had been secured and displaced to a normal standard and the bow visor closed and secured on departure.

According to the JAIC, the accident was caused by a technical fault in the design of the ship. The bow visor locks, installed by the Jos. L. Meyer GmbH shipyard in Germany, weren't strong enough to withstand the wave forces on the night of the accident and they broke.

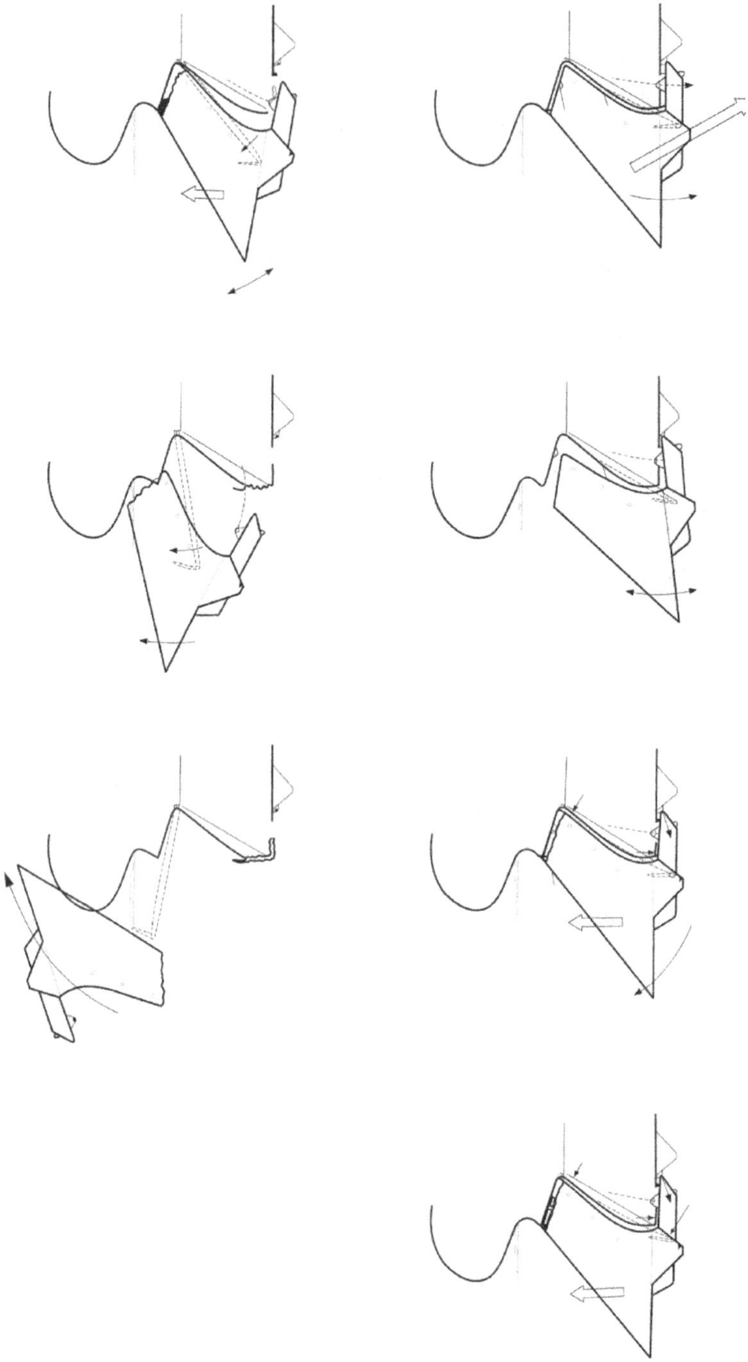

50 THE HOLE

FIG 14 Probable failure sequence of the bow visor
The JAIC theory of the bow visor detachment.

Shortly after the Final Report was issued, the JAIC disbanded.

More than 750 bodies still remain in the wreck at the bottom of the Baltic Sea, about 38 kilometers (24 miles) off Finland's coastal island of Utö.

The *Estonia* sinking claimed 852 lives. It was the world's sixth worst peacetime shipping disaster and the largest peacetime loss of life in European waters in the 20th century.

The Logic of the Hole

September 28, 1994
The *Estonia* ferry sinks in about 35 minutes:

01:14 Bow visor falls off
01:22-01:24 Mayday messages from the *Estonia*
01:30 Ferry on starboard side at 60-70 degrees
01:50 Ferry disappears from radar

Stories of the final poignant hours on the *Titanic* describe passengers playing blackjack in the liner's casino and singing hymns. Children played with the ice that had been knocked onboard after the iceberg collision until an officer told them to return to their cabins. A survivor remembered her father as he said goodbye from the deck of the sinking ship. Glass of brandy in hand, he supposedly said, "I'll see you in New York."

The *Estonia* ferry, however, sank with such speed that the Joint Accident Investigation Commission (JAIC) later calculated a passenger had only 14 minutes to get off the ship and into the water. Escape involved navigating the maze of corridors with plenty of dead ends, up crowded stairwells and across open foyers that had literally become pits to crawl out of while the ship tilted past 45 degrees.[2]

About 250 passengers made it off the ship, though dozens drowned or died of hypothermia in the near-freezing water. Most were sleeping in their cabins and events moved so fast they couldn't react in time.

It was a sudden, catastrophic demise. According to maritime records, the *Estonia* sank faster than some ships that had their hulls torn open by collisions or torpedoes.

But the *Estonia* had no hole, according to the JAIC's Final Report on the catastrophe.

A ship of comparable size with an impermeable hull sinking in minutes rather than hours or days had never been officially recorded before. The *Estonia* in fact dropped to the bottom so fast that it apparently defied physical laws and set an historical precedent for ship sinkings.

Passenger vessels that sank in under one hour*

NAME / COUNTRY	YEAR	GROSS TONNAGE	SPEED OF SINKING	HOLE CAUSED BY
1. Empress of Ireland UK	1914	14,191	14 minutes	COLLISION
2. Admiral Nakhimov Soviet Union	1986	17,053	15 minutes	COLLISION
3. Don Juan Philippines	1980	2311	15 minutes	COLLISION
4. Lusitania UK	1915	31,550	15 minutes	TORPEDO
5. Royal Pacific Greece	1992	3,176	15 minutes	COLLISION
6. Salem Express Egypt	1991	4771	15 minutes	COLLISION
7. European Gateway UK	1982	4263	30 minutes	COLLISION
8. M/V Estonia **Estonia**	**1994**	**15,598**	**35 minutes**	**NONE**
9. Jupiter Greece	1988	6306	40 minutes	COLLISION
10. Express Samina Greece	2000	4455	45 minutes	COLLISION
11. Wilhelm Gustloff Germany	1945	19,350	50 minutes	TORPEDOES
12. Brittanic UK	1916	48,158	55 minutes	EXPLOSION

*Data for the chart was collected from various maritime library sources and then compared to Norman Hooke's "Maritime Casualties 1963-1996." Ships smaller than 2000GT were omitted.

Intact passenger vessels that sank in less than one hour

1. M/V Estonia, 35 minutes

A huge and complex structure like the *Estonia* ferry does not fill like a pail of water. Water is slowed, contained or rerouted by the watertight areas, the hundreds of closed cabin doors of varying strengths, the multiple decks and floors with raised barriers to prevent water entry. Water takes time to accumulate enough force to push away obstacles. Water takes time to fill up a ship as high as an eight-story hotel and twice as long as a Boeing 747-400 airliner. A ship the size of the *Estonia* should float for hours, if not for days.

"This is simple physics," said Werner Hummel, head of Marine Claims Partner GmbH in Hamburg, Germany, a sea casualty investigation firm that was hired by the Meyer Werft shipyard to investigate the disaster.[3]

The JAIC sinking scenario was sharply undermined by Anders Björkman, a Swedish naval architect based in France. Björkman is part-owner of similar ferries in the Middle East. After the *Estonia* sank, he began doing stability calculations because he was concerned his ferries could suffer the *Estonia's* fate.

"We soon found out nothing was correct from the [stability calculations] in the Final Report," he said.

Björkman said that if water flowed onto the cardeck, which is above the water line, the ship would have flipped upside down, "turned turtle" and floated.

"Below the cardeck is the watertight hull, 14 compartments on which the ship floats in a normal situation," he said. "This represents 18,000 cubic meters of trapped air that the ship would float on."[4]

Björkman, who has done extensive research on the *Estonia*, came up with a forceful argument for his position through his drawing of water entry into the ferry. The illustration below is based on his rendering and is hereafter referred to as the "Björkman Scenario."

THE LOGIC OF THE HOLE 57

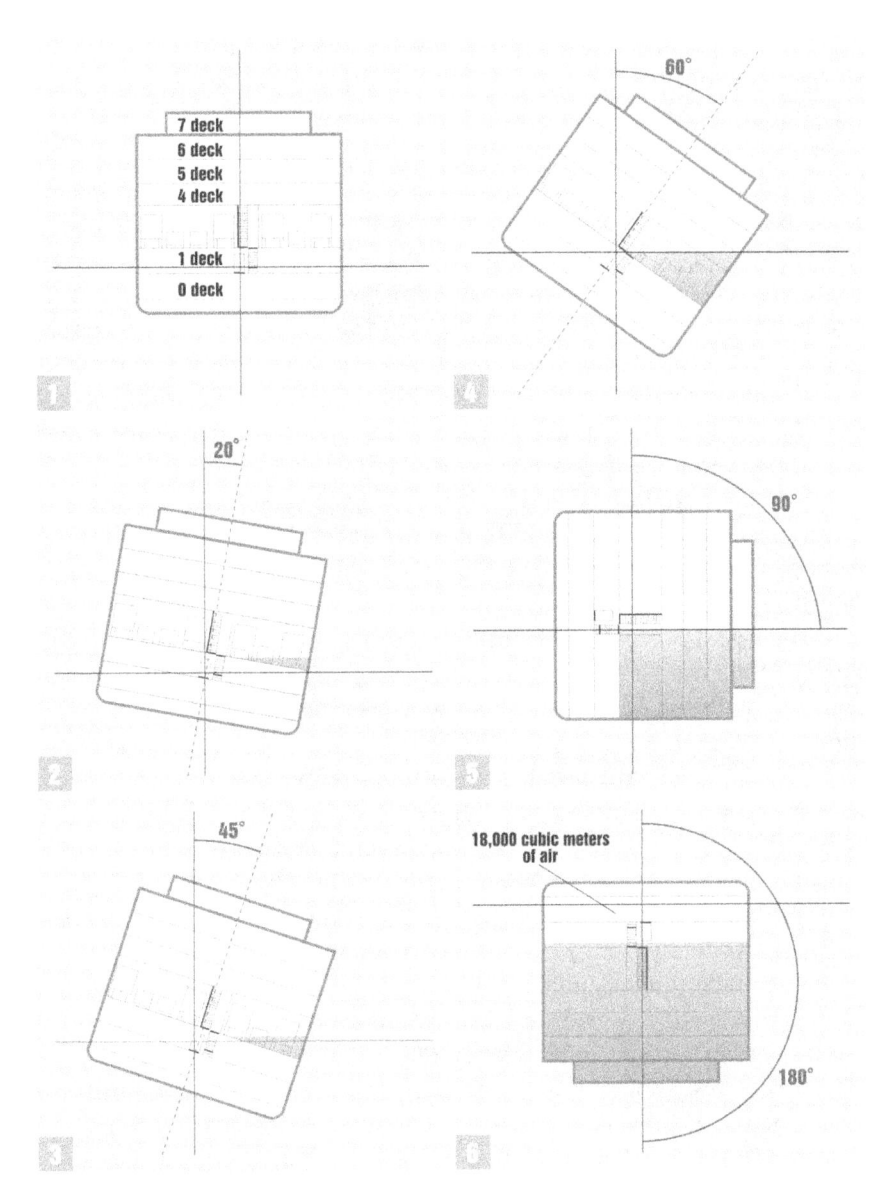

The *Estonia* ferry left Tallinn with a slight tilt to starboard, the right side, increased by the wind. If water enters the cardeck from the bow area, it runs to the lowest point: starboard. As more water flows in (1-5), it adds more weight to starboard, until the ship flops on its side, and eventually turns upside down and floats due to buoyancy provided by 18,000 cubic meters of air in the intact hull (6).

This book contends that the *Estonia* ferry had a breach of integrity below the waterline--a hole or holes or cracks or combination of openings that let water pour in below the waterline.

A hole ties together many of the baffling loose ends. A hole would account for survivors from belowdecks who ran upstairs *before* the ship listed because they'd seen water. It would explain the reluctance of the government-appointed dive team from Halliburton-owned Rockwater to shoot some 70 hours of video of the shipwreck, but not include footage of the starboard side hull area. It would shed light on the reasons for not taking up the human remains and the aggressive moves to prevent any independent postmortem on the shipwreck. A hole would introduce logic into the explanation of why the seaworthy *Estonia* sank faster than the *Wilhelm Gustloff*, a ship punched open by three torpedoes.

Various individuals have talked about the same hole, in the same location--the starboard side hull near the bow. These admissions came from people who one way or another had direct contact with the shipwreck.[5]

The first description is from Rolf Sörman, a Swedish survivor who floated in the near-freezing water for hours grasping an overturned lifeboat and with his other arm holding an Estonian girl, who eventually died from exposure.

From the lifeboat, Sörman said he saw a large, dark spot on the hull near the bow of the sinking ship. "It seemed to me to be a hole," he said. "My evidence was classified as a state secret, so that I myself had no longer access to it. I'm not one hundred percent convinced it was a hole I saw, as it was very dark, but I'm sure it was much darker than the rest of the hull and to my mind it looked like a hole."[6]

Next, talk about a hole came from a prime source. Johan Franson, head of the Swedish Maritime Administration (*Sjöfartsverket*) who supervised the tightly-restricted Rockwater dive mission to the ferry wreck in December 1994, spoke to survivors and journalists at a meeting in 1996. Franson, for all practical purposes, had been the top man in charge of the *Estonia* ferry dive investigation. He was the one of the few men who knew information that was not publicly disclosed.

Someone asked Franson a question: Was there was a hole in the starboard side of the ferry?

"Yes," he answered, "there is a hole in the starboard side, but I don't know anything about it--please the next question!"

This is an astonishing admission. The head of the SMA had admitted publicly the existence of a hole in the hull, starboard side. Present were groups of relatives, journalists and survivors, among them Rolf Sörman himself. Sörman's suspicions now seemed to be confirmed. He figured the investigating commission had discovered a hole and details would be provided in the Final Report, which at the time wasn't completed.

Sometime later, Sörman was again at a meeting of survivors and relatives hosted by the "Board of Psychological Defense," a Swedish government agency that intervenes during crises to give advice and guidance to the public and media. Franson was again present along with other SMA officials. Sörman again asked Franson whether the *Estonia* had a hole in the starboard side. His answer again: "Yes."[7]

There are no rocky outcrops in the well-traveled ferry lane where the *Estonia* sank. Therefore, to admit the ferry had a hole in the hull is tantamount to saying investigators should be looking for criminal negligence or a criminal act.

Franson is no novice. A career lawyer and veteran public servant, he clearly understood the dangers of government officials offering speculation before an investigation is concluded. Representing the Swedish Maritime Administration, he would not make off-the-cuff remarks in front of the press and public. The *Estonia* had a hole; he'd legitimized the idea by stating it publicly.

Later, his story would change.

*   *   *

In October 1999, researchers at a conference about the *Estonia* ferry catastrophe in Scotland presented a sinking theory suggesting that the *Estonia* had a big hole in the starboard side of the hull below water level.

The following year a second conference on the *Estonia* ferry was held, this time in Stockholm organized by a group of relatives of victims known as AgnEF. A number of naval architects and engineers with expertise in maritime accidents attended. One was a Dutchman named Jan de Kat. De Kat is the head of R&D at the Maritime Research Institute in the Netherlands (MARIN). After the conference, de Kat wrestled with the *Estonia* ferry mystery. How could the ferry sink so fast?

MARIN, a private marine consultancy, more than a decade ago developed together with navies and coast guards from the U.S., Europe and Australia, software called FREDYN. This particular program, widely used by the world's navies, predicts capsize behavior of ships as well as damage stability. For example, one function the program performs is to depict what is likely to happen to a ship with a hole in the hull under specified conditions. Such analysis has obvious importance for battles at sea, but can also be applied generically to any vessel.

De Kat decided to use FREDYN to simulate three scenarios for the Estonia ferry. The computer-generated simulation--an animation--is underpinned by a wide range of variables. A short list includes statistical representations of the ferry's internal geometry, size of compartments, wave forces, wind forces and propeller propulsion forces. The ferry starts in a seaworthy condition. Then a breach is created and every half-second, the amount, speed and direction of seawater entry is observed.

Scenario one was the JAIC's version--the official government explanation. DeKat assigned values supplied by the trilateral commission's report to the FREDYN software. He added data corresponding to the ship with the bow doors removed, creating an opening of 107 square feet (10m2) on the cardeck. Two contexts for the ferry were attempted. The first, sailing at the reported speed of 15 knots, showed the vessel in a progressive list. It did not sink. The second context was a drifting ferry. Results were the same--progressive heeling, no sinking.

Using the JAIC data, "It was pretty impossible to get it to do what they [the JAIC] said it did," de Kat said. "We couldn't get the ship to sink. The ship would have capsized, but would have floated, then in 50 minutes it would have turned upside down. So there must be a different mechanism that [allowed] water to flow inside the hull. And how it did, that's the big question."[9]

A second scenario de Kat tried was one proposed by Anders Björkman. Björkman had speculated the ferry had a hole in the hull and the cardeck had not been breached. Data was plugged in corresponding to the ferry with the bow doors closed and a 21.5 square foot (2 square meters) hole on Deck 0, the lowest deck on the ship and below the waterline, starboard side forward. The ferry was simulated sailing at the recorded speed of 15 knots with the engine room flooded and a second time with the engine room dry. In both instances, the ship does not capsize, but a fast change of heel--a flip to the side--can be observed in the first stages of flooding.

The ship would not sink.

Then de Kat decided to try a third scenario. He'd learned at the *Estonia* conference that many surviving passengers from the lower decks said they saw water before the ship listed.

No one recalled massive amounts of water flowing *down* the steps from the decks above. Then how did water get there? He decided to test the hole theory. The data he plugged in for the third scenario corresponded to the ferry with bow door opened (an opening of 107 square feet--10 square meters--on the cardeck) *plus* a 21.5 foot (2 square meter) hole on Deck 0, below the waterline, starboard side forward.

This "double breach" simulation was run in three contexts. In each case, the computer-simulated *Estonia* ferry sank. In each case, the ferry went down in a time sequence and manner almost exactly as described by survivors. In each case, the software proved the ultra-fast pace with which the *Estonia* sank could only be possible with a hole in the hull.[10]

PART THREE

Three Events that Shaped the Investigation

The Cult of the Visor

Had the JAIC ordered a thorough hull investigation immediately after the accident, with methods independently observed and all results disclosed, the truth about the *Estonia* ferry would have been found.

But the maritime experts in the JAIC were not dumbfounded by the 35 minute loss of an intact vessel. Apparently that was a nuance. They instead shifted their core concern to the bow visor and began the investigation. Floodlights fell on the bow visor.

The visor, a chunk of steel acting as the nose of the ship, rises automatically at the push of a button on two hydraulic arms, like a visor on the helmet of a medieval knight. Reverse the operation and it closes.

The JAIC generated hundreds of pages of analysis on the components of the visor system. Visor data printed in the Final Report and its two supplements include design documentation for the visor and locks, strength tolerances of various attachments, order and delivery contracts, color photographs of unrecognizable slabs of streaked and damaged metal that look important and damning but do not deliver a spark of comprehension.

There are graphs and tables and algebraic formulas dealing with the ferry's interaction with the sea that alienate all except those educated in ship design and construction. The data soup is hard for most people to swallow.

The visor over-analysis even sparked criticism from the U.K.-based International Transport Workers Federation, which hired a marine consultancy to evaluate the Final Report. These researchers referred to the microscopic scrutiny of the visor as something "purely of academic interest" that wasted valuable investigative time.[1]

66 THE HOLE

In the end, the JAIC cited inadequate lock design specifications as the reason for the visor detachment, indicating that the German shipyard, Jos. L. Meyer GmbH & Co in Papenburg, was responsible. The German investigators hired by the shipyard maintain that the broken visor system resulted from substandard maintenance and careless handling by the crew. But whether the visor popped off due to design faults or bad upkeep has nothing to do with the accelerated pace of sinking.

An examination of the visor was legitimate and necessary as a contributory cause. The visor's locking system was a relevant consideration, but it was not the *most* relevant consideration. Nonetheless, the visor and locks drew increasing attention at the expense of the other phases of the disaster.

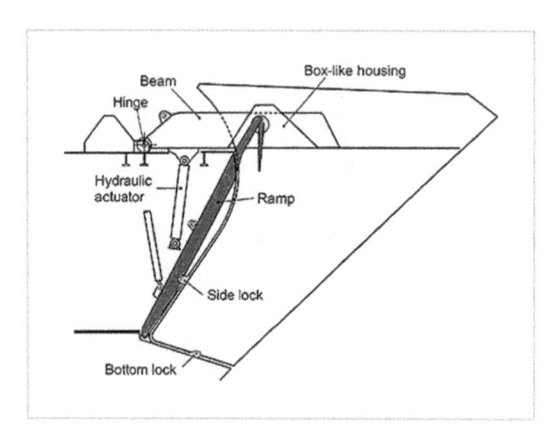

The bow visor weighs some 56 tons and has steel girder construction that resembles on a smaller scale the steel beams of a skyscraper's structure. It's also as big as a garage. The metal cardeck ramp was elongated on the *Estonia* and when the visor closed, the ramp extended into a breadbox-like housing.

THE CULT OF THE VISOR 67

*   *   *

Through political decisions, the visor became the red herring, diverting attention by changing the subject.

The diversion began hours after the accident on September 28 when Swedish Prime Minister Carl Bildt ordered the Swedish Maritime Administration to investigate bow visors on other ferries because "a construction fault might have caused the accident." Bildt based his conclusion on conversations with surviving crew members, who said they saw water on the cardeck before escaping.[2]

In reality, no one knew what had happened. The wreck had not even been found. The director of Estline in Estonia, Johannes Johansen, alluded to a bomb. Earlier bomb threats against the *Estonia* ferry were revealed. Some survivors spoke about a collision, a scraping noise on the hull before the ship flipped on its side. Others said the Estonian crew should be blamed. No one knew the visor had detached. There were no solid facts. But Bildt had forged a tight link between the bow visor and the sinking that would subconsciously influence the course of the investigation.

Sten-Christer Forsberg, technical director of Nordström & Thulin, the ferry's co-owner, was the first to publicly join what would become the cult of the visor. Two days after Bildt's announcement, Forsberg blamed the failure on the bow visor. "There is reason to suspect that this was the main cause of the accident," he said.[3]

Recall that the wreck still hadn't been located. Forsberg didn't hold his speculations to himself, but instead reiterated what Bildt had declared.

The ferry was eventually located on the seafloor by a remotely-operated vehicle (ROV). A few days later on October 2, 1994, an ROV with video camera showed the bow visor was missing from the front of the ship. The visor was not attached. Nothing else was known.

Nonetheless, the Joint Accident Investigation Commission announced visor failure as the most likely cause. By October 4, the investigation seemed to be already concluded. The JAIC issued a press release with details that simply could not have been known at the time:

"The *Estonia* sank due to thousands of tons of water entering the ship through the cardeck. This occurred because the bow lockings were of a design which was too weak, that allowed for a few strong waves to break them, after which the bow visor was torn off, ripping off the car ramp in the process and, as a consequence, the cardeck was flooded."[4]

Everyone was on the same sheet of music.
Instead of starting with all available facts and honing them down to a conclusion, the JAIC started with a conclusion and disregarded or downplayed anything that didn't fit in that box.

The JAIC didn't need persuasion, coercion or even backroom advice to conclude the visor had caused the accident because stakes were high. Nearly 1000 people had died. Enormous pressure was mounting from the public, from international media, from business and government to find answers. The visor provided a safe one.

Each country had its own interests to protect. If the JAIC had found it necessary to cast their investigatory net far and wide to include all probable causes, they would have encroached into highly-sensitive areas. Certainly at the top levels in Sweden, Estonia and Finland, authorities pondered what they would do if their probing began to suggest a country held responsibility, even indirectly, for the ferry disaster. The investigation, therefore, had to proceed delicately, and Bildt's red herring was eagerly swallowed.

Bildt's pronouncement just 16 hours after the accident that the visor came off due to a technical fault was the single most significant juncture in the course of events following the sinking. It was highly motivating to the rudderless commission that had just been formed. Investigating a technical fault tore out the politics. It offered the JAIC an elegant way out of the unknown.

One more step completed the imprinting of the bow visor on public consciousness.

In November 1994, the following month, a Swedish Navy minesweeper and a Finnish icebreaker sailed at night toward the shipwreck. They stopped about a mile from the recorded wreck site. A steel cable with hook was lowered into the depths. The bow visor was hoisted to the surface.

The mangled visor, dredged up from the depths at night on a barge hook like a gruesome trophy fish, became the focal point for widespread rage and despair. The visor detachment scenario now had a forceful image for the media to bring to life. The visor was the culprit. It fully explained the disaster. The JAIC could devalue or disregard anything inconsistent with the visor off, ship down scenario. The JAIC could now adroitly replace doubts with certainties and tame emotions with statistics.

Photo: JAIC

The Dive to the Shipwreck

The divers resembled astronauts on the lunar surface. The difference was that their saturation diving suits were connected by an umbilical cord to a surface ship. Breathable air circulates through one tube inside the cord and hot water through another. The bottom of the Baltic Sea is near the freezing point.

Fixed to each diver's helmet was a floodlight and videocamera. Earphones and a microphone allowed two-way communication to the dive supervisor on the surface, some 80 meters above.

Divers spent 64 hours examining the shipwreck from December 1-4, 1994. Teams of three divers worked around the clock from diving bells hanging near the wreck. The divers were employed by Rockwater A/S, a division of Halliburton Co. The Swedish government bankrolled and controlled the operation. The aim was to determine if the *Estonia* ferry and hundreds of victims trapped inside could be recovered from the bottom of the Baltic.

On board the surface vessel, known as the SEMI platform, were the dive supervisor and support team as well as Swedish criminal police and a Swedish JAIC representative. The dive, however, was not run by the JAIC. Above them all, at the very top of the command structure, supervising and controlling the operation, sat Johan Franson, head of the Swedish Maritime Administration.[1]

The 155 meter-long *Estonia* ferry was nearly upside down. It lay on a downward slope, the stern about 10 meters higher than the bow. At the shipwreck's bow, the starboard side protrusion of the bridge dug deep into the soft mud on the seafloor and was crumpled like paper at the impact point.

Inside the bridge, the floor-mounted swivel chairs where the officers normally sat were on the ceiling. A console telephone hung by its coiled wire.

Also on the bridge were three relatively intact bodies, plus the torso of one person by the entranceway. One of the four may have been the captain of the ferry, Arvo Andresson, an Estonian. Did the captain die on the bridge? If Captain Andresson wasn't on the bridge, was he in his cabin?

The questions are not trivial. For Estonian pride, to stop damaging myths and to contribute to seafaring history, the location of the master's body should be confirmed. Most important, to substantiate the Joint Accident Investigation Commission's interpretation of the chain of events on the bridge, the public record should state where the captain died.

Swedish JAIC member Bengt Schager wanted to know. He was not on the SEMI platform, but he'd requested that bodies on the bridge be identified. This was not a complicated task. The diver need only make a passing glance at the rank insignia on the uniform.

But it didn't happen. Although the divers stood beside the victims, they did not look at the rank, nor were they instructed to. There must be a reason why Franson disregarded such a modest request.

On the SEMI platform above, the officials in their cabins watched the expedition in realtime on television monitors.

Visibility inside the *Estonia's* bridge was limited. Clouds of silt unfurled when divers moved. One diver made a very close examination of a body under a cabinet on the bridge. On the hand was a tattoo. Captain Andresson had no tattoo. Among the small team of officers who were allowed access to the *Estonia's* bridge during this voyage, not one of them had a hand tattoo. But someone with a hand tattoo was on the bridge during the ferry's last moments. The Swedish police started to search their databases.

The divers had zeroed in on and reported a hand tattoo but did not peer at the shoulder rank. Had they been given specific instructions?[2]

* * *

Other divers from the team, mainly English and Scottish, entered into passenger cabins. Breathing mixed gases that included helium, the divers' voices were high-pitched, cartoon-like.

One diver entered a cabin. He looked at the belongings and found a matrushka doll, the common souvenir from Russia. In the next cabin he found a briefcase with a Russian name on it, written in Cyrillic letters. He spelled it aloud several times. Finally, he tells the dive supervisor the name is "Alexander Voronin."

"OK, I'll just see if that name rings a bell up here," answered the supervisor.

"Up here" referred to the Swedish police on the SEMI platform.

The purpose of the dive mission was to assess the salvage of bodies and the wreck. No one explained why an individual named "Voronin" should be singled out for identification with Swedish police.[3]

Alexander Voronin, together with his nephew and father, had escaped and survived.

To understand how the briefcase incident could make sense, it is necessary to mention another detail of the catastrophe. During the dive in December 1994, a mystery surrounded the fate of the *Estonia* ferry's relief captain, the Estonian Avo Piht. Piht was off duty, but onboard the night the ship sank. He'd been seen on deck by more than one survivor methodically distributing life vests to fleeing passengers. State authorities reported Piht was alive. One survivor later said he'd shared a hospital room with Piht. Some stated they'd seen Piht interviewed on television after the accident.

A day after the accident, Swedish news reports referred to Bengt-Erik Stenmark, Sweden's Director of Maritime Safety, confirming that Piht was alive and that he'd already made an initial statement.

Reuters ran a similar dispatch. The U.S. Embassy in Tallinn reported Piht was alive. The *Evening Standard* of London wrote that "a key witness to the events, the second captain of the *Estonia*, has survived. Investigators are waiting until . . . Piht is in a fit mental state to give an account of what exactly happened . . . It was not immediately known where the second captain was being kept or whether he was injured."[4]

The problem was, Piht was missing. By all appearances, he'd survived and then vanished. The relief captain, who intimately knew the ship and who could take investigators through a step-by-step explanation of the fatal events, was nowhere to be found.

Estonian authorities warned of lengthy jail sentences for anyone found responsible for the ferry disaster. Government officials, burning with impatience, wanted Piht hunted down and interrogated. Piht's description was submitted to Interpol as a missing person.

Piht's cabin was 6230. Voronin, to whom the briefcase belonged, was in 6320. But apparently Voronin's nephew, who had shared the cabin with his uncle and also survived, had transposed the numbers in a police statement just after his rescue, a little mistake with big consequences.[5] It now appeared that the Voronin family had been in the cabin of the person who at the time was the most wanted man in Scandinavia. Were the Voronins connected with the missing Piht? What was going on here? There's a strong possibility Swedish police requested the diver enter cabins 6230 and 6320 and look around.

Swedish police, in conjunction with Estonia's KAPO, the equivalent of the FBI, and Interpol, ran a detailed background check on Voronin. Perhaps they'd found something--black rumors and dubious profits were common three years after the fall of the U.S.S.R. Or perhaps they found nothing and Swedish law enforcement chose to conceal from the media what had proved to be misguided suspicion.

Some of this was supported by John Coe, a Rockwater diver. Coe said the divers were directed into specific cabins. "Obviously they [Swedish authorities] had worked out the cabins they wanted to check out. Just verbal directions, cabin numbers. I think they must have had some sort of passenger manifest . . . whether they actually had a hit list of cabins to check out for various people--it seemed that was the case to me. It was not [divers] indiscriminately [coming] across a cabin, [seeing] who's in there, or if there was anybody in there."[6]

Franson categorically denies targeting cabins or individual victims. He explains that the briefcase identification was merely part of a routine survey:

"One of the reasons we had these policemen on board was that if the ship was salvaged, lifted up, they wanted to know what could be found in the cabins and so on," Franson said. "They wanted to get a picture: How would we be able to establish the identity of the people there? [The briefcase] might have been in connection with that, but certainly it was nothing specific we were looking for or any specific person we were looking for. You could find at least 10 myths around this [briefcase incident]."[7]

*   *   *

Andi Meister, chief of the JAIC, found no myths. He just couldn't believe what happened. Divers refused to glance at the uniformed bodies on the bridge, but carefully read and re-read Voronin's name from his briefcase and in another incident rummaged through the cabin of a passenger named Susanne Pundi.

"Why were the two names that had occurred by chance more important than the dead on the bridge?" Meister wrote in *Unfinished Logbook*, his book about the *Estonia*. "Was there an order given for that? On the command deck, the destiny of the ship is decided, if there is anything to decide any more."[8]

Finding bodies in the officer's cabins may have added dimension to an understanding of the ship's last moments and could've been integral to the investigation. But no instructions came over the diver's earphones. Meister was perplexed. How could that be?

He concluded that an earlier dive, undisclosed to the public, must have occurred. That's when the officer's cabins were examined.

"For sure there have been surveys without audience already before the [SEMI] research ship set sail," he wrote. "Can we claim that these [officer's] cabins were ignored? It is difficult to imagine such an illogical decision."[9]

Meister's allegations were supported by other sources citing an early, confidential dive expedition by the Swedish Navy.

The investigative report by the German Group of Experts, commissioned by the shipyard in 1995, mentions such a dive a few times, though it gave no verifiable details. Simultaneously with the first ROV examination of the *Estonia*, the report says, "the wreck was examined by Swedish and other countries' navy divers, which was kept secret until today." Videos of the wreck made by divers of the Swedish Navy "when they surveyed it in the first days of the month of October 1994" have never been made available. The ferry's logbook, according to the report, had been recovered in the early days of October 1994--by Swedish Navy divers.[10]

Nothing could be corroborated. Catrin Tidstrom, spokeswoman for the Swedish Ministry of Transport authorized to answer questions about the *Estonia* disaster, told reporters she had no idea how many dives there had been to the shipwreck.

If an undisclosed naval dive mission to the ferry had been ordered a few days after the sinking, what would the divers do down there that couldn't be made public?[11]

* * *

The Rockwater dive was documented on 19 videotapes and placed in the custody of the SMA and the Swedish criminal police. Rockwater kept one set of original tapes for one week until the divers had decompressed and emerged from the saturation tank without health problems. Then the company destroyed its videos as required by contract with the SMA.

Sweden held the sole original set. When the Swedes sent a copy of the set of videos to the Estonian side, they sent an edited version. The Estonians were enraged.

Meister charged the Swedes with hiding certain parts of the dive operation. His allegations were supported by Aarne Valgma, head of the Estonian Maritime Board's Department of Maritime Safety, who had been on the SEMI platform watching the divers.

Valgma had an odd experience. During the 64-hour expedition, he watched the Rockwater divers in realtime on his personal monitor in his room. At intervals, the picture on his monitor dropped out. What troubled Valgma was that the picture never dropped out on the main monitor watched by the top officials. This was assured, because legal obligations for the health and safety of the divers required that they be continuously observed.

"The corpses had been cut out from the video sent to Estonia," Valgma said. "I cannot say whether also anything else had been cut out."[12]

The videos, Franson later explained, had been edited to protect the dignity of the dead. But from the Estonian perspective, Franson had imposed an informational hierarchy. The Swedes possessed the originals, but no one else could access them. Not even other members of the Trilateral Commission.

Suspicious, the German Group of Experts sent copies of the dive videotapes to a U.K.-based video analysis and production company called Disengage. Analysts scrutinized the videos and found a mess.

The videotapes had unexplained cuts. Some cassettes were missing, others incorrectly numbered. Written dive logs didn't correspond with the video footage. Some editing was out of chronological order and unlogged diver activity occurred. There was no proper video format conversion during duplication of the tapes. Not exactly the meticulous documentary methods expected in an international catastrophe that claimed nearly 1000 lives.

"The fact that the tape cuts repeatedly occur in the same areas of the vessel on different cassettes from different times and dates does not allow us to generate full documentation of a very serious casualty," according to the Disengage analysis report. "This is a particular concern as the areas that lack documentation are very important to the investigation and include the starboard mudline and cardeck."

Franson's claim of creating a sanitized version by clipping only the parts showing the dead didn't ring true. "Very few of the tape cuts that have been documented in this report occur in locations where victims could be or are located and [the cuts] are not due to technical issues, leaving no apparent reason for their existence," read the Disengage report.[13]

On one tape, more than an hour of diver activity had been cut. The dive logbook shows an entry at 14:54 when the supervisor wrote "Diver moved aft to spiral staircase." On the next line, the entry is at 16:00: "Diver returning to outside of vessel."

Between these two entries is something strange: A barely distinct edge line of the type that sometimes appears after photocopying a sheet of paper laid over part of another document.

The German Group determined that a description of diver activity had been written and cut out. The top and bottom of the page were then placed on the photocopy machine and copied into one page.

Neither officials nor media clarified or even addressed the apparent criminal act of tampering with documents in an ongoing investigation.

Curiously, the diver at the time in question was on Deck 0--the floor holding the sauna and swimming pool compartments, areas where critics hold deep suspicions of a hull rupture.

"It is obvious that the JAIC did not desire that the [diving] inspection results were made public," the German Group concludes.[14]

* * *

Franson admits there was censorship of sensitive images in the Rockwater videotapes, and that Rockwater eventually destroyed their originals. But he said there was no withholding of evidence.

"That clause [to destroy original tapes] is designed so they are encouraged to shut up out of consideration for the relatives," Franson said. "You can think of the scenario with divers [telling] gruesome stories to the media. That was the only reason [for secrecy] and I think that was a good and dignified reason for having a clause like that."

The original uncut tapes are with the Swedish authorities, he asserted. No one outside of selected Swedish officials, however, has seen them and no one knows where they precisely are. Not even members of the Swedish parliament who requested to see them.[15]

For Franson, the dive to the shipwreck had answered the questions posed by the Swedish government. The divers had concluded the *Estonia* ferry could be brought up. The bodies could be recovered, though the survey report added that a salvage operation would be substantial and complex.

For others, the Rockwater mission proved a pivotal event. The December 1994 dive prompted Andi Meister, the JAIC's top authority, to resign. It exposed the resentment and divisions within the commission and set the tone for secrecy. It aroused public mistrust and, most important, consolidated Sweden's control over the JAIC's investigation.

Franson, however, said the consequences were unintentional. Controversies related to the Rockwater dive came from poor communication.

"Naturally in hindsight there were mistakes made," Franson said. "For example, we were not communicating with media and the relatives when the diving survey going on. Our information capabilities in the administration at that time were rather bad. I think I slept 17 hours in four days. I simply hadn't the time or stamina to do it. Much could have been avoided if communication had been better."[16]

* * *

Fallout from the mysterious dive was gradual but potent. The issue of identifying the commander on the bridge would not fade from memory and it drove a wedge deeper into the JAIC.

The Rockwater divers, according to their report, saw 125 bodies in total. Most were not decomposed, still dressed, with sex easily distinguishable. Thrown against the walls of the tumbling ship, many were bruised. Franson added that victims were clumped in the stairwells, trapped in the fight to get out of the listing ferry. It was chaos in the last moments--primal self-preservation.

All that detail and not one cursory glance at the three uniformed bodies on the bridge. Captain Andresson, a 40-year-old Estonian, was a traditional Soviet-trained seafarer. He must have stayed on the bridge at the slightest hint of trouble. But then again, Andresson didn't give the Mayday message. Third Officer Andres Tammes did. What happened on the bridge?

Olof Forssberg, head of the Swedish side of the JAIC, told the press that identifying the captain held no importance in the investigation. Meister, Forssberg said, never spoke of ordering a new dive to the wreck to film the bridge. "Although expensive when compared with the results that one would get, Meister has the right to do it," Forssberg said.[17]

Here the public caught a glimpse of the spoiling relationships within the three-state commission. Forssberg's stinging reference underlined the fact that Sweden and Finland were picking up the tab for the investigation. Estonia, lacking economic resources, wasn't paying its own way, yet was making demands.[18]

The Swedes even politely elbowed the Finns out of the picture. Two members of the Finnish side of the JAIC had arranged to visit the SEMI platform to observe the Rockwater divers. After all, the Finns were part of the trilateral commission and also had the right to monitor the survey. But the trip didn't work out. On the last day of the dive, the Finns were told by the technical chief of the JAIC, Swede Borje Stenstrom, that the operation was over. Their presence wasn't necessary.[19]

To Meister (the Estonian chief investigator of the commission who was heading the entire tri-state commission at the time), the Swedes were manhandling the investigation and operating with deceptive tactics. It reminded him too much of Soviet times. He resigned as head of the JAIC in July of 1996 citing "health reasons." Perhaps his health was declining, but his statement also holds cynical humor in the region. Five years earlier when Kremlin plotters told the world Mikhail Gorbachev was relieved of his official duties due to "health reasons," the phrase became a blatant excuse to justify the usurping of power.

Later, Meister was more direct. "The diving mission was one of the reasons why I resigned as chairman of the committee," he said. [20]

Concrete Blanket

What was about to happen next was the last thing anyone expected. Sweden's actions would highlight the dominant role of a state and its subjects, polarize opinion and introduce a pervasive and lasting public distrust.

Johan Franson, who had carefully supervised the Rockwater dive, emerged as the dominant voice in matters concerning the *Estonia* ferry wreck.

The Rockwater dive report had been issued. The divers concluded that the bodies and the wreck were salvageable. Relatives of victims anticipated the retrieval and forensic identification of the human remains, in modern times an obligatory government practice after disasters, partuclarly in Western nations.

Franson, however, held a radically different idea. He'd been privy to all the Rockwater video footage in realtime. After watching the salvage divers cautiously step through obstructed sections in the wreck, he began to think it was possible that someone intent on looting could easily enter the *Estonia* and pick it clean.

Franson's solution, which was announced in early 1996, was unprecedented. As the highest official with responsibility for the *Estonia* wreck, he decided that hundreds of tons of concrete would be dumped over the ferry to encase it, to cover it forever in a concrete blanket.

What was down there worth the risk of a complicated and expensive dive? Paper money? Currency doesn't deteriorate quickly in salt water. Casino and duty-free shop money had been collected before the accident. Both businesses had closed early due to the rough ride. About one million Estonian Kroons ($77,000) were locked in the ship's safe. By definition a locked safe is highly problematic, even for a well-equipped diver.

Bottles of alcohol from the duty-free shop could be targets for souvenir hunters, but they presumably broke as the ship flipped upside down. Some passengers had cash and valuables, but not much. Estonia in 1994 was a destination for thrifty tourists. The Estonian citizen earned an average monthly wage of around $200.

Moreover, breaking and entering the ferry would be an extremely complex undertaking even for the most professional diver.

According to the Rockwater report:

> The survey work demonstrated that the recovery of individual targeted items was only possible within the bridge and not in the public areas due to the chaotic arrangement of debris. The recovery of targeted valuables to reduce the risk of plunder is not practical with the vessel in its current attitude.[1]

The Rockwater divers also mentioned mud stirred up by movement, broken glass, hanging wires and ropes, inaccessible corridors and stairwells congested by human remains. The practical tasks and potential hazards a plundering operation would involve ensured the shipwreck's sanctity.

There was additional protection. Swedish authorities had declared the wreck a grave and drawn up symbolic legislation known as the Gravesite Treaty (see Chapter 14), which Stockholm lobbied neighboring countries to sign. The regional agreement in effect banned expeditions to the *Estonia*. Enforcement involved 24-hour surveillance, apparently in perpetuity, from Swedish Navy and Finnish coast guard patrol boats as well as nearby Finnish military radar installations that peered at the site.

Moreover, the JAIC assured the public that the ferry was tightly sealed by the Rockwater divers on departure, with any access holes welded shut.

If rogue divers did want to break in, they would need a floating surface ship to locate and idle over the wreck, underwater tools to cut through metal, floodlights, radio communication and a somewhat reckless dive team. In short, big money and a surface ship that would have to avoid detection by the 24-hour patrols assigned to the wrecksite. It would be a high-profile effort for a few souvenirs or pocket money.

The truth was, no dive enthusiasts could get near the sunken ferry, much less inside of it.

Franson, however, was convinced they would.

"It would not be proper, if one leaves the ship down there, not to protect her out of consideration for the relatives. It would not be very nice if Aunt Augustus' necklace suddenly emerged on the market because someone had gone down and pinched it. That risk was real at the time (in 1996)," Franson said.[2]

Therefore, he declared that the *Estonia* shipwreck would be covered in concrete and left as an underwater tomb. It would be sealed forever.

*   *   *

Franson has a legal background. He was appointed as head of the SMA after his predecessor was forced to resign for publicly criticizing Sweden's Prime Minister Carl Bildt.

Franson is a reed-thin man, pale, soft spoken and polite. Based on initial impressions, it is hard to believe he has been called at various times by people associated with the catastrophe an "evil genius," a "skillful government plumber" and a "master manipulator" in blind obedience to the Swedish state.

Yet due to his actions, an aura of duplicity, whether justified or not, surrounds Franson. As mentioned earlier, he became infamous after telling a gathering of the relatives of victims in March 1996, "Yes, there is a hole in the starboard side, but I don't know anything about it--please the next question!"

What did that mean? There was a hole in hull? Did he see it on the ROV videos? How much did he know about it? How big was it? Why won't he talk about it? Such a revelation by a senior official would normally make headlines and elicit demands for explanation. Swedish journalists did not press him. Neither did politicians. Relatives were perplexed.[3]

Franson kept a tight leash on information. Some survivors and relatives wanted to know why unedited videotapes of the Rockwater dive weren't available to the Estonian commission members or to Swedish politicians. How many minutes were edited and where exactly on each videotape? The list of questions that could be put to Franson seem endless. His vague and ambiguous answers tended to mystify rather than clarify.

Questions about the concrete blanket elicited the same unsatisfactory responses. There are no precedents for encasing a shipwreck that resulted from a civilian transport accident. Furthermore, Franson wanted to cover it before the investigation had even been completed. Legal action against the shipyard and the certification organization (and for a while against Franson's own SMA) was also underway.

Franson said he thought up the concrete covering idea after meetings with relatives and survivors. "My interest is to safeguard," he said. "That's the way I look at it and therefore I was something of a public figure and in some circles I am probably notorious, but that's something I'm paid for."

Plans for the concrete blanket went forward. The Swedish government awarded a $45 million contract to Nordic Marine Contractors, a consortium involving Norway's Jebsen group and Dutch salvage firm Smit Tak. On the order of Swedish officialdom, 25,000 tons of gravel would be dumped around the shipwreck as the foundation for a gigantic 12" thick concrete sarcophagus. A 65,000 square meter sea floor area around the wreck would be covered with a layer of textile, stone, rubble and sand. Elaborate plans included transporting prefabricated concrete mattresses to the site where they would be wired together to form the impenetrable quilt that would cover the entire ship.

The macabre project confounded nearly everyone connected to the *Estonia* disaster, at all levels of society, in all countries, including Sweden. It caused offense and despair among relatives and friends of victims, who believed the concrete blanket would rule out recovery of remains and seal the truth forever.

As preliminary work on the seafloor began in early 1996. Gunnar Bendreus, chairman of the International Support Group, an umbrella organization that represented more than 3,000 victims' relatives in 24 countries, claimed that more than 90 percent of those who lost loved ones were against the plan. He said the group's lawyers in Germany and France interpreted the move as "violating the process of truth."

The plan also stirred widespread public suspicion. The $45 million allotted to blanket the *Estonia* was roughly the same cost to salvage the ship and bodies. What was going on? What was inside that had to be sealed? The sunken Russian nuclear sub *Komsomolets* had to be covered because radioactive seepage from torpedoes could have serious environmental consequences over time. The dangerously defective Chernobyl nuclear reactor was encapsulated in concrete for obvious reasons. Why the *Estonia* ferry--a tourist ferry? Why was it necessary to quickly undertake an operation that Franson had unilaterally decided would be done?

Despite these questions thrown at Sweden, the consortium was instructed to continue with the initial work, and furthermore complete it all by the end of 1996.

Relatives were enraged.

Bendreus compared the Swedish government to a dictatorship for its refusal to heed protests. He complained that the prime minister had all along ignored pleas for a meeting--and it was now approaching 500 days since the disaster occurred. "They just don't listen," Bendreus said.[4]

"The Swedish government has forced, against the will of a vast majority of relatives in 24 countries, a plan to put our dead and missing loved ones under concrete . . . The Swedish Maritime Board does not have any feelings or empathy for us. They are cold-blooded, heartless people," Bendreus said.[5]

Lennart and Birgitta Berglund, who lost relatives on the ferry, went further. They said if Sweden continues with the sarcophagus plan, they would mobilize a salvage raid to the site beforehand and seize the remains of Birgitta's parents. Berglund, who represents another group of relatives, said they would send divers to recover the bodies using a European company specializing in underwater operations that offered its services to the victims' families for free. Berglund said he didn't fear lawsuits because taking care of relatives' bodies couldn't be seen as criminal.

"It is not the bodies themselves that are so important. It is that you have done what is expected of you as a human being," he said. "You are supposed to put a family member to rest, whether it takes one year or 50."

Some family members even threatened to lay mines near the wreckage to prevent continued work.[6]

As the first steps on the seafloor continued, in Tallinn relatives took to the streets for the first time since opposing the Soviet occupation. A poll showed Estonian families overwhelmingly against the plan.

"It was when Sweden wanted to cover the wreck in concrete that we suspected something was really wrong, that it didn't sink the way they said it did," recalled Estonian Aina Lee, who survived the sinking with the help of her husband, crew member Aulis Lee.[7]

Even those satisfied with the JAIC Final Report felt apprehensive. "It's like a swamp on the sea bottom," said Estonian Ander Paeorg, who lost his wife on the ship. "I thought it was a strange idea to cover it because [the covering itself] would sink. It's not a nuclear boat anyway."[8]

As the victims' relatives battled the Swedish establishment, Franson's plan got hit from an unexpected front: Finland.

The ferry sat not far from a national archipelago park off the Finnish coast, where many species of birds made their home by feeding on the fish population. The ferry still contained 400 tons of fuel and oil. Officials at the Finnish Environmental Institute (SYKE) didn't like it.

"We believed that when the wreck started to corrode, maybe in 20 to 30 years, the oil and fuel would leak and the wildlife was vulnerable," said Erkki Mykkänen an engineer at SYKE.[9]

Earlier, SYKE had successfully extracted fuel and oil from the shipwreck Victory, which lay in Finnish territorial waters, from a 1941 Finnish battleship and from the submerged ferry *Sally Albatross*.

Now they wanted the *Estonia's* hazardous liquids removed and their engineers sketched out implementation plans. Moreover, the Finnish and Swedish governments were expected to share the cost of the pollutant-removal operation.

Franson rejected their plan. Perhaps time was running short. Maybe he cared less about potential leaking fuel than he did about encasing the wreck. Or maybe he didn't want any unauthorized engineers nosing around down at the ship.

Franson instead promised the environmentalists that fuel and oil removal would be performed as a side task by the companies covering the shipwreck in concrete, Netherlands-based Smit Tak and the consortium of Nordic Marine contractors. Smit Tak would use saturation diving--men in dive suits attached to umbilical cords--to pump the liquids out.

But SYKE found Smit Tak's proposed plan superficial and in part founded on erroneous assumptions. "During the negotiations, it became clear that the work coalition did not even intend to remove heavy fuel oil," according to Mykkänen. "We were afraid the Dutch company would say they took it up and then just show us some of their fuel and oil and claim it was from the *Estonia*."[10]

SYKE firmly insisted on controlling the removal of the liquids to ensure it was done properly.

After traveling to Sweden to speak to Franson, SYKE officials were finally given permission to remove the potential pollutants–under certain conditions. SYKE would work without interrupting the wreck covering operation. The concrete tomb mission got priority.

The final condition: No humans. There would be no saturation divers. There would be no curious people down at the shipwreck.

Mykkänen and head engineer at SYKE, Kalervo Jolma, scratched their heads. They went back to Finland and formulated a novel plan based on Nordic thriftiness. For the first time, their organization would pump out the fuel using only remote control robots and ROVs. They would do it without interfering with the concrete blanket operation.[11]

All the while, SYKE's engineers scoffed at the attempted ferry encapsulation, which they believed was doomed from the start. From a sheer technical point of view, the concrete covering was ill-conceived. It would sink.

"The bottom there is like yogurt," Jolma explained.

* * *

Meanwhile, back on land, fury mounted. Legal wheels began to turn. The *Estonia* Disaster Victims International Support Group (DIS) recruited a Swedish lawyer. DIS believed they should have the possibility of obtaining new evidence from the wreck in legal proceedings planned against the Meyer Werft Shipyard and the Bureau Veritas, which certified the ship. Allowing the initial ferry-covering work to proceed further would preclude that possibility.

Could the Swedish state be dragged into international court for concealing evidence relevant to a pending court case? No one knew for sure, but lawyers were on the sidelines assiduously preparing for a fight.

It may have been the distasteful prospect of defending the covering decision in court, but Sweden eventually backed down. In June 1996, all preliminary work was halted and the project abandoned.

The relatives had won one battle. No more concrete tomb. The more intriguing issue is why the operation even got started.

Franson had obviously scrutinized the Rockwater dive report, which described "very soft silts and clays" around the wreck. Presumably the consortium did its own geological seabed tests. Their engineers and geologists studied the results and made calculations. Smit Tak is an international expert in salvage and recovery. The company re-floated the *Herald of Free Enterprise* ferry, covered the Russian *Komsomolets* submarine and later would be the primary contractor in the *Kursk* submarine salvage.

Some of the top salvage experts in Europe drawing from a $45 million contract all agreed to pour rocks onto yogurt. Incompetence or directions from the top levels? Either is hard to prove.

The aborted entombing did result in a couple key changes. The consortium, in its partial preparatory work, shoved the shipwreck forward about one meter and deeper into the soft silt, according to SYKE. These salvage companies had also accomplished something else. Hundreds of tons of sand had been dumped on the seafloor around the *Estonia* before the workers quit. But the biggest accumulation was conspicuous in one place--near the starboard side bow area.

The hill of sand is evident in videos taken in 2000 during an unauthorized expedition to the shipwreck.

American Gregg Bemis, who helped organize the dive, had been told that the Rockwater divers who inspected the wreck immediately after the sinking were able to gain access through a hole in the bottom near the bow.

"We were never able to find that particular hole," Bemis said. "Could it have been covered up by raising the adjacent sand levels?"[12]

PART FOUR

The Backdrop

FORMER SOVIET UNION 1994

When communism collapsed, violent decentralization followed. Ethnic tensions flared. Conflict prone areas (spark) emerged and armed conflicts (flame) broke out. Russia saw itself surrounded by small hostile powers. Moscow believed separatists were working to break up Russia itself.

Brutal civil wars also raged in Yugoslavia and Afghanistan. The first Gulf War had ended three years earlier, creating a stream of refugees across Russia looking for escape to the West.

Russia's weak central authority bred corruption and organized crime, which spilled over open borders.

1994: Chaos Unleashed

The Estonian nation had more crises in the first four years following its 1991 independence from the Soviet Union than Finland and Sweden suffered in peacetime during the entire 20th century. All the major calamities within the loose contours of Estonia during the 1990s resulted from the collapse of the U.S.S.R. and held a direct link to Russia:

The Narva Referendum Crisis, an attempt to carve out a Russian autonomous region within Estonia; Russia's claims to part of Estonia's Northeast border territory and efforts to confiscate it; invigorated organized crime that walked over the law with impunity; the 1994 hijacking of Aeroflot flight TU-134-B; the flood of refugees into Estonia; the hunger strikes, protests and hostage taking at the Oru Peat Factory; the "*Jaagrikriis*"--a violent conflict between factions within the newly-forming Estonian army.

To pluck out the *Estonia* ferry sinking from its proper milieu and obsess over the vessel's mechanical parts is the equivalent of concluding the 1986 Chernobyl reactor meltdown was a generic technical event that could have occurred in any country.[1]

Yet that is exactly what happened. The Joint Accident Investigation Commission investigation was an enormous cut-and-paste job. The ferry catastrophe was casually torn from its historical context and put into the more narrow and predictable world of engineering. Contributing factors, relevant supplemental information and other plausible causes were ignored.

The *Estonia* was not sailing routinely from one port to another. It was literally moving between two starkly contrasting worlds, one full of instability, grinding poverty and violence, the other a wealthy kingdom long run by a caring and peace-loving government.

From February 1993, when the Estonia began sailing the Tallinn-to-Stockholm route, to the time the ferry sank in September 1994, the country of Estonia held a highly fragile independence. Estonia was still entwined politically, socially, ethnically and historically with an imploding Russia. Each groan, crack and thud of the Russian superstructure rumbled through the former Soviet Union (FSU). Estonia lay precariously on the fault line of the rearrangement of the world.

* * *

The fall of the Soviet Union is clearly one of the most important events in the political history of the 20th century. An appreciation of the general course and broader consequences of the U.S.S.R.'s disintegration is worth reviewing not only for historical interest, but essential background that gives validity to the proposed alternative explanations for the sinking of the *Estonia*.

This chapter examines Estonia's flashpoints in 1994, which form the backdrop for the *Estonia* ferry disaster. The main point is that during the 1990s, Russia could not be disentangled from Estonia, despite the 1991 re-establishment of Estonian independence. This equation will consistently appear throughout the book as facts are presented.

Collapse

Macro events had moved with intensifying speed. In November 1989, the Berlin Wall fell and Germany began the process of reunification. Long-shackled Eastern Europe broke free. The Baltic States re-established their independence. The creaking structure of the old and rusty U.S.S.R. finally gave way and the communist system, which provided stability to the planet's largest land mass, stretching from Scandinavia to the Far East, fractured and collapsed. Russia, the largest remaining fragment, "was fraught with anarchy, sabotage and large-scale terrorism," in the early 1990s, according to the man in charge, Russian president Boris Yeltsin.[2]

Breaking away from the Soviet Union one by one, the Baltic States,

Georgia, Moldova, Armenia and Azerbaijan either ignited into armed conflict or were hot to the touch. Chechnya's 1991 sovereignty declaration would soon erupt into two devastating wars lasting nearly a decade. Tajikistan fought a five-year civil war beginning in 1992. Higher stakes came when Ukraine broke away and forced the nuclear Black Sea fleet in Crimea to swear allegiance to the government in Kiev, infuriating Moscow. Afghanistan's internal war exerted a dangerously destabilizing effect on the Central Asian states.[3]

Russia was encircled by armed conflict, real and potential, which the outside world barely noticed.

Internally, Russia seemed to be disintegrating. State-run enterprises stalled because their customers and suppliers in the Soviet Union erected borders and circulated new national currencies. The ruble shed value to a laughable level, turning life savings into pocket money and tearing out the social safety net. Doctors, policemen, professors and politicians alike earned less than the equivalent of $40 per month, and the eroding ruble debased and corrupted core institutions. Mass unemployment and looming starvation prompted worldwide food donations and international security concerns.

Russia's domestic turmoil and disoriented leadership moved civil war into the realm of the possible.

Of course, Russia and Estonia were officially separate countries pursuing their own interests. But in a practical sense, this was not true. Previous centuries of Russian domination and decades of captivity inside the Soviet Union had nearly sewn Estonia into Russia. Therefore, Russia's social upheaval following the collapse of the U.S.S.R. often spilled into the Baltic nation.

Not every crisis erupting in Russia had consequences in Estonia. But there is no doubt that all major crises in Estonia during the early 1990s held direct links to Russia.

Sources of Conflict

A problem in re-examining the 1990s is hindsight. Threats and perils in the former Soviet Union circa 1994 are today often mentioned in the flippant tone used to expose urban legends.

Estonia leapfrogged from a wooded naval outpost of the Soviet Union to a renewed sovereign state and member of the European Union and NATO in little over a decade. Maybe the speed of progress tends to blur and soften all that came before, and when constructive changes flow by fast and frequently, they leave a fainter rendering of the bad stuff in the human memory.

The former despondency, lawlessness and poverty in Estonia have been redefined in people's minds from stark reality to exaggerated difficulties. The lit fuse of apossibly explosive ethnic conflict is today remembered as the dud firecracker it had always been. Contract killings and uranium smuggling are downplayed or forgotten.

But viewing the ferry accident in context means confronting all sorts of unpleasant things. Because when a nuclear empire covering one-sixth of the planet came to an end,, dangerously ratcheting tensions between Russia and its former republics began. Estonia was no exception.

Chechnya 1992 – 1994

Estonia helped trigger the fall of the U.S.S.R. In 1988, a year before the Berlin Wall came down, Estonia officially declared its own laws higher than Soviet laws. The boldness evoked sympathy and respect from various parts of the world. Among the sympathizers were the Chechens, who would soon become Russia's most reviled enemy.

Chechens perhaps found their deepest kinship with the Estonians. War, mass arrests, killings and deportation to work camps under Soviet rule had cut Estonia's ethnic population to below one million and choked the nation's birthrate for generations. About 90 percent of the country was ethnic Estonian in 1939. Fifty years later the figure was 65 percent. Russians made up most of the rest.[4]

Later, Moscow's Russification policy encouraged Russians to move in and put down roots in Estonia. Russian language was introduced into pre-school.[5] Some historic parallels with Chechnya could easily be drawn.

These two diverse ethnicities were bound by an unconscionable thought: How close was their ethnicity to irrelevance if not extermination?

The unlikely mutual respect between Estonians and Chechens can largely be assigned to Dzhokhar Dudayev, who commanded a TU-22 nuclear bomber base in the Estonian city of Tartu in the final years of the Soviet Union.[6]

Dudayev, a native Chechnyan, respected the Estonians assertion of national identity and took their side. In January 1991, clamor for independence from the Baltic Republics was met by beatings and bullets from the Soviet forces in Lithuania and Latvia. In the city of Vilnius, 15 citizens were killed and over 500 wounded. Riga, the Latvian capital, counted five deaths. Estonia braced for similar violence. Dudayev, however, declared his troops would not move against Estonians, and they didn't.[7]

In August 1991, when the Baltic States broke free from Moscow's grip, Dudayev was inspired. He flew to his native Chechnya, won the presidential election and abruptly declared his native land the independent republic of Ichkeriya. The terrible consequences are well-known today.

"A lot of Estonian people from the [Estonian] resistance movement kept in contact with [Dudayev] and he was quite impressed with how we had moved to independence," recalled Mart Laar, Estonian Prime Minister in 1994.

Moscow burned with anger. To the beleaguered Russian authorities, cause and effect were obvious. Estonia's defiance of Soviet rule encouraged Dudayev's push for Chechen independence--for which the newly-restructured Estonian parliament had voted support. Estonia was also apparently a link in supplying arms to Chechnya.[8]

Russia both loathed and feared Dudayev, who they categorized as the Don of the former Soviet Union's largest mafia group, illegally establishing a state backed by criminals. Dudayev had praised Ayatollah Khomeini and Muhammar Khaddaffi and declared he would turn Chechnya into an Islamic republic. By the autumn of 1994, Dudayev was already tagged a terrorist for attempting to blackmail Moscow with bombs and destruction of nuclear plants. Up to his death in 1996, Dudayev would evolve into something like Russia's equivalent of Osama Bin Laden.

In Estonia, Dudayev was respected and memorialized.

To Moscow, the situation was clear. Treasonous bonds had been forged against Russia in its enfeebled condition. Estonia was an instigator, destroying the prestige and power of Russia. Spreading the virus of separatism would not go unpunished.[9]

NATO

An even more humiliating threat that made Moscow politicians pound desks was the acronym for the arch Cold War enemy, NATO. The creeping NATO presence represented a potential stab in the heart of the Russian state. Once again, Estonia was directing the knife.

Initially, the entry of the Baltic Republics into NATO was a nervous whisper. But in 1993, retired U.S. Special Forces Colonel Alexander Einseln accepted the invitation of Estonian president Lennart Meri to become the head of Estonia's Armed Forces, or "Defense Forces" as they were called. His mission was to revamp a corrupted and ill-disciplined Soviet force into a small army fit for a democracy.[10]

Einseln, a U.S. citizen, was born in Estonia. He'd fled the country as a child in 1940 when the Soviets walked in and took over. Einseln was calmly determined to ensure occupation would end; thousands of Russian troops still remained in Estonia. He hammered together a Baltic States peacekeeping battalion called BALTBAT, in reality a stepping stone to NATO.

The Partnership for Peace (PfP) program was launched, officially to enhance cooperation in peacekeeping missions (Russia became a PfP member), but unofficially as a NATO apprenticeship, allowing aspirant countries to get their feet wet.

Escalating threats from the highest offices in Moscow thundered across the region and served as a caution to the more determined voices in the NATO enlargement camp. If NATO expands, "the flame of war would burst out across the whole of Europe," Yeltsin would blare at a Moscow press conference. He was followed by Defense Minister Pavel Grachev:

"What is the line at which Russia starts a military build-up and seeks new military alliances? The limit--please!--is when the Baltic countries become NATO members." Communist Party leader Gennady Zuganov said the Baltics joining NATO would mean "80% of the people in Northeastern Estonia, who are all Russians, would vote for joining Russia. This would mean the division of Estonia."[11]

NATO would build forces on Russia's doorstep. It was unthinkable to many top Russian officials still in denial of the new realities. A few short years ago, they remembered, in the Estonian Soviet Socialist Republic, Soviets had dominated the Baltic Sea from Paldiski submarine base on the Estonian coast. A foreign tourist couldn't even step on ESSR soil without prior authorization from the Soviet state.

Such thoughts riled some Russians each time Einseln worked his connections to invite NATO cadre to Estonia or to suggest a U.S. military ship dock in Tallinn harbor.[12]

Russia's loss of Baltic bases and ports tore a hole in Russian-Baltic relations and Moscow perceived it as an immediate security problem. To the Kremlin, NATO cooperation was the clever work of opportunistic enemies advancing their stronghold. The Baltic States and the Baltic Sea had been the private property of the great Soviet Empire. Now aggressive NATO circles were taking them away.

Narva Powder Keg

"The Estonian people emerged from the darkness of an empire into the bright sunlight of freedom," according to Estonian president Arnold Rüütel.[13]

Not exactly. If the sunlight was bright, it was also dangerously hot and steadily rising in degree. There was little protective shade.

Russians living in a suddenly free Estonia fell hard and fast. Many local bureaucrats, factory and bank directors, military and support personnel, police, transport workers and others who a short while ago held the elite jobs in the country were now officially aliens. They were now legally obligated to learn the language of the country they lived in, effectively barring many from positions of authority.

Former KGB and other security officials were sacked without benefits. There were rumors that Russians would be evicted from their flats. Estonians were even talking about arresting individuals for past war crimes.

The Russians' descent from ruling class to suspect minority group was not a series of steps but a plummet. It was a crushing humiliation.

Organized trouble began in the summer of 1993 when Estonia enacted the "Law on Aliens," infuriating its Russian community who said the action was "equivalent to declaring war against the Russian-speaking population." Russians believed the law didn't guarantee their legal rights.

Narva, a city in Estonia's northeast on the Russian border with a population of more than 90 percent ethnic Russians was the flashpoint. Fist-thrusting Narva residents promised to shut down power stations, blockade the border post and flood the streets with protestors. They found comrades among nationalist politicians in Moscow.

Russia had been in the process of withdrawing its Baltic naval fleet from Estonia. A few days after the law's enactment, that stopped. Russia also cut off the supply of natural gas on which Estonia depended and would soon impose trade sanctions against its tiny neighbor. Yeltsin accused Estonia of ethnic cleansing and apartheid.[14]

Narva's mayor called the situation tense. The Russian language *Nezavisimaya Gazeta* wrote "Only a single spark is needed and the powder keg could well explode." The previously passive Russian community in Narva is now "practically up in arms."[15]

Estonia had moved from boisterous discontent in its Northeast region to a tripwire situation that lit up warning lights in the U.S. Just as conflict seemed imminent, a U.S. frigate fresh from NATO maneuvers unexpectedly plowed into Tallinn harbor while a U.S. Navy aircraft landed in Tallinn's little airport for ostensibly routine reasons.[16]

The Swedish Prime Minister Carl Bildt slipped into the protector role. He emerged at the height of the Narva crisis and applied his diplomatic skills on Estonia's behalf.[17]

Under pressure from Europe and sensing escalating ethnic trouble, the Estonian Parliament, the *Riigikogu*, diluted the Law on Aliens. But Narva Russians weren't mollified. They threw down an ultimatum in the form of a referendum. The Narva City Council passed a decision to hold a plebiscite with one single question: "Do you want Narva to have the status of national territorial autonomy in the Estonian Republic?"

In essence, the question meant, "Should we partition Estonia?"[18]

Russian emotion was quantified when 98 percent of Narva voted yes.

Some noticed a disturbing parallel. The referendum appeared to be a backdoor attempt to install the same post-empire model that seemed to have clicked for the Russians in the Trans-Dniester region of Moldova in 1991. Politicians in Tallinn condemned the referendum, declaring it unauthorized and deeming it invalid.[19]

If the seeds of civil war hadn't sprouted, they were at least planted and watered.

The Moldova plan was a three-step strategy. First, encourage social unrest in Estonia. Second, send in Russian troops to protect Russian citizens and restore order. Third, announce that the soldiers are "peacekeepers" not occupiers, with no definite date to withdraw.

It was a game, because both sides were aware of the historical ironies. Hitler had used a similar tactic when he sent his army into Czechoslovakia claiming that the rights of Sudeten Germans were being violated. But it was a game with very high stakes.

Events soon took a more ominous course as Russia's internal political turmoil had repercussions in Estonia. In October 1993, a few months after the Narva crisis, a second coup attempt in Moscow was quashed after Yeltsin ordered tanks to blast the Russian White House, where renegade parliamentarians were holed up. The October events were followed by the sweeping Parliamentary election victory of the misnamed Liberal Democratic Party, headed by the unpredictable ultra-nationalist, Vladimir Zhirinovsky. For the next few years, Zhirinovsky would bedevil Estonia.

Zhirinovsky's rising influence, validated by the December 1993 elections, unnerved the international community and empowered the radical Russians in Estonia.

Zhirinovsky's desire was restoration of the Russian Empire, and he promised that the unruly Baltics would be the first repossession. "I'm telling you honestly that I'm doing everything possible to liquidate the Baltic [S]tates. I'm saying this openly so that there will be no cause for baseless accusations later ... You feel that you are independent, but this will end for you with your own blood," Zhirinovsky told the Estonian press in one of many inflammatory statements.

Now the Russian minority seemed to have a powerful ally in Moscow. Estonia would again feel the power of Russia and hop to its whistle.[20]

In a declassified February 1994 memo from U.S. Ambassador to Estonia Robert Frasure to U.S. Secretary of State Warren Christopher, Frasure describes the Zhirinovsky effect:

"The negative results of the December 12 Duma elections resonated deeply here," Frasure wrote. "Russian radicals were refreshed. Estonians dug in ... In this uncertain context and following on Zhirinovsky's success in the Duma elections, Russian hardliners have gleefully arisen from their shallow political graves."[21]

As Russia turned right, actions in Moscow once again impacted on Estonia. Thousands of resentful Russian soldiers were still parked on Estonian soil. More divisions were a few hours away, across the border in Pskov. Nothing at all ensured that Estonia wouldn't erupt into bitter ethnic violence or be reoccupied, perhaps this time by "peacekeeping" troops. Politicians and analysts on both sides of the Atlantic were busy assessing the impact on East-West relations should Russia invade the Baltic States.[22]

Would Estonia be forced to trade a chunk of its Northeast, including Narva, Kohtla-Järve and Sillamäe, to get Russian soldiers off its soil? Were any of the 600,000 Russian speakers in Estonia working as Zhirinovsky sleeper agents who would clandestinely help accomplish his goals? Could Zhirinovsky be democratically elected as Russian president in the elections slated for 1996? At the time, all seemed possible.

In many instances, threats against Estonia appeared only in rhetoric, gossip and graffiti. But perceived threats are highly dangerous. They create an atmosphere in which conflict can erupt on mere rumor.

More sinister acts magnified the Narva protests. Police investigated a number of cases involving Russian troops selling their weapons for cash. Estonian police confiscated "500 kilograms of high explosives from a Russian non-commissioned officer, which experts say is enough to blow up the World Trade Center in New York," according to the Estonian Ministry of Foreign Affairs. In the same cache, police seized 12,000 rounds of ammunition, which were intended for sale.[23]

Russian military structures took no responsibility for missing weapons. The clock was ticking. Their scheduled date to withdraw from Estonia was under negotiation at the high political levels. Many senior officers and soldiers saw pullout as surrender; even more, they did not want to return to Russia, where other soldiers were bartering for food or even living in tents.

Where were all these weapons going? How close was Estonia to degenerating into a Balkans-style ethnic conflict that could engulf Latvia, Lithuania, and Northwest Russia?[24]

The Bandits

Estonia's potential ethnic conflict held another insidious dimension. Organized criminal groups were colonizing the Baltic Republics.

With buzz haircuts and Makarov pistols, they favored Mercedes and BMWs and paid for them in cash. Many of these individuals had military or professional sports backgrounds and had shed their hopeless careers for one of ruthless brutality that paid in hard currency.

The criminal groups tended to have friends in high places. In the tangled logic of the early 1990s, Russian politicians, businessmen and the military collaborated to enrich themselves. The lines blurred so much between armed forces and criminals, analysts were referring to Russia's military as "Mafia in Uniform."[25]

In 1994, Estonia was part of their turf. The end of the Soviet state, the presence of demoralized Russian military and lax border controls in the Baltics allowed both local and foreign criminal organizations to operate with unprecedented efficiency. Illicit trade, extortion, open prostitution, bribery of officials, contract killings and largescale fraud were in their portfolio.

Smuggling weapons and drugs was not a fringe activity, but an alarming mainstream practice.

Arms were freely available. Estonia had launched its own currency, the Kroon, and pegged it to the expensive Deutsch Mark. Thus, a Russian soldier's ruble salary fell in value daily to the Kroon. Selling weapons, ammunition, artillery and other ordnance for dollars was often a survival strategy for the individual soldier.

The U.S. estimated Estonia's black economy in 1994 generated over one-third of GDP, "much of it involving organized crime and related activities."[26]

The spike in criminal violence came in 1994 and originated in Russia. 1994 was the year the *Estonia* ferry sank and the year blood flowed freely across much of the FSU. 1994 was also the year Yeltsin called Russia a "Superpower of Crime."

"The bloodshed that was unleashed in 1993-4 was special," wrote the journalist Paul Klebnikov in his book on the looting of Russia. "Generations of criminals fought for the scattered assets of the weakened Russian state."[27]

Estonia's crime rate rose in correlation with Russia's bloodiest years; local criminal activity held direct connections to crime in Russia. Murder picked up substantially. In 1993, Tallinn was declared one of the world's most violent capitals with 259 officially reported murders, the highest rate in Europe.

Meanwhile, only 21 percent of all reported crimes were being solved as of mid-1993. Passengers on the *Estonia* ferry were commonly arriving in Stockholm with cans of mace or sometimes even knives and pistols in their pockets for self-protection.[28]

Baltic ports were the domain of the criminal world. With East Germany gone and war raging in the Balkans, the Baltics became the focal point for moving illicit goods out of the FSU to the West. Criminal groups took advantage of the 13 million tons of legal Russian cargo shipped annually from Baltic ports to move arms, drugs, human refugees, stolen cars and anything else that would sell for hard currency.

Criminal entrepreneurs encouraged thousands of Third World asylum seekers to pour into the Baltics. Many were displaced Iraqi Kurds, uprooted by the first Gulf War, who had traveled thousands of miles across Russia to what they saw as the last barrier to the sanctuary of Europe. Hundreds of refugees were guided to Estonia and to the busy Tallinn port with a direct shipping line to Sweden. Criminal gangs and freelance smugglers took upwards of $1000 per head and packed them on ferries and small boats to Sweden.[29]

In February 1994, Kurdish refugees from Iraq, sealed in a container and loaded on to the *Estonia* ferry's cardeck, nearly suffocated on the night crossing to Sweden. They were rescued when a crewmember heard banging inside the truck.

Many incidents involving the unauthorized movement of strategic material were documented. Between 1993 and 1995, 11 cases of confiscated radioactive materials were uncovered and officially reported in Estonia. Of these incidents, eight cases involved cesium-137, one involved radium, and two involved uranium, according to government figures. (See Chapter 10)[30]

Estonia began appearing on intelligence threat assessment reports in the West. Estonia didn't have radiation detection equipment or expertise to stop the flow of dangerous materials and the 60 Kroon (about $5) monthly salaries of the military conscripts who policed the border posts encouraged bribes.[31]

Nightmares about nuclear appliances smuggled out of the FSU haunted Clinton's White House in the fall and winter of 1994. Agents from Iran and North Korea had been in the FSU studying weapons sites. The unthinkable question was uttered in highly-classified meetings in Washington: Radioactive material passes through porous Baltic borders, so why couldn't criminal elements sneak a nuclear bomb out of Russia's unsecured stockpiles?[32]

In 1994, the former Soviet Union turned out to be a very odd place indeed. Images of U.S. warships blockading Soviet vessels from approaching the Cuban coast were no longer needed to make your hair stand on end.

De-occupation, August 1994

The Balts cheered, but the Russians moved home with mute resentment. The August 31, 1994, Russian troop pullout after more than 50 years of occupation was celebrated by the civilized world as an end to totalitarian rule and a victory for international diplomacy. President Clinton sent a message of congratulations predicting "a new era of regional stability and cooperation." Estonian President Lennart Meri pointed to the end of "the saddest chapter of our history." "I say Estonia is now independent," added Prime Minister Laar.[33]

In reality, the Russians had been pried out. Cajoled, rewarded, scolded, assured and threatened. They never wanted to leave.

Indeed, The Russian voice was laced with vengeance. *Izvestia* wondered how long the troops were leaving for "this time." The military analyst of another newspaper, *Nezavisimaya Gazeta*, said Russia's "uncivilized withdrawal" had caused "incredible and sometimes irreparable" losses to Russia's wealth and national security. Even worse, he wrote, was the "humiliation" to Russia and the Russian-speaking citizens still in the Baltics.[34]

The withdrawal itself was without official fanfare, a condition stipulated in the agreement shaped by the negotiators. But the pullout was clouded by disturbing facts.

Estonia had 10,500 retired Russian officers who stayed put despite their ruble-based pensions in an expensive Kroon-based economy. These were the very same officers who had faithfully kept Estonia in Moscow's grip, together with retired security services personnel, some who were associated with repressions and executions. Estonia viewed these stay-behind military men as a national security risk, a possible clandestine subversive organization working within Estonia to further Moscow's aims--a fifth column.[35]

Anxiety over a fifth column among Russian Diaspora spread as Zhirinovsky continued to make dramatic threats. Leaders of a new group called the Union of Russian Citizens of Estonia were supporting a second referendum for autonomy in Northeastern Estonia.

The U.S. again took notice. They came up with a scheme to give Russian officers $10,000 vouchers for an apartment in Russia on condition they moved out of Estonia. But the voucher program wasn't embraced by Russia. U.S. Ambassador Frasure found it odd that Moscow was fighting so hard to keep recently retired officers in Estonia rather than letting them accept housing in Russia essentially paid for by the U.S. government.[36]

The sleeper cell theory was not paranoia. With colonial experience in Estonia, Russia had the trained manpower, generations of friendships, easy economic ties, institutional knowledge and police and intelligence service files to do whatever it wanted.

A possible fifth column was no joke in the West, either. It was a topic for U.S. defense analysts. Carl Bildt held strong suspicions. Sweden allocated money for Estonia to examine possible risks inherent in the presence of retired Russian military in the country. Lt. General Einseln found that many ethnic Russian soldiers serving under his command in the de-Sovietized Estonian army were loyal to Russia. He also discovered two Russian military intelligence (GRU) officials held high positions in the Estonian Ministry of Defense.[37]

Assertive Sweden

The tumultuous times in the Baltic region were kept in check by unlikely stewards.

Sweden's Carl Bildt and Finland's Esko Aho, both barely 40, and Estonia's Prime Minister Mart Laar in his early 30s, all closer to the age of post-graduate students than seasoned statesmen, were thrust into high-stakes chaos management positions.

Carl Bildt emerged as a key figure in the Baltic Sea region. Bildt was driving the chariots of state in Sweden. His assertive leadership style and bold proposals that are standard qualities for a U.S. politician disquieted some circles in placid Sweden.

Under Bildt, Sweden, which hadn't seen a war for 180 years and officially maintained neutrality during the Cold War, would loosen its nonalignment policy, sign up for NATO's Partnership for Peace program and hold consistent debate on the topic of joining NATO.[38]

To the Russians, he was no doubt a troublesome figure. Bildt had always taken a strong anti-Soviet position, backing freedom and democracy in Eastern Europe long before it became fashionable to do so. He rose to power in Sweden by organizing the campaign to expose what he claimed were Soviet submarines trespassing in Swedish waters. Post-Cold War, he quickly saw Sweden as Europe's "northern pillar" of power.

Bildt was outspoken for a Swede. He closely watched and criticized Russia's behavior toward the re-established Baltic republics and called the post-war replacement of Estonians with Russians in Narva ethnic cleansing.

He worked on Estonia's behalf with the breathtaking energy of a man who must right a wrong. Sweden had, after all, in effect officially recognized the forcible annexation of the Baltic States into the Soviet Union; the majority of the democratic countries went on record to say they did not. Estonian gold deposited in the Swedish National Bank for safekeeping in 1939 had been handed over to the Soviet Union. Sweden had also sent back to Stalin an estimated 30,000 Estonians who had made treacherous escapes across the Baltic to Swedish shores following the 1940 Soviet occupation of Estonia. Most of them were executed.[39]

That was Sweden's historical record; now it was time to make amends. It was Bildt who initiated the new ferry line between Estonia and Sweden. Visiting Soviet Estonia in the late 1980s, he acted as a matchmaker between the Estonian state-run shipping enterprise and Nordström & Thulin AB on the Swedish side. The ferry line would be co-owned. A general agreement for the joint venture ferry line was signed in August 1989.

N&T EstLine AB, better known as "Estline" was the name of the cross-Baltic joint venture. Estline was a product of Soviet President Mikhail Gorbachev's new "regulated market economy," a hybrid between a genuine free-market business and a state-owned concern that allowed Gorbachev to insist that he had not abandoned communism.

Everything about the new ferry line was political and highly symbolic. Bildt believed he was creating a lifeline between free Estonia and the West. Regular service on the route started on June 17, 1990, exactly 50 years after the Soviet Union had occupied Estonia.[40]

In the first years Estline ran the ferry *Nord Estonia*. Later it was replaced by a larger luxury ferry purchased from Finland. It was christened the *M/V Estonia* and started service in February 1993.

Parked in Tallinn harbor, bearing the name of its patron state, the ship flew the Estonian flag--blue, black and white--and sailed to Stockholm with the swank of a gloating nation. It was lit up by floodlights and frequently repainted to keep it gleaming white. It evoked association with the grand maritime tradition of a venerable Europe.

In a sense the ferry was a concrete manifestation of Bildt's Baltic strategy — integration with the West, commerce and progress.

There is no *M/V Sweden* and no *M/V Finland*. But there was the *M/V Estonia*, so named because it was such a crucial tool for a modest, austere country. The Estonian state cared deeply about image. In fact, image was Estonia's security. The more the world knew Estonia, the more world opinion would rally behind it during the nasty divorce from the U.S.S.R. The tactic later became known as the "CNN defense."

Traffic on the big ferry began slowly. Estonians who could scrape together some travel money went to see Sweden, for them a first glimpse of the real West. Swedish citizens were curious about Estonia, but aggressive marketing would be necessary to overcome fear of the post-Soviet crime wave blighting the Baltic nation. Sweden also had a large Estonian émigré community. Many held positions in business, government and the armed forces and showed an intense interest in helping rebuild their homeland. They sailed frequently to Tallinn.[41]

The ferry was a money-losing venture from the day it started, something that should have been closed down in the ruthless shipping industry. But the *Estonia* kept going because political will in Sweden kept it alive. The ship was an unabashed celebration of growing Western links. It was independence in physical form.[42]

Not everyone appreciated the Republic of Estonia and accompanying symbols of the state freedom. "Ferry and air travel across the narrow Baltic is developing rapidly, enabling Balts who have money or rich relatives to become acquainted with Sweden's 'achievements of material culture,'" wrote one commentator sarcastically in the Russian newspaper *Sevodnya*.

> "The stream of tourists going in the opposite direction, however, is small, because they're frightened by the crime situation in the East . . . On the whole, however, Stockholm is happy that the Soviet empire's Baltic bastion has collapsed, thereby removing a military threat to Sweden . . . Now the Swedes want to reclaim their historically and geographically justified influence."[43]

* * *

Given the dangerous instability in the FSU during the 1990s, Estonia nonetheless made a remarkably peaceful post-Soviet transition compared to some other countries. Its swift integration into the EU and NATO, efficient economy and transparent government make Estonia something of a showpiece in the new Europe. Certainly credit is due to the behind-the-scenes diplomatic efforts of Western authorities as well as the Estonians themselves. Estonians intelligence, unbreakable cohesiveness as a people and unique temperament that makes them slow to anger, prevailed and brought tangible progress in creating self-sustaining, indigenous institutions.

But juxtaposed with the vigorous rebuilding of a nation was the spillover of chaos from a nuclear superpower that often seemed to be nearing anarchy.

Across Russia, surreal events played out to an increasingly impoverished and indignant population. A state electric company turned off power to an airport control tower while dozens of planes were in the air, including one carrying President Yeltsin. An army base commander dispatched tanks to an electric power company, forcing it to restore power that had been cut due to non-payment of bills. A Russian man who saw petty bureaucrats take his money, apartment and passport, hijacked a domestic Aeroflot flight that landed in Tallinn without casualties. After Estonian authorities agreed to turn him over to Russia, he hung himself in a Tallinn jail cell.[44]

On September 27, 1994, a silent and sure military buildup was underway in Chechnya. Moscow officially pledged that Russia wouldn't intervene. No one could predict Chechnya was about to be hit by stunning barbarity, with an estimated 20,000 people killed in the first three months of the coming year.On the same date in Tallinn, the wind was picking up during a late autumn afternoon. Leaves were already yellow and maroon. Estonia's far Northern latitude in late fall meant dusk arrived early in the day.

At 19:15, the *M/V Estonia* left port for Stockholm. Europe was less than seven hours away from its worst sea catastrophe since World War II.

PART FIVE

Alternative Scenarios

Alternative Scenarios

The *Estonia* ferry sank suspiciously fast. Russia's descent into lawlessness and violence provides fertile ground for suspicion of foul play.

But the JAIC's one-dimensional approach prematurely eliminated every possible influence except those related to the complex technical interactions between the visor system's mechanical parts. As a result, the official "visor off, ramp open, ship down" is an incomplete rendering of the sinking. It is, in fact, a distortion.

Passenger ships, seaworthy and properly handled, do not sink in 35 minutes because of water on the cardeck and an autumn rainstorm. Something had to greatly accelerate the sinking.

Assuming the ferry was not a piece of junk and the crew competent, the only conclusion is that the ferry had a hole. And a hole could only come from a collision or an explosion.

External factors, however, were not addressed by investigators. The commission didn't closely collaborate with the Swedish and Russian security services, the FBI (which by compelling necessity had set up in Russia and the Baltics), or other relevant authorities. How deep and how long anyone followed a criminal trail is unknown. Nothing indicates that investigators followed a systematic procedure to categorically rule out a collision or explosion.[1]

Moreover, Sweden, a country long held aloft as the world's model of openness and fairness, suddenly clamped down on information about the *Estonia* and shut the doors on public debate. Stockholm quarantined the shipwreck. Specific *Estonia* documents are classified as state secrets. The principal actors in the investigation are not talking.

This section contains speculative scenarios based on coherent and convergent evidence that points to a collision or an explosion. No scenario can be conclusively proven as fact, but a theory need not be conclusive in order to be indicative of the truth.

A final point about speculative theories comes from viewing the *Estonia* ferry disaster in its historical timeframe, which is a sobering exercise.

In January 1995, three months after the ferry had sunk, the nuclear suitcases carried by President Yeltsin and his top command were activated. The Russian military had mistakenly identified a Norwegian high-altitude research rocket as a threat. Russian leaders were forced to decide whether to launch a retaliatory strike against the eastern coast of the U.S.

> "Lights flashed on the [nuclear] suitcases. It must have been a terrible moment as the suitcase owners reached for their keys. This had never happened before, not even in the worst moments of the Cuban missile crisis. Out across Russia, the missile operators went on high alert. They were 15 minutes or less away from launching a massive nuclear strike on the United States . . . The decisive vote on whether to launch or not belonged to Yeltsin and Defense Minister Pavel Grachev, who the month before had assured the president that Grozny could be taken in a matter of hours."[2]

When the rocket didn't head for Russia, nuclear forces went back to normal alert status.

The times were such that sections of the planet could be annihilated as easily as misreading a map or making a wrong turn.

A collision or explosion at sea seems much less preposterous.

Hit and Run

The Baltic Sea is ideal for submarine training operations. Relatively shallow depths dropping off to deeper canyons create an exacting mission for a submarine crew. Depths vary widely, from 30 meters to 300, sometimes within kilometers. Frequent surface vessel traffic, mainly passenger ferries and cargo ships connecting the Scandinavian ports, provide targets of opportunity for submarine tracking and escort techniques, as well as concealment for underwater vessels trailing in the noisy wake of a surface ship's screws.

The tens of thousands of islands along the Finnish and Swedish coasts serve as excellent hiding places for submarines. After the U.S.S.R. collapsed, Estonian authorities asked the Swedes to search for underwater caves somewhere between Narva and Tallinn where Russian submarines could hide.[1]

Rumors that a string of mines left over from the Cold War stretches across the seafloor have circulated since the Soviet Union fell. Some say it extends underwater from Utö a Finnish Island, to Ristna in Estonia and was planted by NATO in secret cooperation with Sweden; others say it runs from Narva to the Finnish coast, in front of Hoaglund Island, set by the Russians to prevent intruders into St Petersburg. After 1991, both Finnish and Swedish military found individual mines in Estonian waters laid by the Russians during the Cold War, but they did not report finding a string of mines.[2]

Submarines speckled the undersea depths of the Baltic for decades. In a length of sea measuring 500 miles, from Kaliningrad to St Petersburg, the Soviet Union had diesel submarine bases at Baltisk in Kaliningrad, Klaipeda in Lithuania, Liepaja in Latvia and Paldiski in Estonia, not to mention the enormous St Petersburg naval bases and construction facilities that repaired damaged subs and designed and tested new ones.

Sweden ran its own twelve diesel submarines of Swedish construction. Norway, Denmark and Germany flexed their NATO muscles by sailing stealthily under the surface of Baltic waters. Subs from the U.K. and U.S. were frequent visitors, checking on Soviet activity, conducting maneuvers and sometimes visiting Swedish territorial waters.[3]

After the U.S.S.R. dissolved, some Russian submarines still roamed the Baltic Sea in denial of their dwindling regional dominance. During the 1990s, Sweden produced acoustic signatures of submarines and videotapes of minisub tracks on the seafloor in its territorial waters. Bildt connected the incursions to Russia.

Sweden had been suspicious of underwater trespassers ever since 1981 when a Soviet Whiskey-class submarine got stuck on rocks in the Swedish archipelago. The apparent post-Soviet incursions were given the highest priority in Sweden, culminating with Bildt's 1994 visit to Moscow where he said he was convinced the submarines were Russian and that they probably entered Swedish waters without Yeltsin's knowledge.

Around this time, the Swedes acknowledged that some 20 percent of the acoustic readings they previously thought were submarines were actually "biological phenomena" a euphemistic phrase for, among other wildlife, schools of swimming minks.[4]

However, Sweden's claims were corroborated by Finland. According to former Finnish Prime Minister Esko Aho, Russian submarine made incursions into Finnish waters during that same period.[5]

Meanwhile, passenger ferry sailings started to increase. With onboard, duty-free alcohol up to five times cheaper than in Scandinavia, Baltic ferries gained a reputation for drink and dance parties at sea.

Like much in the Northern Baltic region, innocent surface activity for decades masked the menacing reality underneath.

* * *

Ruins of Viking ships, trading vessels, warships from numerous countries and different epochs lie scattered across the relatively small

Baltic seafloor, reflecting its bloody history.

Estonia, Latvia and Lithuania for hundreds of years were vital for Russian naval defenses. Considered tactical prizes for any dominant Baltic power, they were contested in the Middle Ages by Danes, Swedes, Poles and German Teutonic Knights. Russia did not acquire control of Estonia until 1721 when it defeated Sweden in an imperial war.[6]

In the 20th century, a period of independence was short lived. Estonia became a sovereign nation for two decades until the Nazis and Soviets brutalized the Baltics. In 1940, the three countries were forcibly annexed by the U.S.S.R.

The region became the very heart of the Soviet Union's maritime potential and one of the most heavily militarized areas in the world. It served as a kind of Berlin Wall of the sea, separating East from West. A short list of the Soviet Baltic Fleet in the mid-1980s included 45 submarines, 260 naval aircraft including bombers and strike fighters; 45 anti-submarine warfare (ASW) aircraft, 55 tactical support and 45 utility aircraft.[7]

The fall of communism brought a drop in Baltic Sea submarine transit, but by no means the end of it.

Post-Soviet Russia, broke and chaotic, had trouble making obligatory payments to state institutions in the 1990s. The military received no economic assistance and was forced to survive in the new free-market jungle.

Naval forces suffered harshly. As the Russian military pullout from the Baltics became a reality, the Baltic Fleet was gutted. Submarines were moved to Kaliningrad or left to sit in port where they were often looted for metals or equipment that were sold on the black market. In Latvia, about 30 abandoned subs and military vessels lay half submerged in the harbor, protruding above the surface.[8]

Military salaries went unpaid for months because the state was broke. Personnel in sub design bureaus fled Russia to work for hard currency in foreign countries. Fuel, repair and maintenance costs limited submarine missions.[9]

"Defense conversion" to peacetime applications was touted by the United Nations as Russia's path to redemption. "Under-the-ice delivery" of cargo using nuclear submarines in the Arctic was one idea. The Malakhit Submarine Design Plant in St Petersburg suggested using submarines as floating power plants or to lay communications cable under the Arctic. In the Northern Fleet, finances were so bad that Victor III class submarines removed their torpedoes so they could shuttle potatoes to Siberia for some cash.[10]

In reality, naval submarines have no commercially-viable peacetime use.

But there was another solution to generate revenue and it was neat. Naval authorities found that idle submarines could be sold for cash. Without going through the stricken central command in Moscow, base commanders could sell submarines to pay salary arrears and perhaps enrich themselves along the way.

There was no shortage of buyers. A British entrepreneur grabbed a used 85-meter long diesel Foxtrot submarine from the Russians in 1994. It sailed over from Latvia. "We bought it from a company set up by the Russian government and Navy," the entrepreneur explained. "It's part of their drive for foreign currency."

A Juliet-class diesel cruise-missile submarine was hawked to the Finns. It became a paying tourist attraction in Helsinki harbor. The Russians also sold a Zulu submarine to the Netherlands and a Whiskey class to Sweden.[11]

Third World countries keen to bolster their sea defense forces lined up to make deals. Iran became the first state in the Persian Gulf region to acquire a submarine when in 1992 it bought a vessel from Russia and sailed it thousands of miles from St Petersburg to Bandar Abbas. Iran then inked an agreement to procure two more.[12]

China purchased four diesel-powered Kilo-class submarines. Chile, India, Algeria, North Korea and Pakistan also bought diesel-electric Kilo class submarines from Russia in the 1990s.

In January 1994, news got out that Russia signed contracts with North Korea for the sale of 10 Golf II-class submarines. Some presumably came from the Vladivostok naval ports, though locations weren't disclosed.[13]

By 1994, submarine sales were in full swing. In eight years, Russia's submarine fleet had been reduced to 99 vessels from 186.[14]

Selling military vessels to Third World countries remained a highly-sensitive issue in the West. President Clinton kept prodding President Yeltsin to stop strengthening the navies of countries run by dictators. The problem was, these countries happened to be Russia's best clients.

Despite official assurances, submarines continued to change hands through more quiet deals that were veiled in the cloth of classified military business. Selling off state resources also handsomely enriched many individuals. Viktor Mikhailov, head of energy ministry Minatom, was cutting backroom deals on his own with Iran to sell dual-use nuclear equipment without the Kremlin's knowledge.[15]

Hawking assets was also a matter of survival. Sometimes the state did pay military salaries, but the amount wasn't adjusted for inflation. The steadily declining value of the ruble bought less and less. Most Russians believed the hard times would worsen. What admiral or shipyard director wouldn't want to sell a rotting submarine when he could do it fast and discreetly? Rogue states were ready to pay hard currency for the secondhand vessels.

*   *   *

In 1994, more than 20 developing countries possessed 150 diesel attack submarines. Many of these boats were obsolete, poorly maintained or operated by ill-trained crews.[16]

Some of these submarines were purchased from St Petersburg. To minimize attention from the politically-sensitive sales, the submarines had to slip out through the Gulf of Finland finger and make a discreet run through the tight Denmark Straits to the open sea.

But the run was more of an obstacle course. The Swedes had a dozen coastal patrol submarines and some snooped on Russia's underwater activities. Moreover, Sweden's underwater surveillance equipment fenced in the Swedish territorial waters with some extra miles thrown in for good measure.

In fact, the Swedes had already sighted one purchased submarine heading home to the Middle East. An Iranian crew sailing a Russian diesel Kilo class submarine was detected sailing between the Danish Island of Bornholm and the southern tip of Sweden in the summer of 1993. The sighting coincided with a NATO naval exercise in the Baltic Sea.[17]

The sighting persuaded U.S. officials to stridently accuse Yeltsin's administration of arming rogue states.

If another sub tried to sail from St Petersburg to the open ocean, more detailed strategic planning between seller and buyer would be necessary to avoid getting caught again. Russian submarines are sheathed in a special rubber coating to help reduce the risk of acoustic detection. Still, the sub would have to pass the prying eyes of Sweden, then maneuver covertly through the Denmark Straits, a 10-mile wide bottleneck spilling into the Kattegat and Skagerrak areas near Norway's Southern coastline, which were dotted with underwater acoustic listening posts.

How could a sub sneak onto the high seas?

A possible answer appeared about mid-1994, when NATO released a press statement outlining several joint naval exercises that would take place in European waters in the coming months.

NATO's post-communist training exercises attempted to show that the organization had a big heart. Under the auspices of the Partnership for Peace (PfP) program, NATO invited the former East Bloc countries, the Baltic Republics, Russia and Sweden for various joint exercises in or near the Baltic Sea. One such event would start September 28 and was called "Cooperative Venture 94."[18]

It was during just such an exercise in 1993 that the Iranian crew was spotted near the Swedish coast sailing their acquired Russian sub. But Cooperative Venture 94 was different in a striking way. The massive PfP training exercise would take place in the deep water of the Skagerrak area of the North Sea as well as much further north in the Norwegian Sea. As they arrived, the sea vessels, ASW aircraft, fighter jets, land-based weaponry and troops would for a time create some expected confusion in the area as they installed themselves *en masse* hundreds of kilometers away from the Denmark Straits.

The naval exercise would unintentionally create a cover for a submarine that intended to slip into the high seas undetected.

* * *

By the morning of September 28, military personnel and vessels from 14 countries were orienting themselves, prepping units and interlocking with the command center. The multi-nation exercise would run ten days. Cooperative Venture 94 was ramping up when the *Estonia* ferry went down.

The exercise included a NATO flotilla requiring considerable men and resources for training, supplies and support. Though details of Cooperative Venture 94 remain classified, presumably the Swedes had sent at least one submarine from their main base in nearby Karlskrona. The Russian Navy also participated.[19]

Coordinating these sprawling multinational exercises between mismatched countries that rarely if ever trained together tied up substantial military resources. NATO attention would be fixed squarely on the Skagerrak area of Southern Norway and even further north as the exercises progressed. Underwater surveillance posts that typically monitor sub traffic would be disturbed by the ships and submarines arriving at the site, testing vessel maneuvering and communications and acting out training plans.

A window had opened on September 27. That day would be ideal for sailing a diesel submarine out of St Petersburg, through the Gulf of Finland and then south to slip through the Denmark Straits toward the broader ocean.

ASW planes from Kaliningrad participating in the exercise could serve a second function, watching for any NATO subs along the militarized Karlskrona area in Southern Sweden and monitoring military vessels as they arrived and clustered near the Skagerrak waters of Norway's Southern Coast. The intelligence would be useful to the submarine crew, helping them avoid detection.

The plan, crudely sketched, would start with the foreign crew setting sail from St Petersburg at night, presumably on or near the surface to enhance navigation. As the sub crosses the Baltic and passes south of Denmark's Bornholm Island, it then follows slowly behind the noisy wake of the next passing surface vessel to frustrate any hydro-acoustic posts.

A surveillance gap created by the mass redistribution of resources more than 300 kilometers miles north of the Denmark Straits could let the sub enter the North Sea right under the noses of the NATO-friendly forces. Although secondhand, the diesel sub is remarkably quiet, employing Soviet underwater stealth technology developed more than a decade before the *Glasnost* period.

Soviet Russia's use of distractions and ruses to support clandestine submarine movements was standard practice during the Cold War. Now, however, the old familiar tactics would be used to avoid bad press and diplomatic unpleasantries.[20]

Perhaps a small crew from the navy of Iran, North Korea, Libya, Pakistan or other client state set out from St Petersburg under the cover of night on September 27, 1994 with one clear directive when delivering the purchased sub to home port: Don't get caught.

120 THE HOLE

SEPTEMBER 27 - 28, 1994

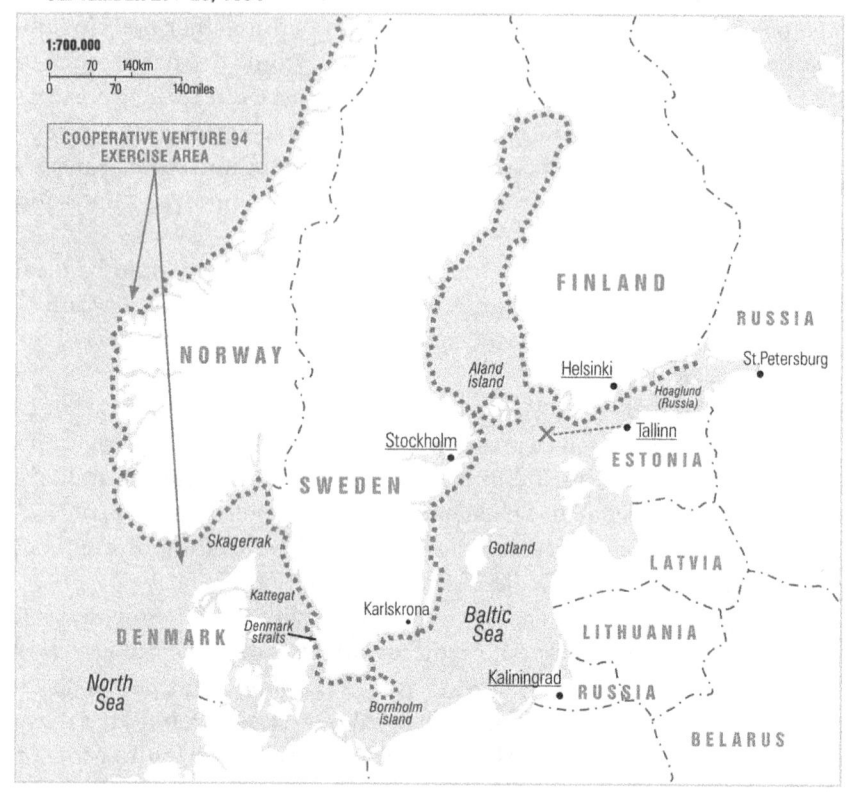

    The coastal broken line represents probable undersea listening equipment that can detect submarines. A submarine leaving St Petersburg could stay near the Baltic Coast to avoid detection, then sail toward the Denmark Straits to open seas. Surveillance resources would be diverted to coordinate the huge NATO sea exercise, Cooperative Venture 94, which gathered at Norway's southern coast but moved further north.
    In 1993, a Russian kilo class submarine purchased by Iran sailed from St Petersburg during a similar NATO exercise. Equipment picked up the sub near Bornholm Island and disclosure prompted the U.S. to publicly criticize Russia's military equipment sales. Iran held a contract for more Russian subs, as did other Third World nations.
    The *Estonia* sunk in position X, but the first indications of trouble occurred about a half hour prior to reaching that position.
    Navies from the 14 nations involved in Cooperative Venture 94, which included search-and-rescue training, were indeed deeply preoccupied with their own exercise. They did not respond to the catastrophe on the night of September 28, supporting the contention that a sub sneaking out during the exercise would have evaded detection.

Scrapes

Extracts from survivor statements appear in the Final Report not as evidence, but only in the most generic form. Testimonies weren't mined for patterns that could shed light on the initial stages of the catastrophe. No statements that contradicted findings were assembled. The excerpts seem to be neutralized and added with much reluctance.

Luckily, the German investigators ferreted out the entire uncut collection of survivor testimonies and included them in the GGE Report. In their signed testimonies to police within days after the accident, survivors described a remarkably similar chain of events. Taken together, as one takes a list of numbers and averages them, the result is enough sensory evidence to suspect a collision. The key elements are loud, unnatural bangs not caused by waves, a crash and abrupt stop that threw some people to the floor, followed by a hull scraping noise and powerful list to starboard.

Crew members' playback of events are especially noteworthy. Crew members are limited in details they can give. Any comments indicating something was wrong with the ferry's upkeep would reflect badly on their employers--the Swedish company Nordström & Thulin and the Estonian state shipping company ESCO. Any suggestions that a fellow crewman made errors in judgment would hurt the regenerating country of Estonia, which had been thrust into the harsh glare of international media.

On the other hand, as experienced seamen, miscellaneous ship voyages in various seas have given crew members a mental catalog of acceptable noises and motions. Crew members often have crisp recollections of any ship behavior that just did not seem right.

Silver Linde, the A.B. Seaman of the watch during the critical hours of the accident, said "a particularly `hard sound' was heard from the bow, a sound that stood out from the others. The sound was accompanied by a heavy vertical ship movement that made him fall . . . the blow sounded like two heavy metal pieces clashing together with great force."[21]

Third Engineer Margus Treu "perceived two heavy waves, one after the other, and they could really be felt . . . he had never before experienced such powerful blows against a ship."[22]

Elmar Siegel, the ship's motorman, lay in bed on the seventh deck, portside. The sound was as if the "the vessel had hit something with the bow."

Here it is useful to emphasize the fact that no rocks, underwater reefs or other hard objects obstruct the heavily traveled Baltic Sea anywhere near where the ferry encountered trouble. September was too early for ice.[23]

The most vivid testimonies come from the first deck cabins, which were located belowdecks, under the water line. The first deck budget cabins tend to amplify the noisy machinery belowdecks and resonate louder from wave impacts than do the upper decks.

Passenger Carl Erik Reintamm suddenly heard a sound like the vessel was proceeding through ice, "a scraping noise . . . After he had realized that it couldn't be ice during that time of the year, he finally thought that the vessel ran over something. About half a minute later, the vessel heeled to starboard."

Holger Wachtmeister, another passenger, was "awakened by a scraping noise and a hard bang--the scraping noise continued."

On Deck 4 the scraping noise was also heard. Passenger Kerim Nisancioglu read:

> "--shortly before the heeling started, the vessel began to roll equally in the waves from side to side . . . In connection with this rolling, the vessel heeled to starboard and he heard something below them sliding over to starboard . . . [The noise] . . . came from some place below them and must have been some large object; shortly after this noise he felt that the vessel heeled more to starboard."[24]

The peculiar scraping was so widely reported that the sound even makes it into the Final Report, though the remark is left unexamined: "In the lounges 10 to 15 people were sleeping and resting. All were awakened by a scraping sound and by the ship's list."[25]

Even passengers on the top decks some 20 meters or more above the waterline corroborated observations of those on the lower decks.

On Deck 7, British survivor Paul Barney was asleep on a bench when a loud noise woke him. "The fear came to me that we hit rocks. I thought we were in the [Swedish] archipelago. It was the bang and the fact we had a permanent list, not a rolling list. Ships don't do that."[26]

Most telling is the abrupt stopping of the ferry, reported by dozens of survivors. The motion was separate from the list and was sudden.

Rolf Sörman, a Swedish survivor who was in the Admiral's Pub on the fifth deck, recalled that "the boat stopped immediately. It wasn't that the ship's propellers were above water because then you would hear the propellers spin, which I didn't hear. It stopped. I thought we must have hit something. A submarine was one of the first thoughts I had."[27]

Nikolas Andreyev was asleep in his room on Deck 1 in the lower bunk,

> "--when the vessel heeled so much that he fell out of his bunk on to the floor . . . at the same time he heard and felt an extremely hard bang which was so hard that he was thrown against the cabin wall . . . He was unable to identify from where the bang came, but it felt as if the vessel had collided with something and at the same time was heeling over extremely."

Also on the first deck, Carl Övberg heard "a really extreme crash . . . in connection with an abrupt stopping of the ferry which was so sudden that I was thrown against the front wall of my bed; it was a short, sharp intense crash as if the ship had struck against something."[28]

The "scraping noise" and the sense that the ship had "hit an iceberg" or "grounded" or "collided" with something has been repeated by at least seven survivors in different parts of the ship in interviews immediately after the disaster. It is important to emphasize survivors felt the abrupt stop *before* the ship listed, as if something hit the ferry then slid out from underneath.

The JAIC assumed aberrant "monster waves" violently ripped the visor from its metal attachments, creating the strange sounds in the process.[29]

Certainly each individual has his own perceptive filters. Personality, culture, past experience and other factors shape memory. Each person's description is vulnerable to distortion, and the weird metallic noises and uncomfortable ship motions are ripe for multiple interpretations. The solution is to respect general descriptive patterns, not specific ones.

Could the energetic disassembly of the visor apparatus at the nose of the ferry mimic a scraping noise along the hull--the belly of the ship? That could potentially explain the scraping, but there is no apparent physical logic.

Equally puzzling is how a tumbling 60-ton visor could halt a

16,000ton ferry. Could a visor torn off by waves really fling people to the floor or throw them out of bed? The visor was about the size of a family garage. But the *Estonia* ferry was two city blocks long. The tail does not wag the dog.

What could cause a 16,000ton ferry to stop forward motion abruptly at sea, even momentarily, if not an impact with another object?

*   *   *

Hidden trouble waits inside a secondhand Soviet submarine. Although the foreign crew could have included a Russian technical advisor, vital equipment may have been poorly repaired, ill maintained or simply inoperable.

Poor workmanship during the 1970s and 1980s plagued the U.S.S.R. Stories about tractors sitting idle in Poland because they had to wait for spare parts approval from Moscow illustrate the crippling inefficiencies of the centralized system. The result was buses, trams, cars and military equipment as a fact of life had to be jerry-rigged to keep society moving.

Submarines exemplified the downward trend. During a clandestine salvage operation of a Soviet sub in 1974, the U.S. discovered welding that was "uneven and pitted . . . Hatch covers were crudely built, and one compartment was reinforced with wooden beams. Another section was full of a few tons of lead weights, which were evidently manually moved back and forth to trim the sub's center of gravity during maneuvers."[30]

A political element also hobbled Soviet subs. The underwater vessels were designed without ample backup systems on the assumption that they would never have an accident. Western subs had three redundant systems to provide power in an emergency, for example; a Soviet sub had only one.

Soviet subs reflected the U.S.S.R.'s political philosophy. Design engineering attention focused on the most important asset--the boat, not the people. Submarines were built with immense strength, girth and stealth. Consideration of human factors came last if at all.

Prominent design aspects of a submarine were standardized. Details and nuances were not. In fact, inconsistent design of crucial equipment caused the Soviet sub S-80 to sink in 1961. The S-80 surfaced during a storm when waves poured in through the open hatch. Strenuous efforts by a crewman to close the hatch wheel failed and the sub went down. Later investigators found the reason: The hatch wheel on the S-80 turned the opposite way than wheels on other subs in the fleet, a fatal mistake discovered too late. Life and death hinged on such a detail.[31]

Environmental confusion is another factor. A foreign crew in the unfamiliar Baltic Sea during a building storm could veer off course despite thorough training. Getting lost at sea doesn't only happen to foreign crews. A nuclear sub during a 1993 NATO exercise ran 14 kilometers off course and struck rocks off the Norwegian coast.[32]

Sub and ship collisions have been recorded all over the world. Surface vessels are highly vulnerable. The U.K. has a list of fishing boats tangling with submarines, the worst incident coming in 1990 when the Scottish boat *Antares* caught its fishing nets on the *HMS Trenchant* submarine and was dragged below the surface, killing four crew members.[33]

After the *Antares* accident, Scottish authorities even set up a submarine warning system designed to give fishing boats at least four hours' advance warning of submarine activity in their vicinity.

Just two weeks before the *Estonia* ferry went down, a Canadian man on his 15-foot sailboat saw a submarine burst out of the fog and destroy his boat. The sub belonged to Chile and it was on a classified "cooperative fleet exercise" with the U.S. Navy when it smashed the sailboat off the coast of Canada.[34]

In the Baltic Sea itself, two Polish seiners (net-haul fishing boats) in separate incidents in 1994 had their nets caught by submarines they claimed were Russian, but the Russian Navy denied it had subs in the area. A year earlier, an unidentified submarine in the Baltic got caught in the fishing net of a Dutch seiner.[35]

*   *   *

Sophisticated sonar and other sensors are fallible. Even the British Royal Navy admits privately that its state-of-the-art submarines are incapable of detecting the presence of trawlers in all circumstances. Imagining potential defects in an older model Soviet sub is not hard.[36]

A submerged boat uses sonar to detect how far away surface vessels are in order to avoid a collision when it surfaces.

A sub has two types of sonar, active and passive. Active sonar sends acoustic signals out into the water and receives incoming echoes--the "pings" often depicted in movies about sea battles. But the pinging also reveals the submarine's presence to anyone listening. To sail in stealth, to sail covertly, a sub uses passive sonar, which basically listens for noise.

Both types can give false readings, depending on sea conditions. Different layers of salinity and temperature, common in the Baltic, confuse sonar operators. If the sea is choppy, active sonar may not provide a return ping. Moreover, surface ships can emit signals that block the echo of another ship nearby. A foreign crew manning a secondhand sub during a Baltic Sea storm is inviting trouble.

The Baltic's shallow waters also create wind-generated waves at noise levels up to 100 times higher than waves in deep ocean water. The resulting background signals, like static on a radio, can mask a sonar signal from a nearby surface ship. A storm, such as the one building on the night of September 27, could easily drown out sonar detection of a ferry.

Submarines are most vulnerable when ascending. The surface had better be clear.

The French nuclear submarine Rubis rose from total immersion to periscope depth and hit the oil tanker *Lyria*, tearing a five-meter gash in the tanker's hull. The *Lyria's* captain thought he'd glanced off a drifting wreck and continued sailing to his destination port, unaware of the collision. Later, the French navy confessed, blaming bad sonar transmission.[37]

Commanders have no room for error. The most experienced among them have made devastating mistakes. In 2001, Commander Scott Waddle was faulted for ramming his submarine, the *USS Greeneville*, into Japanese research ship *Ehime Maru* as the sub attempted an emergency surfacing maneuver for the benefit of civilians on board. "Behind schedule and confident all contacts were distant, CDR Waddle took the periscope and conducted a non-standard, abbreviated search that failed to account for safety of his own ship and surface vessels," according to the court of inquiry.[38]

* * *

Circumstances could have combined to create ideal conditions for a submarine to collide with the *Estonia*. Presuming a foreign crew was manning the sub, a Russian specialist would likely ride onboard to assist them during the journey home. But nonetheless, at night, with a building autumn storm, the sub could have slipped partially off course toward ferry traffic. If it had been submerged, environmental confusion could have prevented the crew from verifying the surface was clear before rising. The sonar may also have been turned off or simply ineffectual. After all, it was a used sub.

Suppose a submarine moved at periscope depth, three meters or so beneath the surface. If the *Estonia* ferry was heading toward it, wave swells up to four meters that night could confound the sub crew. They could misjudge the *Estonia's* distance and direction or miss it altogether.

A head-on collision seems unlikely. But if the ferry in relation to the sub sailed angled to port or starboard, the sub literally faces a 155-meter long wall.

Sonar cannot see aft. Suppose the *Estonia* came up behind the surfacing sub at an angle. Imagine a car merging onto a highway when suddenly another vehicle swerves into the merge lane. Both sub and ferry would strike hard, though inertia is in the same general direction. The initial impact loosens plating on the *Estonia's* hull or opens a breach. The sub slides under the ferry, its antenna and radar in the sail scrape across the ferry's hull, breaking off.

Or the *Estonia*, churning through water, struck a sub that was sailing at periscope depth, scraping metal on metal and careening off, behaving something like a stone skipping over water. The ferry could also have grazed hard against the sub's sail or simply ran over it. Hard contact is enough to crack a sloppy weld or smash corroded hull areas that would subsequently start taking in seawater.[39]

A ferry skimming over a sub would be equivalent to contact with a reef or rocky outcrop just beneath the surface. In 2000, the Greek passenger ferry *Express Samina* hit underwater rock, leaving a gaping hole in the hull. Like the *Estonia*, the *Express Samina* listed immediately and went down in 45 minutes.

Perhaps neither sub nor ferry understood what happened and both vessels quickly put distance between themselves. Like the captain of the *Lyria* tanker who misinterpreted the striking sound of the French submarine *Rubis*, maybe the *Estonia's* captain attributed bangs to the battering of waves. The impact loosened some hull plating and it took the ferry another half hour plowing through rough seas at 15 knots before the hole opened wider.

A bang-up at sea could also explain the odd visor detachment. The bangs from the Russian submarine's sail reverberate through the *Estonia's* hull, sending shockwaves that are absorbed by the poorly-maintained bow visor locks and attachments. In seconds, fine cracks enlarge, sloppy welds shift and the visor incrementally loosens. After 10, maybe 20 minutes, as wave impacts batter the moving ferry, something gives. The visor runs its detachment scenario--only now there's also a breach of integrity below the waterline.

As the visor locks split and bust, the visor yanks the cardeck ramp slightly ajar, a meter at the top on the port side, enough for seawater to flow inside the deck.

By now the ferry has stopped. It's not moving "like a whale with an open mouth" but rather drifting and bobbing like a cork as seawater seeps in through the sides of the cardeck ramp and gushes in from below through the fresh hull plate opening. With leaks from both above and below, the ferry lists to starboard but doesn't float upside down. It sinks in 35 minutes.

A foreign sub commander on a sensitive mission and under orders to avoid detection at all costs would have every reason to flee the scene, the equivalent of a hit-and-run in the sea. No deliberate collision, no act of war, just an accident.

In any case, standing orders from the high circles in a dictatorship have a way of crystallizing thoughts. The sub, the strategic asset, came first. The prime directive was to move from point A to point B without delay. Rules of the road only apply in their own territorial waters. Ethics and morality are defined by the needs of the state.

* * *

Submarines are not fragile, but passenger ships are. Subs are built for conflict, constructed to withstand crushing water pressure at great depths and all potential impacts--ice, depth charges, rock formations, surface vessels, other submarines. Passenger ships are engineered for comfort, not battle. A ferry's hull is not weak. However, butted by a submarine, it would crack like an eggshell.

When the USS Greeneville, for example, shot out of the water on an emergency maneuver in 2001, it split the Japanese fishing vessel Ehime Maru into two pieces. The submarine returned to port on its own power. Some exterior coating on the sub's hull was chafed and the hull plating had scratches. There was no structural damage.[40]

Soviet technology lacked nuance but it emphasized durability. Maximum size, weight, strength and capacity were the criteria of design and manufacturing. Some of the U.S.S.R.'s subs had ice-hardened sails specially designed for frozen Northern seas. Others had a second reinforced inner hull that served as added protection from breach. If the Estonia was ruined by the thump, the sub suffered only cosmetic damage.

Submarines have sailed away from strong collisions before. The USS Baton Rouge, a Los Angeles class nuclear attack submarine and a Russian Sierra class sub collided in 1992 near the Northern Russian city of Murmansk. The Russian sub had slightly damaged her sail while the Baton Rogue streamed back to port in the U.S., a journey of two weeks, before inspecting for damage.[41]

A periscope and antennas, however, are brittle. If a collision took them out, a sub commander's ability to see and report is lost. An impaired sub could have hugged the eastern Baltic coast and sailed to the submarine port of Baltisk in Kaliningrad, the tiny Russian enclave sandwiched between Poland and Lithuania. Former German territory and Russia's prize from World War II, Kaliningrad hosted an enormous Russian military presence. Thousands of Russian troops withdrawn from Germany, Eastern Europe and the Baltic States were sent there.

Kaliningrad was the bane of Europe after the Soviet Union broke up. The region fell under suspicion as the biggest staging ground for

Baltic criminal activity during the 1990s. Stolen cars, drugs, strategic metals and other contraband were shipped out of Kaliningrad ports. In August 1994, three men were arrested there trying to sell plutonium.

Moscow planned to beef up Kaliningrad with troops and weaponry. The enclave, now Russia's lone presence in the Baltic area, would serve as a counterbalance to surrounding countries that were expected to be the first to join NATO.[42]

The lawless and heavily-militarized Kaliningrad would be a safe port for a crippled Russian submarine to dock. A naval team ordered to repair the sub wouldn't be told what happened, and would know not to ask.

Damage Control

September 28, 1994. In Stockholm, about 250 kilometers away from the accident site, Carl Bildt and his Moderate Party associates were gathered for a farewell dinner at a restaurant in the Rosenbad government building in Stockholm. Bildt's party had lost the elections, he was leaving office, and the dinner reuniting his colleagues one last time stretched into the early morning.

Bildt was on the top floor. Sometime after 01:30 a.m. (02:30 a.m. Estonian time), he quickly descended the stairs trailed by two aides, attracting the crowd's attention. He raised his hand to silence the hall. "Something terrible has happened," he said.

In Helsinki, a ringing phone roused Esko Aho from a deep sleep. His personal secretary called him in the middle of the night. In Tallinn, the Estonian Crisis Committee woke up Mart Laar.

Bildt, however, said he does not recall who first notified him. Nor does he recall when. His two closest aides also forgot these specifics. Three cases of amnesia concerning a state emergency call that follows a chain of command procedure are strange. Some believe that Bildt and his aides do not want to reveal that the initial notification came from Swedish or U.S. intelligence services, a detail that would raise questions as to why intelligence services were monitoring the routine sailing of a tourist ferry.[43]

HIT AND RUN   131

*   *   *

Dawn broke. At 07:00 a.m., five hours after the ship went down, survivors were still being plucked from the freezing waters.

Bildt, Aho and Laar agreed to an urgent meeting in Turku, Finland, at the beginning of the workday. The three heads of state had in the past worked together frequently assisting Estonia build the foundation of a modern democratic state.

Many *Estonia* survivors suffering from hypothermia were billeted at the Turku hospital in various states of psychological and physical pain. Recuperating, their bodies warmed by hot liquids and warm blankets, the conscious survivors would be visited by the three leaders.

Third Engineer Margus Treu and Systems Engineer Henrik Sillaste, two Estonian crew members, were keen to talk. Together with another crewmember, Hannes Kadak, the three had been in the engine control room and were able to observe the cardeck one deck up through a closed circuit video monitor. The three had narrowly escaped.

Kadak and Sillaste scrambled up a ladder mounted on the interior wall of the ferry's chimney funnel when the ship listed 40 degrees. Kadak had burned his hand when in the darkness and hurry he'd grabbed a boiler pipe. Treu followed minutes later and fell into the sea without a lifejacket.

Treu who had turned 30 the previous month and Sillaste, who had turned 25 just two weeks earlier, spoke broken English and smatterings of Swedish and Finnish, but they managed to convey to Aho the idea that water had entered the cardeck at the bow.

Bildt and Laar came by. Laar, an Estonian who is fluent in English, listened as the distraught crew members told a more detailed story in Estonian, which he translated to the other two heads of state. Finland's Aho recalled that "[the crew members] said they saw how the water came in and they said something had happened with the front, the bow visor." However, they did not specifically talk about the visor coming off, instead, "they spoke about water coming in."[44]

But water flowing onto the cardeck was a routine matter on ferry journeys. Drivers who previously rode the *Estonia* recalled sloshing through seawater to get to their cars on arrival in Stockholm harbor.[45]

Bildt, however, made his move. He immediately gave legitimacy to the nervous statements of anguished crew members Treu and Sillaste, who, in some accounts, had described "the visor lifted from below."[46]

The "lifted visor" description makes no sense. They could only have seen the visor "lifted from below" if the cardeck ramp was wide open, just as the front porch is not visible from inside the house without opening the front door. And if the ramp had been open, no crew member would be left alive to make any observations. An avalanche of water would have roared in, bashing any living soul against the parked cars and trucks, unless he was lucky enough to drown instantly.

What the crew members had seen, on a video monitor in the dry engine control room belowdecks, was water spraying through the edges of the closed ramp--like a car window not quite closed during a rainstorm. In fact, Sillaste later sketched in tranquility a picture that flatly contradicted "the visor was lifted from below" statement. It explicitly showed water spray entering from the sides of a closed ramp.[47]

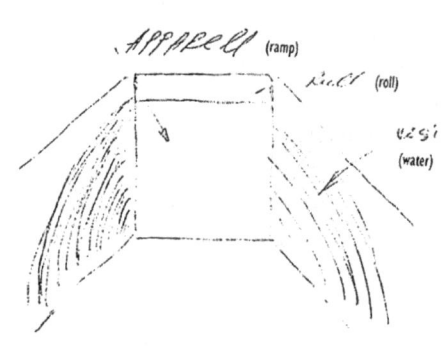

Sillaste's drawing of water streaming in from cardeck ramp edges.

Closed cardeck ramp on *Estonia*'s sister ship *Meloodia*.

But Bildt latched onto the visor movement, even though it was physically impossible for anyone onboard to have witnessed it. Apparently, he persuaded the others that the 60-ton nose had fallen off. When Aho, Laar and Bildt were ready to leave the hospital, they were in consensus that the visor had fallen off, according to Aho.[48]

Imagine the crew members just plucked from the icy water and shaking in hospital beds, physically ill, haunted by screams of fleeing passengers, hounded by media, overwhelmed by fear and perhaps guilt, their colleagues dead. In this diminished condition, the crew's vague descriptions should be taken at face value.

A more ominous factor shaped the stories of the Estonian crew. The Estonian Minister of Transport, Andi Meister, who crew members had never before met, was now standing nearby with some serious state officials. Their cold faces implied that any guilty parties would be found and summarily dealt with.

State pressure on the crew should not be underestimated. Topics like seaworthiness, maintenance, repair and stewardship were implicitly off limits. On safer ground was the explanation the crew eagerly volunteered to the three prime ministers: Something happened to the bow visor that was due to a "technical fault."

As Bildt prepared to leave Turku, he phoned the Managing Director of Estline in Stockholm, Hans Laidwa, from the airport. Estline was the Swedish-Estonian joint venture company that owned the ferry line.

Bildt told him not to worry. A technical fault was the reason for the sinking.

He also rang his staff and ordered an investigation of bow visors from the Swedish Maritime Administration as "a construction fault might have caused the accident."[49]

By these words, spoken just hours after the disaster, Bildt reduced every person looking for answers to an audience. Never mind that no one knew where the shipwreck rested. No one knew what condition it was in or even what had happened. Certainly no one knew that the visor had actually separated from the vessel.

Confusion reigned. The press kept struggling to tally an accurate casualty count. Hundreds of Swedes and Estonians went down with the ferry and were entombed inside the sunken carcass. Technical experts from Sweden, Russia and Estonia debated whether people were still trapped alive inside air pockets that remained in the sunken ferry.[50]

But Bildt was determined to grab control and shape the course of the investigation.

That same day, Bildt's righthand man stepped forward with an uncharacteristic demand. Commander Emil Svensson, one of Bildt's close aides who had accompanied him to Turku, was a career military officer who by training and experience would be far from squeamish. Svensson had played an assertive role representing the Swedes when they confronted Russia with submarine incursion accusations.

Suddenly Svensson, by profession a man shaped by the military code that demands the dead be brought back home, apparently lost his bearings. The morning of the disaster, he took a strong stand against salvaging the wreck. His reason: The bodies inside would be unpresentable.[51]

The statements are remarkable. The question of salvage was not a key topic at the time. As a state representative, Svensson had declared the official position of the Kingdom of Sweden a little too early. Helicopters and ships were still searching the accident site for survivors. Sweden would never retreat from Svensson's position.

Bildt worked more discreetly. He was careful not to make a premature statement to the press. In the afternoon, before leaving Turku, Bildt, Laar and Aho staged a press conference. The mainly spoke about caring for survivors and grieving relatives and the ongoing search-and-rescue efforts. The three prime ministers also decided a Joint Accident Investigation Commission (JAIC) with members from Sweden, Estonia and Finland, would be set up as an investigatory body. The JAIC would conduct an open investigation and look at all possible theories. No stone would be left unturned, Bildt pledged.

But as the commission was formed, Sweden's head of state had tacitly handed them the cause, and one of the top military officials had effectively discouraged--and later prohibited--anyone from second-guessing it.[52]

* * *

Back in Estonia, the visor scenario wasn't so easily swallowed. Laar's instincts told him other more menacing factors could've influenced the disaster. Laar was the only one of the three prime ministers to grow up in the Soviet Union, where truth was defined by the state.

Experience told him dark intrigue sometimes whirled behind unfortunate accidents.

Laar, who had sailed on the *Estonia* ferry in the past, initially believed a collision occurred. "Of course we suspected foul play," Laar recalled. "We had all possible scenarios. We did not rule out any reasons. Mostly we thought it could be a terrorist attack but also any accident with another ship, a submarine, because of the two or three loud bangs, who knows?"[53]

Rumors of Russian military involvement were circulating in the Estonian media, rousing the Russian embassy in Tallinn and consulate in Narva, which monitor the domestic press. Emotions burst. An Estonian journalist at a press conference asked Estline management: "Why don't you consider a Russian submarine version? Russians used to send us to Siberia by thousands. It's a trifle for them to kill another thousand human beings."[54]

The next day, a spokesman for the Russian Navy issued a statement:

> "The senior officer on duty at the headquarters of Russia's Baltic Sea fleet, Alexander Gorbachuk, said no ships or submarines of the fleet had been in the area where the disaster happened... The Baltic Sea fleet's two guard ships and a tanker, which he said were the only vessels Russia had on the sea at that time, had been in the North Sea outside the straits of Skagerrak... Because of the storm no other vessel left the bases in Kaliningrad or Kronstadt, the officer said."[55]

The key words are "of the fleet," meaning the Baltic Sea fleet. A sub acquired by another country would no longer be a Russian Naval sub, making Gorbachuk's statement technically accurate, but disingenuous. Additionally, given the discretion surrounding weapons sales to Third World countries and the way that state assets were looted by quiet deals, it's possible that a sub deal was cut without his knowledge.

Other Russian ships certainly were near the *Estonia* ferry that night, though apparently they were not "of the fleet." On September 28, a day before Gorbachuk's denial, the Russian Maritime Rescue Service reported that "the Russian rescue service received no Mayday signal from the `Estonia' ferry... Russian ships in the area did not receive any distress signals either," according to the duty officer.[56]

Another Russian vessel, the *Leonid Bykov*, was caught by the Finnish coast guard in an erratic maneuver just one hour after the ferry had sunk. Finnish authorities warned the ship in three languages it was headed toward rocks, but received no response. Although only 65 nautical miles from the catastrophe site, the *Leonoid Bykov* didn't respond to the *Estonia's* distress calls.

Presumably the *Leonoid Bykov* likewise was not "of the fleet." But the Russian Navy often employed dual-use vessels that looked like research ships or freighters but carried out military missions, a characteristic tactic of Soviet Naval Forces. Post 1991, semi-privatized firms ran these ships, putting the activity in the gray area between state and private.[57]

Krasnaya Zvezda ("Red Star"), a right-wing newspaper highlighting the Defense Ministry perspective and with preferential access to high-ranking military officials, ran Russia's second denial about a week later:

> "Chief of Russia's Main Naval Headquarters Admiral Valentin Selivanov has categorically refuted all allegations about a possible involvement of Russian submarines in the recent ferry disaster in the Baltic Sea. . . .`Any intelligence service in the world can confirm there were no Russian submarines in the Baltic Sea at the moment of the *Estonia* disaster.' This statement was made in the wake of allegations by some Estonian ultranationalists that a Russian submarine might have been involved in the accident."[58]

Military sources likely vetted *Krasnaya Zvezda's* articles before publication. Maybe the well-crafted phrase "at the moment of the *Estonia* disaster" is subtly misleading. Because about 30 minutes before the disastrous events, some survivors reported loud impact noises. For example, a Swedish survivor, policewoman Maria Fägersten, reported "the vessel ran against something" about midnight and she and others moved to the windows and looked out in the dark storm, but could see nothing. The impact experiences, coming 15-20 minutes prior to the fatal chain of events, were therefore not "at the moment of the accident," making Selivanov's literal statement true.[59]

* * *

While Laar kept an open mind when facts were unknown, even suspecting a collision, Bildt chose the visor as the centerpiece, and he chose it for a good reason.

In 1994, Estonia and Russia faced each other in a dangerous peace. Finland's Aho believed that any Russian moves that compromised Estonian independence would not be met with passive resistance. "I was very convinced that the Estonians will never give up," Aho recalled. "They made a mistake maybe in 1940 when they gave up too easily, but now they were not going to give up. We tried to say that to the Russians that it is now a fact that these three [Baltic] countries are independent and they want to stay independent and there is no alternative left."[60]

On the Russian side, Estonian independence provoked institutional humiliation and national resentment. The Russians had been all but evicted from the Baltic Sea, an area they had dominated for more than 300 years.

By mid-1994, four of the five Russian naval bases on the Baltic Sea were held by foreign powers. Twelve of the 16 bases of the Baltic Fleet "are no longer ours," mourned the *Moscow News*. "We have lost 64% of all repair facilities, 75% of navigation equipment, 25% of aviation, 50% of surface ships and all of our submarines."[61]

This was the generation that lost that proud traditional stronghold. It happened on their watch. Against their will, they'd surrendered control to Estonia, which many senior officers still considered a region of Russia.

When the ferry went down, emotional springs were tightly compressed on both sides. Estonians were looking for responsible parties. The *Estonia* ferry had been the mythical great white ship, reconnecting Estonia to European civilization. Now it was gone, as were hundreds of Estonians. The inclination was to blame the traditional enemy to the East.

Bildt stepped in. Bildt had been the most aggressive foreign politician pushing Estonia through progressive phases of post-Soviet sovereignty. With quiet tenacity, he'd won pledges of support from the U.S. and Europe, parried Russian objections and encouraged the impression that a Western coalition stood behind fragile Estonia.[62]

He knew any hint of incidental Russian involvement in the catastrophe--even if a Russian shipyard had merely sold a submarine anytime during the autumn of 1994--could undermine all previous diplomatic efforts. Delicate compromises between the two countries could be smashed. Worse, it could ignite the violence he and others worked so hard to prevent.

Bildt keenly understood the frailty of Baltic independence. He pointed out in an article that Russia's behavior toward the Baltic region will be the "litmus test" of Russia's new direction. The article's subtext underscored the potential for violent rupture between Russia and the former U.S.S.R. territories, and the severe "repercussions [that] will be felt beyond the region" should relations shatter.[63]

Estonia, Bildt knew, had no ring of steel.

There was one more thing. Unexpressed, in the back of Bildt's mind, was perhaps the notion that the rogue groups he believed operated within the Russian Navy may have been involved. Bildt had stated publicly his belief that renegade units may have been responsible for Sweden's submarine incursions. Yeltsin, he suggested, was not in full control of the military. Was there any connection between these factions and the ferry accident?[64]

An ethnic fire in Estonia would signal an emergency situation, evoke a *force majeure* clause in political agreements. The firemen would be the very Russian troops who had just been evicted one month earlier after negotiators used everything in the diplomatic tool kit to get them to leave. These Russian soldiers would be labeled "peacekeeping troops," not occupation forces, and they would keep the peace indefinitely to protect the ethnic Russians living in the "near abroad," the Kremlin's phrase for the Baltic Republics.

Moscow was now peppered with nationalists who howled at the gates of power. Vitalized by the threatening rhetoric of Zhirinovsky, they cried for restoration of the great Soviet Empire, starting with the Baltics. Yeltsin leaned right in an effort to gain their approval.

Nothing less than Northern European peace and stability was at risk. For reasons of regional security, Bildt hastily fixed attention on an engineering fault without providing evidence. In practice, he pulled off what has diplomatically become known as an honorable deception.

In one masterful stroke, Bildt swept all the threatening rumors, emotions and uncertainties into a hat and out popped the visor theory.

As a result, representatives from Sweden, Estonia and Finland, who comprised the JAIC, were unconsciously persuaded to put a fence around the investigative field.

The day after Bildt's announcement, Sweden's head of Sea Safety Inspection, Bengt Erik Stenmark, publicly scoffed at Bildt's visor statement and was promptly fired. He was eventually replaced by Johan Franson, the organizer of the secretive Rockwater dive and father of the endgame stratagem to entomb the shipwreck in concrete.

Down the road, Olof Forssberg would be appointed to head the Swedish side of the JAIC. Forssberg had previous experience in charge of a Swedish government-acknowledged whitewash concerning the Soviet shootdown of a Swedish DC-3, a scandal only declassified in 2000.

Transport Minister Mona Sahlin would later consolidate decision-making power over the fate of the shipwreck and bodies.

In short order, Sweden took full charge of the Estonia ferry disaster investigation and dominated the JAIC until the commission officially disbanded three years later.

140 THE HOLE

Seafloor Antics

Nobody could definitively rule out a collision without first removing the sand that was covering up key areas of the *Estonia's* hull and openly conducting a comprehensive hull survey. The JAIC did not bother with that. They simply directed their attention to the visor.

A submarine bumping a civilian ferry would immediately become a matter of state security. If some material from that collision littered the seabed, the highest levels of state would be informed. A confidential underwater investigation would be warranted in order to confirm it happened. Especially in a part of the world where a former empire tearing apart at the seams was provoking global anxiety.

Finnish vessels located the sunken ferry on September 30 about 80 meters depth and nearly upside down. The Finns took side-scan sonar photographs of the wreck and they were presented at a press conference. News reports announced that the sonar pictures seemed to show a large object on the seabed 9-18 meters from the bow. No one knew what it was.[65]

For the next two days, air bubbled out of the wreck. Big air bubbles. A Russian news report quoted a technical expert saying that people were probably still trapped inside the wreck in air pockets and that his institute had the specialized equipment to rescue them.[66]

Other authorities denied people could survive. A ship's walls are not designed to withstand underwater pressure, so cabins would soon implode. Until then, near freezing temperatures and lack of oxygen would send any survivors into shock and a quick death.

The media speculation stirred victims' relatives, who couldn't face the sudden and irretrievable loss. They latched onto the fantastic hope that loved ones perhaps could be rescued.

It was against this backdrop that Dr Jouko Nuorteva, sonar expert and sector manager at the Finnish Naval Research Institute, stepped in to analyze four other sonar photographs taken of the found wreck.

Waves and air bubbles distorted the sonar photographs, but Nuorteva finally managed to discern a satisfactory image of the wreck on the sea bottom. In all photos, something appeared to be sitting on top of the wreck in the bow area.

Not 9-18 meters away, as the first batch of sonar photos had shown. On top.

The object's shape and dimensions resembled the bow visor. Was the visor still attached to the front of the ferry? Speculation flew: The visor hadn't wrenched free after all.

Nuorteva confirmed nothing but the "observation of a large object."

He was being deliberately vague in accordance with government instructions. Officials had asked Nuorteva not to publicly mention air bubbles percolating from the wreck to avoid cruelly rekindling false hopes. "What I saw [on the sonar pictures] could have been air bubbles," Nuorteva recalled. "But I didn't want to say this. We were under a little pressure not to say there was still air in the ship because then the public may get the idea that people are still alive down there."

So he stuck with "large object."

According to Nuorteva, the big object "on top" of the bow in the sonar photographs--suspected to be the bow visor--turned out to be a reflection from the warped side of the cardeck ramp. The steel cardeck ramp is in a closed position, slightly twisted open on portside about half a meter. This ramp damage created the reflection.[67]

Fair enough. But what about the analysis of the other large object, the one the first sonar images appeared to show lying on the seabed 9-18 meters from the bow? Apparently, it was ignored.[68]

A few days later, Kari Lehtola, head of the Finnish side of the JAIC, in a fax to his Swedish counterparts, wrote "there is a 10 [meter] long and 5-7 [meter] broad object on the bottom. It is probably of metal. The form fits well with the visor. Depth is 70 [meters]."

An ROV with video was sent down to the ferry. Videotape obviously presents a far more accurate rendering than the wavy lines of sonar images. On these *videos*, something large was seen 14 meters from the wreck. Lehtola also saw it, then wrote a second fax, stating: "The large object turned out to be a steel plate."[69]

So that the reader will not be thrown, a short summary is necessary. Officials first interpreted sonar pictures as showing a large object 9-18 meters from the sunken ferry. Four other sonar photos showed a large object *on top* the ship, which Nuorteva said turned out to be a reflection. Lehtola confirmed by fax the existence of the first large object 9-18 meters away seen on sonar photographs. When an ROV provided *video evidence* of the large object, Lehtola dismissed it as a "steel plate."

The Baltic Sea is littered with hundreds, if not thousands, of wrecks and their remnants, from sunken ships to downed airplanes. Most are casualties of the two World Wars, but vessels and debris range from

Viking times to recent times. Perhaps the mysterious object had indeed been part of the undersea rubble well before the *Estonia* went down.

Then a strange thing happened. Videotape of the wreck from the government-supervised Rockwater dive in 1994 and later the *One Eagle* expedition in 2000 found nothing even near the large object's reported size. "Ten meters long and 5-7 meters broad," according to Lehtola's fax. The size of a small vessel. What was it? Where did the large object--the "steel plate"--go?[70]

Misinterpreting the squiggly lines of sonar reflections as a large object is entirely plausible. The disappearance of a large object *videotaped* sitting on the seafloor is not.

Equally confounding--or telling--the three governments were not even curious about it.

* * *

Misreadings of sonar images. A missing object. But still no visor. Where was the bow visor? The search for the 60-ton pyramidal chunk of steel continued.

According to Tuomo Karppinen, a Finnish member of the JAIC, the visor search first concentrated on the area near the wreck, then moved outward. They believed backtracking on the ferry's route would yield results, perhaps even retracing the route as far as two hours before the ship had sunk.[71]

Finnish naval forces assisted. If the Finns didn't find the visor in one week, then Swedish mine-hunting vessels equipped with more sophisticated detection gear would move in.

Scouring the uneven terrain of the Baltic Sea could take a long time. Nuorteva, the sonar expert, thought the heavy visor could have sunk deep into the soft clay on the seafloor and disappeared. Scattered junk on the seabed also slowed the search by registering false positives.

Sweden offered to send three mine hunters "at least 2 on the security scale." A "2" means only people with an elevated security clearance would be on board. Although Lehtola requested the military vessels and they were put on standby, both Lehtola and Karppinen deny the mine-hunters were involved in the visor search.[72]

Still, a Swedish mine expert, a Commander Tönnström, was on

the vessel *Tursas*, which lifted the visor from its found location. There are suggestions that Tönnström was with Swedish military intelligence (MUST). If so, his presence would be standard procedure. He would want to visually inspect any visor damage that could indicate a collision. MUST would want to know the details.

"Tönnström knew we would lift the visor and he would see the conditions of the accident and that was good for him to know," Lehtola explained, rather cryptically.[73]

A second interpretation considers Tönnström's involvement peculiar. Mine-hunting ships and personnel holding secret clearances mobilizing to help research vessels look for the bow visor seems a disproportionate response. Military ships would be better suited searching for a set of keys than for locating a trailer-size chunk of steel. Perhaps the *Estonia* ferry fell on or too close to Swedish underwater surveillance equipment. Or maybe something had to be taken care of down at the wreck and the mine-hunters would support activity on the seafloor.

Refer back to the large object seen on video that nobody had questioned. The object that Lehtola reported to be "10 meters long and 5–7 meters broad" roughly corresponds to a minisub. Perhaps the sonar images or the ROV video glimpsed a minisub, which, after completing its work, sped away.

There is nothing nefarious about clandestine examination of the wreck. The military has a look before the public does in order to collect intelligence related to the catastrophe. In August 2000, when the Kursk submarine sank, the Russian Navy sent two deep-water *Mir* submersibles to the sunken sub to find and collect any fragments and debris from what officials thought had been collision.[74]

Sweden could have sent a few divers from its elite *Bassak* underwater unit or a minisub that discharged divers down at the *Estonia* ferry carcass to scour the nearby seafloor for physical evidence of a collision.

A minisub shape could be what registered on sonar. After finishing underwater work, the divers would enter the minisub and leave the scene. As a result, subsequent sonar photos show no large object. The old sonar pictures with the "10 meters long and 5–7 meters broad" object were dismissed as metal reflections.

But the problem is that the ROV videotape captured the minisub image. The *videotape* would then have to be edited. If a JAIC member had seen the videotape, he would be instructed not to disclose any information due to state security concerns.

Some minisubs move about on conveyor belt tracks that provide seafloor traction. Advanced navigation and battery technology allow minisubs to operate over long distances and run for days or weeks underwater. Sweden was plagued by these tiny seafloor buses. "[B]ottom-crawling mini-submarines in 1987 drove straight through our secret mine fields just as they drove right into our naval base areas in 1982," lamented Carl Bildt in 1987.[75]

Minisubs can come and go undetected. During the Cold War, Johannes Johansen, former Estonian director of Estline, recalled sailing on Soviet cargo vessels. He knew about Soviet mini-submarines that attached themselves to the hull. When the freighters docked in foreign ports to unload coal or oil, the minisubs would detach from the hull and gather intelligence. Johansen had never actually seen one, but he knew they were there. "When we docked, we would do our business and they would do theirs," he recalled. The minisubs would reattach to the hull well before the ship left port, leaving no traces of existence.[76]

On October 18, the visor was located by Nuorteva's hand-size "sonar fish." Sweden's high-tech military equipment had been rendered non-essential by the little research gadget.

The visor had sunk into the soft bottom, but enough surface area protruded to register on sonar. It was hoisted from the sea nearly 1.5 kilometers from the actual wreck position, sowing suspicion among some of the public that the visor had been beside the wreck and then moved.[77]

It had taken one week to find a bow visor the size of a garage. Waves and weather caused delays. But maybe during that week, divers below needed time to work. Perhaps underwater listening posts were checked for damage or the bottom had to be cleaned up. Some sensitive object may have been carefully extracted from the wreck. If the ferry had collided with something, debris would litter the seabed.

According to the Final Report, the *Estonia* ferry's debris field was detected on sonar 90-300 meters west of the wreck. But that is hard to believe. Because plotting that area on the official map of the *Estonia's* supposed course of events, the "Kalmar Chart" (see Appendix II), would show that the main debris tumbled out when the ferry had a mere 15 degree list.

Nuorteva puts the debris concentration 275-450 meters SW of wreck, based on sonar photographs. The type, accumulation and trail of debris could have provided vital clues in reconstructing the ship's final moments. But the debris field was not videotaped. In fact, it was left completely unexamined--at least by the JAIC.[78]

Political necessities are not the sole explanation for intrigue at 70 meters underwater. The questionable object and a prolonged visor search could simply be human mistakes that occur when nations sit clueless in the aftermath of a trauma and investigators face relentless pressure from all possible fronts.

One such repercussive foul-up happened when Lehtola wrote down the shipwreck position erroneously. His miswritten coordinates remained on record for months and when research vessels couldn't find the 155 meter-long wreck, they had to employ sonar to relocate it.

Lehtola explained that Nuorteva told him the wreck position over a mobile phone while at sea. The transmission was dropping out and Lehtola unfortunately did not read the coordinates back for verification. He wrote down the wrong wreck position. "I made a mistake," Lehtola said.

The erroneous coordinates could have been crosschecked by examining the logbooks of ships that had already been to the wreck site just after the ferry sank, he pointed out.[79]

But the German investigators saw trickery. They surmised that the Swedes and Finns on October 1 or 2 had found the visor next to the bow of the wreck "but decided to keep this secret as well as the actual position of the wreck and to continue the search for the visor. The Estonians were sent to search to the east (where the visor definitely never was) while the Finns with the help of Swedish mine hunting experts and vessels clarified something around the wreck."

The German Group believes Lehtola's wrong coordinates were intentionally passed off as the official wrecksite in order to allow completion of some classified underwater work. In support of the theory, the Germans mention a cryptic letter Lehtola had written to the Swedish government explaining that he had possibly "exceeded his authority" when "isolating the wreck."[80]

Lehtola explained that the phrase was misconstrued by the German Group. What he was referring to was a directive he'd issued declaring that no unauthorized vessel can go near the shipwreck. His statement was the equivalent of running police tape around an accident investigation site on land. But technically, the shipwreck was in international waters and therefore he had no legal right to issue that directive. The terms he used in the letter "exceeded his authority" in "isolating the wreck" expressed his doubts about the legality of cordoning off the wreck.[81]

Honest mistakes happen. Before the Estonia sank, the sea accident of the largest magnitude the Finns had dealt with was an overturned barge. Errors probably stemmed from pressures to which they were unaccustomed.

Regardless, the JAIC is unable to dispel suspicions regarding the activity surrounding the visor search.

Unaccountable Incidents

A submarine hit-and-run could explain several peculiar phenomena on the night the ferry sank.

Communications throughout the Northern Baltic Sea were disrupted during the time of the accident. When two nearby Finnish vessels, the *Mariella* and the *Europa*, heard the *Estonia's* Mayday and used their ship radios to alert rescue centers in Finland over the emergency VHF Channel 16, there was no answer. They changed to channel 2182, which covers the whole Baltic Sea. Again, no answer. After some time, they pulled out their mobile phones, found the phone numbers of the land-based rescue centers and called them.

Not far away in St Petersburg, Russia's State Marine Rescue Coordinating Center also drew silence. The SMRCC was linked to a series of U.S. and Russian satellites that pick up any emergency beacon signal and send the exact coordinates of the ship in distress. Called COPSAS-SARSAT, the collection of relay satellites forward the data to rescue co-ordination offices.

But the satellites picked up nothing because the *Estonia's* EPIRB emergency buoys had, against all known convention, been switched off.[82]

Signal jamming of all radio communications apparently occurred on the Southern coastline of Finland as the accident unfolded.

Werner Hummel, the German investigator, said that his group has documentation showing that the regional telephone network servicing the catastrophe site failed just as it was needed most. The malfunction was truly a startling coincidence. The telephone company stated its entire radio communications network, for unknown reasons, had been down from 1:03 to 1:58 a.m.--almost exactly the time the Estonia first encountered trouble until the time it disappeared from radar.[83]

Another communications mystery was a continuous radio signal sent from Russia's Hoaglund Island transmitter. Rear Admiral Heimo Iivonenile, a Finnish commission member and radio communications expert, believed the Hoaglund signal blocked VHF channel 16, the international mayday channel.[84]

Hoaglund Island (known as *Suursaari* in Finnish) is a closed Russian military island a little more than halfway between St Petersburg and Helsinki. In the past, as a possession of Sweden, then later Finland, the island was a resort area with casinos until Soviet Russia took it in

1939. Finland fought and won it back briefly, but in 1944 Hoaglund was incorporated into the U.S.S.R. as a strictly off-limits area.

After 1991, the island remained under the authority of the Russian military and was home to a radar system and radio transmitter, which, for unexplained reasons, always seemed to be left on. Because Hoaglund was a closed Russian base, Finland and Estonia were limited in what they could do to get someone to turn the transmitter off.

K. Jaak Roosaare, a returning Estonian émigré from New Jersey and member of Estonian parliament in 1994, called for a Russian government explanation. Roosaare also asked the parliament to inform the UN because jamming distress signals would be against international law. Parliament never followed through. The Finns had contacted the Russians in the past on the wayward transmitter with no result. Later, Admiral Iivonenile wavered and said it was only possible the transmitter interfered with the Mayday. The issue was eventually dropped.

A series of comprehensive malfunctions in regional communications systems all at once, and all at the exact time the ferry had sunk suggest military or intelligence service involvement. Was a distress call intentionally blocked? If so, why?

Another unaddressed question concerns the NATO exercise Co-operative Venture 94, which was gathering in the Skagerrak area with naval forces from 14 nations conducting "peacekeeping, humanitarian and search-and-rescue operations." Why didn't the NATO communications units set up for the exercise overhear the distress calls? Why weren't they contacted for help? The massive exercise with dozens of sea vessels, planes and helicopters were ready to go just the other side of Southern Sweden.

Were there specially-equipped rescue helicopters or other aircraft that could have assisted? Survivors who didn't die from hypothermia while floating on upturned boats or flotsam in the biting water waited four-six hours for rescue. NATO search-and-rescue personnel and equipment could have saved some lives. Flying time was under one hour. Why didn't they respond to the distress traffic? What happened?[85]

*   *   *

Movements, figures, commotion. The submarine collision hypothesis resembles a film viewed through an unfocused lens. Occasionally a recognizable image appears, then reverts to a blur.

The *Estonia* ferry encountered trouble in the first hour of September 28, 1994, Estonian time. Because of the time difference, the accident happened on September 27 in Sweden. On that very day, the Swedish military documented six airspace violations.

Could these intrusions have any connection to the *Estonia* ferry disaster? In response to inquiries, the Swedish Armed Forces declassified two incidents as German aircraft. A good guess would be zealous NATO pilots taking a shortcut across Sweden to the Cooperative Venture exercise in the Skagerrak area.

Four airspace violation reports, however, remain classified.[86]

Why, almost two decades later, four presumably innocuous airspace incursion reports could cause damage to Sweden's national security on release is, like so many circumstances in September 1994, wide open for speculation. Some reasons for the fly-ins could have been civilian aircraft with an inexperienced pilot straying in and out four times; additional high-fliers charged up for Cooperative Venture 94; an incursion report that mistakenly identified Sweden's own homemade fighter jets as intruders; NATO jets on a classified mission associated with the raging Balkans war; faulty early-warning equipment.

While it's possible that declassifying any of these incidents could point out weak points in Sweden's air defenses, the information would be circa 1994. Technology has leapfrogged ahead since then, and few people are interested in studying antique air defense systems. Releasing merely the intruding aircraft's country of origin and time and date they were spotted would expose nothing.

There is one exception. If the four trespassers were Russian ASW planes from Kaliningrad, that could draw a line under the word submarine. Similarly, when the *Kursk* submarine disappeared, Russian IL-38 aircraft flew the Norwegian coast searching for a foreign submarine that they believed was the guilty party.[87]

ASW planes dropping sonar buoys could be searching for a lost submarine that was supposed to have made contact hours earlier. The aircraft could have circled the southern Baltic, stretched the search area a bit too far and crossed into Sweden's airspace.

Or ASW planes could be reconnoitering the Karlskrona area in southern Sweden, the location of the country's main submarine base, to confirm that the coast is clear and a sub may proceed.

Disclosing the intruder's country of origin could give away the game, and Sweden's clampdown on the raw data indeed suggests Russian aircraft. From 1992-1995, the Russian military air force violated Lithuania's airspace more than 5,300 times. Unauthorized flying through Swedish airspace wouldn't make much difference.[88]

Aircraft from the East crossing the Swedish demarcation line has precedents. In 1984, a Soviet jet fighter trailed a civilian Airbus 310 jetliner some 50 kilometers into Swedish airspace. Radio intercepts showed the Sukhoi-15 fighter had armed and locked on its air-to-air missiles. Fortunately, the suspense ended without incident. But the Soviets, offering testimony and documents, vehemently denied it ever happened.[89]

Later, when Bildt's trespassing accusations centered on submarines, Moscow stuck with the official policy of denial.

The quilt of secrecy that Sweden carefully places over documents unnecessarily deepens suspicion of a collision. In fact, Sweden itself does not escape the speculative net. In 1994, Sweden had 12 patrol submarines plus one midget sub. Not a bad size fleet for a neutral country in a post-Cold War world. Finland, by comparison, has no subs.

Of Sweden's 12 submarines, four of them were docked for the three-day period September 27-September 29, 1994, according to the standard logbooks. Logbooks from six of the remaining eight boats can in principle be inspected. According to the Swedish Naval Press Attaché, logbooks from the latter half of 1994 for the other two submarines--the *Sodermanland* and the *Ostergotland*--are today still classified as secret.[90]

The Swedish Navy also maintains two sets of logbooks: The standard daily logbook records the submarine's own movements and the "war diaries" record details of what the submarine had detected while roaming. War diaries are classified.

More suppressed information comes from submerged military listening posts. If any submarine had rammed the *Estonia*, the underwater impact noise should have been recorded by submerged acoustic equipment.

The Sound Surveillance System or SOSUS, is a cluster of underwater microphones buried in the seabed, with the cable running to monitoring equipment on shore. Underwater sounds are monitored and recorded, building a library of sound signatures that enable analysts to distinguish a Russian sub from, say, a French one. SOSUS posts were sprinkled around the globe in open seas, in certain choke points and along strategic coasts to track the movements of unfriendly submarines. In other words, the oceans are bugged.

Not much is known about SOSUS, a secret still closely guarded by the U.S. Navy even though the listening posts were dramatically scaled down after the Cold War ended. The Navy keeps the precise locations of SOSUS units confidential.[91]

SOSUS works best in the open sea. A submarine's signature noise close to shore will be disrupted by fishing trawlers and ferries' propellers as well as bad weather and echoes, just as the background noises of a city can drown out a lone voice.[92]

The Finnish Navy has some sort of SOSUS-equivalent undersea listening posts along the south littoral area and the U.S. draws intelligence from the Finns about the comings and goings from St. Petersburg. Unfortunately, the tangled politics of the region prevent official disclosure of the system outside of intelligence circles. Proof of eavesdropping on strategic Russian military areas would cause a political row and create lingering mistrust between Russia and its Scandinavian neighbors, a situation unwelcome during Russia's rocky transitional years.

Sounds recorded on September 28, 1994, in the Northern Baltic Sea can be tossed onto the growing pile of the *Estonia* ferry's official secrets.

None of the incidents--the pattern of submarine purchases by dictatorships; the 1993 verified sighting in the Baltic of an Iranian-crewed Russian sub; the missing large object seen on sonar near the *Estonia* wreck; the lock on information concerning NATO's Cooperative Venture 94 exercise and the four airspace incursion reports--even though they coincided with an enormous sea catastrophe nearby, can be considered part of a definitive answer without other corroborating data.

The submarine collision hypothesis has partially interlocking parts. Like a badly cut jigsaw puzzle, some pieces fit together, others don't but seem like they should. At the same time, nobody acquainted with the unraveling of the Soviet Union can devalue it.

Dark Signature

In the summer of 2004, thunderous noises tore through the Baltic States. In Tallinn, store picture windows wobbled and people froze in their steps. NATO jets soaring faster than the speed of sound created sonic booms that signaled in an odd way the country's arrival into the security of the trans-Atlantic alliance.

Ten years earlier, explosions of an ominous origin erupted throughout the Baltic States. Lithuania had two bombings of its railroad line. In Latvia, a blast hit near the Russian-occupied military base of Skrunda and a special squad disarmed another timer-controlled device attached to a load of TNT. The U.S. State Department referred to these incidents as "acts of terrorism" springing from "ethnic tensions."[1]

Estonia had 63 reported bombings in 1993, along with 50 car bombings. Two years earlier, no detonations had been reported. Explosions that hit shops and businesses were related to protection rackets or rival mafia gangs settling accounts. A huge bomb blew out the windows in an office building and caused extensive damage to a church in Tallinn's Freedom Square next to the hotel where a journalist was staying. "The incident was strangely underplayed in the newspaper," she commented.[2]

Later investigations proved criminal organizations were executing some politically-inspired violence and getting away with it.[3]

On September 28, 1993, exactly one year prior to the ferry accident, a bomb exploded on the roof of a building in the courtyard of the American embassy in Tallinn, taking out the embassy's satellite communications antenna and part of the roof. Toompea Castle, the seat of the Estonian government, received bomb threats, resulting in tighter security of offices, TV and radio stations.[4]

One month before the ferry sank, a device with 4.5 pounds of TNT blew up under the office of the Mayor of Narva-Jõesuu, a resort town in Northeastern Estonia, destroying one-third of the building and causing a fire. Prime Minister Laar said the act was a "direct challenge to the Republic of Estonia and its local governments." Later, leaders of criminal groups were arrested in connection with the politically-motivated bombing.[5]

Blasts erupted so freely and frequently that in early 1994 Swedish policemen arrived to help Estonians conduct several bomb threat exercises on the *Estonia* ferry. According to the German investigators, government agencies in Estonia and Sweden were aware of bomb threats to sink the *Estonia* ferry; the last threat appeared on September 27--the day of the ferry's final departure.[6]

Thus, on the days following the catastrophe, the word "bomb" was on the minds of many people.

Prime Minister Laar carried a hunch about foul play. Andi Meister, head of the JAIC, would not exclude a bomb. Johannes Johansen, Estonian director of the Estline company operating the ferry, told journalists "Last year there was a very vague piece of information that there may be an accident in the Baltic Sea . . . We reacted in a very, very sharp way, informing our colleagues and stepping up security. I don't know if it was someone's stupid joke."[7]

Ats Joorits, a member of the Estonian embassy staff in Stockholm, went a step further. He "disclosed sensational news heard at the harbor: there had allegedly been a bomb on board."[8]

Several Estonian newspapers analyzed the possibility. The *Post* reported a rumor that the ferry had been one mafia group's prime smuggling conduit until a rival group "bombed their competitor." The story seems more imaginative than real, the article said, because the rival group could have simply tipped off Stockholm customs about the arrival of illicit goods.

Also examined by the media was political terrorism from "the dark forces of some foreign state," a fairly obvious reference to Russia. An Estonian journalist pointed out that Swedish Prime Minister Ingvar Carlsson, Bildt's successor, declared shortly after he took office that Sweden would remain neutral in a Baltic conflict.

"A year ago, Carl Bildt had promised that in case of a Baltic crisis, Sweden shall not be passive. Sweden was the only state which promised to help if we [the Estonians] are in trouble. During the days that followed the catastrophe of the *Estonia*, that promise was revoked. Let us hope this was not a cause-and-effect."[9]

Estonia's bomb epidemic does not necessarily mean that deliberate blasts sank the ferry, but it certainly does provide a barometer of criminal activity in the tiny republic circa 1994. It was no great leap from bombing the U.S. Embassy courtyard or a mayor's office to attaching explosive devices to a passenger ferry gleaming with political symbolism.

As time passed, anxiety about a bomb ebbed as the JAIC microfocused on the visor mechanics. Shouts of foul play faded to murmurs, then infrequent whispers. The bomb theory collected dust.

By 1998, Swedish State Prosecutor Tomas Lindstrand ruled that his preliminary inquiry into circumstances of the *Estonia* ferry sinking be closed. Nothing had been found to prove that the disaster had been caused by a premeditated crime. Lindstrand wasn't saying definitively no criminal action occurred, just that his office had found no proof. Justice parked there.[10]

* * *

The same year, some private citizens decided to examine more meticulously the four-year old videos from the official Rockwater dive. The 70-odd hours of videotapes were publicly accessible, though parts had been edited by Swedish authorities.[11]

On one tape, as the camera drifts along the wall of the ship's hull, a rectangular shape momentarily appears. Closer inspection revealed the rectangular box-shaped thing was affixed to the portside, near the fifth deck. What was a box doing attached to the port side bulkhead of a shipwreck?

The German team brought the images to explosives experts in Germany and Sweden. Both identified the rectangular box with about 90 percent certainty as an underwater explosive charge.

All videos were then carefully scrutinized. The ROV footage taken just a few days after the catastrophe revealed another surprise. German investigators spotted a cube-shaped object near the port side locking devices of the visor. It was orange. Experts from Sweden, the U.K. and Germany were called in for visual analysis. They identified the orange packet "with a high degree of probability as an `explosive charge.'"

The video analysis experts then examined another set of videotapes of the same area shot two months after the ROV footage--during the Rockwater dive. The package had disappeared, suggesting that someone down at the shipwreck had removed it.

The German Group hired a former U.K. Royal Navy diver and military explosives expert, Brian Braidwood, who analyzed the orange cube and concluded:

> "--[T]he suspect package could have been an explosive device containing between one and three kilograms of plastic explosive . . . Finding such a device near the visor side locks suggests an attempt to damage the ship at a particularly vulnerable place," he continued. "--When or how the cube got there must remain a matter of conjecture. It can only be emphasized that the act of placing and arming such a charge takes only a few seconds as the firing time will have been set beforehand. A determined saboteur might well decide to increase his possibility of success by placing more charges, at similar vulnerable points elsewhere on the ship."

But the most telling visual evidence Braidwood found was the dark signature of an explosive force--a hole with petalled metal. The starboard side damage includes outward-folded petals, like a flower, damage that is structurally inconsistent with the port side tearing.[12]

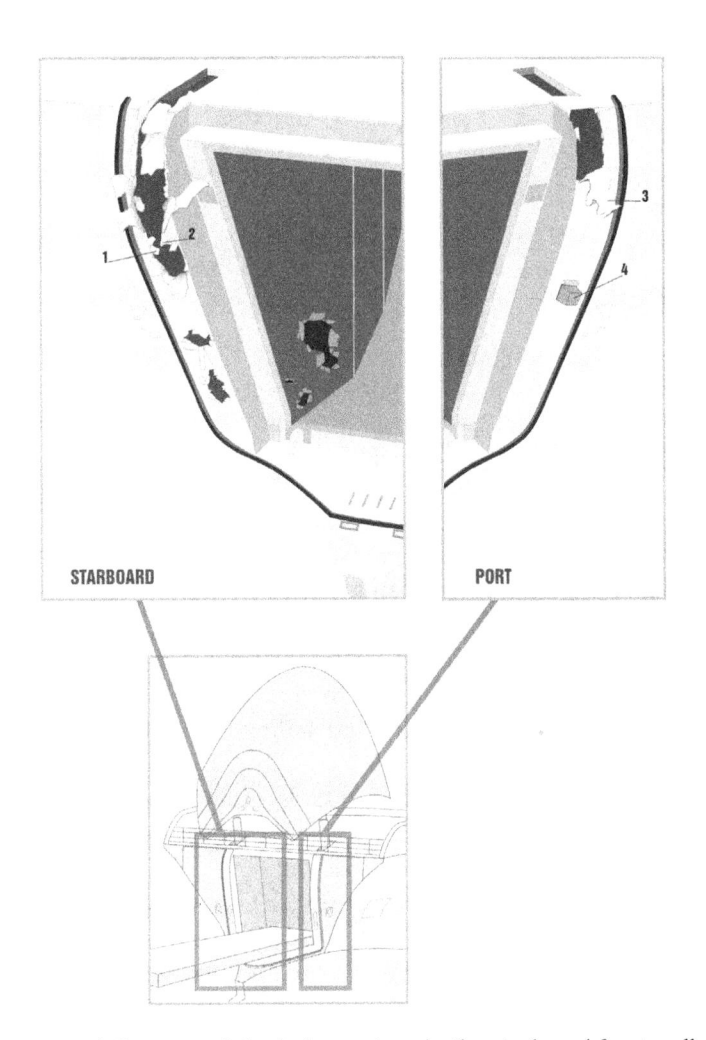

A 2 meter x 0.6m hole was torn in the starboard front wall with the petalled metal signature of an explosion. By comparison, the port side damage #3 shows a distinctly more linear damage pattern, with no petalled metal.

Metal samples were taken from #1 and #2. Bemis and Rabe brought the samples from #1 to independent laboratories in the U.S., U.K. and Germany, where they tested positive for an explosive force. Metal showing structural damage from a force above 1000 meters per second is categorized as an explosion; above 5000 mps is categorized as damage resulting from military explosives. The *Estonia's* samples were determined to be in the 3000-5000 mps range.

Note the interior wall of the starboard side, also with a hole bordered by petalled metal.

#4 is the location of the orange packet seen on video, which military demolition experts identified as an unexploded bomb.

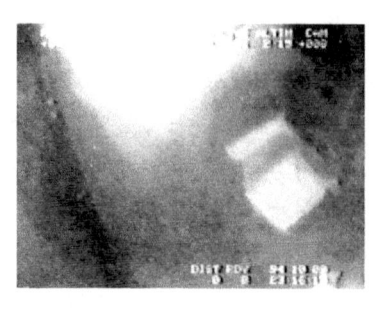

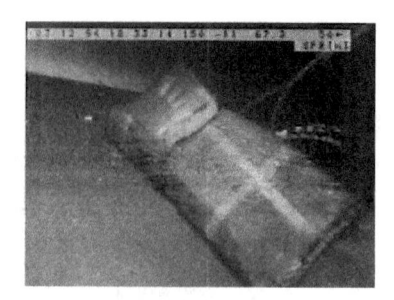

Left: Orange cube fixed to portside bulkhead.
Right: Rectangular box discovered portside, near the fifth deck.
Explosives experts say they are underwater explosive charges.
The JAIC claims they are floating debris.

Suddenly, key missing pieces seemed to have been found and they started to snap together. The two unnatural bangs heard by survivors at the bow; reports of the ferry coming to an abrupt halt and people falling to the floor or thrown out of bed--before the list; the freely available demolition material; the rash of bomb explosions in Estonia; previous ferry bomb threats. One passenger told how the *Estonia's* Captain Arvo Andresson looked edgy the night of the final sailing. It all seemed to cohere.

The Germans hypothesized that the portside orange packet was one of several explosive charges. For some reason it didn't detonate, yet the corresponding device on the starboard side did.

Backed by the reports of explosive experts, the German investigators were reasonably certain a series of small bombs played a role in the ferry sinking. International press picked up on the findings, revitalizing public debate.

The commission responded. Lehtola, the JAIC chief in Finland, pointed out that Finnish police ran laboratory tests on the retrieved visor. They took several paint samples from inside the visor and ran thin layer chromatography, liquid chromatography and spot test analysis that revealed no vestiges of explosives.

But Lehtola's explanation wilted when Hummel, the German investigator, went deeper. He countered that the sampled area had been underwater for almost seven weeks, skewing those tests.

"Since the investigation of the TWA 800 crash [in July 1996] it is public knowledge that explosives cannot be traced by means of the methods applied by the laboratory when the objects have been under water for more than one week. It would, even today and in 20 years time, be possible to prove explosion damage by scientific methods by means of which the destroyed molecular structure is examined. This, however, was not done according to the available documents," Hummel said.[13]

Lehtola concluded that the two discovered objects--the rectangular box and the orange cube--were not unexploded bombs. He claimed one was part of a broken pallet and the other a tarpaulin. The orange spot on the wreck, rumored to be a box of explosives, is not actually orange but appears to be due to the artificial light used in underwater filming, he added.

"A bomb explosion is excluded both as the cause and a contributing factor to the sinking of the ferry," Lehtola said.[14]

* * *

August 2000. In the seemingly slow motion of underwater video footage, a coiled telephone cord stretches from its base, swayed by mild currents. Stuff is scattered: wooden deck chairs, drawers spilling from a bureau, loose chrome metal trim, white deck railings. As the ROV videocamera moves closer to the stern, two human remains, essentially clothes and bones, lay with arms folded over chest, sad commentary on Sweden's assurances that during the last official dive to the wreck all bodies were sealed inside the ferry.[15]

The video footage was one result of an unauthorized dive to the *Estonia* ferry organized by American Gregg Bemis and German journalist Jutta Rabe. The August 2000 research expedition infuriated Swedish authorities, who claimed the crew violated the controversial Gravesite Treaty.

The dive was launched from the ship *One Eagle*. Its efficiency was compromised because the *One Eagle* had to sail 850 miles from Germany, the nearest country that is not signatory to the treaty. The *One Eagle* couldn't retrun to Germany each night to replenish essential supplies such as gases and fuel, so everything necessary for a one-shot dive expedition was estimated and loaded.

The expedition, therefore, had limited supplies onboard and that meant time was precious. Unfortunately, time was unnecessarily wasted because the Swedish government ordered a flotilla of ships to encircle and harass the *One Eagle*. Stockholm had dispatched naval forces against a retired CEO and a middle-aged mother sailing on a research vessel in international waters. A Finnish destroyer lurked in the background, endorsing the threat.

The reason for the menacing maneuvers is not clear. To protect the bodies in the ferry? Stockholm had civilized and more effective ways to ensure non-interference with the human remains. Months before the dive, Bemis and Rabe had invited Swedish observers on board. Surely a group of Swedish bureaucrats on board the *One Eagle* could have checked every move the divers made and reported any grave desecration.

The Swedish Defense Ministry, which initiated the farcical operation, had also crossed a line. The *One Eagle* was in international waters, meaning no one on board was subject to the Gravesite Treaty. Sweden's systemic harassment of the research ship could likely be defined as a criminal act had it been challenged in court.

Sweden's odd aggression also confounded the U.S. Embassy in Stockholm, which said it was disturbed by the possibility that Swedish forces would imperil the divers. They noted that Sweden had used "bubble-making equipment" to deter a past attempt to dive on the *Estonia*.

Meanwhile, the *One Eagle* crew went about the expedition, trawling the Baltic with a 1.5-meter long sonar fish in attempt to locate the wreck. During one of the ship's maneuvers, the line to the instrument was cut and the fish disappeared. Bemis suspects Swedish marine forces were involved in the loss of this essential and costly locating tool.[16]

The *One Eagle* then relied on publicly-released grid coordinates, sonar and a depth finder to locate the *Estonia*. But the ship's satellite navigation system (SATNAV), which pinpointed its own position in the sea, behaved erratically. It had worked fine before arrival. Bemis believes the military jammed *One Eagle's* satellite navigation. If the SATNAV system is one degree off, the *One Eagle* could be off 450-900 meters, missing the wreck entirely.

Because of constant SATNAV interference, the *One Eagle* had to hold position with its bow thrusters, which Bemis described as analogous to "riding the clutch in a car so long it can burn out."

Each extra hour locating the ferry consumed fuel and supplies that could've applied to dive time.

Divers wore tanks strapped to their backs containing tri-mix gas, an adjusted combination of oxygen and nitrogen with helium added to minimize narcosis, and therefore weren't bound by a support line. But they had a time disadvantage. Divers descending to the wreck and simply orienting themselves on the seafloor took five minutes. After an additional 15-20 minutes inspecting the wreck, divers would then need to surface, which took about two hours. A diver had to decompress by waiting at various depths to eliminate excess helium and nitrogen gases absorbed into his body.

The constraints cut short the actual inspection work. Moreover, the *One Eagle* had to save enough fuel to sail back to Germany. Docking in a nearby port to replenish supplies meant immediate arrest, as Sweden had lobbied all surrounding countries to sign the Gravesite Treaty.

Soon Swedish military in an amphibious assault raft skimmed up to the research vessel. They wanted to assist, they said, and shouted the numbers for the sunken ferry's exact location. But their figures didn't make sense when compared to the official grid coordinates.

The showdown came soon enough. The top Swedish Coast Guard officer demanded boarding rights and the *One Eagle* acceded. On board with a security team, he said the *One Eagle* crew was making an illegal dive and insisted on seeing a crew list to verify that no one from signatory countries was participating.

"We told him we have a right to be here and furthermore it's his job to protect us," Bemis recalled.

The *One Eagle's* captain didn't give up the list, something that the Swedes had in their possession all along.

Despite these provocations, the *One Eagle* stayed put and eventually found the *Estonia*, though they'd lost valuable time without even stepping into the sea.

Divers did manage to take a cutting torch down and burn off two pieces of metal from the bow bulkhead. The two pieces of metal, taken under rushed conditions, would prove to be the only concrete evidence ever produced by independent investigators, and it would prove to be damning evidence.

In the U.S., Bemis hired a San Antonio, Texas firm, Southwest Research Institute, to analyze the two metal samples the divers had cut off. The institute's report concluded one of the samples showed signs of a deformation process called "twinning," that is, evidence of "shock loading," an explosive force.

The report left no room for ambiguity. One possibility is a cryogenic situation--exposure to minus 100 degrees centigrade, for example. But the ship was never exposed to such extreme temperatures. The only other possibility is a "running shear fracture," technical jargon for an explosion.[17]

Jutta Rabe in Germany also had samples from the same piece of metal. She brought them to Brandenburg State Laboratory (*Materialprufungsamt Brandenburg*) in Germany, which does analysis for the German police. The lab found "characteristics . . . which are consistent with the effects of a detonation," according to the report.[18]

Later, Dr Kurt Ziegler from the Brandenberg lab told the U.K. newspaper *The Independent*: "The results show changes to the metal similar to those seen by high detonation velocity. That would be consistent with explosives such as Semtex or Hexa Composite. That kind of material will send shockwaves straight through the metal and is designed to destroy it."[19]

Semtex, an extremely powerful explosive made in the Czech Republic and familiar to military professionals worldwide, is a soft, putty-like plastic harmless to those handling it. Easily available on the black market, Semtex can be molded like clay around locks, confining damage to a specific area. A blasting cap or piece of detonating cord is required to set it off. Bemis recalled that similar malleable plastic explosives were placed around the driveshafts of the *Lusitania* wreck to carefully blow off the propellers, which were hazardous to divers.

The Brandenberg lab's explicit descriptions gave the bomb theory a new legitimacy. Metallurgical examinations were hard science--measurements and analysis. Not conjecture.

Survivors and relatives of *Estonia* victims rallied and demanded a new investigation. Public pressure energized the bureaucracy in the Ministry of Transport. After years of silence and a palliative posture toward the relatives, Stockholm's position now had to change. The Bemis and Rabe expedition results had shredded the JAIC's conclusions. Sweden had to act.

Now, it was assumed, the Swedish state would live up to its obligations and unlock the mystery. Authorities would order recovery of the bodies. The wreck would be raised and independent experts would conduct an open investigation of the bow area. These actions would begin to restore public trust and allow relatives to move toward closure. Foul play in the deaths of 1000 people would not go unpunished; no Western government could ignore that.

But that is not what happened.

Bemis and Rabe sent the lab reports to heads of state in Sweden, Finland and Estonia, presenting their scientific evidence that a bomb had exploded on the *Estonia* ferry.

"[Transport minister] Mona Sahlin has seen this letter," Camilla Buzaglo, a spokeswoman for the Transport Ministry, told the press, "and she wants to remind people that the expedition by Bemis and Rabe is being investigated as a crime."

No amount of prompting would get Buzaglo to move from this position, wrote one journalist, "not even the possibility that a potentially far more serious crime had been committed."[20]

* * *

Suppose the accident happened as the commission describes. Enormous waves jerked the visor off, in the process popping out a series of metal locks and attachments. Could the violent ripping of metal mimic the physical effect of an explosion on the metal? The researchers at the metallurgical labs have said it could not.

> "There are mechanical forces and explosive forces," Bemis explained. "Mechanical forces are *not* sufficient to produce `twinning', but explosive forces are. This distinction is important because all three labs deduced twinning in the metal. Hence the theory that the visor was wrested off the front of the ship does in no way explain the evidence of the explosion at the site of the bulkhead."[21]

The Brandenberg report, carefully read, gives nourishment to the explosion theory.

It's essential to recall that the commission states the visor had play, that is, continual wave bombardment jarred it loose from its attachments. The play successively enlarged, and locks and attachments were eventually torn from their mounts. Progressive detachment. The bow visor did not fly off as fast as a sneeze; that defies logic.

Yet Dr. Ziegler from the Brandenberg lab said his examination showed the "event" had a velocity of "more than 5,000 meters per second" and that could only result from a massive explosion or something traveling at that speed and hitting the ship.

Lloyd's List pointed out that the Concorde jet cruised at about 1/10 that speed. No 60-ton block of steel, progressively detaching, could soar off its locked restraints ten times faster than the Concorde.[22]

Even though two labs had reported evidence of an explosive force, Rabe didn't stop there. She brought the fragments to the *Institut für Materialprüfung und Werkstofftechnik* in Clausthal-Zellerfeld, Germany. Their report stated that areas of the metal "have been heated up to 700-720° C during cracking (deformation) . . . As the deformation of the investigated samples has not been created in a testing laboratory, we have to proceed that the cracking of the material was induced by a detonation or some projectile."[23]

Germany's *Der Spiegel* television program, where Rabe worked as a journalist, believed a sensational story had been uncorked: One of the worst peacetime catastrophes in 20th century Europe was actually an act of sabotage.

For added assurance, *Der Spiegel* management brought the metal to a fourth lab, the Federal Institute for Materials Research (*Bundesanstalt fur Materialprüfung* or BAM) in Berlin, a government organization. This was the last stop. A total of three labs had analyzed the *Estonia's* metal samples and concurred that evidence of an explosive force existed. A fourth would be insurance.

BAM, however, tried a different method. Instead of basing their findings solely on analysis of the metal taken from the shipwreck, BAM tested on fresh metal of a type similar to that used in constructing the *Estonia*. Researchers applied explosive forces by various means. Then they compared the fresh metal and the actual *Estonia* metal fragments. They concluded that the samples from the *Estonia* do not prove an explosion occurred.

BAM added that structural changes in the metal fragments were superficial and resulted from a shipyard process to clean away rust known as "shot peening."

Shot peening, in principle like sand blasting, is a cleaning process that shoots small particles of metal onto a metal surface before painting. Bemis explained that shot peening would only have affected the outside surface of the metal. It could not have possibly caused structural changes deep in the metal's interior, "which was what alerted the experts to the fact that there was an explosion." Shot peening as the cause of such deep structural damage was an amusing thought to the Southwest lab examiner.

There was one more detail. The Meyer shipyard, which built the *Estonia* in 1980, searched their records and found that the *Estonia's* steel had never been subjected to shot peening.[24]

Nonetheless, the negative results from BAM gutted the bomb theory. Sweden's Ministry of Transport and commission members pointed to the BAM lab findings as the definitive answer--even though the lab did not analyze the actual metal samples from the ferry.

To bury all talk of explosions, the Finnish JAIC mentioned recordings from the Institute of Seismology at the University of Helsinki, which operated a measurement station about 160 kilometers from the casualty site and can detect blasts caused by as little as 800 grams (two pounds) of explosives.

The Institute's records showed no evidence of an explosion in the Baltic Sea on the day of the accident. If the *Estonia* had suffered bomb blasts, goes the logic, the acoustic readings would have recorded the sound like they did when the *Kursk* submarine was torn by explosions in August 2000.[25]

Once again, analysis appears to corroborate the JAIC's position, but is subtly misleading. The *Kursk* explosions occurred more than 30 meters underwater. The *Estonia's* "unnatural bangs" occurred above the waterline (where the visor attachments are), on the surface of the sea, and were likely drowned out by high winds and the ferry bouncing through rough seas. If the visor banging against the ship and thudding off the bulbous bow didn't register on the Institute's underwater acoustic devices, surely a surface explosion wouldn't.

Monitoring stations typically keep watch on phenomenon like seismic activity deep under the sea floor, underground nuclear testing and illegal dynamiting of fish. Submerged microphones detect sounds that originate in the silent depths, undisturbed by wind and weather. Just as a swimmer several feet underwater can better hear the propeller of a motorboat some distance away than he can hear people shouting on the surface.

For several years, German prosecutors continued to probe the issue of the metal samples and the bomb theory, appearing at Hummel's doorstep, visiting his home, repeatedly quizzing him about the *Estonia* case. In November 2002, the German prosecutors closed the criminal investigation after finding no evidence to support allegations of an explosion aboard the ship.

Three independent labs from different countries concluded the metal samples from the ferry show an explosion likely occurred. One German government lab that didn't analyze the actual metal samples did not concur.

To say one non-positive result from the state lab renders three positive analyses wrong is an arrogant oversimplification and hardly a reason to close the file. But that is exactly what happened.

When the government latched onto the BAM report and summarily rejected the other analyses, critics were left in the wilderness. Even those with open minds began to question why someone would want to place explosives on a passenger ferry sailing to, of all places, Sweden.

Splinters and Fragments

"I'm absolutely convinced that all this time, from 1990 to 1996, the shadow of a Time of Troubles, a civil war, hung over Russia. Many Russians believed with utter despair that everything would come to this: a new military coup, a junta, the breaking up of Russia into numerous small republics--in short, a Yugoslav debacle... It was a terrible prospect. And it was possible...."

Boris Yeltsin writing in *Midnight Diaries*, the third volume of his memoirs.

About one month after the Estonia ferry had sunk, Moscow journalist Dmitry Kholodov from the newspaper *Moskovsky Komsomolets* was deep into an investigation of crime and corruption within Russia's military.

On October 17, 1994 he received an anonymous phone call instructing him to pick up a briefcase at Moscow's Kazansky Railroad Station that supposedly contained hard evidence to nail the kingpins of the military mafia. Kholodov collected the briefcase and returned to his editorial office. When he clicked open the latches, the case exploded and he died. A professional had wired it to detonate on opening.

The chilling news spread and renewed widespread concern about the degree of criminal influence in Russia. Eventually, a former intelligence chief in the paratroopers, four paratroop officers and the deputy head of a private security firm--a quintessential rogue group--were arrested, then acquitted. The acquittal was overturned until 2004 when they were acquitted a second time and the statute of limitations on the murder expired. The case is still unsolved.

The mention of Kholodov's murder here is not an attempt to associate him with the *Estonia* ferry. But his assassination underscores the fact that in 1994, renegade groups within the Russian military were active, secret and striking with deadly professionalism.[26]

Further proof of active breakaway military units comes from Carl Bildt himself. Bildt was convinced submarine visits into Swedish territorial waters in the 1990s were initiated by rogue units within the former Soviet navy. He did not pull the idea out of thin air. Bildt had access to Swedish intelligence and almost certainly was privy to intelligence from the U.S. and NATO, to whom he had forged a close post-Cold War relationship.

In 1994, Bildt delivered a letter to Boris Yeltsin saying that it was not too farfetched to assume "that the responsibility for this [submarine incursion] activity could be laid in the hands of ex-Soviet structures or patterns of behavior."[27]

Bildt apparently saw Russia as a country torn by competing factions of power. Because it is one thing to broach a topic in a tactful manner with high-level Russian functionaries in Stockholm and quite another to deliver in writing, from one head of state to another, accusations that a president is not in control of his own military.

Bildt was as subtle as a sack of concrete. To make such a gutsy move, he must have been sure. He must have read unambiguous intelligence reports from varied sources tracking the activities of renegade factions in the former Soviet military.

Such splinter groups would certainly find a home among the political extremists and revenge-seekers camped out in the Baltic Republics. Other likely comrades may have been found among the 2500 Russian military personnel who defiantly remained in Estonia after the August 1994 troop withdrawal, a group suspected by Western authorities of acting as a Fifth Column.[28]

* * *

The *Estonia* ferry sinking coincided with the rising influence of extreme nationalists in Russia. Dozens of radical organizations flourished in 1994. Moscow's nationalist voices blamed outsiders, describing Russia's ills as a result of the "Gulliver effect," a giant power beleaguered by many smaller forces.

Besides Vladimir Zhirinovsky's Liberal Democratic Party (LDRP), the largest among them were Russian National Unity and the National Bolshevik Party, both participants in the Moscow militarized confrontations of October 1993. Some organizations had tentacles in the Baltics and some had track records of violence.[29]

Russian nationalists exploited Estonia's ethnic divisions for political currency at home. They hammered home the idea of regaining lost territory, with hegemony re-established in the Baltics as an easy first step. Their fiery vision invigorated some of the thousands of stateless Russians living in Estonia.

The rhetoric likewise had a forceful appeal in Russia's power ministries. When Moscow relinquished East Germany and Eastern Europe, the former KGB, generals and many party leaders weren't consulted. They were now demanding "with much more emotionalism" that there be no concessions on the Baltics.[30]

Moreover, Russian Defense Minister Pavel Grachev found "extreme bitterness" among servicemen over poor accommodation, "the fall in their social status, and chronic impecuniousness." Many felt humiliated by the "precipitate" withdrawal from Europe and some are in "a strongly revanchist mood" and are allegedly even "prepared to return with tanks to defend their compatriots" in the Baltic States. He ordered divisional commanders to forbid contacts between servicemen and representatives of the political opposition.[31]

The new Baltic Republics stirred a particular hatred among some in Russia's officer corps. Not only were Estonia, Latvia and Lithuania seen as energetically pioneering the Soviet Union's disintegration. Estonia and Latvia had also been the objects of Russia's ambitions since the 15th century. Senior Russian officers still saw them as strategically vital.[32]

In Estonia, Commander-in-Chief Einseln and Defense Minister Hain Rebas, both returning émigrés, combined energies in attempt to assemble a military force fit for a democracy. The Soviet officers they found in charge of the military held high expectations for promotions in rank and took offense when Einseln revoked their privileges, which ranged from drinking on the job to rape.

Rebas said that the Soviet officers' mentality "was that of a big army in a totalitarian state and we tried to build a small, tiny defense force in a democratic state. They had great mental problems in adjusting. They were quite aggressive and not very likeable men."

Einseln recalled integrating ethnic Russian soldiers with Estonians for the first time. A disturbing issue arose: Should an armed confrontation with Russia occur, some ethnic Russian troops would not be loyal to Estonia.[33]

When Einseln fired more than a dozen of the officer staff in the first eight months he took over, a potential rogue unit was created.

Estonia had its own extremist factions. The Defense League, known as the *Kaitseliit*, was in the early 1990s a hyper-patriotic volunteer group that refused to join with the regular military forces. The leader and some members had criminal backgrounds. They distrusted Russians and were eager for confrontation. One incident involved *Kaitseliit* members shooting at Russian military cars and capturing soldiers.[34]

The times were volatile, with coiled hatred on both sides. In 1993, an incident known as the *Jaagrikriis,* abruptly became a decisive moment in Estonia's post-Soviet history.

The incident began due to worsening criminal activity at the Russian-controlled Paldiski submarine base near Tallinn. Paldiski hosted two nuclear reactors and the Estonian government held security concerns. Authorities ordered an Estonian army unit to take over parts of the base.

Two big mistakes were made. The particular unit storming the base was an overzealous team of soldiers that had previously comprised a paramilitary group. They were eager for confrontation and in an act of mutiny, didn't follow chain of command orders. Second, neither the Paldiski Naval Base Commander Admiral Aleksander Olkovikhov nor other Russian naval personnel had been informed about the operation.

Estonian Coast Guard boats blocked Paldiski harbor. Several hundred troops rushed in. The Russians armed and mobilized.

If anyone needed proof that the seeds of a Balkan-style conflict had been planted in fertile ground, here it was. An armed standoff between the Estonian army and Russian military, and Moscow had no knowledge and no involvement.[35]

* * *

Some 300,000 stateless Russians lived in Estonia in 1994--one-fourth of the country's population. A large portion of them were moderates who simply wanted slower adaptation to new citizenship rules. Most of Estonia's Russians did not want conflict, but some of them did.

Piotr Rozhok offered one such example. According to reports from Robert Frasure, at the time U.S. Ambassador to Estonia, Rozhok was a simple Russian chauvinist living in Narva. Zhirinovsky's rising influence after his Liberal Democratic Party won election victories in Russia changed that.

> "[Rozhok] rocketed from relative obscurity to instant notoriety as the self-proclaimed leader of the unregistered liberal-democratic party in Estonia...he took the line that Estonia is ancient Russian

land and called for retired Soviet military officers in Estonia to resist with arms any attempt to throw them out of their apartments," Frasure wrote in a confidential memo to the U.S. State Department.

In 1994 Rozhok "called on retired and reserve Soviet/Russian military officers to form paramilitary units," according to a memo from U.S. Assistant Secretary of State Richard Holbrooke. As head of the Estonian Union of Russian Citizens group, Rozhok said Russian servicemen "may bring Estonia to the brink of a civil war."

A confidential source talking to Frasure disparaged Rozhok, adding that "while the leaders of the veteran's groups are appropriately aware of Rozhok's inflammatory remarks, there are a lot of hotheads just below them."[36]

Rozhok is not linked to the *Estonia* ferry disaster. But others like him with less public visibility certainly roamed the former Soviet Union, looking for their own rise from obscurity. It does not take much imagination to see other "hotheads"--as Frasure's confidential source calls them--emboldened by Moscow's ultranationalist politicians and finding common interests with alienated military or criminal elements that have few misgivings about damaging the state of Estonia.

The U.S. Embassy in Tallinn worried about these destabilizing influences and wanted to "help Estonia cope with the threat that foreign-financed organized crime poses to Estonian sovereignty."[37]

Foreign financed is perhaps a reference to the mixture of political agendas and crime common in the 1990s. Assassinations, bombings and vice acted as a socially-destabilizing force in Estonia that tried to undermine law enforcement and government. Collaborating in crime could be men from the security services, the political extremist, the military officer and the suddenly rich "New Russian" businessman.

Each contributed expertise. The businessman had money, connections and the veneer of respectability. Russian military or elite *Spetsnaz* (*spetsnazncheniya* or "special designation") soldiers offered access to weapons and specialized knowledge in using them. The ex-KGB and the politicians played the traffic cop role, steering them around legal potholes and bottlenecks.[38]

The profit and power that traditionally bonded criminal groups took on a deeper meaning after 1991. Money equaled survival. Those who had never flirted with crime were now drawn in and committed by necessity. The monthly salary of a Russian officer was the ruble equivalent of about $30. In Estonia, the Russian solider had to buy goods in the expensive Kroon currency that was pegged to the Deutschmark.

Organized crime offered salvation. Handsome profits on weapons sales and an $800 street price for a contract assassination could provide a *Spetsnaz* thousands of dollars per month. Soldiers and officers in elite units typically found well-paying work at private "security firms" a common euphemism for criminal organizations.[39]

For all parties--nationalists, security services, criminals and military--collaboration was a win-win situation.

It doesn't take much to connect the dots. Political extremists pledge to protect Russian interests in Estonia and imply the need for a provocation. Local nationalists conspire with military and criminal contacts. A few hardened men then put suggestions into practice.

* * *

Though the filter of foul play, the *Estonia* ferry tragedy shows the marks of orchestration. In fact, timing brings a disturbing sensibility to the bomb theory.

The *Estonia's* fatal chain of events began by many accounts at exactly 01:00. At that hour, the ship's route always put it in the open sea, far away from the enclosed protection of the Gulf of Finland and nearby populated areas. One o'clock also brought a crew shift change on the ship, and the captain would typically retire until early morning to guide the ferry through Stockholm's archipelago. One o'clock was also a confusing date change. In Estonia and Finland it was September 28, but in Sweden September 27 became the 28th. One o'clock also arrives when most passengers are asleep in their cabins.

If explosive were set to detonate at 01:00, they would create the maximum amount of confusion. The choice of 01:00 would also suggest planners that were familiar with the ship's route, approximate speed and crew schedules.

Macro events also seem to cohere. On September 28, the Swedish government floated in a transition phase. Carl Bildt and his conservative Moderate Party had been voted out of office. In fact, the night of September 27th, Bildt and colleagues were at a farewell event. It was his final day in office.

Boris Yeltsin was in the U.S. (the accident occurred around 7 p.m. Washington DC time on September 27, 1994) and had addressed the UN General Assembly on September 26th. Yeltsin's schedule was publicly known for weeks. The trip included his scandalous return via Shannon Airport in Ireland when he didn't get off the plane for a planned official visit because he was ill, or, as many speculated, drunk.[40]

That left Estonia's Mart Laar. The Prime Minister's resignation had been the subject of speculation since at least September 22, with the chairman of Laar's Isamaa (Pro Patria) parliamentary faction denying rumors that Laar himself had said he wanted to resign.[41]

On September 26th, when the *Estonia* was still in Stockholm port readying to return to Tallinn the next day, the Estonian Parliament turned gossip into reality and delivered a vote of no-confidence in Laar, effectively removing him from office.

Thus, on September 27, 1994, the night of the final journey of the *Estonia* ferry, the governments of Sweden and Estonia were in transition periods and the Russian head of state was out of the country. Institutions are at their most vulnerable during changes at the top. Outgoing officials devote attention to their new opportunities and incoming officials orient themselves, bring in new personnel and struggle through a learning curve.

Micro and macro events aligned gracefully. To saboteurs, September 27 must have looked exquisite.

Macro Events

SEPTEMBER 27-28

Sweden: Bildt leaving office

Estonia: Laar's resignation made public

Russia: Yeltsin in the US

Micro Events

SEPTEMBER 27-28
01:00 Estonia time:

Loud, unnatural bangs, scraping noise, list

Crew shift change

Ferry at midpoint of voyage

Time zone change

Telecommunications in the area goes out beginning at 01:03

Time the trouble began

Time of decisive events	12:30-1:00	Just Before 1:00	1:00	1:00-1:15 (JAIC)	1:20
Number of survivor confirmations	13	1	29	3	5

Controversy exists over the time the *Estonia's* fatal chain of events began. The majority of survivors, some who wore watches or had alarms clocks in their cabins, identified the loud bangs and start of trouble at exactly 01:00. Yet the JAIC report states the ferry's trouble started at 01:15, supported by three survivor statements.

* * *

In 1994, a passenger ferry could be sabotaged with unsettling ease. Anyone could carry weapons onto a commuter ship. Ferries, unlike airlines, had no metal detectors, obligatory passenger searches or baggage inspections. In the post-September 11 era, transport security measures are slightly stricter than before. But in 1994, boarding procedures on the *Estonia* ferry were no different than boarding a city bus.

Explosives could easily be brought on board. Still, if sabotage was involved in the catastrophe, why weren't explosive devices placed in delicate areas where they would be expected to sink the ship?

The dark signature–the hole in the bulkhead with petalled metal-- was above the waterline, away from the visor hinges. If someone wanted to sink the ship, the argument goes, they made a dumb mistake. They'd set explosives in the wrong place.

There were so many options. Even an amateur could park an explosives-laden truck on the ferry's cardeck. The driver exits the boat well before departure and at night the blast sprays ferry fragments into the sea.[42]

The *Estonia* also had a nightclub, restaurant and shops that tended to fill up just after leaving port. Semtex in a gymbag timed to go off at night could have been hidden under chairs, in a baggage room or inside passenger lockers. Criminals like to take the path of least resistance. Why didn't they?

The question is actually a demand for a motivation, which ultimately can only be a guess based on the atmosphere of the times. Maybe the wanton act of killing a shipload of passengers wasn't what anyone wanted. In 1994 Estonia, it would be an act of war.

Crippling the ferry is quite different. Estonia's fiercely-guarded international image would suffer. In a symbolic bombing no one would be hurt, but maybe key decision makers in the US and Europe would wonder what is wrong with a state that cannot even secure simple transport lines. The flow into Estonia of international advisors, state functionaries, businessmen, students, tourists--the catalysts of economic development--would slow to a trickle. A disaster, after all, often reflects internal decay.

Newspaper articles with the semblance of objectivity would raise serious doubts that Estonia could ever meet the rigorous standards of NATO. Seemingly fair analysis would imply Estonia's institutions were weak and incapable and its government dysfunctional, perhaps in competition with organized crime. Russian nationalists would relish such commentary, which would also send an implicit warning to other regions that insist on declaring independence.

Diminishing Estonia's international image, maybe disqualifying it from immediate entrance into the Western circle, would be a far more viable and effective strategy for the extremist side than sinking the ship.

* * *

The theoretical motive for someone placing explosives on the ferry clearly has limits. The accident resulted in the death of nearly 1000 people, not the shaming of the Estonian nation. Accepting the rogue faction hypothesis means assuming that the perpetrators' plans somehow went awry. Speculation ends here.

Some officials doubt the possibility of nefarious perpetrators due to the lack of police leads. Money, connections, political needs, threats, violence or a combination of the above would certainly squeeze a few drops of information from the insiders. There would be a leak.

Heike Arike, Estonian Interior Minister in 1994, said the ministry never received any clues pointing to criminal involvement in the disaster:

> "Estonia is an extremely small country . . . It [wasn't] possible to hide something . . . At that time, Estonia had no special laws or acts concerning confidentiality. Officials were not bound by those laws and they tended to speak about everything. People can have secrets today. Our government in 1994 had been different."[43]

However, mafia-like groups that came together as the U.S.S.R. disintegrated continue to taunt authorities with their track record of avoiding discovery. A rogue group inside Russia's elite Alpha troops is suspected of storming the Vilnius television station in 1990, but no arrests have been made. Lithuania, after several years, identified the perpetrators of the 1991 murder of seven Lithuanian border guards at

Medininkai customs outpost, but are unable to extradite them. No conclusive evidence that journalist Dmitry Kholodov was killed by a military hit squad exists, though that is where the compass points.[44]

Perhaps criminals who were instrumental in sinking the ferry later fought in the bloody gang rivalries in Russia and the Baltics that turned thousands into anonymous dead, their murders still unsolved. They took their secrets with them. Others died by the thousands in the killing fields of Chechnya. The luckier gangsters just disappeared into the world, maybe serving a new multi-millionaire boss in Cyprus, Spain, Israel or the U.S.

Critics can argue that Russia is regarded as the traditional source of misery for Estonians, and suggesting Eastern involvement in the ferry disaster is an oversimplification. But the important distinction is between the official Russian government, which operated under constitutional constraints, international obligations and an unforgiving press, and the semi-legitimate factions of the early 1990s that freely used state institutions for their own ends without the Kremlin's knowledge.

Another contention is that the rotting Soviet Union can be relied on to explain away almost any eventuality, tie together every loose end. Because the ferry sank during years of social upheaval doesn't automatically mean the tragedy was a product of the times. But just as a technical glitch and pilot error could cause a plane crash in a war zone, the suspicion and scrutiny should be directed at the battlefield.

Desperation characterized the decade that saw the end of the U.S.S.R. Russia's institutions had been on the edge of the precipice. Colonel Robert Bykov, veteran of Russia's nuclear missile forces, felt impelled to come forward and issue an ominous warning.

In ancient times, Bykov wrote in the newspaper *Komsomolsky Pravda*, Herostratus burned down the great temple at Ephesus simply to perpetuate his name. "Officers manning control desks are also people," he continued. "We have no guarantee today that some Herostratus will not turn up in Russia's missile forces."[45]

When the Russian high command publicly admits an anguished soldier could intentionally launch a nuclear strike as an act of self-assertion, limits to plausible acts are removed. No institutional controls are in place. A few mean and miserable men affixing explosives to a ferry would pass unnoticed.

178 THE HOLE

In 1991, when Soviet tanks rolled into Tallinn, Estline Company operated a ferry line to Stockholm. (Photo: Tõnu Noorits)

Chechen leader Dzhokhar Dudayev commanded a Soviet airbase in Tartu, Estonia and was inspired by the Estonians independent spirit. (Photo: Tõnu Noorits)

Ultra-nationalist Vladimir Zhirinovsky gained popular support and political influence in Russia and repeatedly threatened the Baltic States.

Right to left: Russian president Boris Yeltsin, Estonian president Lennart Meri and Russian Foreign Minister Andrei Kozyrev discussed disagreements over the withdrawal of Russian military in Estonia. (Photo: Polar Film, Tallinn)

President Meri struck a closed-door deal with Boris Yeltsin to get Russian troops out of Estonia, officially ending the occupation in August 1994. (Photo: Polar Film, Tallinn)

The evicted Russian military took some heavy weaponry out of Estonia by sea (top). In Paldiski harbor, they abandoned vessels and left a mess. (Photos: Polar Film, Tallinn)

Paldiski base near Tallinn contained working nuclear reactors for Soviet Navy submarine training. No Estonian was allowed on the territory for decades. (Photo: Polar Film, Tallinn)

After 1991, Paldiski grew criminalized. A dangerous armed confrontation on the base between Estonian forces and Russians resulted in the resignation of Estonia's Defense Minister.

Admiral Aleksander Olkovikhov was in charge of Paldiski and oversaw the highly-secretive decommissioning of the nuclear reactors. (Photo: Polar Film, Tallinn)

Under exclusive Russian military control, a specially-designed train was brought in to carry 20% enriched uranium out of Estonia. (Photo: Polar Film, Tallinn)

182 THE HOLE

Alexander Einseln (left), a retired U.S. military officer, returned to his native Estonia to help de-Sovietize the military. He accepted appointment as head of Estonia's armed forces and walked into a political minefield.

Estonians showcased their symbol of independence for visiting political leaders. From left, Toivo Ninnas, head of ESCO, Kazakhstan President Nursultan Nazarbayev, *Estonia* Captain Avo Piht and President Lennart Meri. (Photo: Courtesy of Sirje Piht)

The *Estonia* ferry. The big white ship connected the re-established Estonian state to the West. (Photo: Tõnu Noorits)

The *Estonia's* two captains, Arvo Andresson (left) and Avo Piht. (Photo: Courtesy of Sirje Piht)

Carl Bildt (right), who played a vital role in ushering Estonia back into Europe with Estonian Prime Minister Mart Laar (left) at Paldiski base. (Photo: Tõnu Noorits)

Depiction of the *Estonia* ferry disaster by Latvian artist A. Halturins, which is hanging in Tallinn's Maritime Museum.

Siiri Same, the *Estonia*'s accountant who survived the disaster. She fought her way off the sinking ship and waited for hours in icy waters for rescue.

Estonia survivor Jaan Stern fled after seeing seawater on the floor of his cabin, which was belowdecks. After a wave shoved him into the sea, he was pulled onto an upturned raft and waited for rescue until morning.

Corridors and stairways were little more than a meter wide, jamming up quickly in a rush to the exits.

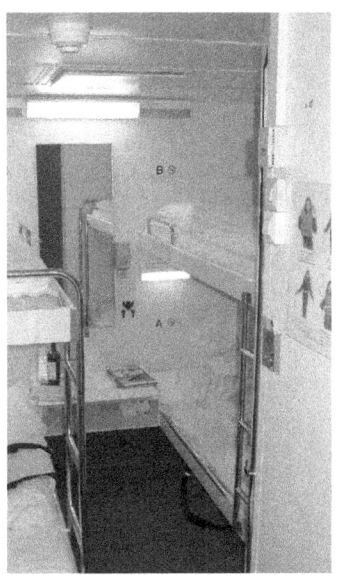

A four-bed economy cabin on the *Meloodia*, sister ship of the *Estonia*.

Stairwells from belowdecks led up to wide open foyers that were treacherous to navigate during the ferry's list.

186 THE HOLE

Johannes Johansen, managing director of Estline, the joint venture company that operated the ferry line. Estline was about to turn a profit and had ordered a second ferry when the *Estonia* sank.

Johan Franson, head of Sweden's Maritime Administration. Franson supervised the official dive to the shipwreck and initiated the controversial operation to cover the *Estonia* ferry wreck in concrete.

Werner Hummel, the head investigator hired by the German shipyard that built the *Estonia*. Hummel's report discovered plenty of undisclosed information and raised crucial questions about the government findings.

Kari Lehtola (left) and Tuomo Karppinen, members of the Finnish side of the JAIC. Despite the JAIC's conclusions, Lehtola wanted to maneuver an ROV into the sunken ferry and examine the bridge and cardeck.

Finnish sonar expert Jouko Nuorteva who found the *Estonia's* visor with his sonar fish. Misreadings of his sonar pictures created lasting suspicions.

Gregg Bemis and Jutta Rabe on board the *One Eagle*. Their unauthorized expedition to the shipwreck brought back metal samples that indicated the *Estonia* had been subject to an explosion.

Baltic Drainpipe

Smuggling is a fact of life in port cities. Shipping has long held a rough and permissive reputation, and the idea of the outlaw waterfront has an almost mythical status.

But when the U.S.S.R. shattered, illicit export activity spiraled out of all known proportions. This was not routine smuggling. Contraband and dangerous materials could ship across the Baltic Sea as easily as a container full of shirts.

In Estonia, authorities were preoccupied with radical structural changes that were crucial to renewing the nation. Criminal activity simply overwhelmed the country's resources. Law enforcement faced threats and challenges they were unprepared to meet.

Pivotal events were the pullout of Russian troops from East Germany and war in the Balkans, which had disrupted established drug routes from the poppy fields of Central Asia and Afghanistan to Western Europe. A supply chain bottleneck formed.

About the same time, Baltic borders to the West were flung open. Nimble criminal groups seized the opportunity. They redirected much of their inventory across the Baltic Sea to Scandinavia and then to Europe. The massive shift of distribution channels laid the groundwork for thriving Baltic criminal activity.[1]

Large Russian and Baltic cities were soon divided up by the most ruthless and effective criminal groups. In the post-Soviet environment, gangs routinely required businesses to pay for protection, or a *krisha* (roof). If the service was refused, consequences were swift and ranged from physical destruction of the business premises to murder. Many of these gangs operated under the guise of "private security services" and employed former military, particularly special forces, and professional athletes to carry out threats.

Criminals dressed like B-movie gangsters. Black leather jackets and baggy pants, gold neck chains and buzz haircuts were the common outfit. The lower-level street muscle wore the unmistakable fashion of the time: a two-piece nylon sport suit and sport shoes. These thugs were typically visible in Baltic and Russian cities during the 1990s.

The gangster militias discovered the most efficient route for moving bulky weaponry or large quantities of illicit goods was by boat.

The Baltic States' communication and transportation links with the West, combined with newly-opened borders and corruption among police and customs officials, elevated what had been contraband to the status of commodity export.

In addition, Estonia, Latvia and Lithuania proved ideal places for drug smugglers to launder their profits. Newly-founded private banks badly needed hard currency for startup capital and, unlike Western banks, wouldn't necessarily question where the money came from.[2]

Drugs were the first phase. Drugs came from Central Asia. Heroin couriers protected by paramilitary squads moved largely unhindered through the rubble of the former Soviet Union. They then shipped, for example, from the port of Tallinn across the Finnish Gulf to Helsinki. The idea was to get the goods into a Western port and re-ship to points worldwide; cargo arriving from Finland held little interest for Western customs officials. Estonia in this sense was a sort of smuggler's bridge between two worlds.

In 1991, most of the 400 tons of heroin that ended up in the West followed this route.

South American drug runners also took advantage of the new, unclogged channels. They were shipping cocaine hidden in cargo ships into Baltic ports and then trucking it into Western Europe.[3]

The flow of narcotics through the Baltic States was so rampant, alarm bells rang in the U.S. State department. In a 1995 report, Washington was explicit:

> "Estonia's location between Russia and the Nordic countries and its modern transportation links make it attractive to drug traffickers for smuggling operations...The majority of the drugs enter Estonia via railway from Russia and are transshipped out of Estonian ports."[4]

Drug smuggling also inspired other explanations for the ferry sinking. According to the Moscow-based Felix Group, a shadowy think tank with purported ties to Russia's security services, Swedish customs had been tipped off about a heroin shipment on the ferry and were waiting in Stockholm. The crew tried to dump the cargo by opening the bow doors at sea, but the visor snapped off and the ship sank (see Chapter 13).

References to crew involvement also appeared in the 1999 Russian language novel, *The Clash of the Triads* by Russian writer Oleg Benukh. His book contains a lengthy, undisguised section on the sinking of the *Estonia* ferry. In Benukh's version, the *Estonia* was sunk by bombs, the result of a war between two drug gangs, one from Central Asia and the other Hong Kong's infamous triads. The *Estonia's* captain and some crew members acted as accomplices.

Benukh's novel is fiction, but he said it is based on fact. Benukh said he spent time in Estonia talking to people who confirmed his own research on the drug gangs.

"For ten years before the accident everything with the ship was ok," Benukh said. "After the tragedy they're saying the ship was not designed right. From my point of view that's laughable. The people [responsible] are not in Estonia. They're in Central Asia and Hong Kong."[5]

The outlaw courier network could naturally be expected to have crewmember friends who would ensure seamless passage of their cargo. And in all likelihood the *Estonia* ferry was shuttling contraband. But no evidence ever implicated any crewmember in smuggling operations on the *Estonia* ferry.[6]

The ferry's master, Arvo Andresson, had special incentive to stay clean. From a practical angle, Andresson earned the equivalent of about $3000 per month in Estonian Kroons. He was 40 years old. In the context of 1994 Estonia, he was a wealthy and fortunate man, among the top bracket of wage earners. The median monthly salary in 1994 was $138, if a person could find a job. Unemployment and consumer prices were rising and the social safety net was in tatters.

Andresson also had an unlimited contract with ESCO, meaning if he lived up to his responsibilities he would stay the master as long as he wanted to.[7]

Only an irrational man would gamble his prestigious career and comfortable guarantees for some black money. Some have even suggested Captain Andresson was coerced into collaboration. But there is no factual foundation for either view.

* * *

Drugs weren't the only goods concealed on ships. Refugees roaming the unlocked territory of the former Soviet Union eventually walked into Estonia and became human cargo. Those with money were shuttled to Sweden at $2500 per head. The Estonian interior ministry cited refugee trafficking as a well-organized activity carried out by Russian mafia groups.

In February 1994, 64 Kurdish refugees from Iraq were found near suffocation inside a container on the *Estonia* ferry's cardeck after a crew member on watch heard them banging on walls of the truck.[8]

A more ghastly fate befell more than 100 Iraqi Kurds who were reportedly sealed inside a truck that went down with the *Estonia* when it sank on September 28. If they remained conscious after the truck somersaulted over cars, they presumably had to bear the slow rise of seawater seeping in through the door seams.[9]

Items trafficked across Estonia's borders included rare religious icons, pre-Revolution antiques, stolen cars, armaments and strategic metals. Sometimes speedboats loaded with prohibited items shot across the Narva River into Estonia, in some places only a 25-meter run. Russian customs officials told of several failed attempts to smuggle non-ferrous metals to the Baltics by loading them on planes stationed at military air bases in the St Petersburg and Pskov Regions.[10]

"Every goddamn thing was for sale," recalled Alexander Einseln, then head of the Estonian Armed Forces. "Just pay the money."

Einseln, who has the military officer's habit of speaking his mind, loudly condemned corruption in his native country. He was shocked by the breadth of graft in post-Soviet Estonia.

Einseln did not just gripe about it. In 1994, he organized a customs sting operation. The result was that "every border guard and customs official who was offered a bribe accepted it," according to a confidential memo from the U.S. Embassy in Tallinn to Washington DC.

"[Einseln] attributed part of the problem to the $5 per month salary of servicemen and border guards," the memo said.[11]

Weapons were hot items. When communism fell, conflicts flared and weapons flowed.

Arms were readily available. Former Soviet army troops still stationed in Estonia were eager to make deals. When smugglers paid $100 to a soldier for a Kalashnikov rifle, they effectively gave him one year's wages. Officers supported the sales. "Troops ought to sell army property and material. It's the only way they can survive," a Russian military officer told the Russian newspaper *SM Sevodnya*.[12]

Munitions and other equipment were also stolen from storage sites by criminals, often in collusion with military sentries. The problem was particularly acute in areas near Russia's periphery.[13]

Estonia and other liberated Soviet vassal states had underdeveloped national institutions and little experience running their own affairs. Estonian borders were secured largely by inexperienced personnel on the ground, which made the exfiltration of military goods easier. Nonetheless, Estonian authorities fought back and sometimes won.

Customs confiscated 21 Soviet armored personnel carriers and thousands of anti-tank rockets intended for buyers in Europe and the war-torn Nagorno-Karabakh region bordering Armenia and Azerbaijan.[14]

Local police also caught a shipment of 3,000 TT pistols in the port of Tallinn addressed to the Estonian Flaterno company. Chinese-produced TT pistols sold in Estonia for $350 each and resold in Moscow for up to $1300. Driving demand was Russia's underworld, which preferred the gun because the 7.62 caliber bullet easily pierced a bulletproof vest.[15]

Despite several contraband seizures, the international arms dealing network persevered. Law enforcement authorities were up against formidable groups with plenty of cash, political muscle and a growing international customer base.

When Estonian customs intercepted a batch of 15,000 Makarov pistols intended for the Isle of Man off Ireland's coastline, speculation was that the arms were headed to the Irish Republican Army. Customs officials added that the pistols seized in Tallinn were "probably not the first and not the last." Three days later, 25,000 of the same guns were nabbed in Helsinki.[16]

Another revenue stream for smugglers was the unconventional metals business. In the early 1990s, Estonia turned into one of the top exporters of rare metals on the planet.

Tiiu Silves, "Metal Queen" of Tallinn, started the trade legally in 1988 by offering imported televisions in exchange for scrap metal, according to *Forbes* magazine. Her Silves Enterprise Corp. in 1992 earned $310 million in revenues and she hired the former head of the Estonian

KGB as part of the management team.[17]

With a market established, rare and strategic metals exports turned into a major contraband problem for Estonia. Shadowy commercial structures easily conspired with broke state-run enterprises that held the stockpiles. Management gives the material away, writes it off inventory documents as waste and receives a cut of sales in return. In 1992, more than $500,000 worth of metals, including titanium and aluminum, were illegally shipped through Estonia, *per day*.[18]

"Consider precious metals and ask how Estonia can be the second largest exporter of precious metals in the world when it produces no precious metals," was how the phenomenon was phrased in testimony before a U.S. Senate Committee.[19]

Some controlled metals had nuclear weapons applications. As early as 1992, Ukrainian officials detained a plane believed bound for Estonia loaded with 3.2 tons of zirconium, a dual-use nuclear material and 800 kilograms of hafnium, used in nuclear control rods. Two planes from Kiev are believed to have smuggled more than six tons of these materials to Estonia.

The same year, Finnish and Russian customs in two separate incidents intercepted large Estonian shipments of zirconium.[20]

Business was often conducted in cash. "Buyers, accompanied by bodyguards carrying suitcases of cash and by their own scientific experts for testing the goods, filled hotels in Baltic ports, where Russian smugglers congregate," according to a *Time* magazine investigation. "The sellers are most likely to be mafia-connected hustlers or former KGB agents--some of whom have even set up joint ventures with former CIA agents to smuggle strategic materials."[21]

Border guards were in many cases unable to detect contraband or unauthorized to stop it. Estonia had no law on the books that required export licenses for strategic goods such as nuclear, biological and chemical materials and technology until November 1994, two months after the ferry sank.

As 1994 approached, smuggled goods began to turn from drugs, guns and controlled metals to far more dangerous things. Esoteric substances few had ever heard of were turning up in connection with Estonia. Finnish police collared smugglers with radioactive californium-235. The material was routed from Russia through Estonia to Finland, with Germany the final destination.

Thefts of fissile materials from the state-owned Fosforit Combine in Kingisepp, a Russian city 20 kilometers from the Estonian border, included several measuring devices containing radionuclides and cesium-137. Devices turned up in the Estonian towns of Sillamäe and Narva and five were found on a ship about to leave Tallinn.

Estonian police arrested two Swedish men for allegedly carrying a 28-kilogram lead container of cesium-137 onto a ferry from Estonia to Sweden. It is unclear whether it was the *Estonia* ferry.[22]

Cesium-137 is a radioactive metal resulting from nuclear fission in a weapon or reactor. It is used in various industrial measuring devices and in cancer treatment. As a radioactive substance, it is also a potential component of a dirty bomb when coupled with several pounds of TNT.

During 1994, several bars of cesium-137 with radioactivity up to a lethal 200 roentgens per hour popped up in Estonia, Sweden and Finland. When police traced the cesium's origins, they often led to one point: the Saku Repository near the city of Saku, outside Tallinn. Saku, previously a radioactive waste facility, had one security guard watching 72 hectares and a broken alarm system. Saku was looted.

In one heist, an Estonian man carried a bar of cesium-137 in his coat pocket for a few days and died from the intensive radioactivity. The bar was traced back to Saku.[23]

Illegal trafficking became so severe that about three weeks before the *Estonia* ferry sank, Estonia was forced to shut down a border crossing to Russia. Prime Minister Laar said the closing was important to help police cope with the underworld.

"Crime has been imported to us from the Eastern neighbor," Laar said.[24]

Between 1993 and 1995, 11 cases of confiscated radioactive materials were officially reported in Estonia.[25]

As with smuggling most anywhere in the world, what is seized can be only a small fraction of what actually flowed through the channels.

So far, no material through the Baltic nation had been weapons grade. Some smuggling was amateurish, the result of desperate people dreaming of a big cash sale to Western buyers. But responsible officials worldwide braced themselves every time laboratory-grade materials turned up in the police net.

Deadly goods drained out of the former Soviet Union under the guidance of organized crime. The concern was that extremists, military dictatorships or terrorists could far more easily procure a wide range of deadly material than in the past.

Nuclear device smuggling was the biggest fear internationally, and it was not misplaced. In 1994, Russia acknowledged 700 incidents involving the theft, or attempted theft, of nuclear materials. In many cases, thieves stole without much effort, climbing through a hole in a fence or bribing grossly underpaid guards. A line was crossed when Russian authorities caught two workers at a Russian nuclear plant who had taken warheads home in their pickup truck and stored them in a garage.

If security of nuclear stockpiles was so lax, what would stop experienced criminals from sending one by ferry, packed inside a container of jeans?[26]

Estonia was not an exclusive smuggling point, but the belief was that highly lethal cargo would follow rare metals and be smoothly integrated into the existing commercial shipping route. It was precisely that idea that stung Swedish customs officials:

> "We have information from companies [in Sweden] that they have received offers to buy plutonium and all other types of material via fax from the former Soviet Union," Hans Ohlsson, head of customs in eastern Sweden, said in 1993. "The nightmare is that we will be swamped with life-threatening substances . . . Sweden lies in the way of all the legal and illegal traffic over the Baltic Sea."[27]

Scandinavia hadn't lived with such consistent threats since the Second World War.

The peak came in the last eight months of 1994, when four chilling incidents involving high-end product were revealed. Four seizures of *weapons-ready* material believed to have originated in Russia occurred in different countries in Europe, though not in Estonia.[28]

After those incidents, FSU smuggling networks entered a higher threat category. Red flags went up in Washington, London and Moscow, at the UN, NATO, Interpol, the FBI, the CIA and at just about every other place that bore responsibility for preventing the illegal flow of materials that could wipe out large sections of the world.

"The Baltic States" were linked with Russia in warnings from intelligence services and security analysts. General Alexander Lebed, formerly the Secretary of the Russian Security Council, stunned the world when he told a visiting U.S. Congressman in 1995 that he'd ordered an inventory of Russia's suitcase-sized nuclear bombs and 84 were missing. Such a device could be prepped by one person in 30 minutes and kill 100,000 people. Although uncertain about their location, he speculated that they could be somewhere in Georgia, Ukraine or the Baltic States.[29]

Estonia did not report nabbing any weapons-grade material. Estonia did have several attempts to peddle U-238, a controlled substance that could be enriched for weapons use. Estonian authorities took the problem seriously and later apparently launched a sting operation, which was successful. Two unemployed men from the town of Haapsalu attempted to sell five kilograms of U-238 to an undercover policeman for $45,500.[30]

"The unprecedented leakage of nuclear materials from the former Soviet Union in 1994 signaled a clear shift in the nature and significance of the nuclear smuggling problem," read a report from the National Defense University in Washington DC.

"Of special interest is the role played by the Baltic countries of Estonia, Latvia, and Lithuania, whose territories have served a transshipment function for material leaving the FSU en route to other parts of Europe."[31]

Just as reports of intercepted goods capable of unimaginable destruction peaked, the *Estonia* ferry sank.[32]

The Consignment

Paldiski Naval Base stretches about 100 square kilometers along the northwest coast of Estonia. About a half-hour drive from Tallinn, Paldiski was a Soviet installation with shoebox-style apartment blocks that housed naval troops and their families. At one point, 16,000 Soviet military personnel were stationed at Paldiski. Like any military base, it contained schools, a post office and shops and was secured by barbed wire and guard towers.

But Paldiski was a level higher than many other bases. It was top secret and didn't appear on maps. Soviet submarines docked in its sheltered deepwater port. Navy personnel with security clearances from around the Soviet Union attended courses in the enormous main building that housed the crown jewels: Two functioning submarine nuclear reactors used for hands-on instruction.

The well-guarded base was Moscow's territory, an enclave within Estonia ruled by its own authority and subject to its own laws. Even though Russian troops withdrew in 1994, few Estonians ever set foot in Paldiski until Russia officially handed it back in September 1995.

Paldiski's fate mirrored that of the U.S.S.R. Central control fell away, decay and corruption ensued and criminality dominated.

One journalist described a visit to Paldiski in late 1993:

> "--[R]ocket launchers and other boats lie stripped or half-submerged in their berths, leaking oil steadily into the sea . . . Buildings housing [the] two research nuclear reactors . . . and other port facilities have been gutted, contents carried away or destroyed. Underground cables have been ripped up by scrap metal merchants

and equipment stolen . . . As we drive into the compound, our guide points to a neat two-storey building in the compound. 'Mafia headquarters,' he said. 'This is where they have all their guns and bombs.' . . . These gangs have weapons and are probably made up of soldiers who have become skilled at auto theft, armed robbery, kidnapping, extortion and drug or arms smuggling."[33]

In early 1994, Estonian police discovered a military train near the nuclear reactor in Paldiski pulling 22 wagons loaded with anti-tank mines and bombs. In some train cars, the contents had been unloaded and sold. "Presumably these weapons are now in the hands of local criminals," reported the Estonian Foreign Ministry."[34]

During the troop pullout negotiations, the Russians argued unsuccessfully to keep Paldiski base until year 2000. Vandalism and looting coincided with the troop withdrawal, according to Einseln. Departing Russian forces poured cement down sewer pipes, locked guard dogs in a room for two days without food and left graffiti on the walls that said "We'll be back." Anything of value was torn out and taken.

The house of Rear Admiral Alexander Olkovikhov, the Paldiski base commander, mysteriously burned down the day after he was supposed to turn it over to the Estonian state.

Fortunately, the nuclear reactors were unharmed.

Environmental damage was far worse. Nuclear material had been tossed away without regard for safe disposal. Radioactive waste remained in liquid form, against all modern conventions of storing it in solid form. In 1994, a civilian died after coming across radioactive waste near the base.

"This was not radioactive waste storage, this was a radioactive waste dump," said Henno Putnik, deputy director of Estonian Radioactive Waste Management Agency (ALARA Ltd.), a state-owned company set up by the Estonian government. "Everything radioactive was just thrown in the same spot, with no segregation, no packaging."[35]

Paldiski base was relinquished, but the Russians were given authority for one year over the section where the nuclear reactors sat. Admiral Olkovikhov and a small team of Russian military specialists remained behind to remove the total of 460 nuclear fuel rods from the two reactors.

The fuel rods, each about three meters long, contained 20 percent enriched uranium. Though the uranium would require further enrichment to make a weapon, 20 percent enriched falls into the "weapons useable" category. Plutonium could be extracted from the fuel rods, though that would require reprocessing, according to Putnik. Nonetheless, it was highly-sensitive material.

The press wrote about the decommissioning negotiations and the dismantling schedule was published. Before the first reactor was taken apart in August 1994, the Swedes offered to act as neutral observers to monitor the procedure. But Russia still controlled the reactor site and Admiral Olkovikhov refused, demanding tight secrecy.

The Russians handpicked the personnel for the nuclear fuel removal process because it was actually the reversal of standard operating procedure for loading nuclear fuel into a Soviet submarine. Thus, they considered the operation a military secret.[36]

On September 20, 1994, Russian specialists began to dismantle the second reactor by lifting the lid and removing the fuel rods. By September 27, the date the *Estonia* ferry would sail from Tallinn port on its final voyage, a crane was loading the rods onto special train wagons modified to carry nuclear material.[37]

On October 15, the operation was done. The Russian military team stated that all the rods from both reactors containing the 20 percent enriched uranium rolled out of Estonia to Russia under guard.

They supplied no documents to backup their claims.

In fact, no report on the decommissioning procedure was made. There is no summary. There is no inventory record or chain of custody verification. Not one document exists that certifies all 460 fuel rods containing weapons-useable uranium were indeed on that train and sent back to Russia.

It was merely announced.[38]

While military interests can arguably require confidentiality during the reactor decommissioning phase, the routine practical matters of counting, loading and locking the fuel rods in the train cars have no basis for secrecy.

The Estonian government was forced to trust the words of the occupying force they had just uprooted. This was the same Russian military force who had looted and vandalized Paldiski base, who were heavily criminalized, who were impoverished and vengeful and had been evicted, as they saw it, from the naval base Russia had held since Peter the Great ordered it built in the 18th century.

All the fuel rods are back in Russia, they said. It was hard work, but they got it done. As if they'd finished moving office furniture and not some of the deadliest material known to man.

It does not require much imagination to see that some of the weapons-grade uranium may not have been loaded onto the Russia-bound train. Without a documented chain of responsibility for the fuel rods, without any external monitoring, they could be appropriated as easily as the glut of other illicit material had been.

No evidence shows fuel rods were on the *Estonia* ferry. However, evidence clearly shows that Estonia's well-oiled smuggling channels enabled criminal groups to provide a turnkey solution for purchasers of any black market goods.

Several three-meter long fuel rods required the use of a crane to lift them. A few could fit snugly into the seven-meter trailer of truck, which could drive onto the cardeck of a ship, the most viable long-distance transport for bulky items.

A buyer could have been found months earlier and delivery date prearranged; the decommissioning negotiations and dismantling dates were publicly known. Terrorists are not the most likely customers. Any state with nuclear ambitions or any country that is assumed to have nuclear capability and perhaps operates an undisclosed refinement facility would covet 20 percent enriched uranium. They would also cherish discretion and pay well.

The strategic material goes from Tallinn to Stockholm, where it could be driven onto a Swedish-flagged cargo ship. From there, it could be shipped to a buyer in the Middle East or Asia and evoke far less suspicion than if the ship sailed from an FSU country.[39]

Local operatives would profit. Russian and Estonian law enforcement officials could be completely unaware of the shipment. Inventory of nuclear material and weapons at storage facilities in Russia was notoriously sloppy, if done at all.[40]

Speculation that something radioactive sat inside the *Estonia's* cardeck spread wildly after Johan Franson's concrete blanket idea was unilaterally approved by the highest levels of the Swedish government. The planned covering was a thick-walled, tightly-sealed concrete tomb.

The two decommissioned reactors at Paldiski Base and, as mentioned earlier, the Chernobyl reactor and Russia's nuclear-powered *Komsomolets* submarine that sank in the Norwegian Sea were all covered in concrete sarcophaguses for compelling practical reasons: fear of radiation leakage.

Sweden attempted to hastily implement the same solution in attempt to encase a ferry full of tourists, businessmen, students and senior citizens.

*   *   *

German journalist Jutta Rabe had long held suspicions about forbidden cargo on board the *Estonia*. Rabe's general course of events begins with sensitive goods appropriated by the U.S. government by questionable means. The sellers may have been Russian businessmen, perhaps linked to corrupt officials and criminal groups. The U.S. secured the cooperation of the top echelons in Sweden, who would wait for the *Estonia* ferry to arrive in Stockholm, pick up the shipment and drive it to a Swedish airfield where it would be loaded on a U.S. military aircraft.

Supporting the theory is the survivor testimony of Carl Övberg. He stated that just before the *Estonia* ferry sailed from Tallinn on September 27, passengers were temporarily blocked from the port, an action taken by the military, presumably the Estonian Defense Forces. Moreover, two trucks, presumably containing the strategic cargo, were then driven onto the cardeck and secured before routine boarding resumed.

Perhaps Russian intelligence agents found out about the unauthorized sale and placed explosives on the ferry, if not to sink it, then to force its return to Tallinn.[41]

Guesses about the contents of the suspect cargo include classified Soviet space technology, osmium, cobalt, plutonium and biological agents.

Western states were indeed taking advantage of opportunities to acquire strategic material from the former Soviet Union. Post 1991, French intelligence officers were involved in a clandestine operation to acquire Russian torpedoes on the black market in Poland. The scheme involved recovering the torpedoes at the bottom of the Baltic by submarine, then loading them in a specially-requisitioned railroad car for transport to France.[42]

Russia was a shopping mall for war materiel. Libya, Iran, Iraq and North Korea as well as factions in ethnic conflicts worked out whisper deals with Russia and their representatives and quietly scoured the country to buy all that was unobtainable before 1991.[43]

The U.S. was also a buyer of controlled Soviet military hardware. When communism fell, the Pentagon bought from Russia an advanced nuclear power plant designed to be shot into space called "Topaz." It had been top secret and went up for sale in late 1991. Two C-5 military transport planes delivered it to the U.S. where authorities studied the system for use in outer space.

Another instance involved a U.S. military cargo jet delivering the entire S-300 system, the Soviet equivalent of the Patriot missile, including a "flatbed carrier with its computers, radar, and missiles" to a military base in Huntsville, Alabama.

"There was a lot of movement of sensitive technology out of Russia in the early 1990s," said Fritz Ermarth, former CIA bureau chief and National Security Council official. "The supplier and middlemen arrange transport and the Western end takes delivery of it when it arrives. A lot of technology was of value to the U.S. Everything from submarine-quieting systems to information on how Russians used Japanese machine tools to work on the propellers on their subs."[44]

The illicit cargo theory was continually ridiculed by critics, especially the JAIC, as fantasy. In 2004, ten years after the disaster, those same critical voices fell abruptly silent when a retired Swedish customs official, a whistleblower, revealed information that helped prove the *Estonia* ferry had indeed transported Russian military equipment on two voyages. Orders had been issued from the top levels instructing Swedish customs to allow the cargo to breeze through the standard inspection.

A subsequent investigation by the Swedish government confirmed that the *Estonia* ferry had indeed been used to transport Russian military equipment in two instances in September 1994, but not on the night it sank. Swedish authorities said the cargo had not been explosives or weapons, but refused to reveal what it was, who it was for, why it was allowed to forego customs checks and why military goods were allowed on an international civilian passenger ferry. These details will remain classified for 70 years.[45]

Rabe had been one of the most vocal in suspecting that something classified was stored on the *Estonia's* cardeck. But curiously, the gut feeling even extended to members of the official commission, the JAIC. Publicly, the JAIC scorned alternative hypothesis or ideas suggesting clandestine activity. Privately, they were so convinced something was foul that they acted, with some rashness, to prove it.

* * *

It was April 1996. The sun shone on the fractured ice still floating in the Northern Baltic. In the distance, a ship with a crane approached the site of the sunken ferry. Loaded with stones, the black ship would dump the white gravel on the seabed 60 meters below, launching the process that had been ordered by the Swedish government: entombment of the *Estonia* ferry.

In five days, another ship was due to bring geo-textile material to carpet the stones and provide a base for the concrete tomb. When the mission finished, the *Estonia* would be like a nut under a cup.

Meanwhile, the Finnish ship *Halli* was anchored over the wrecksite. Erkki Mykkänen, an engineer from the Finnish Environmental Institute (SYKE), was supervising the oil removal operation from the *Estonia's* storage tanks. As environmentally-conscious Finns, SYKE wanted a clean sea. They did not want oil or fuel from the sunken ferry leaking into their fishing waters over time.

Mykkänen hoped no technical glitches would interrupt the fuel vacuuming operation. Because when the ship with the load of stones arrived, SYKE by contract was required to stop work and wait. Therefore, SYKE stuck to a strict schedule, planning to finish oil removal by June. By then it would be impossible to drain fuel because the concrete walls would be going up.

Mykkänen got a call on the ship from Kalervo Jolma, head engineer at SYKE.

"[The Finnish JAIC] want to visit the bridge and are asking if they can break a window [on the ferry]." Jolma said.

Kari Lehtola, the Finnish head of the JAIC, was apparently haunted by suspicions that he never openly acknowledged. Sweden's decision to seal the shipwreck in concrete had been bizarre. In addition, there were Andi Meister's public accusations--the Swedes were withholding evidence and the Rockwater videotapes had been selectively edited. Circulating rumors spoke of radioactive material that had been loaded on the *Estonia* ferry. Who knew what was true?

Only one thing was sure--the April 29th arrival of the geo-textile materials vessel would seal the truth, forever. Time was running out.

Lehtola decided to make an urgent, discreet investigation of the wreck before it was encased. His idea was to break a window on the bridge with the ROV that SYKE was using, and have a look.

But the SYKE engineers had little time to assist. The most pressing concern was to extract the fuel before the arrival of the geo-textile materials vessel.

Lehtola was persistent. His next request was specific. The ferry's car ramp was slightly open and with a small ROV, it was possible to go inside the cardeck. Lehtola asked the engineers if it was possible to detect radioactivity. By coincidence, the SYKE's ROV had equipment for monitoring radiation underwater. (In the past, the same ROV had investigated dumping of a radioactive container by the Russians in the Gulf of Finland).

But Mykkänen explained that seawater was an excellent insulator. Water insulates radioactive cores in nuclear reactors. The salinity of seawater is an added shield. A detection device would have to sit on top of the radioactive material to click. How could anyone find the precise piece? The cardeck was like a toolbox turned upside down.

Lehtola was unperturbed. He wanted to try. The commission, he said, would work the phones to make sure the geo-textile vessel arrived a few days late. Then the ROV could poke around the bridge and possibly the cardeck. Time was tight. The race was on.

Lehtola dispatched commission member Tuomo Karppinen to the *Halli*. After Karppinen arrived by helicopter, the *Halli* positioned over the bow of the wreck, readying the ROV for descent. But poor visibility in the April Baltic Sea thwarted the operation. They waited and tried again. The small ROV was prepared and expectations ran high.

Then technicians noticed a double slash on the ROV's umbilical cable. Nobody knew how the slashes occurred, though presumably it was accidental. In the end, poor visibility below 60 meters depth prevented examination of the cardeck and bridge.

One month passed. Lehtola would not give up. He again called the engineers on the *Halli* and this time asked directly if any Swedes were on board. When Mykkänen said there weren't, Lehtola repeated his request for an ROV investigation of the *Estonia*, specifying the bridge and bow area. The ROV went down and shot some footage of the bow. Unfortunately, deep-water visibility remained poor, and the bridge wasn't videotaped.[46]

* * *

SYKE went on to successfully complete the fuel and oil extraction and in doing so had accumulated several hours of shipwreck video footage, which was passed on to the Finnish JAIC.

When Tuomo Karppinen watched the videos, he noticed something disturbing. The Rockwater divers in 1994 had cut through the ship's steel walls in some places or enlarged window areas in order to safely enter the ship. At the end of their work, divers covered the access holes with thick metal plates or steel gratings and welded them shut.

In the video, some of the metal covers were missing.

The metal plates weighed more than 500 kilograms, according to the German investigators. Intruders at the ferry were not souvenir hunters. Only divers using special tools in a lengthy operation could dislodge these manhole covers welded to the access holes. The evidence corroborates the public statement by Gustav Hanoliak, a diving expert who was hired by the Swedish Maritime Administration. Hanoliak said that bars welded over an access hole made by the Rockwater divers in 1994 had been removed, indicating someone had broken into the *Estonia* shipwreck. Swedish state officials, who solemnly vowed to safeguard the wreck, did not investigate nor comment on the matter.[47]

Olof Forssberg, head of the Swedish JAIC, explained it all with a shrug by saying the covers simply "slid away." The Finnish JAIC was slightly more analytical, suggesting that violent sea floor currents or fishing trawler nets were responsible for breaking the welds.

Andi Meister, the Estonian JAIC chief who resigned in protest, scoffed at the flimsy excuses in his book about the disaster.

"Deep down there must be quite a wonderful rapid that breaks the welded parts of an iron plate open and lifts away extremely heavy metal covers, but does not carry away mud and clay from around the ship!"

Meister also emphasized that dangled nets are just not strong enough, and any trawlers fishing near the *Estonia* ferry would be shooed away by the vigilant coast guard assigned to protect the wrecksite.

"--[W]hy does no one want to think of the possibility that a man has visited the ship?" Meister asked.[48]

Another peculiarity of the ship's condition suggesting visits by outsiders, according to Meister's book, is a broken bridge window seen on one of the Rockwater videotapes:

> "The window was broken... It would be more correct to say that it had no glass, as its frame did not have sharp glass pieces that would have had interfered with the diver on entering. Just as if the opening had been prepared in advance... That particular window had no obvious reason for breaking as the ship was sinking... Why had the window broken so clean and without any pieces?"[49]

German investigators also voiced concerns about the condition of the bridge. The *Estonia's* T-shaped bridge on the top deck was 25 meters wide, protruding from the sailing ferry like the head of a hammerhead shark.

On the sea bottom, the ferry is nearly upside down. The underside of the bridge wing, portside, appears to have been torn open or pulled back after the vessel had come to rest on the seabed.

The sheltered location of the underside wing and the localized, curled-back metal, rule out sinking-related damage. Recall that the ferry tilted on its starboard side, thrusting the portside of the bridge into the air. As it sank stern first, the portside bridge--had it hit bottom hard-- would have shown a dent. But the videos show no such damage.

"It... has to be assumed that this [pulled back metal] was caused by interested parties searching for something particular hidden inside the void space between the bridge floor and wing underside..." the German investigators wrote.[50]

Hiding contraband under the floorboards of the bridge would ensure smooth transit. Customs officials by protocol typically do not inspect the bridge.

* * *

Who was capable of interfering, at an early stage, with the shipwreck?

There is anecdotal information about a special unit of Russian navy divers visiting the wreck, though years after the ship sank and largely for the purpose of underwater training. Moreover, vehicle tracks on the seafloor near the wreck were captured on videotape during the dive in 2000 (see Appendix VII). They are similar to the underwater vehicle tracks on the videotapes Sweden submitted in 1993 as evidence of Russian incursions into Swedish territorial waters.[51]

The Swedish Navy was also capable. In 1994, Sweden possessed an underwater rescue vehicle, the URF (*Ubats Raddnings Farkost*). The URF could descend with four crew members down to 350 meters and carry up to 25 people. The URF is only about 12 meters long and three meters wide and operates autonomously, without umbilical cord running to a surface ship. The Swedes also ran the midget submarine *Spiggen II*, about 11 meters long and two meters wide. The *Spiggen II* can sit underwater for two weeks and cruise at five knots.[52]

Could one of these small submersibles have descended to the announced grid coordinates and discharged naval divers? As noted earlier, a minisub corresponds very roughly to the size and shape of the "large object" seen on sonar images that later disappeared. The same object also appeared on a videotape that the German Group said was edited.

Militaries worldwide use ROVs outfitted with grasping arms to perform underwater investigative research, including the search and recovery of evidence such as discarded weapons, aircraft crashed at sea and human remains.

Suppose Swedish military divers descended to the wrecksite to check radiation levels and assess recovery of the strategic material. The sensitive mission would evaluate the potential underwater hazard and threat to the region without alarming the public.

Looking into the cardeck, divers discover an impossible pile of twisted metal wreckage and report that search and retrieval of a specific container would be dangerous and time-consuming. Their equipment detects no radiation--water is an excellent insulator.

A few top political leaders are informed of the findings. They decide to leave everything in place. The Rockwater divers could then be cleared to survey the wreck without being exposed to anything harmful, but they shouldn't poke around the cardeck. The military then hands the government a classified report recommending the ferry be encased as a safety measure to prevent radioactive leakage due to progressive corrosion of the hull.

Loose ends now seem to fit. Sweden's refusal to recover the bodies; its active enforcement of the symbolic Gravesite Treaty preventing independent investigation; Franson's concrete blanket project; a variety of government documents related to a Scandinavian passenger ferry accident that are inexplicably classified as secret. It could explain Bildt's reactionary visor-as-cause statement that steered the JAIC and the public toward the explanation of a shipbuilding fault.

Clandestine cargo, however, would not explain why the ship sank unless it is convincingly linked to a bomb or collision scenario. There's also the possibility that dangerous cargo was unrelated to the accident.

In the end, no satisfying synthesis of the miscellaneous elements in the theory can occur. The assertion that radioactive material was carried on the *Estonia* ferry cannot be confirmed, but it certainly cannot be dismissed. An unfettered, independent examination of the shipwreck, however, would reveal the truth.

As far as Sweden is concerned, dangerous cargo is not within the realm of the possible. "The myth with radioactive cargo, the myth with the Russian mafia, etcetera, these are myths," said Johan Franson. "You could find at least ten myths around the *Estonia*."[53]

Cocktail Effect

A modern transport accident rarely results from a single event. Preexisting conditions – known or unknown vulnerabilities in systems and the vessel – are aggravated on each journey. They eventually combine to produce optimal conditions for failure: what is known as the cocktail effect.

Soviet mentality was arguably to some extent an accessory cause for the sinking. No academic studies have examined the culture of safety in the U.S.S.R. But history is filled with tragic instances resulting from the careless Soviet attitude toward safety.

Every country struggles with homegrown disasters. But the U.S.S.R. was unique. It provided no form of independent public inquiry. On the contrary, accidents were often concealed for political reasons. A mishap was seen primarily as a vulnerability that foreign political enemies could exploit. Moreover, the all-powerful state does not show citizens its weaknesses.

The lawsuit, the instrument that tends to keep Western corporations at the cutting edge of safety, didn't exist in the Soviet legal system. Incompetence and negligence that lead to a catastrophe didn't necessarily result in punishment. Jail terms could be avoided by leveraging the right Communist Party connections.

Calamities aggressively concealed and denied include: an anthrax outbreak; the launching pad explosion of a manned Soyuz space mission; orbiting nuclear reactors falling to Earth; an enormous tunnel explosion in Afghanistan that killed thousands; a civilian airliner crash kept secret from families of the victims.[1]

The repression inherent in the Soviet system nearly ensured that the hardest lessons were never learned.

Post-Soviet Union, the general disregard for safety in Russia seemed to intensify, despite the lessons of Chernobyl. Alcoholism, official toleration of corruption and the general lack of morale invited accidents.[2]

After Western aid and business cooperation began, unfamiliarity with Western technology added another dimension of risk. It contributed to the cause of the 1994 Moscow-to-Hong Kong Aeroflot crash that killed all 75 on board. The pilot allowed his children to play at the controls of the leased Airbus 310. He wasn't aware that the Western-made airliner's design allowed the autopilot to be easily disengaged; in a Soviet jet the procedure was not simple. By the time cockpit crew understood the mistake, the jet had begun to soar nose first into the Siberian tundra.[3]

Also in 1994, the International Airline Passenger Association condemned the former Soviet Union, strongly recommending no one fly over Russia or any other part of the old U.S.S.R. "Overloaded airplanes, lack of cockpit discipline, pilot error, aging aircraft," are all common, the agency said, in the first such warning it had ever issued.

Procedures taken for granted in the United States, like safety inspections and regular maintenance and renewal of pilot licenses, were often disregarded in countries finding their place in the post-Soviet world.[4]

Estonia of course is not Russia, and airliners are not ferries. With a long seafaring tradition and previous experience as a relatively democratic, independent state, Estonia was always seen as more Western-oriented than other Soviet republics. Estonia's strong work ethic today is self-evident. The country's startling achievements over the last decade offer the best proof that Estonians had reawakened existing virtues, not developed new ones.

But the values and institutions of the Baltic States were also deeply shaped by the communist system during the five decades of their forced incorporation into the U.S.S.R. Communism thrived by exploiting human weaknesses, such as laziness, irresponsibility, envy and deceitfulness. Local party functionaries ensured Soviet values and practices were instilled in the army, police forces, judiciaries, central banks, and health and education systems of the occupied states for generations.

Consequently, Russia's post-Soviet maintenance and safety culture was reflected to some extent in the Baltic States. The two main organizations that investigated the *Estonia* ferry accident--the JAIC and the German Group of Experts--took contrary positions on that idea.

*   *   *

"On departure from Tallinn on 27 September the *Estonia* was seaworthy and properly manned. There were no outstanding items either from the authorities or from the classification society's surveys. The maintenance standard of the vessel was good as witnessed by various instances."[5]

The statement from the Final Report implies that the crew and Estline management are clear of any charges related to bad maintenance and poor inspection. The technical cadre that comprised the JAIC, as stated earlier, concluded that the accident was caused by shortcomings in engineering design and blamed the Meyer Werft shipyard, which built the ferry in 1980.

The JAIC's main point was that inadequately designed locks weren't strong enough to hold the bow visor in place as it was buffeted by waves.

"The visor attachments were not designed according to realistic design assumptions, including the design load level, load distribution to the attachments and the failure mode. The attachments were constructed with less strength than the simplistic calculations required . . ."[6]

Second, the JAIC pointed to the *Estonia's* ramp design. On a typical ferry, the cardeck ramp lifts and closes over the cardeck opening, fitting neatly into the recessed perimeter like a castle drawbridge. The *Estonia's* ramp, however, extended higher. The elongated cardeck ramp, when closed, extended above the forecastle deck and tucked into a housing, which resembled the convex lid of a treasure chest. In other words, the bow visor and cardeck ramp were interconnected.

Therefore, in the JAIC's view, management and maintenance were not key issues. Had the visor and ramp not been mated by design, a detached bow visor would have left the ramp in place to act as a barrier to the sea. The ferry would not have sunk.

The German Group of Experts, hired by the shipyard to investigate the disaster, emphasized instead the human factor. According to the GGE report, written guidelines for maintaining the *Estonia* were often disregarded. The crew's maintenance methods involved banging, prying, stuffing and cutting, all with a casual disregard for safety standards.

Numerous examples are spelled out. To secure the bow visor at the bottom, an 18-inch "Atlantic" iron bolt slid through a series of steel sleeves, like a door latch. Estonian crewmembers, however, had to hammer it through the sleeves, which were in a damaged state. Visible fatigue cracks in the visor's hinges went unnoticed. A shoddy welding job someone had performed on the vital visor locks was ignored.

But the ferry was always regularly painted white so it looked sharp.

Additionally, the GGE reported that both ramp and visor were misaligned, and during a given journey the space between them filled with seawater that squirted through the broken edge seals and flowed freely onto the cardeck.

Water is heavy. While ship designers can estimate wave impacts in a specific sea and integrate them into design specifications of locking mechanisms, their calculations do not include an extra 150 tons of seawater between the visor and the ramp continuously sloshing from side to side.

The visor and ramp misalignment bolstered the GGE's conclusion that seawater poured onto the cardeck on nearly every voyage. To limit the spray, crewmembers stuffed mattresses and bed sheets around the ramp edges.

The German report proposed that the Estonia's crewmembers and possibly the ship's owners didn't respect the rules for upkeep and operation, resulting in a weakening of crucial parts of the ferry--in particular the bow visor system. It also suggested the ferry may have sprung a leak below decks due to systemic neglect and poor upkeep, which bordered on criminal negligence.

Of course, hammering bolts shut and stuffing blankets in gaps do not mean that the ferry was doomed. Shipping is a rough business and imperfect boats sail all the time. As practical men, crewmembers often choose a stopgap solution rather than adhering to the instruction book. After all, a ship only has to float, not soar into the air lifting thousands of tons.

Coarse practices and crew improprieties, if true, certainly did their part on the night of September 27 by desensitizing the crew to trouble. Loud banging and water ingress on each voyage could have been seen by the crew as more of a familiar nuisance than an impending danger, hastening the course of events.

* * *

How two highly competent investigative teams comprised of maritime experts and engineers, could study all the available evidence and arrive at such divergent conclusions is indicative of the powerful interests involved.

Although the GGE claimed to be independent, the fact that they were hired by the shipyard creates a conflict. The GGE operated with the ultimate aim of clearing the shipyard of blame. However, the Germans did not exclude any relevant information they uncovered and worked openly, outside the restrictive parameters set by state interests. They turned over every rock possible.

The JAIC by comparison only targeted specific, pre-determined areas. The commission left out the crew's maintenance practices and made other terrific omissions mentioned earlier, which permanently marred the Final Report as biased.

Pointed JAIC criticism came from Bengt Schager, a former Swedish member of the commission who resigned. Schager summed up the commission from an insider's point of view:

"In Sweden, the chairman of the [JAIC] reports to the Minister of Transport and the Minister could be one of those who could be blamed for an accident involving transport, so I don't think this was a very healthy organization."[7]

The JAIC's aversion for probing too far came under fire from other sources as well. The London-based International Federation of Trade Workers hired a marine consultancy to go over both the German findings and the Final Report. They were baffled by what had been skipped:

"It is surprising that for a supposedly comprehensive and objective [final] report, a significant amount of the evidence on the maintenance and repair of the system, which is contained in the German Experts Report, is not discussed . . . "--[W]hilst the maintenance issues referred to in the Joint Commission report would probably not have been material in terms of the accident, the allegations made in the German experts' report might have been. Even if the supporting evidence is inconclusive, we would expect it to have been taken into account by the Joint Commission."[8]

The Final Report also danced around the issue of ship inspection. Two Swedish journalists, Mats Holm and Susanna Popova, reported that serious faults on the ferry had been found a few hours before the fatal trip. In their book "Protokollet *Estonia*," they pointed to managerial failures at the Swedish Maritime Administration, which supervised a last-minute inspection in Tallinn port on September 27th known as Port State Control (PSC).

The PSC is hotly disputed by the Swedish government, which contends the inspection was merely a training exercise.

In summary, on September 27, 1994, the *Estonia* sat in Tallinn port undergoing cabin cleaning, touch up painting and replenishment of food and beverages. Swedish Maritime Administration personnel were training Estonian ship inspectors on the fine points of vetting a ship. The Estonian government in 1994 encouraged many such tutorial programs to help them reintegrate with the West.[9]

On that day, the Swedish instructors chose to examine the *Estonia* ferry, probably assuming the country's flagship stayed in tip-top shape and would be a quick job. Though the PSC was only an exercise--trainees listening to professionals--the Swedish-Estonian PSC team recorded 14 faults, five of them labeled "Code 17," meaning the captain was obligated to ensure the fault was rectified prior to departure.[10]

"The vessel may not, in other words, leave port until all the faults have been dealt with," said Mats Holm, the Swedish journalist who co-authored the book.

Negligence and irresponsibility regarding the PSC has been sharply denied by Stockholm. According to Catrin Tidstrom, the desk officer at the Transport Ministry:

> "[Inspectors] didn't find anything that would keep this ship in the harbor if the ship had been in Sweden, and our seaworthiness inspector, that's what he told me. They found some things they should have looked into before [the *Estonia*] left port, but they had no authority to drive these questions through. But there was nothing that would keep a ship in the harbor, that's what it came to."[11]

She emphasized that the PSC was a training exercise and Swedish instructors in Estonia had no legal right to stop a ship from leaving a foreign harbor.

COCKTAIL EFFECT   **217**

Tidstrom's explanation is bewildering in light of the German report, which located the legal agreement between Sweden and Estonia. The contract considered the "training" an authentic inspection by properly authorized inspectors.

Moreover, just before the *Estonia* left on its final voyage, the Swedish inspectors told Arne Valgma, head of the Estonian Maritime Board's Department of Maritime Safety, that the ferry should under no circumstances sail in its current condition. The warning "was said to have been rejected by him and subsequently by the Estonian authorities up to the highest level," the GGE report claims.

The Germans concluded "--it is quite obvious that the *Sjöfartsverket's* [SMA's] inspectors had found the *Estonia* to be unseaworthy."[12]

*   *   *

Bengt Schager has strenuously argued that the human factor was central to the catastrophe. Schager, a Swedish maritime psychologist who resigned from the commission in frustration, said the JAIC simply would not thoughtfully consider mistakes by the crew.[13]

The JAIC was hypersensitive to criticism directed at the Estonian crew, Schager said. In some cases, that resulted in shouting matches between Schager and Andi Meister, the Estonian who was chairman of the JAIC. When Schager studied the testimonies and wrote that during the accident "some of the crew members were paralyzed" he was challenged.

"Every time there was some hint of criticism or something to show [crew members] weren't mastering the situation, they were upset. And we had to take this out of the report in order to have silence in the house."

Schager also had plans to interview a dozen or so survivors. Suspicious of crewmember spin on events, he wanted to listen to service-oriented crewmembers who had not committed to the visor-as-cause explanation. But the Swedish JAIC chief Olof Forssberg instructed him not to do it. The reason, Forssberg said, was due to budget considerations.

Someone also edited Schager's email exchanges with other JAIC members as the messages were forwarded up the hierarchy. After seeing repeated instances of bias and obstruction that he thought compromised an honest and open investigation, he resigned.

Today, Schager still cites the ferry's excessive speed as a major factor in the accident. Had the ferry's officers heeded the warning provided by the unusual banging sounds, they could've slowed down and taken other measures to interrupt the fatal chain of events, he surmised.

"Any ship can lose a visor," Schager said. "Still, they were going full throttle and had indications of metallic noises. That was not good seamanship. It shows lack of judgment."

Anders Hellberg, a journalist for the Swedish daily *Dagens Nyheter* who co-authored a book about the *Estonia* disaster, is convinced the ferry's speed was the sole cause of the accident. Without a doubt, if speed had been halved that night, she would not have sunk, Hellberg said.[14]

Captain Andresson perhaps believed the ship's solid German construction could readily withstand the forces of nature. Plowing through waves without due respect for the sea perhaps reflected the captain's unwavering trust in the superiority of Western technology, a dangerous misperception that stemmed from post-Soviet euphoria and illusions.

But facts do not support the accusation of excessive speed before the banging noises were heard. At 00:30, about half an hour before the fatal chain of events, the *Estonia's* average speed reached 14-15 knots, slower than the average 15.4 knots of the *Silja Europa* ferry, a much larger boat that was sailing that night parallel to the *Estonia*.[15]

One theory holds that Captain Andresson ran the ferry hard to make schedule, keeping the ferry line competitive and pleasing the owners. Estline was finally nearing profitability in 1994. Management planned to launch a second ferry on the Tallinn-Stockholm route beginning September 28, which turned out to be the day of the catastrophe. Had the accident not happened, Estline was expecting roughly $4 million in net profit for 1994. Andresson, some speculated, intended to do his part in sustaining Estline's profit.[16]

Running a ship hard and fast to beat the clock certainly creates a nice context for error. Some suggested that the master of the *Jan Heweliusz* ferry, which sank in the Baltic Sea in 1993, had been forced to leave port under severe weather conditions in response to the shipping business mantra, "time is money."[17]

The captain of the *USS Greeneville*, the submarine that rammed a Japanese research vessel, had been 30 minutes behind schedule. "In response, the CO took several actions that created an artificial urgency in the Control Room that directly contributed to the collision," according to a court of inquiry.[18]

Andresson had sailed at similar speeds many times before, sometimes in meaner wind and wave conditions than on September 27. No complaints about speed had been brought to board meetings. In fact, more passengers were buying tickets on the *Estonia*. The speed of the ferry only became a contentious issue after the accident, a fact that suggests it was not central to the sinking.

Heiki Lindpere, formerly legal director and member of the board of ESCO, knew Andresson as a practical man who wasn't afraid to make decisions. "He wasn't locked into his cabin. He was taking trips around the vessel, checking himself to see if everything was ok. Some masters take things much looser," Lindpere recalled.

Moreover, Andresson fortunately hadn't fallen victim to the insidious Soviet disease. He was sober.

"Everything was in good order under his command," Lindpere said. "There was never any doubt of his capabilities. That was also the attitude of the Swedish [joint venture] partner. We would have changed the master if they'd said to do so."[19]

But the Swedes did indeed hold a conflicting opinion. Hellberg, the Swedish journalist, reported some scathing critical comments about Andresson's abilities and argued that the disaster resulted from the autocratic Soviet management system.

Hellberg claimed that when Andresson took over the *Estonia* ferry in early 1993, he made revealing mistakes as he got ahead on the learning curve, including mixing up port and starboard and damaging a quay in Stockholm. Andresson was "arrogant and nonchalant" and "strictly upheld discipline and the hierarchy on board."

He was a product of the Soviet system, Hellberg wrote, and no bridge crew would dare touch the controls without Andresson's go ahead.

"On a Swedish ferry the mate first reduces the speed and does thereafter inform the master about what he has done. [In] regards [to the] *Estonia*, it was the other way round," one source said.

The Estonian side of the joint venture was devoted to Andresson, according to Hellberg. Complaints about the captain from the Swedish side were rejected.[20]

It's unclear whether the book's criticisms described an ongoing situation or were confined to the early 1993 period, when the Swedish-Estonian ferry line was immature and Andresson was finding his footing as commander.

Moreover, Hellberg began writing the book fresh after the accident, when Swedish objectivity often gave way to emotions running at full tilt. The myth of Swedish seafaring expertise contrasted with nautically-inferior Estonians in much the same way Anglo-American heroism rose above the cowardice of third-class passengers in early discussions about the sinking of the Titanic.

In reality, the *Estonia* ferry carried Prime Minister Laar, the Interior Minister Heike Arike and the board of directors of Estline--Captain Andresson's bosses--who often held their monthly meetings in the ferry's conference room as it sailed. The politically-inspired ferry represented more than a bus ride across water. It symbolized a reunion with Europe and a long-awaited return to the boundless freedom of the sea. These facts are hard to reconcile with the caricature of a somewhat incompetent captain who consciously permits his decrepit ship to routinely cross the Baltic Sea.

In summary, the ship design, the question of seaworthiness and Soviet-influenced practices were to some extent accessory causes of the sinking, acting as catalysts. But they do not answer the core question: Why did the ferry sink in 35 minutes?

PART SIX

Hidden Agendas

Detours

Disinformation has a long and venerable history in Russia. Traditions go back at least to Lenin's provocations and deceptive tactics in playing one political group off the other. The *Cheka*, the first Soviet secret police organization, had a disinformation desk. Their successors, the KGB, devoted an entire department to disinformation. The Russians are arguably the undisputed masters of the game, and deception was a well-worn instrument of Soviet policy.

Disinformation involves the spreading of false information. At its most accomplished level, disinformation subtly diverts discussion rather than stating crude lies. Fabrications are camouflaged by the appearance of objectivity. Two hallmarks of the technique are the use of anonymous sources and lack of verifiable details.

In 1983, Korean Air Lines flight 007, a commercial airline, was shot down by a Soviet fighter jet supposedly after it strayed into Soviet airspace. The KGB spun disinformative tales to make the crime seem ambiguous. Articles in U.S. newspapers began to appear claiming spy gear had been placed aboard at Andrews Air Force Base in Maryland; the Korean pilot had boasted to friends about his specially-equipped spy plane; the pilot privately shared anxieties with his wife about "a particularly dangerous" mission. Unnamed sources were cited.[1]

During the Chechen War, Russian press reports stated in a matter-of-fact way that the "White Tights," a unit of female blonde snipers from the Baltic States, volunteered to fight Russians in Chechnya. "They get $1000 per day plus $1500 for each Russian officer they kill," according to Itar-Tass.[2]

No one ever corroborated the news story, but the sensational report made a politically expedient link between the Baltics and the raging Chechen War.

During a catastrophe, disinformation materializes just as naturally as opportunistic viruses infiltrate a weakened immune system. In the aftermath of the *Estonia* ferry disaster, disinformation took many forms.

About a week after the ferry went down, the Estonian press was reporting rumors of Russian involvement, pressuring the Russian military into addressing the accusations.

The chief of Russia's Main Naval Headquarters, Admiral Valentin Selivanov, denied through an interview in *Krasnaya Zvezda* ("Red Star"), the unofficial mouthpiece of the Defense Ministry, that any Russian submarines were involved in the ferry sinking. In a riposte, he gave his own explanation of the maritime tragedy:

> "`There was water-diluted fuel aboard the *Estonia*,' he maintains. `It could have been diluted either in the fuel depot or aboard the vessel to sell the surplus on the side. This made the engines stop, which caused the ferry to fall athwart. At that time, the motor vehicles in the cargo hold, which were not properly secured for there were more of them than allowed, moved to one side, thus adding to dynamic list, which made the vessel capsize' . . .
>
> "This version, the Admiral holds, is also backed indirectly by the testimony of few surviving passengers who said they had heard some strange noise before the ship capsized."[3]

Reports from a nationalistic Russian newspaper, however, don't usually persuade mainstream opinion. Soon the big guns in disinformation would roll in.

The Felix Report

As bureaucrats firmed up the plans to pour cement over the shipwreck, a Russian language report dated February 1995 and titled "International Narcotics Trafficking and the Former U.S.S.R." appeared on the desks of journalists in key newspaper offices across Russia and Estonia.

The report's author was one Ivan Ivanov of the Research Group "Felix," an organization that had released previous research reports on various political issues.

This particular document detailed Russia's connection to international drug smuggling operations in Latin America, the U.S. and Europe. In clinical terms, the Felix Report explained the heroin transport routes from Central Asia through Russia to the Baltic States and Europe. It named and linked specific Russian generals and international politicians to drug gangs and various scandals, listing the roles they played and money received. Above all, the report offered evidence that implicated Chechens as leaders of the underworld nexus expanding across the former Soviet Union.

The Felix Report appeared to be derived from official KGB archives or Russian Interior Ministry files. Deep into the 81-page report, the reader abruptly comes across three pages that purport to explain the sinking of the *Estonia* ferry on September 28, 1994.

A broad sketch of the Felix Report scenario [relevant pages are reprinted in English translation in Appendix III] is as follows:

> The captain of the *Estonia* and his close aides agreed to carry a "large quantity" of heroin and 40 tons of cobalt in collaboration with "Lesnik" [Mart Laar, the Estonian Prime Minister] and "Yuri" [Yuri Toomepuu, Lt. Colonel (Ret.) U.S. Army, member of Estonian parliament 1992-96].
>
> When the vessel left Estonian waters, Estonian Defense Commander Alexander Einseln found he'd been cut out of the deal. In retaliation, he leaked information about the shipment. Word got to Swedish customs that a large bundle of narcotics on the *Estonia* ferry would arrive in Stockholm harbor.
>
> But the tipoff was somehow overheard by a powerful Moscow boss of the narcotics trade. He was ex-KGB, a cohort of Lesnik and Yuri, and was very angry. The boss called Lesnik, who called Yuri, who called the captain of the *Estonia*, demanding that both the heroin and the 40 tons of cobalt be dumped into the sea.
>
> Yuri told the captain that when Swedish customs found the heroin, they would continue searching and probably find the cobalt, and the Swedes would be difficult to reach an agreement with. These conversations were wiretapped by the former second man in Estonian customs, Igor Kristapovich.
>
> The captain refused to comply, saying such an operation was too dangerous at sea during a storm. Yuri insisted in the coercive

terms used by criminals, and the captain finally relented.

In the middle of the voyage, the captain ordered the bow visor mechanisms unlocked. The crew maneuvered the vehicle containing the heroin and cobalt toward the cardeck ramp. But the worsening storm tossed the ship and the unlocked visor was torn off, punching a huge hole in the ship that caused it to sink.

Kristapovich, who had recorded the telephone conversations, was later assassinated in Tallinn.

The Felix scenario ignited the suspicions of most everyone impacted by the disaster: it offered an official explanation. At the time, the Final Report had not been completed. Previously, the concrete blanket project and resignations of several commission members had evoked cynicism and opened minds to darker ideas. The Felix Report filled the information vacuum.

Russian journalists corroborated some facts and excerpted parts for articles. Internet chat groups were ablaze with the sensational explanation. It was investigated further by the German Group of Experts. Two novels grew from the Report, one by Russian author Oleg Benukh called *Clash of the Triads* and the other by Estonian author Juhan Paju--*Katkenud Roman (An Interrupted Novel)*.

The Felix narrative spread quickly out of Scandinavia. The report reached the desk of the merchant marine section of the Cypriot Ministry of Transport and went as far as the Xinhua News Agency in China, which reported on it. The CIA received a copy. Even Kari Lehtola, head of the Finnish side of the JAIC, would read a translation of the Felix Report.[4]

As it was disseminated, the stated events underwent further shaping and molding.

Moscow author Oleg Benukh's novel, *Clash of the Triads* was based on the Felix Report. The plot concerns rival Asian gangs competing for ownership of the drug smuggling mule, the *Estonia* ferry. The crew was involved. The rivalry intensified. When one gang parked a truck filled with a large stash of heroin on the cardeck, the competing gang set bombs on the ferry.

Fiction aside, Benukh believes drug gangs did sink the ferry. He was interviewed in the Russian news magazine *Itogi*:

"Unfortunately, the most probable version [of the *Estonia* ferry sinking], in my opinion, is the version about deliberate flooding of the ship. According to some information, hidden inside the luggage compartments of three cars parked onboard the ferry was about 500 kg of pure heroin. And in three trucks, about 50 tons of cobalt. There are very serious reasons to believe that when it came to shipments of drugs (and the route is Singapore - Delhi - Moscow - Tallinn - Stockholm) the police, customs services, port and border guards were bought. The route was established by the most terrible drug mafia in the world--the Hong Kong "triads" . . . supposedly the arrival of the ferry with a large shipment of drugs became known to the main competitors of the "triads"--the Colombian drug mafia, and they took the utmost measures to ensure the cargo did not reach Stockholm."[5]

Werner Hummel, the head of the German Group, received calls from interested parties purporting to corroborate the Felix Report. They ended up modifying it. Hummel gave the following description to a Moscow News journalist in Hamburg:

"At the end of this February [1996] Dr. [Peter] Holtappels, our commission's chairman and a lawyer specializing in maritime law, was in Tallinn at the opening of an international humanitarian foundation to aid the relatives of the victims of the catastrophe. After two to three weeks we received a letter from Estonia detailing the off-stage maneuvers surrounding the ferry, which to a great degree proved the Felix report.

"It is assumed that the captain of the *Estonia* and his close aides were carrying about 100 kilograms of heroin and 40 tons of cobalt. When the vessel left Estonian waters, [General Alexander] Einseln, speaking to the captain by mobile telephone, ordered the heroin to be dumped into the sea, and somewhat later the two trucks containing the cobalt. Einseln said that Swedish customs had been informed by a competing gang. At full speed and with the storm raging, the captain ordered the cargo hatch in the bow of the vessel to be opened, knowing that if he didn't follow the order, it would cost him his life.

"It's said that Kristapovich was able to give [recorded telephone conversations between Einseln and the captain] to the Russian and American security services, and they are now there. Naturally, our commission would be interested in getting the authentic copies of these recordings from Moscow if, of course, they do exist. We are interested in contacts with the Russian security services."[6]

Perhaps the Felix Report roused the Germans because of striking similarities to another ship that was deliberately sent to the bottom in 1977, the *M/V Lucona*. Udo Proksch, a wealthy and well-connected Austrian businessman, was suspected of organizing the explosion of the *Lucona* on wide open seas for insurance money. Proksch was tightly protected by several Austrian politicians. Ultimately an investigative journalist collected enough evidence to implicate him.

Elements of the *Lucona* affair paralleled the Felix Report's description of the *Estonia* disaster: Corruption in high office; questionable cargo; a well-connected villain with ties to the defense ministry and involved in illegal trade of weapons; the menacing background presence of the KGB; a mysterious sinking at sea; use of military explosives to sink the ship.[7]

The Germans knew an offhand dismissal of sinister scenarios was unwise.

On close examination, however, the Felix Report crumbles. No sources are provided for the assertions. Lacking in any specifics that would allow corroboration, the report's depiction of the ferry sinking has value equal to an urban myth. Even the author's name is sketchy-- "Ivan Ivanov" is a Russian name comparable to "John Smith"--and no contact information for the Felix organization is supplied.

The Felix Report also mixes in what is known as *kompromat*, broadly defined as compromising material on an individual that purports to be factual but withers under the verification process. If disinformation maligns institutions or countries, *kompromat* tends to target specific people or companies.

Boris Yeltsin himself recalls how *kompromat* infiltrated the Kremlin and slighted individuals. When he attempted to verify the charges, gross distortions came to light. Usually *kompromat* was written by fired officials or former members of the security services who had been paid by a business competitor or political rival to slur the reputation of another.[8]

The men incriminated in the Felix Report, by nature of their professions and personal politics, were juicy targets for a black propaganda campaign.

The Felix version shoots obvious quarry--Mart Laar, Yuri Toomepuu and Alexander Einseln. The three are certainly disparate figures, yet alike in a very broad sense. Each man was actively de-Sovietizing Estonia in his own unique and controversial way. Maybe the only common thread running through them was energy in purging Estonia of all things Soviet.[9]

"Lesnik," who in the Felix Report is implicated in a variety of scandals, is a barely disguised Mart Laar. "Lesnik" is the diminutive for "man of the forest," or something like "little woodsman." The cynical nickname snipes at Laar's historical chronicle of Estonian resistance fighters, the "Forest Brothers" who terrorized the Soviet occupiers for decades. Called *War in the Woods, Estonia's Struggle for Survival, 1944-1956*, the publishing of the book provoked a critical attack on Laar in the Soviet newspaper Pravda in the late 1980s.

Laar was staunchly anti-Soviet and as prime minister he could influence legislation that put long distance between Estonia and Russia. Laar fought the Russian old guard practice of allowing communist mangers to take part in privatization, limiting the Soviet *nomenklatura's* grab for state assets. Isolating this powerful group of Red Directors who felt a strong sense of entitlement created tough enemies.[10]

"Yuri" another villain in the story, is an American citizen of Estonian birth, Yuri Toomepuu, who retired from the U.S. military as Lieutenant Colonel. Toomepuu returned to Estonia after independence and for a while served in parliament as the head of the Estonian Citizen ("Eesti Kodanik") party, which was described as "dangerously radical nationalist." Toomepuu's supporters were "bitterly anti-Russian" and they "formed a `Decolonization Committee' to help usher the Russians off Estonian soil," according to one report.[11]

The third target of defamation, the head of Estonian Armed Forces, Alexander Einseln, is a former resident of Mountain View, California. Einseln was born in Estonia and fled at age 12 after Soviet troops had literally walked in and taken over. He became an American citizen, enlisted in the U.S. Army and served in the Korean War and in Vietnam in a Special Forces unit. He later worked for the U.S. Joint Chiefs of Staff as NATO-Warsaw Pact and European Division Chief and served in the U.S. Pacific Command before retiring in 1985.

In 1991, when Estonia broke free of the Soviet Union, officials in Washington with close ties to Baltic émigré groups recommended Einseln and others to the neo-Estonian government. Lennart Meri, then president, soon asked Einseln to serve as Commander of the Armed

Forces, a position that carried the rank of General. Einseln would use his broad military experience to begin reforming Estonia's fighting forces into more of a "citizen soldier" ideal.

But soon the U.S. Department of State objected, referring obliquely to Russia. "We remain very concerned about any steps that could be misinterpreted about U.S. intentions in the region," a spokesman said.

Einseln believed hands-on help for his homeland outweighed perceived Russian sensitivities. In May 1993, he accepted the appointment, and walked into a nightmare.

The U.S. State Department stopped Einseln's U.S. military pension and threatened to haul him back on active duty and institute court martial proceedings.[12]

The real trouble came in Estonia. Getting down to work, Einseln found staff officers drinking on duty, routine insubordination, theft and the brutal practice known as *dyedovschina* or initiation of new recruits--all part of the Soviet army legacy. He fired more than a dozen of the most troublesome officers in the first eight months, deepening existing resentment in the officer corps, which by design was largely non-Estonian.

Einseln also clashed with Estonian politicians. When an unannounced cache of broken weapons arrived from Israel, Einseln demanded they be returned. Millions of dollars of state money had been spent, and Prime Minister Mart Laar hadn't told Einseln about the purchase.

"My reaction was, take the junk back and let the seller pay the transport fees," said Einseln, who had submitted his resignation due to the incident. "But you don't do that because bribes had been paid. I became very unpopular."[13]

Einseln had a bit of the crusader in him. Direct, assertive and devoted to renewing his motherland, he obviously did things that angered certain circles. He ran a border guard sting operation and ordered secret taping of a middleman offering kickbacks for more weapons purchases. He initiated a Baltic States peacekeeping battalion (BALTBAT) that was a thinly-disguised NATO apprenticeship. On Estonian TV he talked tough, condemning domestic institutional corruption. He also told viewers he'd issued an order for troops to fight if Russian soldiers came across the border.[14]

Einseln also leveraged contacts in the U.S. Defense Department, Army and NATO to put his native country under the international spotlight. Western officers and U.S. military made occasional symbolic visits to Tallinn. Einseln let the big neighbor know that Estonia had new friends.

Einseln was not just a good target for *kompromat*. He was celestial.

The Felix Group

After the Felix Group gave anonymous interviews to Russian newspapers, the public learned it was named after the feared Russian secret police founder Felix Dzerzhinsky. It claimed to be a private assemblage of former KGB and GRU (military intelligence) officers. They said they formed the Felix Group out of concern for Russia's moral and social decay and indignation over the impunity of those who profited by it.

By some accounts, the Felix Group had 60 members. They claimed to be set up just before the disintegration of the Soviet Union in 1991 to investigate economic crimes. The public debut was December 1993, and over the years Felix issued several incendiary reports to the media.

The reports appeared to mix intelligence briefings and police records with a propaganda message. Sometimes they were over the edge. Many reports from the group "contain patently false, inflammatory material of a nationalist bent," according to Victor Yasmann, a political analyst who studied the group's handouts.

Various Felix reports stated at different times that Israeli Special Forces had participated in the storming of the Russian parliament in October 1993; that the West had organized a plot to destroy Russia's nuclear potential; that Moscow had plans to reoccupy the Baltic States. The group also openly proposed assassinating Prime Minister Viktor Chernomyrdin and former KGB First Deputy Chairman Filipp Bobkov for their allegedly corrupt activities that were destroying Russia.

"Felix is partly truth, partly disinformation," Yasmann said.[15]

In 1995, a man connected to the Felix Group finally appeared--in Washington DC. A Russian delegation was invited to Washington, organized under the auspices of NATO. Anton Surikov, a Russian researcher at a Moscow think tank, was in the delegation. Surikov handed the February 1995 Felix Report to Fritz Ermarth, formerly one of the CIA's top Soviet analysts and director of the National Intelligence Council. Ermarth went over the document and passed it to CIA colleagues. To his knowledge, the CIA did not act on it.[16]

The CIA believed Surikov himself had written the report. Ermarth concurred, but thought he must have had help. The report's extensive details could not have been assembled by one man alone. Surikov probably accessed Russian intelligence service files, Ermarth thought. That assessment turned out to be dead on.

In reality, Anton Surikov was a post-Soviet Wizard of Oz. The thunderous Felix Group made up of 60 powerful and patriotic ex-intelligence officers was really one guy behind a curtain pulling levers.

"The Felix Group was only me," Surikov admitted almost ten years after the ferry disaster. "I wrote the reports."

He conceded that in compiling information, he worked with the Russian security services. "The main goal of the Felix Report was to show Chechens as a criminal force," Surikov explained. "The Felix Report was not directly connected to the government, but certain interested parties would commission it. At that time somebody paid for the reports and you did it."[17]

The *Estonia* ferry events described in the report, Surikov said, offer one version. Sources for the *Estonia* section were former KGB and businessmen living in Estonia.

He explained that in the 1990s, Estonia held a leading position in drug transit, especially after the Russian troop withdrawal from East Germany, which shifted the drug pipeline to the Baltics. Narcotics moved from Afghanistan to Tajikistan, Russia, Byelorussia, then Estonia and out to Europe. "This was the main stream of drug trafficking," he said. "Chechen criminal groups controlled the Baltic States and the goal of the Felix Report was to make the image of Chechnya into a den of criminals."

Surikov has a shadowy background ideal for developing high-level disinformation skills. He held the rank of Major in Russian military intelligence (GRU) with expertise in psychological operations. The media reported Surikov had been a member of Russia's elite *Spetsnaz* and allegedly held links to a number of notorious characters including Shamil Basayev (Russia's most wanted man at the time of this writing) in Abkhazia in the early 1990s and Arab millionaire and suspected arms dealer Adnan Khashoggi. As a GRU officer, he was posted to Tajikistan in 1993 after the start of the civil war that brought President Imomali Rakhmonov to power.[18]

Official facts show that Surikov served in the government of Yevgeny Primakov in 1998 and 1999. He was an assistant to First Deputy Prime Minister Yuri Maslikov. Just as Surikov joined the Primakov administration, the Felix Group vanished.

Surikov held a solid Russian nationalist position on the Baltic States in the 1990s, fitting form with the Felix Report's harsh anti-Baltic tone. In an interview with the Estonian newspaper *Postimees*, Surikov said that if NATO decided to expand into the Baltic States, then military conflict between Russia and Western nations would be unavoidable.[19]

Indeed, the anti-Baltic agenda, if not already clear throughout the report, appears obvious at the conclusion of the narrative:

> "Most of this information [about the attempt to dump contraband off the ship] had been given by [murdered Estonian customs officer Igor] Kristapovich to one of the chiefs of the FBI in the U.S. What ensued was a difficult conversation in the Washington White House. Having mentioned the names of Lesnik and Yuri, [the FBI chief] supposedly asked: "How is it possible to render political support to these people [the Estonians]? They are not simple contraband smugglers. On their conscience are the lives of hundreds of people."

Surikov had woven enough actual intelligence into the Felix Report to make the ferry scenario carry the semblance of truth. But the dumping of the drug-laden truck in mid-voyage seems clearly contrived. The death of 1000 people could generate an entire Felix Report, or at least serve as the centerpiece of one. Instead, the Felix Report allots 79 of the 81 pages to sundry criminal activities such as smuggling routes, Chechen bandits, profiteering Russian generals and corrupt nationalists in the Baltic States. The ferry sinking gets shortchanged with a mere two-page description lacking in details, maybe because it was an afterthought.

Since the report was released in February 1995, Surikov was probably close to completing it when the ferry sank on September 28, 1994. His intelligence connections in Estonia saw the catastrophe as a way to blacken reputations and even political scores.

Local media provided fodder for the Felix narrative. Just one month after the accident, an Estonian newspaper presented a graph entitled *Folklore*, listing a menu of possible causes: It was sunk by a Russian submarine; it was blown up by a competing mafia group; the captain of the ship, fearing Swedish customs would find drug cargo, sank the ferry; the shipping company sent the ship to the bottom to collect insurance; the accident was the result of a terrorist act.

It is a fact that Estonian customs officer Igor Kristapovich was murdered in October 1994 in Tallinn. The linkage between his murder and the ferry sinking was first proposed in November 1994 in the Estonian newspaper *Eesti Aeg*.[20]

Therefore, concocting the tale was easy. Surikov's Estonian sources could have offered ideas for the Felix Report just by skimming the local newspapers.

The Submarine Fax

Not only did the Felix Report plot or variations thereof filter into books, interviews, TV documentaries and dinner conversations, it spawned an unsettling three-page document that rolled off the fax machine of a lawyer in Sweden. Hereafter referred to as the "Submarine Fax," the anonymous document, derivative of the Felix Report, also puts forth reasons for the ferry sinking (the entire text is reprinted in Appendix IV).

The narrative thread begins with Washington D.C. arranging for Alexander Einseln to lead the Estonian Armed Forces. U.S. officials wanted to acquire classified Russian weapons from Paldiski naval base. Two trucks were loaded with a large computer with highly-sensitive data belonging to Estonian Lt. Kitti Jurgens, as well as a small quantity of osmium and some very heavy equipment containing cobalt.

The shipment sat on the *Estonia* ferry on the evening of September 27, 1994, destined for Stockholm. The Russians desperately wanted to prevent the contents of the two trucks from arriving in Sweden and by extension the U.S., so they sank the ship.

> "[T]he *Estonia* was deliberately sunk by explosives or by a submarine. This was known since the early stage [sic] by the Swedish, Finnish and Estonian governments. It is even possible that these governments knew before that the Russians would do something like this (remember the shooting down of the Korean Air Jumbo near Sakhalin Peninsula) and tried to counteract, but in vain."

Like all disinformation, the Submarine Fax is appropriately hollow when probed.

The U.S. State Department did not shoehorn Einseln into Estonian defense force headquarters. On the contrary, the department's fist came down in firm opposition to it. The response is well documented, as is the department's retaliatory punishment after he went ahead and accepted the post anyway. Moreover, by September 1994, no operable Russian submarines docked at Paldiski base. The stolen computer of Lt. Kitti Jurgens that was "too large to be transported by bag or suitcase" was actually a personal laptop computer with no sensitive information.[21]

The Submarine Fax did not provide sources or verifiable details and the author was anonymous--the hallmark of disinformation. Still, the Fax had an effect.

Germany's *Spiegel* television program contacted Einseln for an interview in November 2000, just after the *One Eagle* dive to the wreck. The *Spiegel* TV reporter said a former military officer in Estonia implicated Einseln as the main gangster in the Estonian mafia who gave orders to the ferry's captain to dump drugs into the sea. This unnamed source said he had proof: a telephone call record from Estonian military headquarters to the ferry on the night of the disaster.[22]

As Einseln saw it, *Spiegel* TV was out to malign him. The German newsmagazine *Der Spiegel* had alluded to Einseln's criminal involvement with the ferry sinking in past articles. Fed up with accusations, Einseln agreed to the interview with the hope of setting the record straight.

During the interview, Einseln talked about the Estonian state infected with corruption, the ease in moving illicit goods, the U.S. State Department's anger when he accepted his post and rising resentment from discharged officers and domestic politicians. "There was a very strong move to get rid of me," he explained.

Einseln added that his last stand came after he apparently infuriated Estonian politicians by saying on television that internal corruption represents a far worse threat to Estonia than the Russian military. Shortly afterward, he was asked to resign.[23]

Spiegel TV never aired the Einseln interview. The path that led to Einseln had been a detour.

* * *

In conclusion, the Felix Report was a highly-effective diversion from the truth. Contributors were most likely former KGB, ex-communist party functionaries and others who resented the new realities. The Estonian parliament had proposed a bill to punish former agents, requiring them to leave the country or be deported. This *nomenklatura* class held vivid memories of affluence and dominion. But things had changed. They bitterly refused to accept privation and political impotence.[24]

Portraying the state-owned flagship as a drug shuttle, denigrating the Republic of Estonia, provided a way to strike back.

Russia also consistently worked a provocation strategy, often with defamation as the goal. Laar believed psychological warfare was the only effective weapon the fallen empire had.

"There were intelligence games, there was the wrong information they tried to send through the intelligence services -- they had infiltrated and...will try to kill us," Laar recalled. "Psychological warfare was very strong. Because actually the Russian goal was to not let us out of their influence, not let us out to the West."

Most consequentially, tainting Estonia's image would scare away foreign investors.

> "[The Russians] played very much on instability and played very much on showing that Estonia couldn't manage on its own. We needed those investments, needed that economic recovery, those fast reforms, and Russia's aim was of course not to let us do this. They couldn't stop us militarily because they were themselves very weak. And so it was necessary to have such psychological warfare . . . This was the game."[25]

Detours flourished because the JAIC and Sweden had created optimum conditions. Disinformation works best in an information vacuum. Openness burns away conspiracy. In the 1987 *Herald of Free Enterprise* ferry accident in the North Sea, the bodies and wreck were recovered. No material was classified. An open investigation and public inquiry were held, responsibility was established and justice served. Today not even the most fringe conspiracy voices are suggesting key questions remain in the *Herald* accident investigation.

The *Estonia* ferry investigation didn't follow those precepts, encouraging detours that blur fiction and reality.[26]

Strategic Compassion

"Missing" is perhaps the most terrifying word in the English language, in almost any context. People can better adapt to the harsh reality of a yes or no. The uncertainty packed in "missing" is a continuous torment.

For more than a decade, the word has afflicted many of the families and friends of the *Estonia* ferry disaster victims. To this day, most of the 757 missing people remain trapped inside the wreck.

Throughout history, states have organized dangerous and sometimes hopeless attempts to recover victims regardless of cost, time, technical limitations or individual objections.

At the site of the World Trade Center in New York, teams of recovery specialists have been sifting through rubble for years to find body parts and chunks of bone for forensic identification.

About half of the 2,792 people listed as missing in the Sept. 11, 2001 attacks on the Twin Towers have been identified as of this writing. The medical examiner expects several hundred people will never be found; nonetheless, the huge, concerted effort to identify the dead is expected to continue for years.[1]

Technical challenges don't prevent action. The *Ehime Maru*, the Japanese trawler accidentally destroyed by the submarine *USS Greeneville*, sank in 670 meters (2,200 feet) of water off Hawaii. Only nine people were missing. But the wreck was re-floated and towed to a depth of 35 meters, where U.S. Navy and Japanese divers recovered remains of eight of them.

Terrain makes no difference. Disaster workers in India attempted to extract 25,000 bodies buried in an earthquake in Western India's Gujarat. Taiwan authorities recovered 225 passengers from a China Airlines flight that crashed into the sea off Taiwan. When a Gulf Air Flight went down in the Persian Gulf, all 143 bodies were recovered.

Financial considerations don't get in the way. In Tanzania, rescuers went into a mine and brought up bodies of 32 miners who had died of suffocation. The Russian government, cash-strapped when the submarine *Kursk* sank in 2000, spent about $100 million to raise it and identify the bodies of recovered crew members.[2]

Length of time does not matter. Years after the 1995 Srebrenica massacre, 4,000 body bags await DNA analysis that will help Bosnians reach an emotional conclusion and perhaps move forward. The U.S. is still on a quest to account for 8,000 missing soldiers from the Korean War in 1950, using DNA methods to identify what remnants of bodies they can find. Even soldiers' bones from World War I, found in 2003 in trenches at Ypres, Belgium, will be identified and buried with full military honors.

From sunken ships, crashed airliners and space shuttles, from beneath fallen rock and collapsed skyscrapers, authorities in all countries reflexively launch efforts to retrieve human remains after a civil catastrophe. Governments do not squabble and debate the practice, which seems to transcend all political, economic and religious differences around the globe. Recovery work and forensic identification are more of a moral imperative than legal procedure. It simply gets done because it is right.[3]

The breathtaking exception is Sweden's decision not to recover the *Estonia* victims. Inside the rusting hulk just 38 kilometers southeast of Finland's Utö island are citizens of 17 countries, ranging from two-months old to 87-years old. Despite public promises by various prime ministers, despite the anguished urging of victim's relatives, despite an independent commission's recommendations and the countless examples set by the civilized world, Sweden has refused to recover them.

*   *   *

Psychologists propose that a person in grief needs to see actual remains of the deceased in order to authenticate the reality of loss and say goodbye. A land burial then provides a physical space for religious rites.

Survivor guilt is a related issue. Some passengers strong enough and lucky enough to get off the ferry ran past children clinging to stair railings and elderly men pleading for help. One survivor " . . . between the outbursts of aggression . . . remembered with self-contempt how he had trampled over injured people when escaping in panic from the ship."[4]

Survivors therefore may feel an overwhelming unconscious motivation to ensure the dead are pulled from the sea and returned to land.

Another issue involves the relatives' disquieting sense that they've been forced to become accomplices in the abandonment of their loved ones.

"Annika is too beautiful to be lying at the bottom of the sea," One mother said of her daughter during a demonstration of 300 relatives of victims who demanded the raising of the *Estonia* ferry wreck.[5]

Such powerful instinctual feelings initially seemed to be misinterpreted by the Swedish government as overpowering grief. Authorities regarded the pleas of the relatives with something like benign apathy.

"The response they have been giving these last years is that the ship has the sanctity of the grave, and the ship shall remain there," said Bertil Calamnius, a Swede who lost his daughter on the *Estonia* and who serves as the head of AgnEF, one of the relatives' groups.

"All people who had lost someone on the *Estonia* found that they were not regarded as fairly intelligent normally functioning people. The relatives were treated with kid gloves 'It's so sad you have lost somebody.' They more or less patted us on the head."

Calamnius' daughter had been in Estonia on a volunteer program arranged through Sweden's Upsaala University to help de-Sovietize Estonia. Her summer work in Tallinn at a marketing company had come to an end and she planned to sail back to Sweden on the *Estonia* ferry. When the *Estonia* arrived in Tallinn on September 27, a university friend disembarked and handed her the return ticket to Stockholm. She boarded the ferry.

"I would like to get my daughter home eventually," said Calamnius, who like many relatives have deep doubts about the JAIC's explanation for the sinking. "I haven't changed my opinion on the bodies; they should have been brought home."[6]

Catrin Tidstrom, the desk officer in Sweden's Ministry of Transport tasked to answer questions about the disaster, said the ministry held in high regard the wishes of some relatives and survivors who did not want the ship raised or the subject of salvage discussed. She was less sympathetic toward Calamnius and AgnEF, however, and disparaged relatives who were vocal in demanding a dignified land burial.

"The relatives I've spoken to don't go out to the papers, don't scream, don't send in long notes--and they don't go through journalists," she said, her voice evoking the image of closing a file and putting it away.[7]

* * *

A year after the catastrophe, some relatives felt the Swedish government's time for redress had expired. Denied access to their kin, some took on the task themselves. Two attempts were made to reach the sunken wreck using hired boats and divers in order to retrieve bodies. They were intimidated by Swedish patrol ships and sailed away from the site.

Families then planned to jointly raise funds for a recovery operation. Confronted with the group's plans, Ines Uusmann, Sweden's Transport Minister at the time, turned the tables and bitterly condemned the relatives plan as "morally atrocious."[8]

Soon, all dives to the wreck were banned by a legal experiment known as the "Gravesite Treaty," even though the *Estonia* shipwreck is a civilian passenger ship that lies in international waters. The agreement, drawn up by Sweden and signed February 23, 1995, designates a two kilometer (1.5 mile) square area around the *Estonia* site as an off-limits burial ground. All countries touching the Baltic Sea except Germany are party to the treaty, which prohibits citizens from the signatory countries from any involvement in dives to the wreck.

The Gravesite Treaty, according to Swedish officials, protects the bodies from adventure divers and looters and therefore the *Estonia's* victims don't have to be recovered. The narrow emphasis on security sharply diverged from the relatives' broad moral arguments. Officialdom has refused to budge from their position.

Camila Buzaglo, spokeswoman for the Transport Minister, reminded the public that just sailing through the no-trespassing zone is analogous to digging a coffin up out of a grave.[9]

"This is a graveyard," added Tidstrom. "We still see this as a graveyard. All the countries around have agreed this is a graveyard and no one should dive or take things from it. It's a criminal offense."[10]

The Transport Ministry's view, however, contradicts the position of the highest religious officials in Scandinavia. When senior church officials from Sweden, Estonia and Finland arranged a special memorial service at sea with a choir, they deliberately avoided blessing the site as a final resting place, according to Gunnar Weman, Archbishop of the Church of Sweden.

Swedish authorities pioneered the Gravesite Treaty allegedly out of concern for the suffering of relatives. The treaty transforms the ferry into a protective shell that is assigned the status of a tomb. The dead will remain undisturbed. These claims, put forward with some official righteousness, were later proven, in a horrifying way, to be false. During the August 2000 *One Eagle* expedition, an ROV passed by several bodies outside the wreck.[11]

In reality, the Gravesite Treaty is a ruse. It does not secure and dignify the dead, but is instead a government tool used to thwart, limit and discredit independent investigations of the shipwreck.

The treaty is closer to a handshake between state bureaucracies than an internationally-recognized legal document because the *Estonia* wreck rests in international waters, outside of national jurisdiction. The treaty's biggest challenge came in August 2000 when the *One Eagle* sailed from Germany, a country that is not signatory to the treaty. Nonetheless, the organizers of the expedition, Bemis and Rabe, face arrest should they set foot in Sweden.

Bemis consulted with maritime lawyers who found that the treaty could not be defended on a legal basis. "You cannot draw a square in international waters and say no one can go there," Bemis said. "That's why it is called international waters."

Bemis, who owns the rights to the *Lusitania* wreck and has been working with diving expeditions for decades, acknowledged the need to protect bodies and personal effects. Before the August 2000 dive, he explained to Swedish authorities that the dive's purpose was to examine the wreck's exterior for structural damage. Divers would not disturb the human remains. He invited Swedish observers onboard as monitors, but received no response.[12]

Later, Tidstrom did comment. "I don't think many people would like you to dig up your grandmother because they want to make an investigation."[13]

The Re-established Europeans

Estonians are not Soviets and they are not Russians. With Finno-Ugric roots, they have more Finnish influence than Slavic as well as a short but important history as an independent country before Soviet occupation. Estonians hold a deep conviction that they belong in Europe. They have consistently hammered on that point to the outside world since independence from the U.S.S.R. in August 1991.

Mention that Estonia was a "newly independent state" after August 1991 and an Estonian will probably take the time to correct you. Not "newly independent" but a state that "regained its independence." They're quick to point out that Estonia had for 20 years been an autonomous country sharing European values before forced incorporation into the U.S.S.R.

Estonia is indeed an amazing story by many measures. Estonians shrugged off the Soviet legacy, avoided conflict and survived economic shock therapy despite relentless difficulties. The country set high goals and reached them.

Marju Lauristin, a Tartu University professor and former Estonian parliament member, writes that the Estonians' enduring drive to reunite with the West nourished the collective will, enabling progress. "This is the main source of their patience, so much wondered at and admired by the Western world."

Lauristin draws a "civilizational conflict between the Russian-Soviet Empire, the `New Byzantium' of the 20th century, and the Baltic and other East European nations, representing the Western traditions of individual autonomy and civil society."[14]

Yet no civilization conflict exists when these nations are actually challenged to make practical decisions on matters concerning life and death. On the contrary, the body recovery issue shows the Swedish and Estonian position smoothly aligning with that of the Soviet Empire, which as a matter of policy outlawed independent investigations and dismissed any state moral obligations.

Moreover, Lauristin herself opposes recovery of *Estonia* victims for the most un-Western reasons, in particular, the notion that abandonment fits with some kind of natural order. "The sea as a gravesite has always been part of tradition," she concluded.[15]

Western officials do not yield to superstitions in tragic circumstances. Tribal beliefs that equate the sea with a grave do not form the basis of institutional decision making. In civilized countries, governments have a compulsory duty to exploit technology and resources in the service of the public to mitigate suffering.

The 757 bodies in the *Estonia* were not Vikings longing for combat and the smell of blood. And unlike those drowned on warships, the truck drivers and students, schoolchildren and tourist groups, cooks, waitresses, dancers, musicians, police officers and civil servants did not agree to risk their lives in the service of their country when they took a fun overnight cruise.

Stepping onto the *Estonia* ferry was no different than boarding an evening flight to Stockholm.

*   *   *

Estonia's connection to the sea dates back to the Stone Age. Hollowed-out tree trunks were used as the first boats. Centuries of seafaring experience and myths, passed down through generations, are woven into the Estonian psyche.

In ancient times, when a boat overturned all souls could be lost. Nothing could be done. For spiritual comfort, people embraced the notion that the sea was actually a hallowed grave. A meaningful symmetry was involved: The sea gives food for life; it also takes life. Deaths at sea were accepted as sacrifices that pleased the gods, thus enabling tribes to put death aside, aiding survival.

Centuries later, with inventions like the life vest, a man overboard could be saved from drowning. Sea accidents no longer translated into certain death. Eventually, ship design, rescue apparatus, safety equipment and diving and recovery techniques all appeared and advanced in sophistication, allowing those to sail the sea with far less risk than before.

In 21st century Europe, the mythological gods of the sea no longer need to be placated, and a slab of rusting steel is no longer elevated to a holy resting place.

But Estonian President Lennart Meri disagreed. "Even if it is technically possible to raise the ship, all ethical reasons speak against [this]," he said. "I want to follow the old traditions and let the site between Sweden, Finland and Estonia be a sacred place."

He added, "The sea from time to time needs sacrifices. This is very deeply rooted in our culture."

Meri has been described by international media as "eccentric" and by one journalist as "almost callous." But perhaps that's not entirely fair. Meri in a sense does share a system of beliefs with other politicians, in particular, the mayor of a Haitian city hit by a ferry tragedy in September 1997, which took the lives of 200 people. The Mayor, Simon La Pointe, also adhered to his culture's revered traditions. He announced to the grief-stricken relatives that voodoo was involved in the ferry sinking.[16]

Indeed, Meri's counterpart, former KGB agent and Russian president Vladimir Putin, took the higher ground. After initial missteps in handling the *Kursk* catastrophe, Putin told the families that efforts would be made to recover the bodies. He stuck to his promise.

Meri's superstitious and insensitive stance substituted for modern leadership. His irrational attitude on the recovery issue suggested he was more of a village chief than a statesman moving his country forward. His refusal to insist on repatriation of victims after such a devastating tragedy was perhaps his greatest failing as president.

Salvage Realities

Marine salvage experts and naval architects concur that the *Estonia* ferry can be raised. The Dutch salvage firm Smit Tak, as early as December 1994, concluded that the *Estonia* was salvageable and some of the easily accessible human remains could be brought up first, the rest remaining inside until the entire ship was raised. The Rockwater dive survey report confirmed that bringing home the victims was possible.

Raising the wreck is well within the realm of engineering. Some salvage experts have suggested a slow and cautious lifting of the 155-meter ferry with balloon-type devices or some sort of buoyant cradle, then floating it to shallower waters. Divers could then work relatively unfettered, removing the remains from the inner recesses of the ferry.

David Mearns, director of Blue Water Recoveries Ltd who assisted in the deep sea investigations of the *M/V Derbyshire* and *Lucona* shipwrecks, said raising the 16,000 ton *Estonia* would be a challenge, but not an impossible task. He suggested that slings throughout the vessel that ran up to floating derrick barges might be one of several ways to lift the ferry in a controlled manner.[17]

Anders Björkman, the naval architect who has analyzed the *Estonia* disaster, also proposed ways to re-float the wreck. Essentially his plan involves removing all the cars and trucks from the cardeck onto the seafloor, then inserting pontoons into the cardeck and filling them with air. The *Estonia* can then be floated to shallower water for body retrieval.[18]

Providing reassurance for the *Estonia* salvage is TWA Flight 800, which exploded and crashed into the sea off Long Island, New York in 1996. On a far more dangerous mission, divers made more than 4000 dives and faced entanglement in electrical cable and punctures and tears from the sharp jagged metal of the jet's pieces. The TWA dive was likened to a swim through razor blades. Nonetheless, the wreckage and all human remains were recovered.[19] (see chart Appendix I).

The ferry is a far less challenging target. Unlike the exploded airliner, the *Estonia* isn't spread over miles of seafloor. Oil and fuel have been removed. The depth of 60-80 meters is not great. The *Estonia* could be brought close to the Finnish military island of Utö, where the victims could be removed and forensically identified in privacy.

Successful identification is uncertain. But the Baltic Sea environment where the ship sank has particular characteristics that may have kept remains in a physical state suitable for effective forensic testing. A body submerged in water decomposes naturally just as it does buried in the earth. But cold, deep water delays decomposition so that bodies may be surprisingly well-preserved after a long period of immersion. These sea conditions also favor the formation of adipocere, a brown, fatty, waxlike substance, which may help slow decomposition.

It is unrealistic to expect the *Estonia* victims' bodies will be intact; it is, however, a reasonable assumption that bones and teeth would be in suitable condition for DNA identification.

At the wreck site, the sea's features are extreme. A low salinity (the Baltic is less than 1/3 of world ocean salinity) and low oxygen content severely limit macro and micro fauna, the natural decomposing agents of organic material in the sea, according to Pekka Alenius, senior scientist at Helsinki's Finnish Institute of Marine Research (FIMR).

Macrofauna is the main feeder on organic material in the sea. Soft parts of the human face are particularly vulnerable to fish, and crustaceans can turn a body into a skeleton in a couple days. Yet macrofauna are scarce in the area where the ship sank.

The Baltic is also too deep and cold for the toredo worm, a hungry creature that devours almost all organic material in salt water.

Microfauna, such as bacteria, are also decomposing agents. Yet in the area where the *Estonia* sank, microfauna are scarce. For example, from 1997-2001, either no microfauna or only 1 - 100 of them per square meter were found, according to the FIMR.

The 50-80 meter sloping shelf where the *Estonia* rests is on the outer edges of the sea's "greatly impoverished zone" where bacteria don't like to colonize. There's just not enough oxygen for them. "It is uninhabitable for organisms other than anaerobic bacteria," Alenius said.[20]

Though low in salinity, the Baltic's salt water could still act as a preservative. Salt water tends to dehydrate submerged bodies. "This is sometimes evident in brain tissue," said Jamie Downs, forensic examiner for the Savannah, Georgia, Bureau of Investigation. "Intact brain tissue has been found in shipwrecks from the early 1900s."[21]

Significantly, the temperature at the site is estimated to remain close to 34 degrees Fahrenheit (1.2 degrees Celsius), barely above freezing. The low temperature acts as refrigeration, putting the *Estonia* ferry in cold storage.

The main factor working against body reclamation is attrition resulting from intense water pressure. Roughly every 10 meters of depth adds one atmosphere. The *Estonia* victims, at about seven atmospheres, have unusual pressure exerted on protective tissues. An extreme example of the effect is the human remains from the *Titanic*. Bodies, including the bones, dissolved because the wreck was at a depth 12,500 feet (about 4000 meters), Downs pointed out.

In a recovery operation, all the casualties assumed to be in the *Estonia* would not be found. Those seen on the seabed by the *One Eagle* ROV have probably dispersed; others may have worked their way out of the wreck via deep currents. But the majority of victims inside the wreck still have a reasonable chance of being positively identified. A major advantage is their containment inside the ferry and further encasement inside cabins. Searching the seafloor for remains is unnecessary.

Bringing up the victim's remains would encourage psychological closure and could settle many outstanding issues and dispel myths. Forensic identification could help clarify the mystery of the second *Estonia* captain, Avo Piht, who was seen by survivors distributing lifejackets and was officially reported as a survivor, but has not been found. Disturbing theories have emerged to explain why. Several other crewmembers had also been identified one way or another as survivors, only to disappear.

Forensic identification would work on several levels. First, documents in the clothing of the individuals would be used to determine identity. Credit cards and driver's licenses in wallets may still be in some pockets. Plastic does not easily dissolve in seawater. Everybody had a passport on the international trip. Familiar watches, wedding rings and other jewelry, clothing and shoes would bolster chances of positive identification.

The next level would be the presence of medical devices such as a pacemaker or hearing aid. Then the victim's teeth would be compared to dental records. Teeth are resilient and an individual's genetic code can be obtained from the pulp inside.

Forensics experts would study a set of teeth and compare them with dental records, which like fingerprints or DNA evidence, is one of the most accurate methods available. In general, teeth remain intact in submerged human remains. "Teeth are very durable," Downs said. "In some cases you could even ID based on one tooth."[22]

The next level would be DNA identification. Forensic experts obtain a sample from the victim's remains and they compare it with either a sample known to come from that person (from a hairbrush, toothbrush or undergarments, for example), or DNA samples from close relatives (mother, father, or children). But because the *Estonia's* deceased are in various stages of decomposition, standard forensic DNA techniques based on non-degraded tissues would probably be of limited value.

Forensic identification, however, has entered a golden age since September 11, 2001. New techniques that deliver results from damaged or obliterated remains overwhelmingly build the case for giving identification a try.

In badly decomposed tissue, the scientist uses mitochondria that are separate from the nucleus of the cell and have their own DNA. Mitochondrial DNA, or mtDNA, is inherited from the mother. Mitochondrial DNA can survive in hair, teeth and bones. Because mtDNA is inherited only from the mother, samples used for comparison with a victim's samples must come from either a maternal relative or the victim's personal effects.

So if the missing victim is female, samples obtained from her mother, maternal grandmother, siblings or children can provide useful comparisons. Comparative mtDNA samples from a male victim can come only from his mother, maternal grandmother, maternal aunt or uncle or any sibling, but not from his children.

A famous case of ancient mtDNA testing involved Russia's last czar, Nicholas II and his wife Alexandra, who were murdered by Bolsheviks in 1918. Their remains were exhumed in 1991 and positively identified a few years later through laboratory tests in Britain and the United States, 73 years after death.

Mark Stolorow, executive director of forensic science at US-based Orchid Cellmark Inc, which assisted in identification of 9-11 victims, cautioned that the many variables in the Baltic's specific environment over the years make the condition of the victims' DNA uncertain. In addition, no meaningful scientific studies about the persistence of DNA from underwater cadavers exist. With so many unknowns, speculating on the rate of success in DNA typing is unwise.[23]

Even if DNA testing failed to identify everyone, relatives of the missing would be no worse off than they are now. It may turn out to be a partial solution, but it is vastly superior to no solution at all. Recovery will not bring happiness, but perhaps for many less anguish.

No

"I think we should do everything in our power to re-float the ferry," said Carl Bildt, Sweden's Prime Minister, as he left office just after the ship went down in 1994. Ingvar Carlsson, who followed Bildt as head of state, also said efforts should be made to bring up the wreck. In Estonia, Economics Minister Toivo Jurgenson concurred: The *Estonia* ferry must be salvaged.[24]

The same year, the technical examination from the Rockwater dive reinforced the apparent political will by confirming that recovering the bodies and the ship was possible. But shortly after the report was out in December 1994, expectations hit a wall. Sweden's Ethical Council, which advises the government, issued the determinative recommendation: No.

The judges of human ethics cited an unpresentable condition of the bodies, which was actually the public position of Sweden's high military Commander Emil Svensson just hours after the ferry sank (see Chapter 8 section "Damage Control"). The ethical team had picked up Svensson's remark and ran with it.

Svensson's excuse would be trotted out in several venues in different countries. It had the effect of instilling terror in relatives who simply wanted a proper land burial. Like the cautionary tale "The Monkey's Paw," the excuse tapped primal fears.

"Many of the bodies would be exposed to air and summer temperatures causing quick decay, as the operations would have to be carried [out] when waters are calm and free from ice," according to the Ethical Council. "If the ship is salvaged, many will see it as an unworthy manner to handle corpses."[25]

Johan Franson at several meetings described how disgusting the bodies would be, how the archipelago would smell if a recovery operation began and the difficulty in identifying people.[26]

There has never been an incidence in modern history when recovery of civilian casualties depended on the tasteful appearance of the remains. Countless other victims in far worse shape have been recovered. The TWA 800 passengers had been subject to an explosion and submerged in seawater. PanAm Flight 103, which blew up over Lockerbie, Scotland in 1988, resulted in the recovery of 270 human remains scattered over 75 miles. Less than half of them were rendered "viewable" to the grieving families.[27]

The 9-11 scientists are handing chips of bone, or perhaps an arm or torso. Intense fire from the two jets that plowed into the towers and compression from tons of falling rubble pulverized human bodies with varying effects.

Sweden nonetheless pushed the hypersensitivity issue further:

"Police officers, rescue servicemen, pathologists and other personnel were prepared to perform their duties. But the number of corpses would expose the staff involved to severe psychological strain. In spite of debriefings and other support measures, psychiatrists confirmed such risks."[28]

Sweden's compassion broke new ground. A pathologist protected from handling the dead? How about a surgeon shielded from blood and an undertaker kept away corpses? As the authorities' apparently sincere concern became overzealous, it began to suggest they had a different agenda. Compassion began to look like a strategy.

When the Ethical Council's statements failed to sway public opinion, someone suggested that the mental health of the salvage divers would be at risk if they brought up remains.

Yet the Rockwater divers in December 1994 saw plenty of bodies in the wreck and handled some of them. John Coe, one of the Rockwater survey divers to the *Estonia*, had in the past worked on recovery of the victims from the Piper Alpha, the North Sea production platform that caught fire and killed 167, as well as the collapsed oil platform the Alexander Kielland.

Coe, who had seen bodies in the *Estonia* wreck, said professional salvage divers experienced in dealing with human remains underwater do not suffer psychological trauma. Coe's main difficulty was with the Swedish requirement that the divers be briefed by a psychiatrist. "We've done this sort of thing before, it's not very pleasant. But you recover people so their loved ones can grieve and put them to rest ... what [the briefing] did was it highlighted the experience you were going to go through, that you were going to see women and children. Instead what you've got to do is turn off your emotional side of it."[29]

Specialists in recovery, especially navy divers, approach body recovery in a practical manner. The *Kursk* submarine victims had been subject to an explosion and chemical fire. In preparation for recovery, Russian divers visited a morgue and had courses at the Medical Academy in St Petersburg. Low visibility in the sunken sub sometimes required the divers to search by touching objects. Russian military commanders dismissed advice from the Norwegians that the divers shouldn't look in the face of the victims for psychological reasons.

"Sometimes they had to work for two hours with one body to pull it out," said Rear Admiral Gennady Verich. "If a diver was afraid to look at the face, was afraid to touch it, he wouldn't have been able to get the job done."[30]

The British newspaper *The Daily Telegraph* mentioned one of the Royal Navy divers who recovered bodies from the *Herald of Free Enterprise* ferry, Able Seaman Eamon Fullen, only 19 at the time: "--It didn't slow me up at all, I'd been well prepared years before and expected it as part of my job diving and being in the Navy and life in general."[31]

Disaster recovery divers accept the physical result of death as part of their work, just as do police officers, firefighters and soldiers. Such self-evident truths were never pointed out.

Government excuses labeling a retrieval operation as demeaning continued to pile up. Another objection held that the salvage would never be able to find or positively identify all bodies, so recovery was out of the question.

"Grandma and grandpa take a trip to Tallinn with two grandchildren and you [recover] one child and grandpa," Franson said. "How would that affect relatives? You would get those kinds of very difficult questions to answer."[32]

Peter Örn, who led a government-appointed commission to assess the issue of recovering the bodies, said others held the same opinion. "A lot of people on the ethical board, including church people and so on concluded that there must be some equality. If you can't bring them all up then you can't bring up any."[33]

Sweden was now demanding an ideal solution or no solution at all. Someone could argue that a small group of Swedes unilaterally imposing their own ethics on families from 17 countries is a display of staggering arrogance, but no one did. Mainstream media shied away from debate on a position that is widely divergent with customs and practices of the West.[34]

If Sweden had genuinely wanted an equitable solution for victims from 17 countries, they would have brought up the recovery issue at the United Nations.

Yes -- No

The refusal to expatriate the victims stood in sharp and strange contrast to the standard of Swedish justice, considered a model of fairness throughout the world. But the feeling of responsibility that the living have for the dead touches deep emotional currents and as it turned out, the ethical committee decision was not the final word.

As years passed, the demand for action would not fade away. Families of victims who wanted a proper Christian burial for relatives trapped on the ferry persistently knocked on the doors of Swedish officialdom.

Their efforts resulted in a 1998 decision to appoint an Analysis Group to look into the question of repatriating human remains. Headed by Peter Örn, secretary-general of the Swedish Red Cross, the team was empowered to ask any questions concerning the salvage issue to any person, who in turn was obligated to answer fully.

The Analysis Group's instructions were to avoid the why and how of the sinking and exclusively examine the matter of human remains recovery. Initiated and sanctioned by the Swedish government, the group's implicit aim was to assuage public outrage over the broken promises of prime ministers and the subsequent ferry entombment fiasco. Explicitly, the goal was to make recommendations for action.

After interviewing everyone from victims' relatives up to Carl Bildt, the Analysis Group issued an autumn 1998 report.

"Measures must be taken to recover and identify the bodies that are inside the hull or outside of it," the Analysis Group reported. The goal must be to recover and bury the dead with dignity and according to the wish of their loved ones, it said. "This would likely restore confidence in society."

Örn, the political appointee in charge, went on to tell the press: "We believe that many relatives can't complete their mourning without efforts to recover their loved ones."[35]

Örn had handed Stockholm the answer. The relatives, marginalized and pitied, now had clear political support. They had stated their case to an officially-handpicked representative who had fully agreed with them. In all fairness, the bodies in the *Estonia* ferry would have to be recovered.

Here a brief summary is required. The government made several attempts to rewire the explanation for not recovering the ferry's victims. Sweden's first objection was the scary condition of the bodies. Then an intense concern for the medical personnel and divers who would handle them. Then the demand for an ideal solution--either retrieve all bodies or none at all. None of these worked. Pressure from the relatives of victims continued to mount.

Finally, the state sets up a group to air public frustrations and ideally to close the books on the issue. Unfortunately, the group's answer is directly opposed to the government's position.

What to do?

Sweden's Transport Minister, Mona Sahlin, no doubt carefully digested the Analysis Group's report. She had no moral or legal basis to turn it down. The Swedes had spoken. Heeding the voice of the people, after all, is a fundamental tenet of the modern Swedish state.

But Sahlin found a way out of the dilemma. Soon the trumpet of consensus blared through the Swedish Parliament. Suddenly, ethical decisions made by Swedes alone were deemed unfair. Suddenly, Finland and Estonia held pivotal positions in the affair. Of course they needed to be consulted. The Gravesite Treaty was a government-level agreement.

Sweden had not factored in the treaty, and that was wrong.

Estonia, which had been treated like a stepchild during the investigation, was now a full-fledged *bona fide* sovereign state and key participant in high-level discussions on the bodies issue. Finland, which lost 10 citizens in the disaster, was now respected as a heavyweight in the decision-making process. Although 22 Latvian citizens lay inside the wreck, the country of Latvia, also a Gravesite Treaty signatory country, was elbowed aside.

Sahlin knew what had to be done. In late 1998, she flew to Finland, asked Helsinki officials their position on body recovery, and received a negative answer.

She then went to Tallinn. In Estonia, it wasn't so easy. Relatives overwhelmingly supported repatriating the bodies. Sahlin did things differently. She organized a closed-door meeting with the leaders of the relatives' groups "Memento Mare" and "Memento *Estonia*." She based her whole decision on this meeting, which was not attended by any other Estonians except these two leaders and a few other members on the Memento Mare board. The meeting lasted one hour.

The leader of Memento *Estonia*, Ander Paeorg, had received his wife's body back after the ship sank. Although his perspective was quite different from other relatives who had not been so lucky, Paeorg was being consulted on the pivotal decision for body repatriation.

"There were two votes," Paeorg recalled. "Bringing up the bodies and covering the wreck. We were against both of them. [Sahlin] did not try to convince us otherwise."

Apparently, the group leaders had not discussed the Sahlin vote much with other relatives in Estonia. Veronica Andresson, wife of the ferry's captain, was puzzled over why the ship and bodies hadn't been brought up. "It's not clear why the wreck wasn't taken up at once," she said. "--Like the *Kursk*, [salvage] should have been done at once. I'm not aware of who decided not to do it . . . My only wish was to have the ship taken up as soon as possible."[36]

Sahlin let ignorance of forensic matters feed Estonian apprehension. Estonian relatives held many doubts concerning recovery, which swayed their decision. How could bodies ever be positively identified? Where in the world could we find the people skilled in marine forensics? What terrible psychological problems would the recovery experts have after viewing remains? The Estonians, who had been cut off from Western ethics and technology for five decades had many such questions. They were left unanswered.[37]

"What happens to corpses under the water resembles a horror movie," Paeorg added. That rather dramatic statement was circulated in the Estonian media and all talk about taking up and identifying the victims faded away.

"Sahlin did not try to explain the technical capabilities and expertise involved in a recovery operation," Paeorg recalled. "She did not explain possible scenarios to technical objections."

She simply listened, then flew back to Sweden. From Stockholm, Sahlin announced that Finland and Estonia, official signatories to the Gravesite Treaty that protects the inviolability of the wreck, didn't want the bodies up and therefore they would not be salvaged.

"It was possible to bring them up, possible to identify and bury them. The committee that I led was for it," Örn said. "No one knows what happened then, but it was very clear [Finland and Estonia] didn't want this. I don't know how hard Sweden tried to pressure them. Perhaps we'll never know."

Sweden's *Dagens Nyheter* newspaper reported that because of Estonia's opposition, it is now very difficult, if not impossible, to rescind the Gravesite Treaty.[38]

The Transport Ministry issued an official statement in February 1999:

> "The agreements would have to be renegotiated and laws on the protection of the sanctity of the grave be amended ... even if the governments and parliaments of four countries were in agreement that this should be done, it would be a long process ... many relatives, both those who hope for recovery and those who accept the sea as the final resting place--would be subjected to a long period of uncertainty and the risk of further suffering."[39]

In an amazing display of tactical dexterity, Sweden now tossed bureaucratic obstacles on the heap of excuses. A treaty that arguably has no legal basis and was designed to discourage daredevil divers should not be difficult to reverse negotiate, if not annul.

The bodies would stay in the wreck. Case closed.

* * *

In August 2000, a Russian journalist produced a videotape that shocked the world. It had been secretly made at a conference between Russian Prime Minister Ilya Klebanov and relatives of victims of the Kursk disaster.

A mother was demanding answers from Klebanov, venting rage over her son who'd been trapped on the submarine, shouting at one of the highest officials in the Russian Federation. Lost in emotion, she didn't see a woman jab her with a hypodermic needle containing a strong sedative, and she collapsed.

The chilling incident serves as an apt analogy for the Swedish government's treatment of *Estonia* ferry victims' relatives. Sweden's patronizing approach treated the more vociferous relatives like unruly children who required delicate handling, reinforcing the darkest stereotypes of the nanny state. Stockholm's broken promises and parental admonishments are the psychological equivalent of the forced sedative injection given to the Russian mother. In both cases, the state divested the relatives of the right to judge and justified it by categorizing objectors as distraught.

Örn, head of the Analysis Group, said the relatives of the victims and even some survivors were marginalized. "They were seen as people with no influence on this matter and the matter was left to people with responsibility," Örn said. "No one noticed their frustration."[40]

Sweden has often been perceived as the world's moral benchmark. Its tradition of fair and principled politics injected humanitarianism into international politics, producing people like Raoul Wallenberg and Dag Hammarskjöld. Carl Bildt himself applied his negotiation skills to try and mediate the Balkans conflict, and although Hans Blix is a scientist, his morality could not be suppressed in the lead up to the second Iraq War.

But if the world adopted the Swedish principles underpinning the *Estonia* catastrophe, the TWA Flight 800 bodies would remain seat-belted in the twisted wreckage at the bottom of the sea off Long Island and the relatives of 9-11 victims would have first been polled to establish how they felt about recovery and forensic identification. The world's oceans would be cordoned off into a checkerboard of restricted gravesites and no independent investigations of accidents at sea would be permitted.

* * *

Without conflict for nearly 200 years, the Swedes have relaxed far too long in an antiseptic version of life. Exposed to the germs of reality, state institutions became disoriented. Even the Church of Sweden seemed uncertain about its own role, more concerned about offending groups than it was with steering by religious principle.[41]

Institutional paralysis, however, is inconsistent with Stockholm's sharp and relentless efforts to prevent salvage and recovery of the *Estonia*. Official reasons for the salvage refusal seem more like nervous attempts to rationalize the state's own position. The excuses say more about public servants terrified by the consequences of de-controlling the shipwreck than they do about compassionate government.

Suspicions about strategic compassion extended to the U.S. Embassy in Stockholm. Suspicious U.S. authorities wondered about the abnormal emphasis Swedish officials placed on the sanctity of the grave at sea.

In July 2000, Sweden made urgent appeals to the U.S. Embassy in Stockholm to stop U.S. citizen Gregg Bemis and the *One Eagle* expedition. Intense concern for the feelings of the victims' relatives was the reason given. A U.S. embassy memo classified as "sensitive" implied that the claim of state compassion was strategic, perhaps a smokescreen for something else, something that the U.S. wanted to stay out of:

> "---The embassy has received faxes (being faxed to eur/nb) from . . . organizations in support of [Gregg] Bemis' plan to carry out further investigation. [NAME DELETED] supported the idea that most, but not all, of those with direct connection to the disaster were not satisfied with explanations to date and supported a full new investigation with the caveat that bodies should not be disturbed. In addition, the Church of Sweden has publicly taken the position that it has no objection to such an endeavor. In fact, we understood that Mr Bemis got the idea for the expedition at a conference attended by the families of victims. This suggests that

there is support for Bemis' dive and that the sensitivities of victims' families are not really an issue . . .

"It is not totally clear why the GOS [Government of Sweden] has approached embassy on this matter. The GOS also is not calling on the USG to accede to the [Gravesite] agreement. The GOS already has a dialogue with Bemis and has exchanged several messages directly with him. It has the ability to inform him personally of the risks he assumes by going ahead with his dive. But, it was done in such a way--by the Industry [Transport] Ministry, not MFA [Ministry of Foreign Affairs]--as to hype the role of this action in solving the problem. With strong feelings surrounding this disaster, nearly six years after it occurred, we do not want to be placed in the middle of the ring. We believe that, with the GOS pushing one way and the bereaved families (who do not trust GOS statements on the cause of the disaster) pushing for further study on the other, it is best to remain as neutral as possible."[42]

Peter Nobel, who worked on the formation of the Gravesite Treaty, tried to shape the treaty to keep open some prospect of finding the truth. "I pointed out that the wording of the proposed law [Gravesite Treaty] should not exclude future activities of an entirely acceptable character, e.g. technical research or securing of evidence. Neither remark influenced the wording of the legislation."[43]

Effectively, the treaty locks the ferry in a compartment and gives Stockholm the key. The treaty can continually serve as a pretense to prevent and discredit any independent forensic examination of the ferry's hull. The *Estonia's* structural condition can remain a state secret.

The Gravesite Treaty created a curious situation. Instead of the wreck protecting the bodies, the bodies are protecting the wreck.

Conclusion: A Work in Progress

A review of the *Estonia* ferry investigation and related feats is useful.

The JAIC failed to present a credible accounting. The Final Report's conclusion that strong waves detached a poorly-designed locking system is categorical. The report doesn't acknowledge doubts and questions. Uncertainties behind the commission's judgments were omitted, as were relevant facts.

The bow visor was prematurely labeled as the cause. Perplexing technical analysis drew attention to the bow visor and away from the core issue of rapid sinking.

Most crucial, the "visor off, ship down" explanation is a non-sequitur because the commission ignored the fact that there is a missing link between these two events. "Visor off, ship down" carries an especially high standard of proof since it asserts something incredible: that the *Estonia* sunk in 35 minutes without a hole in the hull.

But officials offered no analysis for the speed of the sinking, which should have been the focal point of the investigation. The fast-paced sinking was treated as a scientific fact, not as an aberration to be confronted. The Final Report is a betrayal of common sense.

The obvious answer, which has been disregarded or ridiculed, is that the *Estonia* ferry must have had a breach in its hull. Not necessarily a gaping hole, it could be as subtle as bent plating opened to the sea. The hull's integrity was violated by a collision, explosion, or some sort of blending of the two, and strategic cargo may have played a role. These conclusions are not sensational when the ferry disaster is viewed in its historical context.

The collision scenario develops out of the anarchy and opportunism in the Baltic region in the 1990s. In the framework of this interpretation, Russia sold a second-hand submarine of the same type it had sold a year earlier, which had been spotted in the Baltic Sea. An accidental impact, perhaps unrecognized by both captains, dislodged hull plating from the *Estonia* ferry on the starboard side hull. Damage progressively worsened as the ferry pounded through rough seas. Soon the ship listed hard; the visor couldn't withstand the angled wave forces and was violently torn off.

News of the accident could have turned hot ethnic tension into cross-border violence. The Swedish state went to work, carrying out politically-expedient decisions. Underwater activity on the wreck by divers may have required demolition work that was related to specific cargo.

The bomb scenario, broadly sketched, holds that the Swedish government, in an agreement with other states, acquired classified, perhaps dangerous cargo from the FSU and routinely transported it to Stockholm using the passenger ferry *Estonia*.

A criminal group or a disaffected military faction could have planted bombs on the ferry for several reasons and may have collaborated with or been influenced by Russian ultranationalists of the time. Explosions in several parts of the ship, combined with heavy waves, tore off the visor and breached the starboard side hull. Perhaps only by coincidence was the coveted cargo on board, and the sudden loss of the ship created urgent difficulties at the highest levels of the Swedish government. The cargo had to be recovered or shielded.

Criminals and state, two completely parallel forces, unaware of each other, each using the ferry to exploit opportunities opened by the collapse of the U.S.S.R. They intersected while pursuing their own interests on the night of September 27, 1994.

* * *

Constructed with unknowns and variables, the framework theories clearly have loose ends. Moreover, no theory at this point can reasonably tie in strategic cargo, which could have been either neutral element or a catalyst.

No scenario--including the JAIC's conception--can be verified. Every explanation remains speculative until the ferry's hull undergoes scientific scrutiny by independent experts, a painless solution that is tactically blocked by Sweden's Gravesite Treaty.

Another dimension of the catastrophe that has spread lasting cynicism needs to be confronted. The *Estonia* investigation is laced with unwarranted secrecy. The public is told the ferry sinking was a tragic but straightforward transport accident attributed to an old construction fault and an autumn storm. Sharply undermining the explanation is the existence of classified papers on the *Estonia* ferry sinking--and the official indifference toward it.

The U.S. National Security Agency (NSA) is the proverbial House of Secrets. Its archives hold a treasure of international intelligence derived from global listening posts and from people on the ground. Signal intelligence (SIGINT) activities, including the surreptitious interception of international communications that impact on U.S. national security, are the NSA's mission. The NSA is ultra-secret, and for decades its very existence was officially denied.

A Freedom of Information Act (FOIA) request to the NSA for any information pertaining to "The passenger ferry *M/V Estonia*, which sank in the Baltic Sea between Estonia and Sweden on 28 September 1994," resulted in three documents for a total of seven pages on the subject. They cannot be released.

"The documents are classified because their disclosure could reasonably be expected to cause serious damage to the national security," according to the NSA. In addition, they are classified as "secret" and "no parts are reasonably segregable," meaning the agency couldn't release the documents even with blacked-out sentences or paragraphs.

Under FOIA privilege, the decision was appealed, but the appeal was denied. In 2009, I requested the documents again, but the request was again denied on the same grounds.[1]

No Americans sailed on the ferry and there was no U.S. assistance during any phase of the accident. Why information related to a tourist transport accident in Scandinavia more than a decade ago would reasonably be expected to cause serious damage to U.S. national security defies understanding.

The NSA's refusal to dislcose information supports the idea that a collision or an explosion is a legitimate field of inquiry.

The existence of classified documents verifies that the U.S. government and perhaps other countries are preventing the public from knowing all the facts about the *Estonia* ferry disaster. The sensitive documents turn up the volume. They cast further doubt on the JAIC's conclusions and potentially move the *Estonia* ferry disaster beyond the expertise of a group of polite Scandinavian engineers. At the same time, no conclusions should be drawn from unknown content.

The NSA employs about 38,000 people engaged in listening to all types of communication through worldwide land and undersea listening posts, orbiting satellites and human sources on the ground. Experts then analyze the data for various agencies in the intelligence sphere.

Intercepting the Soviet Union's communications had been the NSA's single-minded mission since it was founded by presidential order in 1952. Most resources were oriented to Soviet Russia. Most cryptographers, mathematicians and analysts also specialized in Russian language, politics and history. Surveillance gear picked up high frequency signals unique to Russian transmissions. Systems for detecting early warning missile launches and submarine movements, for listening in on telephones and radio communications, were all tuned to Russia.

The Russia momentum continued to roll on well after the fall of the Soviet Union. In fact, the NSA had been criticized for continued emphasis on Russian intelligence and less attention to the post-Cold War terrorist threat.

One NSA task involved eavesdropping on strategic points where Russian subs must pass to reach the open ocean. Secret equipment may dot the Gulf of Finland, in close proximity to St. Petersburg's bases and defense enterprises. If the U.S. has no underwater detection apparatus in the shallow Finnish Gulf, they could in all likelihood be wired into Finnish electronic ears, or Swedish or Norwegian.[2]

News of such an arrangement would cause a diplomatic row and potentially drive a wedge between Scandinavian and Russian relations. Perhaps that's why the ferry documents are secret--they would officially give the surveillance game away. Protecting sources and methods is a primary consideration in classifying NSA material. It could be these SIGINT sharing arrangements that are highly sensitive, not the text of what was heard.

Then again, the primary reason for classifying the material is not clear. In the NSA letter, the first reason for withholding is damage to national security. The letter then states:

"In addition, this Agency is authorized by various statutes to protect certain information concerning its activities. We have determined that such information exists in these documents."

The key words are "in addition," denoting a secondary reason, not a primary one. (FOIA response letters are very carefully worded because they could become part of a legal appeal). Thus, in this interpretation, protecting sources and methods--"information concerning its activities"--was one justification, but not the main one.

Speculation on the main reason for secrecy is easy to compile. Military cargo was on board the *Estonia*; criminal activity unrelated to the disaster was monitored and investigative agencies do not want disclosure to protect their ongoing operations; routine radio communication from a submarine was intercepted.[3]

The documents could also shed light on the reasons for peculiar communications anomalies when the ferry went down (see Chapter 8 section "Unaccountable Incidents").

Suddenly, at the crucial moments, the regional telephone network and international emergency frequency that continuously monitors the communications of every nearby vessel, as well as rescue coordination centers and coast stations, just conked out. As quick as if someone flipped a switch.

How these incidents tie together is unknown. Perhaps they don't. No one knows if they are related to the circumstances of the accident. In any case, the odd coincidences fit the profile of events that would be written up and sealed in the NSA archives.

Another suggestion is that the NSA was monitoring Gregg Bemis on the *One Eagle*, or received SIGINT from Sweden or Finland about the dive. Maybe the NSA was simply curious given Swedish resistance to the dive. But U.S. law prohibits the NSA from deliberately collecting data on U.S. citizens without a warrant based on foreign intelligence requirements.[4]

Moreover, Swedish officials had been invited on board the *One Eagle*, journalists went along for the ride, the ship's communications were on public airwaves and the dive results were released through the media and put on the Internet. The entire dive was open and therefore the NSA had no reason to tie up resources and approach the legal limits of its authority by eavesdropping on the *One Eagle*.

The NSA listens to thousands of ship and shore communications every hour, but not every one of those intercepts are worthy of being written up. In order to be selected from the glut of competing information, formalized on paper and sent up the chain of command, the substance of what the NSA overheard very likely held intelligence value.

*   *   *

Sweden is a remarkably open society. Executive branch politicians mingle with everyone else in Stockholm. Brochures detailing parliamentarians' salaries and travel allowances are free for visitors in the lobby of the parliament building. Swedish citizens are allowed to go through a politician's mail. Sweden's information disclosure laws are perhaps the most liberal in Europe.

But the demystification of the government has limits, something made evident by the intrigue surrounding the *Estonia*. Atypical incidents inside the governing body support the claim that national security concerns underpin the *Estonia* investigation, and that government answers are actually strategic falsehoods.

Mona Sahlin, with ultimate authority for the disaster when she was Sweden's transport minister from 1998-2002, has been a controversial figure. According to Erik Schmill, a Paris-based lawyer who represents families of Estonia victims, Sahlin did something at once both secretive and revealing. After the public announcement that legal action filed by a few families of *Estonia* ferry victims would be heard by a judge in France, Sahlin called the judge. She wanted to privately discuss the case *before* it was presented to him. When Schmill found out about Sahlin's request, he was floored. "They don't do that even in Third World countries," Schmill said.[5]

Inside the machinery of parliament, stranger events have unfolded. Lars Angstrom, a representative of the minority Green Party who has studied the disaster and the critic's views, tried unsuccessfully to launch a parliamentary motion to reopen the investigation. He was not asking for a diving expedition, but a critical administrative review. In other words, listening to the critics, finding out what bothers them, then giving some documents another look and answering questions--customary government tasks.

He rallied others to support the motion. In particular, Angstrom recalls discussing the ambiguities and flaws in the *Estonia* investigation with a member of Sweden's Center Party, Ange Hansson, who listened attentively with an objective ear and pledged his support. But one day

Hansson met with Transport Minister Sahlin and the next day he reversed his position.

"The only way to get someone to give up a personal standpoint is if some important people tell you that this matter has to do with the safety of the nation, that it's very important for the security of Sweden not to dig into it," Angstrom said. "That's one of the few arguments that can change a person's view."

For 18 months, Angstrom tried to get the Swedish Parliament to vote on a motion to re-examine the disaster. In May 2002, the motion was finally included in a state budgetary debate--a maneuver that turned it into a peripheral issue. "[Parliament] didn't argue, they just said there will be no new investigation," Angstrom said. "Usually you refer to earlier decisions or some arguments. I found it disturbing."

Angstrom doesn't necessarily see a political whitewash or cover-up, but more of a widespread moral inertia. Swedish politicians have extraordinary difficulty accepting the idea that the authorities are incompetent or deceiving.

The view of an unflawed society persists, despite precedents that shatter it. Sweden has in the past repeated innocuous explanations for catastrophes that turned out to be lies. In 1952, a Swedish DC-3 transport plane was shot down by the Soviets over international waters in the Baltic Sea. The Swedish government insisted for 40 years the plane was on a routine training mission. After the U.S.S.R. fell, consistent pressure from the crewman's relatives resulted in the truth: The plane from neutral Sweden had been spying on the Soviet Union for NATO. The facts were kept quiet for nearly half a century to prevent perceived damage to Sweden's national security.

The 1986 street murder of Olaf Palme, the prime minister who helped build the modern Swedish state, has never been solved. But the investigation, marred by secrecy and scandal, indicates powerful forces within the country have influenced its course.

Sweden and the U.S.S.R., and later Russia, also share a rich history of espionage scandals that have never been closely scrutinized. There could very well be individuals in or retired from Swedish state institutions intent on concealing treasonous activity of the past. The blackmail potential against these individuals may be one reason why information on the ferry sinking remains blocked.

For Angstrom, the ferry disaster has a close parallel. In 1983, he was chairman of the Swedish Peace and Arbitration Society (SPAS), which obtained secret documents concerning Bofors Weapon Systems AB, a major Swedish armaments producer now owned by the U.S. company United Defense.

The documents showed that Bofors was involved in, among other things, paying kickbacks to secure a $1.3 billion India arms deal. Angstrom and his SPAS colleagues confronted officialdom with the evidence, but nothing happened.

"People told us this can't be true, your peace organization is out on thin ice, these respectable people and companies could not have done this, and that was also the opinion from the media," Angstrom recalled.

After continuous pressure, five years later in 1989 the three highest directors in Bofors were sentenced for smuggling arms.

> "I don't believe that people in parliament knew anything about [the kickbacks]," Angstrom said. "They were honest when they said this could not have happened. This situation was so unusual, society and the justice system were not used to these things occurring in Sweden. I have the same feeling with the *Estonia* disaster. I am convinced that there is something very wrong."[6]

Equally discomfited was Tom Heyman, a retired politician from the Moderate Party. Heyman knew something about ships and the sea. He trained as a master mariner and served on sea-going vessels before he entered politics. Heyman also supported an *Estonia* re-examination. He recalled discussing a draft motion in Parliament. "The chairman in the Social Democrat committee was more or less frightened," Heyman said. "She put the issue on the shelf."

In 2001, just after the *One Eagle* expedition, Heyman found himself on a committee with responsibility for a new motion which, if passed by his committee, would obligate the government to reopen the *Estonia* investigation. In a special meeting with committee members and his party leader, Heyman showed a presentation highlighting the flaws in the investigation. Pledges of support from enough key parliamentarians constituted a majority, and he was sure the motion would pass.

When the vote approached, Heyman's party leader gave all members a direct order not to vote in line with Heyman. "They were prohibited from following their own ideas and it was also said to me, `Do you really have to be present the day of the vote? Can you stay away?'"

The motion was voted down.

More telling, the vote was not split along party lines. "[I'd] been in parliament 14 years and never experienced anything like it. It was obvious there was a main interest this should not happen," Heyman said. "I don't know why the *Estonia* sank, but I'm quite sure it didn't happen like the report said. That is a forgery from the start to the end. Everybody was trying to protect their own interests as best as they could."[7]

Clumsily pulling the national security veil over a transport mishap suggests that full disclosure could send trouble rippling through other states, and one guess would be Russia.

During Russia's traumatic and highly vulnerable period in the 1990s, U.S. and European governments in repeated instances went out of their way to avoid even the subtlest public criticisms, tiptoeing around dangerous blunders that resulted from a state losing internal cohesion.

After the narrowly-averted Russian nuclear launch on the East Coast of the U.S. in 1995, the incident was barely acknowledged by Western governments. No one wanted to undermine confidence in Yeltsin, who seemed to be attempting to democratize Russia. Likewise, in 1994, pilots in a Finnair passenger jet at 30,000 feet near Minsk saw what they thought was a missile fly in front of them, prompting a classified investigation by the Finnish Defense staff. Due to the "sensitivity of the event," it was hushed up until 2003.[8]

The *Estonia* ferry disaster is simply part of the same pattern.

* * *

The notion that the Final Report, despite its bias and incomplete findings, is nevertheless the definitive word on Europe's worst peacetime ship disaster in the 20th century, is a particularly elastic and comforting one. It permits everyone to shrug off reality with an all-embracing reference to specialist engineering matters related to the bow visor.

No knowledgeable central authority in Sweden or anywhere else is available to give satisfactory explanations to questions related to the *Estonia* catastrophe. No one is around to discuss the omissions in the investigation's findings. No mainstream Swedish media outlet is keeping up pressure for government accountability. The JAIC has long disbanded. The principal authorities from 1994 have refused to talk.

Public discontent over the state's mishandling of the catastrophe did force Stockholm to set up an *Estonia* database at the Board of Psychological Defense, which, among other things, is the home of government crisis public relations. The BPD provides "advice and guidance regarding mass media's . . . capacity for dealing with critical strains on society in peacetime." In other words, they put a positive spin on issues of public concern.

The BPD's database or "Factbank," as it is called, has been promoted as the Swedish state's ultimate gesture to ensure accessibility, and by implication accountability, to all documents related to the *Estonia* disaster. That is not the case at all.

The Factbank merely consolidates public material into one place. Some research that is critical of the official findings will not be included. Other documents were excluded because they're classified secret by the Swedish state. The people at the BPD are not central authorities well-versed in the intricacies of the catastrophe and the unaddressed issues in the Final Report. They are more like custodians of the material.

The BPD invites the public to view documents and photographs about the *Estonia* ferry catastrophe that have been available all along.

The Factbank appears to be Sweden's endgame. It represents the discharge of responsibility from the Ministry of Transport to the BPD. The BPD will direct *Estonia* inquiries to the Factbank. The Factbank does not contain answers to what's bothering people, in effect sending critics back to the Ministry. It's a nice taut circle. It wears people down.

The policy of evasion has worked well to distance and defang criticism, and prolong the search for the truth.

By comparison, the amount and detail of information available on the World Trade Center attacks in September 2001 is voluminous and growing every day. The 9-11 commission turned out an exhaustive report, public debate continues in the media, and the finest details of government explanations are relentlessly questioned.

The ferry catastrophe had an enormous impact on small Estonia. But instead of openness and a search for truth in the aftermath, Swedish authorities reined in information, locked up the vessel and chafed at the suggestion of debate. The message to Estonia is accept secrecy and leave official words unchallenged. This propagation of Soviet values has arguably had a negative effect on Estonian media and institutions, which seemed to move from one culture based on deception into another.

CONCLUSION: A WORK IN PROGRESS 271

* * *

The denouement of the *Estonia* ferry disaster has yet to unfold. It is a work in progress. Conclusive proof, the final word on the calamity, sits 38 kilometers off the coast of Finland at the shallow depth of 50-80 meters. The truth gets closer in direct proportion to proximity to the wreck.

An independent research mission to the sunken vessel would unmask the whole story. Without it, all that can be done is to roughly sketch the contours, not fill in the content.

Critics must be careful not to transform possibilities and probabilities into certainties. All facts are not at hand, and corrections and clarifications to the record will come. Any conclusions drawn now would be more potential rather than actual, more intuitive rather than logical.

State authorities may release secrets decades later, when geo-political situations have matured, when the core generation involved has either passed away or retired from their government posts, when the legal action has long dried up and the legitimate criticism has cooled into historical curiosity.

In the meantime, breaks could come from other whistleblowers like the Swedish customs official who revealed something was amiss when the *Estonia* ferry was ordered to breeze through customs checks. Or maybe Estonia or Latvia could be persuaded to begin parliamentary debate on an amendment to the Gravesite Treaty that would permit a private but state-supervised expedition to sail from Tallinn or Riga. If Stockholm is incapable of establishing why the ship sank so fast, maritime investigators from other countries must be allowed to do it.

The JAIC's position is not structurally stable. Small actions could create a pivotal event that leads to a large, sudden shift in the rules--and to a reframing of the disaster. For now, however, the truth about the *M/V Estonia* remains in a governmental black hole.

Resting uncomfortably with the Kingdom of Sweden is the obligation to resolve one of the worst controversies connected to the collapse of the Soviet Union: What happened on the Baltic Sea on September 28, 1994?

Postscripts

Postscript A

The Struggle to Explain the Swift Sinking

"The *Estonia* ferry sank after water breached bow doors and sloshed along the cardeck, making the ship unstable and capsizing the vessel."

The above description, which consistently appeared in slight variations across dozens of news organizations, attempts to summarize the JAIC findings. It is misleading.

The dangerous instability of roll-on, roll-off ferries like the *Estonia* is well-known. Water runs onto the open cardeck, the ship flips on its side and floats on the trapped air inside the hull. The *Estonia* disaster produced ro-ro legislation that requires strengthening of the cardeck door and the ability to remain upright with a half meter of water on the cardeck.

But a listing or even capsized ro-ro ferry is not equivalent to a sunken ferry. The problem is, two separate events--specifically the ship floating on its side and the ship's *rapid* sinking--are wrongly linked into cause and effect. The JAIC should have asked, "The ship is on its side, now how did it get to the bottom so fast?"

Instead, the public got glib statements. "It is clear to every sailor that once water gets onto the cardeck the ship will inevitably go down, and fast," said the head of the JAIC in 1996, Estonian Uno Laur.[1]

Laur, who threw the Final Report at any critical voice, gives no ground to any dissenters.

Behind closed doors, however, the ferry's sudden drop to the bottom confounded commission members. Bengt Schager, a Swedish maritime psychologist and former member of the JAIC who resigned in frustration in 1997, spoke about concealed disagreements:

> "I noticed the stability people in the JAIC seemed to be more certain in 1994 and 1995 than they were in 1997," Schager said. "They were more and more uncertain on the scenario. And I put that on the table, I told them, 'You're not so certain about this chain of events... They were in disagreement in closed rooms [on stability issues]. We did not understand how a ship can sink in 35 minutes. That was mysterious for everyone and it's still unexplained."[2]

Indeed, the JAIC didn't know how to handle the *Estonia's* sinking phase. To say the Final Report glosses over it is understatement. In the 228-page report, only a few paragraphs allude to the swift sinking and conclude: "When windows on the accommodation decks were broken by wave forces, subsequent sinking was inevitable..."[3]

The "broken window theory" is often brought up informally as a rational explanation for flash flooding of the vessel. The theory asserts that when the ship flipped on its side, cabin windows and the large wall windows in the rear accommodation deck broke on impact. With windows gone, the enormous ship was engulfed by seawater in minutes.

Of course, the image is striking. But there's no evidence or even the JAIC's trademark statistical analysis to support it. Conspicuously missing is the Nordic diligence that produced stability calculations, material strengths, significant wave heights and other recondite data that filled a Final Report and two masonry brick-size supplemental reports. The JAIC simply left it at that--broken windows.

No analysis on the type of glass installed on the *Estonia* was conducted. Glass strength is a serious design consideration for a passenger ferry due to safety and comfort concerns. Ferry glass must withstand the fierce wind, rain or hailstorms of the Baltic Sea as well as the acute impact from the drunken tourist who falls against the glass doors and is able to walk away rubbing his head. No ferry company wants to invite lawsuits.

The *Estonia* did not have ordinary plate glass windows. Glass installed on ferries varies by strength rating. Heat-treated, toughened glass, for example, crumbles on forceful impact. Laminated glass shatters but does not break. Windows on ferries are at minimum double-paned, providing an added barrier from the sea.

Most cabin windows on the front half of the *Estonia* are about as big as a person's head. Even if waves broke them all, the openings would hardly be big enough to flood a ship as long as the Statue of Liberty is tall.[4]

Moreover, the assumption that the larger wall-size windows aft acted as "critical openings" for a torrent of seawater is undermined by the available facts. Most windows stayed intact when the wreck was drifting and taking on water. The evidence is from the Rockwater dive on December 4-10, 1994, when divers were forced to break windows with hammers and other tools. Hard physical work was required to make the openings big enough to fit a diver's body through. The description in the dive survey report shows just how few large slots the ferry had:

> "The windows aft on decks [4, 5 and 6] were large enough to allow safe access for divers to enter the vessel when broken. This was achieved by hammering a large marlin spike into the corner of the selected window in order to shatter the glass. The glass could then be removed using a hammer. . .In addition, the forward windows on Decks 4,5,6 had to be smashed and extended by oxy-arc cutting to allow divers access."[5]

Apparently the dive report, written by men who actually walked into the shipwreck, was rejected by the JAIC. The Final Report states: "The first potential openings to be submerged were the aft windows on deck 4 [when the ship was listing 40 degrees] . . . Waves with considerable impact energy would have pounded against these windows earlier. It is unlikely that the windows, although of heavy construction, withstood such impact forces."[6]

Unlikely, maybe. But according to the official dive report, they did indeed endure the impact forces.

There is one more loud detail concerning the broken window theory. The Final Report maintains that the ferry's large glass backdoors aft burst open when the ship was listing 40 degrees. If that were true, debris must have spilled out--especially since the ship had sunk stern first. All kinds of loose material from the officers' dining area on Deck 7 and the cafeteria on Deck 5, both located in the stern area, should be loosely dispersed on the nearby seafloor. Ashtrays, silverware, broken glass, plates, chairs and tables are a short list of cafeteria paraphernalia.

Moreover, the stern hit the bottom with a thud, then the bow fell forward and the ship went under. The thud of the 16,000 ton ship on the bottom would jar lose anything not nailed down--an effect analogous to a pipe smoker who taps his pipe on cement to free spent tobacco.

Therefore, a major debris accumulation from Deck 5 and Deck 7 should be roughly 1.5-- 1.8 kilometers WSW of the wreck--where the JAIC states that the ferry developed a 40 degree list and waves smashed the large rear windows (see Kalmar Chart, Appendix II). A second debris field should be at the wreck's stern, which hit bottom first.

However, sonar photos from the Finnish JAIC suggest only one major debris field at 300-500 meters WSW of the wreck. Emphasis on the word "suggest" because sonar photographs can be easily misinterpreted, even by experts, and the debris field was left unexamined by divers.

If the sonar reading 300-500 meters WSW of the *Estonia* is indeed from rear dining area debris, then the back windows that had been blamed for the fast water ingress were actually very late in breaking open. Thus these large windows aft could not have been a critical factor in the swift intake of water.[7]

Some windows probably broke *after* the ferry had filled up with seawater and descended down to the seafloor, where water pressure intensified with depth and popped them out.

The *Estonia's* windows weren't flimsy, the broken window theory was. The JAIC soon abandoned it. But people continued to ask uncomfortable questions about the fast sinking. The supposedly undamaged ferry, after all, sank faster than the torpedoed *Wilhelm Gustloff* and almost as fast as the torpedoed *Lusitania*.

Officials eventually wheeled out the "ventilator theory."

The theory proposes that ventilator pipes extending from the car-deck level down to the decks below acted as ingress tubes for the seawater, flooding the lower decks quickly.

If such a theory were true, it could potentially account for both the water belowdecks cited by escaping passengers before the list, as well as the rapidity of the sinking. Yet the JAIC devoted a whole three sentences to it: "Ventilation ducts to the car deck were installed at Deck 4 level. According to testimony from a member of the alternate crew the ducts were normally closed. The ducts may however, have opened during flooding."[8]

That is all the analysis devoted to a potentially critical piece of the puzzle. Moreover, during the official dive to wreck, no one instructed divers to even shine a light at the ventilator shafts. The divers accessed the cardeck as well as accommodation Decks 4, 5, 6. If the tubes had been videotaped in the open position, the ventilator theory would have strengthened the JAIC's final conclusions and diminished support for the idea of a hole in the hull.

The JAIC's apparent disregard of the ventilator theory didn't stop the Swedish government from proposing it again. In 2002, Sweden's Board of Psychological Defense was assigned the task of converting disbelievers in the Final Report.

The Board, citing a study outsourced to Swedish engineers, claims open ventilator pipes on Deck 4 acted as a conduit for water to fall belowdecks and flash food the ship. The theory was formally presented, accompanied by the obligatory graphs and arcane calculations, which alienate the general public but give an air of seriousness to the effort.

A basic error taints the theory--the ventilators were not of sufficient volume to flood the ship quickly. According to Swedish journalist Knut Carlqvist, the BPD study misrepresents the size of the shafts and the possibility of water intake through those shafts. Carlqvist used data from the Board's report that stated each shaft measured an area of 0.25-0.30 square meters. Several ventilator shaft openings, each about the size of a book, cannot explain the rapid intake of thousands of tons of water in a few minutes.[9]

First broken windows, then ventilator pipes. As of this writing, the Swedish government has launched another effort into explaining why the ship sank so fast. To borrow a phrase the former head of the JAIC, Uno Laur: The public has heard every government explanation for the *Estonia's* fast sinking except for the UFO version.[10]

Cardeck Ramp

The *Estonia* ferry's cardeck sats just above the waterline. When the ship was docked with visor up, the vehicle ramp located at the front of the ferry came down like a castle drawbridge and cars and trucks drove onboard across a fairly level plane. When the ramp was down, the opening was 5.5 meters wide by 5 meters high (27.5 square meters).

Passengers drove their cars into the open mouth of the ferry and a crew member guided the driver to a parking space. The driver then pulled the parking brake, probably removed the stereo system and put it in the trunk, and then set the car alarm before walking to his cabin. Trucks also frequently rode on the *Estonia* and they came from all over the region, carrying cargo across the Baltic Sea to Europe.

When all vehicles were loaded, the ramp would lift and seal the opening. Then the second barrier, the bow visor, descends and locks.

The cardeck by necessity must have precise design considerations. With trucks and cars from many countries parked on the deck of every voyage, some are sure to have gas or oil leakage or liquid seeping from cargo. Therefore, the cardeck must be designed to accommodate leaks and prevent any fluids from trickling down to the passenger cabins directly below. Ship designers understand that seeping liquids could potentially cause fire, hazardous fumes or cosmetic damage to cars or cargo.

No toilets, sinks or windows were on the cardeck. People weren't allowed to loiter on the cardeck or visit during the voyage. The only openings were the elevators and stairwell doors inside the central casing, which is encircled by a 100mm high curb. The curb's purpose was to block leaking gas, oil--or seawater--from flowing downstairs. Stairwell doors had an additional 130mm raised partition, providing an extended barrier. Stray liquids would be forced to flow out the scuppers--small openings dotting the edges of the cardeck walls that drain into the sea.

Stairwell doors opened and closed hydraulically. Push the button and after a short delay, the door hisses open. They weren't watertight, but served as barriers nonetheless.

In summary, the cardeck can be thought of as an open deck where any liquid would have to accumulate more than 230 millimeters (nine inches) before it could seep out the central casing doors and flow down the stairs.

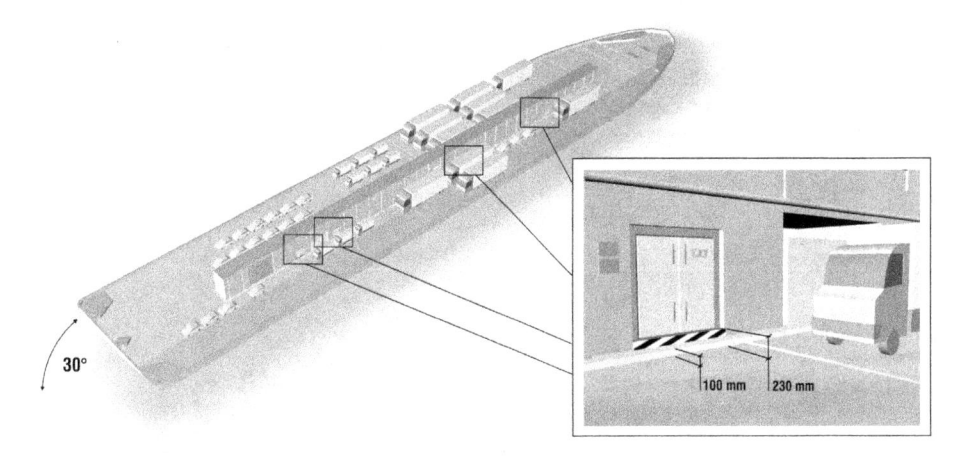

Cardeck. As the ship lists progressively starboard, water has a proportionally higher distance to go in order to reach the doors of the central casing and seep belowdecks. The ship will roll over before that can happen.

INSET: Additional water barriers. A 100mm (4 inch) curb around the central casing; doors had an additional sill for a total of 230mm (9 inches). Passengers had to step over the partition to enter the stairwell.

282 THE HOLE

The *Estonia* ferry also had an unusual design. When the cardeck ramp closed, the top of it extended about two meters into a housing that was connected to the bow visor. Therefore, the reasoning goes, when the bow visor tore off, it naturally yanked open the ramp.

The ramp was cited as a key element in the sinking. The *Estonia* didn't flip on its side because the visor came off. It did so, the JAIC claimed, because the ramp was pulled wide open by the falling visor, opening the cardeck to the sea. An independent report by certification organization Norske Veritas also cited the open ramp as the main cause of the disaster.[11]

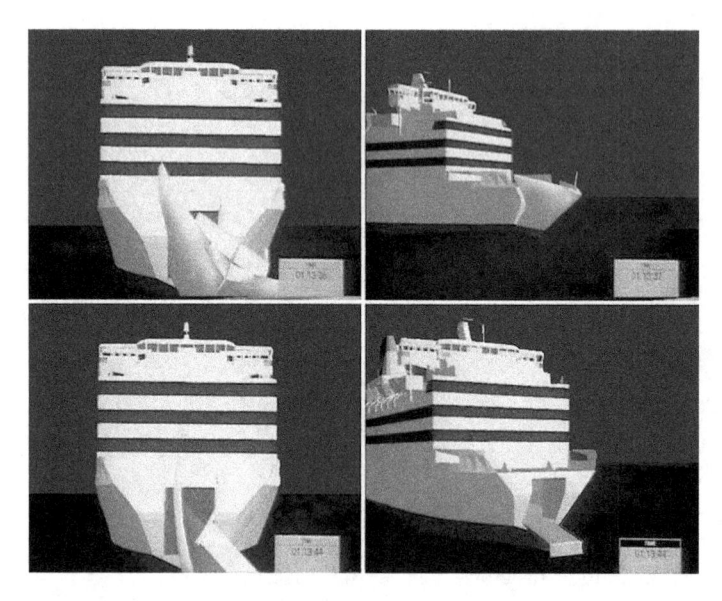

The JAIC detachment process, as seen in this clip from the commission's animation, depends on the ramp being ripped wide open.

To repeat the JAIC's conclusion in the Final Report: The visor fell off, pulling the ramp open; water flooded the cardeck and the ferry sank. Over time, detach-and-sink became conventional wisdom. But for several reasons the scenario is not an accurate rendering of the fatal chain of events. One concerns the ramp. Apparently, it was never fully open.

The cardeck ramp was never proven to be open, only stated so. Divers found the ramp in a closed position slightly *ajar*--less than one meter-- at the top portside. Because the shipwreck rests nearly upside down, the JAIC has claimed that gravity closed the ramp. No attempts were made to prove that assumption. Why the JAIC did not instruct the Rockwater divers to conclusively resolve the ramp question is unknown. Divers could have run a wire cable from the surface platform to the ramp, then start reeling the cable in to determine freedom of movement. Such a quick and easy operation would have bolstered--or shattered--the JAIC's conclusions.[12]

Another inconsistency with the open ramp idea comes from the loading. On the night of the accident, the cardeck was crammed with cars and trucks. It was a tight fit with only about 10 centimeters (4 inches) between vehicles. The cardeck was a parking lot. Securing vehicles with straps that fasten to D-links bolted to the floor proved too difficult under the crowded conditions. Instead, drivers were told to put their cars in gear and pull the handbrake tight. For large trucks, crewmembers shoved wooden wedge blocks between the wheels and the floor.[13]

The last vehicles on board, according to official the cargo list, were two passenger cars. When the ramp lifted and closed, the rear bumpers of the latecomer's cars were an arm's length away from it.

The *Estonia* then sailed out of Tallinn with a 0.5 degree stern trim. As it sailed, water accumulated in the visor, reducing trim from stern until it became bow heavy, that is, the front of the ship sat slightly lower in the water than the rear.[14]

Following this logic, if the bow visor fell off and pulled open the cardeck ramp, creating a 27.5 square meter opening, violent waves would have roared into the ship as the ferry sailed at 15 knots. Thousands of tons of crashing water in a confined space create a lifting effect. The last two loaded cars were in gear with parking brakes pulled tight. But that resistance would be no match for the immense force of the sea pulsing through a 27.5 square meter opening.

Waves couldn't push the two cars backward; the cardeck was packed too tight. But if the ramp was indeed open, nothing prevented the cars from tumbling out the opening. In a matter of seconds, the passenger cars that were parked closest to the cardeck ramp would have been thrown into the sea. During the lengthy and extensive search for the bow visor in the casualty area, no cars were found at the bottom of the Baltic, according to the JAIC.

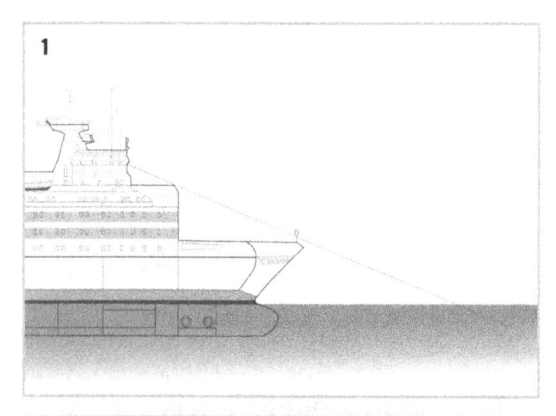

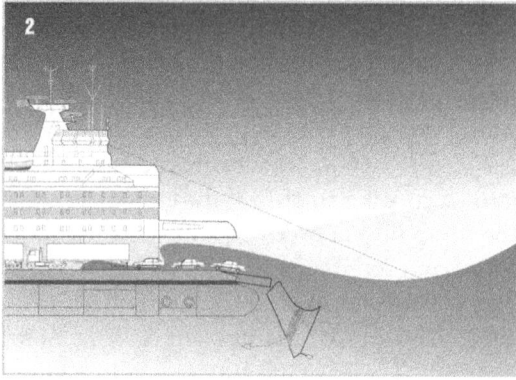

1. In a normal situation, bridge officers can see the blue lamp on top the visor.

2. The Final Report's Kalmar Chart (see Appendix II) shows that the bow visor detached at 01:14, pulling open the cardeck ramp while the ferry continued sailing at 8 knots for six minutes. If true, bridge officers would have instantly seen the blue lamp missing. Light from the cardeck would illuminate the sea. Cars would have tumbled out. Survivors below the cardeck would have heard the rumble of waves washing in overhead. None of these events happened.

More reason to discredit the "visor off, ramp open, ship down" concept comes from the bow visor itself, which was recovered from the sea in November 1994. From its condition, inferences can be drawn.

The starboard side actuator arm is still attached and extended telescopically. The visor is dented on the front, slightly starboard side of the center.

"Vertical orientation of the damage on the visor front side indicates that the ship was approximately upright when the visor fell off," according to Tuomo Karppinen, a Finnish member of the JAIC. "The position of the extensive dent slightly starboard of the centerline indicates that the visor was on the port side when it collided with the bulbous bow..."[15]

Yet the explanation seems counterintuitive. Wind and waves came from portside. The 60-ton chunk of steel would have to jump against those natural forces--while still secured by the starboard side actuator arm.

A possible alternative chain of events could begin with the visor's portside actuator arm breaking. The visor for a time stayed connected to the ship by the starboard actuator. The ferry's engines stopped. The vessel lay on its side, drifting. Battered by waves, secured by only one arm, twisting and rending at the attachment joint, the visor eventually broke off at a late stage in the sinking.

Corroborating evidence for the late-stage detachment comes from several survivors. While standing on the capsized ship, they saw what appeared to be the visor arm swinging.[16]

In other words, the visor fell off *after* the list; it did not fall off and then cause the list, as the JAIC said.

If the visor fell off at a late stage, then the ramp was never wide open and seawater couldn't rush in. Restricted seawater inflow means the ferry would take far longer than 35 minutes to fill and sink.

Instead of a 27.5 square meter hole, which would be the JAIC's wide open ramp, a 2.5 square meter hole--a generous estimate of the *ajar* ramp--slows the fill by a factor of ten. It's comic to suggest a ferry the size of 1.5 football fields could sink in 35 minutes due to a hole the size of a bedroom window.

To summarize, the cardeck ramp was not fully open, as the JAIC asserted. It was pried open less than a meter, as evidence shows. No one has produced any proof that the cardeck ramp was fully open, although the Final Report assumes it to be fact and a government-commissioned computer animation shows the ramp like a wide-open drawbridge.[17]

The assumption is not a minor imperfection, but a fundamental flaw. The *Estonia*, according to the JAIC, suffered no breach of hull integrity. And as Björkman has emphasized, the ship also had 18,000 cubic meters of air below the cardeck that it floats on in a normal situation. Then why didn't the ferry float on its side? Why did it flash flood and sink in 35 minutes when there were no sizeable openings? How is that possible?

Only through the logic of the hole.

Water Below

Crew testimonies about the final course of events should be read with skepticism. Crewmembers have an innate feel for the ship, the sea and rough water sailing, in principle making their descriptions of events valuable to the investigation. But they were, at the end of the day, employees of the state.

Estline, the joint venture company that ran the ferry, was half-owned by ESCO, the Estonian state-owned shipping company. Crew statements, therefore, had to be carefully constructed in order to prevent damage to the Estonian state through legal action or national disgrace. The state cannot be expected to act against its own self-interest.

In such cases, the truth undergoes a careful filtration process. The method was psychological pressure, which shaped crew statements.

Henrik Sillaste, the system engineer who barely escaped the rotating ship by scurrying 23 meters up an escape ladder inside the funnel, told the German investigators that all crew survivors were threatened by ESCO with quick dismissal "if they said anything against ESCO's interests to commission members, journalists or other interested parties and this had scared all of the crew survivors considerably."[18]

Crewmembers were also quizzed several times. Often crucial elements of their stories differed in each interview and revised statements were left unchallenged. Silver Linde, the A.B. Seaman on watch, changed core details of his story several times. He was the commission's star witness.

Bias, conflicts of interest and the molding of crew testimonies went unrecognized by the JAIC. But the commission plowed ahead and used the crew statements as anchors for the official detach-and-sink explanation.

Less contaminated is passenger testimony. They were people from various countries and backgrounds, largely unacquainted with each other and with no obligations to the powerful interests involved in the disaster. Broad patterns derived from passenger affidavits are therefore impartial compared to what crew members said.

Eyewitness accounts, while not always precise or indicative of the cause of an accident, still yield clues. Eyewitness evidence is the basis for the U.S. justice system.

But the full text from more than 100 signed passenger statements are excluded from the Final Report. Instead, the JAIC bled the passenger testimonies, diminishing their importance. They are printed as anonymous summaries. No one compared them to find general patterns. Vital information was sometimes left out.[19]

The unsystematic and unprofessional interviewing methods imposed on survivors immediately following the accident made everything murkier. Ambiguous words, ripe with multiple meanings, were left unclarified. Survivors were sometimes questioned in a leading manner. Police interviewed a number of survivors. Police are trained more for interrogation than for sensitively drawing out unbiased accounts from traumatized people.

Additionally, a person's recollections distort over time, shaped by discussions, myths, fears and the media. Sometimes people remember something they never saw.

For these reasons, the fairest way to use testimony to support a view is to confine statements to the first interview just after the accident and include only passengers, no crew. Moreover, analysis is limited to those on Deck 1 below the cardeck, where the accentuated noises warned passengers of imminent danger earlier than those on the top decks.

Deck 1

Deck 1 is below the waterline, near the bottom of the ferry. A passenger actually sleeps under the water. Deck 1 rooms are cheap because they are noisy. The hull can amplify the wave and engine noises, making sleep uncomfortable. The enhanced sensory experience helped save the lives of 21 passengers.

Taken as a whole, these basement passengers have a story to tell: Water had been on Deck 1 before the ship listed. It did not come from above.

Eight Deck 1 survivors saw water before bolting up the stairs. Nine reported running up the stairs and seeing water leaking out the cardeck doors. Five did not mention water at all--neither confirmation nor denial. No one reported water flowing down the stairs.[20]

The following are extracts from the German Group of Experts Report:[21]

1. Carl-Erik Reintamm in cabin 1094 "left his cabin at once and

found a lot of water in the alleyway [corridor]; when he passed the shower/WC area on his way into the stairway, he saw water about 0.4 m high which was rushing along the longitudinal wall with speed."

2. Carl Övberg in cabin 1049 saw water under great pressure streaming out of two goosenecks next to the cabin wall. He also saw water penetrating the door forward of these goosenecks in the 3rd compartment which belonged to a cleaning room and saw water running over the floor.

3. Holger Wachtmeister in cabin 1047 left his cabin when the ship heeled and noted water in the alleyway.

4. Ain-Alar Juhanson in cabin 1056: "Whilst I was asleep I heard a heavier bang which I had heard before already, but not so heavy. After that bang the vessel suddenly heeled to starboard. All 4 of us woke up, grabbed our clothes and jumped into the alleyway, where we noted water."

5. Antti Arak, also in cabin 1056. "At first I heard screaming and then I saw water running in the alleyway . . . "

6. Yasmina Weidinger and Daniel Svensson in cabin 1027. She heard a loud noise and the vessel heeled. Her cabinmate Daniel shouted that they had to get out.
When Weidinger jumped out of her cabin door, she saw water in the alleyway which trickled from somewhere. When Daniel Svensson stepped out of the cabin, he shouted that "there was water in the alleyway."
Outside the cabin, Weidinger was able to lean against a wall and pull up her jeans when she saw water penetrating the floor in front of the cabin.

7. Jaan Stern in cabin 1120. Stern saw water in his cabin and ran upstairs.

8. Taavi Raba, cabin 1070, was in bed half asleep and became alarmed when the vessel did not roll evenly any more and sud-

denly heeled to starboard so hard that he fell against the wall. He had to jump through a water wall to reach the stairway leading from first deck upwards.

Eight people who saw water where it shouldn't be. No one reported water flowing downstairs. If water didn't flow down from the cardeck, then how did it get on the first deck?

The Final Report breezed over these crucial recollections. Two unnamed passengers, it reports, saw water on the Deck 1. One saw "A thin trickle of water on the floor" and one "saw water coming into his cabin."[22]

The Final Report said two. Signed affidavits show eight. Six testimonies and their meaningful implications have been erased from the historical record.

In the Final Report, the survivor's testimony section begins with a disclaimer:

> "Some details deviate from what the witnesses actually stated. The commission has edited some detailed statements in order not to confuse the reader in cases where witnesses have made obvious mistakes, e.g., regarding deck numbers or other locations on the vessel. Statements concerning timing, estimations of list as well as quotations are, however, at all times written as stated."[23]

A careful reading of the paragraph reveals that the only parts of testimonies "written as stated" are those with numbers--timing and list estimation--or the lifting of an exact quote, which was done selectively. There are no rules that require using all *relevant* quotations. In other words, if a passenger did speak about water, the comment may not be included at all.

Likewise, if a survivor's quotation was paraphrased--not lifted as a quote but restated by the JAIC authors--no rules apply. This clause effectively permits the distortion of testimony.

The Leaky Roof Theory

Nearly five years after the *Estonia* sank, Tuomo Karppinen, a member of the Finnish side of the JAIC, made a thoughtful effort to address, *inter alia*, an escalating debate about survivors who saw water below the cardeck just before or after the big list. In two articles published in *The Naval Architect* magazine, Karppinen's analysis of the contentious issue went well beyond anything that the commission had done on the topic.[24]

But in his attempts to explain water on Deck 1, Karppinen makes a puzzling statement in light of the witness statements: "Testimonies of all 20 [sic] surviving passengers from the passenger compartment on deck 1 below the cardeck, give no support for flooding to have occurred under the cardeck."[25]

For survivors, water on Deck 1 was not a matter of speculation but an intimate, harrowing reality. Karppinen inexplicably contradicts their testimonies.

Informally, others have tried to explain away the Deck 1 witnesses with the leaky roof theory. In this view, any water seen on Deck 1 leaked from above, specifically, through the cardeck elevator shafts.

Potentially, water could pour down through the central casing lifts or stairwells. But the ferry departed Tallinn with a 1-3 degree starboard side list. Loose water would roll along the starboard side wall and accumulate--but never reach a level high enough to spill down the central casing. Physical laws are at work; the ferry tilts further to starboard in direct proportion to the weight of entering seawater. The vessel reaches a tipping point and capsizes.[26]

Water couldn't reach the central casing because the ship would first flip over, following the Björkman scenario (see illustration in Chapter 3).

However, the main flaw in Karppinen's argument is framing water ingress as an either/or proposition. Either water was on the cardeck or it was below the waterline. The answer is more complex, involving water inflow in both places.

Water indeed sloshed around on the starboard side of the cardeck as it continually sprayed in at the sides of the ramp. The cardeck's open space and the *Estonia's* chronic starboard list ensured seawater collected. Survivor statements do not cumulatively contradict that. They do, however, articulate the presence of water apparently from a second breach belowdecks.

The possible conclusion would be seawater spraying onto the cardeck and gushing through a hole belowdecks. Two unsealed areas. One at the bow visor and one somewhere below, perhaps the sauna compartment, indicating a hull breach.

As noted in the preface of this book, only when this particular "double breach scenario" was plugged into the FREDYN ship stability prediction software did the simulated Estonia ferry model sink as described by the majority of survivors.

Postscript B

Historical Spotlight

Stability calculations and model testing can provide useful but usually oversimplified explanations for the behavior of a ship going down. Like avalanche prediction or the interpretation of body language, they remain inexact sciences. Too many assumptions must be made and the results may vary depending on who does the interpreting. When convoluted events create inconsistent findings, authorities turn to history for a benchmark.

Historical facts are on solid ground. Maritime archives provide evidence about the way ships sink that is the closest to empirical evidence as possible. And the records show that every ship roughly comparable in size to the *Estonia* that dropped to the bottom in less than one hour had been holed.

Unfortunately, no centralized database containing detailed information on all reported ship sinkings exists. But organizations and libraries maintain enough records to establish the uncanny fact that the *Estonia* ferry defied all established patterns of sinking ships in recorded maritime history. This is not conjecture, it is an historical reality (see chart Chapter 3).

Historical statistics on ship disasters can be reduced to two general principles. They are self-evident, but need to be mentioned:

1. With no hull damage, stricken ships capsize and float.
2. With hull damage, they can sink in minutes.

The first principle is illustrated by the *Princess Victoria*, a ro-ro ferry with a capacity of 1,500 passengers that shuttled between Scotland and Ireland. In January 1953, a fierce gale swept across the Irish Sea and ripped open the ferry's stern doors, which were used to load cars. The cardeck flooded and the ship listed heavily to starboard. The *Princess Victoria* floated for six hours before sinking.

Another relevant ro-ro ferry was the Polish vehicle and railroad car vessel the *Jan Heweliusz*. In January 1993, it sailed the Baltic Sea in a Beaufort 12 storm, a "junior hurricane" and rolled over, resulting in 55 deaths.

The *Jan Heweliusz*'s hull had not been breached. Seawater flooded the cardeck through previously-damaged stern doors. But the Polish ferry floated upside down for more than a day.[1]

The accident followed the by now familiar pattern: water on the cardeck, instability, unrecoverable list, floating for a considerable amount of hours if not days.

Strikingly similar to the *Estonia* disaster were key aspects of the March 1987 *Herald of Free Enterprise* ferry accident. Evidence that the *Herald* followed the first general principle is inconclusive. But indications suggest that it did.

The *Herald*, also a ro-ro passenger ferry, was about half the *Estonia*'s gross tonnage. In March 1987, the ferry streamed away from port at Zeebrugge Harbor, Belgium with its bow door open. Seawater flowed onto the cardeck and in a few minutes the ferry flipped on its side, killing 193 people.

The *Herald* listed to port, the Estonia to starboard. Still, they both followed the same pattern. As the *Herald* investigation describes:

> "A large quantity of water entered G deck [the cardeck] and caused an initial lurch to port due to free surface instability which was extremely rapid and reached perhaps 30 degrees. The water collected in the port wing of the vehicle deck and the ship became stable again at a large angle of loll. Water in large quantities continued to flood through the open bow doors aperture. Thereafter the Herald capsized to port rather more slowly until eventually she was more than 90 degrees."[2]

However, the sea was shallow. The *Herald* foundered only 1.6 kilometers from Zeebrugge port in nine meters of water. Therefore, the ferry's bottom-up progression halted when the top of the rotating ship hit the sea bottom. The *Herald* rested at an angle on the seafloor, half submerged.

The relevant question is, was the *Herald* on its way to flipping completely upside down, "turning turtle," after which the vessel would float for hours or days? Was the *Herald* following the Björkman scenario?

Investigators did not examine whether the ship would have continued to rotate upside down because it was irrelevant to the accident.[3]

But the *Herald's* list-to-grounding took three-six minutes, implying a fast rotation and momentum in line with the flip-over motion depicted in the Björkman scenario. Following the logic, if the water had been deeper, the *Herald* would probably have floated upside down.[4]

General principle two makes another cogent point. Ships with torn hulls sink faster than ships with sealed hulls. Not the other way around.

The Greek ferry *Express Samina* sank in 2000, claiming more than 60 lives. The ferry's stern hit rock and the impact gouged a hole in the hull. The vessel listed and sank within 45 minutes. The *Estonia* sank faster with no breach of the hull.[5]

The *Admiral Nakhimov* was a Soviet luxury ferry. Like the *Estonia*, the ship offered bars, casinos and restaurants for pleasure cruises. Though not a ro-ro ferry, the *Nakhimov* matched the Estonia's size. It weighed almost the same at 15,280 tons and was 174 meters compared to the *Estonia's* 155 meter length. The night the *Nakhimov* sank, it carried 1,234 passengers; the *Estonia* was carrying just about 1000.

In August of 1986, the *Nakhimov* was sailing across the Black Sea from the Southern Russian port of Novorossiysk when it collided with a mammoth 50,000-ton Soviet freighter. The freighter's bulbous bow punched through the *Nakhimov* under the waterline and ripped a 90 square meter hole in the starboard side hull.

Water rushed in at an estimated 100,000 gallons per second. The ship rolled over and within 15 minutes sank to the bottom in 50 meters of water. 423 people died.[6]

The *Nakhimov* plummeted to the seafloor because the ship had openings in the hull the size of houses. The *Estonia*, with a watertight hull, took only minutes longer.

Then there's the *Wilhelm Gustloff*, a German liner. The *Gustloff*, like the *Estonia*, was a German-built passenger ship sailing in the Baltic Sea during a storm. In 1945, a Soviet submarine spotted the vessel and fired three torpedoes. With hull collapsed, the *Gustloff* listed 40 degrees starboard and after one hour, it sank.[7]

The *Gustloff* sinking underscores the crude ommission of the historical record. To accept the Final Report's conclusion is to accept, without evidence or explanation, that the *Estonia* was the first seaworthy ship in history to sink faster than a thrice-torpedoed ship: a truly miraculous feat.

Appendices

APPENDIX I: Recovery

	TWA 800	ESTONIA FERRY
Date of disaster	July 1996	September 1994
Total number of casualties	230	757 assumed
Bodies recovered from wreck	100%	0
Bodies identified from wreck	100%	0
Wreckage depth	40 meters	50-80 meters
Cost of investigation	$40 million	$3 million
Length of investigation	16 months	36 months
Number of dives to wreckage	4,600	One official dive by teams lasting 72 hours
Result	All bodies and jet recovered	757 bodies left in shipwreck

No expense or effort was spared to bring up victims of TWA Flight 800, a far more challenging task than the sealed container of the *Estonia* ferry. Relatives of *Estonia* victims wanted recovery, which was deemed possible by salvage experts and recommended by a government commission. But Sweden has categorically refused to do so.

Nationalities of passengers and crew

COUNTRY	TOTAL	RESCUED	MISSING
Belarus	1		1
Canada	1		1
Denmark	6	1	5
Estonia	347	63*	237
Finland	13	3	9
France	1		1
Germany	8	3	4
Latvia	23	6	13
Lithuania	4	1	3
Morocco	2		2
Netherlands	2	1	1
Nigeria	1		1
Norway	9	3	6
Russia	15	4	10
Sweden	552	51	461**
Ukraine	2	1	1
United Kingdom	2	1	1
Total	**989**	**138**	**757**
%	**100**	**14**	**77**

* One of the rescued died later in hospital.
** The body of one missing person was found on 17.10.1994 and that of another on 11.5.1996.
Source: Final Report

The *Estonia* ferry disaster was an international civilian transport accident. Citizens from 17 nations perished, though most victims were from Sweden and Estonia. The official death toll does not account for the more than hundred Iraqi Kurds reported to be hiding inside a truck, part of a human smuggling operation.

APPENDIX II: The Kalmar Chart

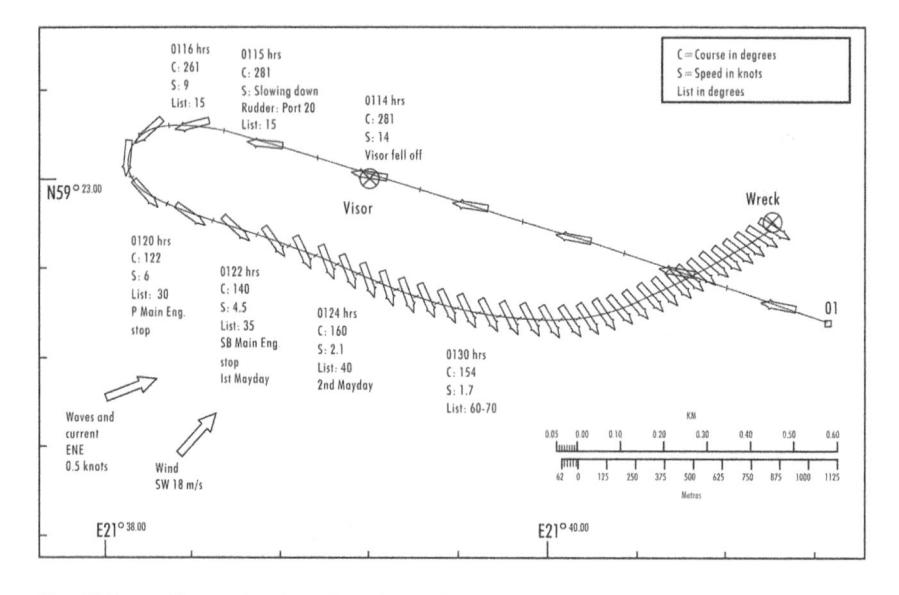

The Kalmar Chart, developed at the Kalmar Marine Academy in Sweden, renders the *Estonia's* final sequence of events according to the JAIC.

APPENDIX III: The Felix Report

The Felix Report is a disinformation document that attempts to discredit, among other things, key institutions and political and military figures in the Baltic States. No sources and no verifiable facts support the claims.

Russia was fighting a war in Chechnya when the Felix Report was released. The report's main goal was to label and condemn Chechens as the FSU's dominant criminal influence.

The following is the author's English translation of a section from the original Russian language document. The key pages concerning the Estonian state begin on page 68 of the report. The ferry disaster scenario begins on page 72.

Research Group "Felix"
International Narcotics Contraband and the Former USSR
Ivan Ivanov
Moscow, February 1995

[p.68]

. . . It is interesting that Latvian mafioso practically pay no attention to the police, who have been deliberately disorganized by the state authorities. The Ministry of Internal Affairs by a state decree dismissed the professionals from their positions (the reason--insufficient knowledge of the Latvian language). Instead, coming into law enforcement bodies are recruits who are politically appealing--people mainly from the countryside. In reality, in Latvia there is nobody to fight criminality.

Because of the dismissals, the struggle against organized crime has been left to the police, who are accused of being connected to mafia, and to the corrupted top levels of the Ministry of Internal Affairs, the Chief Prosecutor and the government. Prime Minister Maris Gailis, suspected of being connected to Chechens, had assigned himself in the autumn of 1994 the duties of the dismissed Ministry of Internal Affairs chief Girts Kristovskis. His connection to the

Chechens went unnoticed. In Riga, the Ministry of Internal Affairs has actually turned into the largest mafioso structure in the republic.

Four officials from the Ministry of Internal Affairs were recently in prison--for large scale extortion. The former Ministry of Internal Affairs chief Cevers' opinion about mafioso at the core of the Ministry of Internal Affairs of Latvia is not far from the truth.

However, Latvia, in terms of total criminalization of all institutions of authority, still falls short of Estonia, which it could compete with in this sphere if it weren't for Chechnya. According to the newspaper "Sevodnya" (18.11.94), only in 1994 and only in Ivangorod have so many weapons been detained that they could arm a whole army. The Russian-Estonian border became the most active smuggling site in terms of the number of offenses connected to the smuggling of weapons.

It is explained away by saying that the armed forces of Estonia, having bought weapons from Israel, discarded Soviet-manufactured guns, which were dumped in Russia. Another reason given is the use of Estonia as a transit hub for illicit weapons from Russia to Europe. But the arms trade is not run by individual criminals. Legal entities closely connected to the state are engaged. The people from the structure headed by the U.S. citizen, Colonel Alexander Einseln is especially involved in the mentioned field. Einseln calls himself "General" and "Commander of Estonian Defense Forces."

[p.69]

Also, members of the paramilitary armed structure "The Estonian Security Center," headed by Jaanus Rahumagi, are close to them, as are employees of the department of Juri Pihl, general director of the security police.

The income from the "weapon business" goes into both the pockets of officials and into the treasury of the republic, which in view of the available facts has turned into a mafia society. The important organizing roles in Estonian weapons smuggling are played by Ministry of Internal Affairs Chief Heiki Arike, Uno Ellen, general director of the police department and the armed nationalist group "Kaitseliit." A member of this group was until recently the known recidivist Vello Kuut, who was three times in court for larceny and once for rape.

Incidentally, Kuut's BMW automobile has a license plate reading "Estonian Defense Force," which is headed by "General" Einseln. The close "business" contacts of this retired American officer with Kuut were, as is believed, reason for a sharp strain in the relations between Einseln and Arike, which occurred immediately after a scandal involving fraud by the firm AVVO. AVVO tried to get from Bulgaria 20,000 AK-47s and two million bullets by using false documents. The deal almost held. However, at the last moment Arike did not divide something with Kuut and finally [Kuut] went to prison.

According to information from a journalist at the newspaper "Sevodnya," Alexander Kudakayev, illegal weapons trade is conducted in the republic of Estonia in a big way, supported by buying the cooperation of police. The weapons are sold in "containers" for cash to people who are identified as members of Kaitseliit. What the Kaitseliit members do with the weapons, nobody can say. To whom the Kaitseliit sold or distributed 28,000 pistols that had arrived in Estonia from Germany and Poland is not known.

However, one only needs to examine the documents of the paramilitary organization the "Tartu League" to see that this organization in the last few months purchased more than 20,000 TT pistols in various places. But in reality the League didn't buy anything, they were just recipients of the huge weapons shipments. Tartu is the largest center of illegal trade in weapons in the Baltic States.

The profitable smuggling of raw materials and illegal weapons trade means the largest Estonian mafioso do not miss an opportunity to make money, and in different ways--from drugs and financial frauds. Playing a particularly important role in these areas of criminal activity is a criminal structure led by a figure named "Lesnik," whom experts put in the same league as Pablo Escobar and Dzhokhar Dudayev.

[p.70]

The greatest accomplishment of Lesnik was that he received money in connection with the two worst scandals in the Baltic States in 1994: the sale of Soviet rubles to Dudayev and the accident of the ferry "Estonia." The man with the most complete information on these events was Igor Kristapovich, assistant general director of the customs department of the Republic. Earlier he was one of the experts in the struggle against smuggling while he was serving in the Estonian KGB during Soviet Times.

Kristapovich, having been involved in such situations and having old connections, had an opportunity to carry out wiretapping of private telephone negotiations conducted by Estonian mafioso. He collected information and documents that were very dangerous for Lesnik, and also dangerous for one more chief Estonian criminal, a retired American Lieutenant Colonel, who was working in structures of the legislative authority of Estonia.

This man, in a January meeting with Moscow's narcotics mafia kingpin, Usman Imayev, called himself in a Russian manner by the name "Yuri." He is a political opponent of Lesnik and at the same time holds close criminal connections and is the main distributor of drugs through Estonia into North America. Apparently, the Estonian mafioso was afraid of exposing the identity of Yuri and had ordered people to "remove" (liquidate) Kristapovich, as was done: Kristapovich was killed by two shots to the head. However, before he died, it has

304 THE HOLE

been said he had time to send materials, in part concerning the ferry "Estonia," to the U.S. and to Moscow.

Other, incidental information from Kristapovich includes a financial scandal involving Lesnik and Dudayev and concerning Soviet money, according to the "Financial News" (12.01.95). The events here were revealed as follows:

In the summer of 1992, Estonia planned to mint and circulate its own currency. To carry out these plans, 2360 million Soviet rubles were first collected from the population of the Republic. Then the Premier Tiit Vahe signed the Russian-Estonian agreement with Igor Gaidar and Alexander Shokhin. One item in the agreement said: "All ruble notes received by the Estonian party will be transferred to the Bank of Russia within one month from the date of introduction of Estonian national currency." Gaidar held the signed agreement in high esteem, having named it as an example of "civilized divorce."

However, almost immediately they forgot about it and Russia did not receive any Soviet rubles from Estonia. A little later, Vahe left office by resigning because of "business" undertaken with Lesnik and with the president of the Bank of Estonia, Siim Kallas. Tiit Pruuli became a close advisor to Lesnik. In December 1992, Pruuli sent on an AN-26 plane belonging to Latvia, the first set of rubles as "diplomatic cargo."

[p.71]

The rubles went to someone in Moscow.

Two weeks later, a plane from the same Latvian airline took away the second part of the "diplomatic baggage" from bank safes, but this time the money came from Riga. A couple weeks after that, the Tallinn customs officers found out Pruuli had received a suitcase containing $300,000. However, after easily deceiving them, Pruuli was released together with the money, and he put it into the budget as the first payment for the weapons that Estonia had bought from Israel.

This weapons deal, in which Lesnik played the most active role, also was investigated in detail by Kristapovich. The criminal background to the deal has connections to the story of one former Lithuanian minister in the same situation, trying to get the weapons from the same Israeli firm. With this purpose, the Lithuanian arrived in Israel. He had doubts about the expediency of the deal's conclusion. Then the Israeli government sellers, to dispel any of the visitor's doubts, gave him as a gift an expensive hunting gun with an optical sight. The Lithuanian initially refused the gift, to the genuine surprise of the Israelis.

"You refuse?" they asked. "Recently `Lesnik' was here. (Naturally they used his real name and not the nickname "Lesnik"). *He* accepted the gift with pleasure and he agreed to support a similar contract between us and Estonia."

History can be astonishing. You would think Lesnik could without problems buy himself thousands of similar gifts. However, when looking at the past, Lesnik's frugality is simply crazy. Having received from his "comrades" 360 rubles for "work" and having signed the appropriate receipt, the next day he wrote back to them a rather curious message. Lesnik repeatedly asked his "comrades" to find an opportunity to compensate him for the cost of the ticket Tallinn-Leningrad-Tallinn," which is hardly more than 10 rubles.

Coming back to Pruuli, it is necessary to point out that the contents of his suitcase, the first ruble-laden diplomatic baggage, was quite modest. Serious business began on March 20, 1993. On this day at the Tallinn airport, a plane from Grozny arrived and brought the Chechens Ruslan Sultuhhanov and Ruslan Salamov.

Under the orders of Pruuli, they would transport three cars and a lorry belonging to the Bank of Estonia.

[p.72]

The cargo of about 18 tons of ruble notes was transferred onboard the plane, protected by 18 men with automatic rifles, and it flew to Chechnya. The next day the plane, accompanied by the same persons, returned to Estonia and loaded a new batch of rubles and again took off to Chechnya.

After 1 1/2 years, in August 1994, the scandal burst. Tiit Vahe accused Lesnik and the Bank of Estonia of selling currency not belonging to them and of carrying out illicit currency operations. It was discovered that they sold Chechnya 1.5 billion rubles through somebody named Marek Strandberg. Strandberg was one of the co-owners of a Finnish-registered Estonian firm, "MAAG" (specializing in buying up and reselling light metals from Russia), who recorded in his books a payment of $1,898,547 to the government of Estonia, which, according to Vahe's honest statement, did not arrive in the government coffers.

As a commission for the [ruble] deal, Strandberg officially received about $1 million. However GOSKONTROL of Estonia considers that he actually had made $5 - $8 million. Thus, from the total 2360 millions rubles, Chechnya was sold only approximately 1500 million. 726 million was transferred to a local firm "as paper for recycling." GOSKONTROL refused to disclose the name of this local firm in order to protect a trade secret. Lesnik supervised this imaginary "paper for recycling" firm and over time he bought petroleum, light metals and wood from Russia.

When "the ruble bomb" went off, Lesnik was compelled to leave the structures of executive authority. Officially, he remained a lawmaker. His cohort, Siim Kallas, presented as a candidate for the post of Prime Minister by the party of Lennart Meri, received a no-confidence vote.

Other big scandals of Lesnik that Kristapovich tried to expose are connected to the "Estonia" ferry accident of September 28, 1994. The version of events follows:

Lesnik, as an intermediary of the Lithuanian police, bought from a person in Vilnius referred to as "Yandarbayev," a large quantity of heroin, which would be sent from Estonia to Sweden to the Estonian-American Yuri in the U.S.

Yuri broke tradition with this heroin transfer. In the past, he had always used the same operatives to move the heroin--Estonian narcotics traders on the ferry "Estonia."

Another Estonian-American already mentioned above and also cooperating with Lesnik in the narcotics business, obviously was not pleased. He had been cut out of this lucrative deal. Deciding to take revenge, he tipped off a DEA [Drug Enforcement Administration] employee of the U.S. about the smuggling operation. In turn, the DEA employee spoke to Swedish colleagues who were engaged in the fight against drugs and asked them to look for a heroin shipment arriving on the "Estonia."

[p.73]

However, somewhere in Sweden there was an information leak about a pending search for drugs, and the leak came to the attention of one of the big bosses of the Moscow narcotics gangs in London.

The information leak, however, came a little too late--the ferry already was underway. The London-based boss called Lesnik. Kristapovich wiretapped this conversation, which took place in Russian, as well as the conversations of other participants, which took place in Estonian language. When speaking with London, Lesnik sounded very nervous. Therefore, he had obviously had prior knowledge about the information leak.

Yuri then contacted the captain of the ferry and said he was obligated to get rid of the drugs on board. The captain agreed to carry out the order. However, it seems Yuri finally lost his nerve. In 20 minutes, he again contacted the captain and ordered him to get rid of 40 tons of illicit cobalt, which was also being delivered on the ferry to Sweden.

The bewildered captain asked the question: "What for?" Yuri began to explain nervously that this time, most likely the ferry will be searched for heroin by people who it will be difficult to find a mutual agreement with. They certainly will find the illicit cobalt and then they could start asking too many questions. So it would be better to get rid of the cobalt. However, the captain began to object: To throw overboard 40 tons in a storm, at night, was extremely dangerous. And moreover the ferry was already very late. But Yuri insisted and the captain at last agreed, having thus shown extreme irresponsibility.

His team began maneuvering a vehicle with a cargo of cobalt, in attempt to move all the illicit cargo to the vessel's front part. Then simultaneously, the speed of the ferry would be sharply decreased while dumping the cobalt into the sea.

The ship was by now so late that the captain ordered an increase in speed up to 15 knots. Moreover, as a further measure to save time, he ordered a loosening of the fixing mechanisms that raise and lower the bow visor, as well as the removal of a part from the latching devices, and all this despite the countervailing effect of the wind up to 27 meters per second and wave heights of six meters.

And finally, having sent some of the crew to the top deck, "so they don't disturb anything," the captain, under the pretext of attending the birthday of the bar waitress, left for his cabin to rest until the "preparatory work" on the cardeck was finished. However, further events changed the scenario. As a result of ship movements caused by the storm, the powerful variable hydro-dynamic loading on the vessel's bow visor complicated the maneuvering of the multi-ton trucks with cobalt. A loosely-fixed bow visor broke from its locks, tearing a huge hole.

[p.74]

The hole resulted in fast flooding of the interior of the vessel. A catastrophic situation resulted. The overdue attempt of the captain to turn the vessel away to counter waves did not help. The crew was mostly celebrating the birthday of the waitress and was not capable of controlling the situation and organizing the rescue of the passengers. At 01:48, the ferry turned over and sank underwater, carrying with it about 900 passengers and members of the crew.

Kristapovich had given most of this information to one of the FBI chiefs in the U.S. What ensued was a difficult conversation in the Washington White House. Having mentioned the names of Lesnik and Yuri, [the FBI chief] supposedly asked: "How is it possible to render political support to these people [the Estonians]? They are not simple contraband smugglers. On their conscience are the lives of hundreds of people."

APPENDIX IV: The Submarine Fax

The four-page fax, another attempt at disinformation, was sent anonymously to several people in Sweden. This book refers to the document as the "Submarine Fax," but it is untitled, unsourced and undated. No editing has been done. All mistakes are in the original, which is in English:

Re: Considerations in relation to the sinking of the car/passenger ferry ESTONIA on September 28, 1994

- After Estonia's independence US-interests arranged for Alexander Einseln/friends to be placed into respective positions. They were taken up with open arms in Estonia as coming from the USA being their most admired Western country.

- Main target of the action were the secret Russian weapons which had to be transported back to the USSR and of which the USA wanted the most sophisticated ones home for examination.

- Einseln, in his capacity as Army Chief, had knowledge of all these operations and had access to most, if not all, sensitive information/documentation.

- The camouflage for the stealing of very few, very selected parts of equipment was the large scale sale of military goods from the Russian troops in co-operation with Russian Generals and many, including Einseln, made quite some private money.

- Whilst smaller parts of the secret equipment were certainly brought out of the country by plane via diplomatic mail or the like, the heavier pieces had to be transported by trucks the normal way. Here the by far easiest way was by NORD ESTONIA and subsequently by ESTONIA as otherwise several borders would have to be crossed by the trucks, whilst on the ferries the trucks were escorted by Army personnel on board at Tallinn and from board at Stockholm without complications and problems. It could not be easier.

- It has to be assumed that several such transports were carried out in the past and there was apparently nothing the Russians could do against it.

- As the last of the secret nuclear submarine bases in Estonia was going to be closed down by the end of 1994 the removal of military goods and transports back to Russia and private sale of common and sensitive equipment went on for several months, i.e. during the entire second half of 1994. The name of this base is Paldiski, located about halfway between Tallinn and the NW corner of the Estonian mainland. In September 1994 still some of the large submarines were stationed there and the base was still at least partly operative. At the coast, on one of the islands, a sender was located which was active whenever the subs were exercising out in the Gulf of Finland and in the Baltic.

- According to the militaries, from this base, a small quantity of osmium and some equipment connected to or containing cobalt, but very heavy, were loaded on two trucks and shipped by ESTONIA on the evening of September 27, 1994 from Tallinn to Stockholm.

- Inquiries revealed that these two trucks were brought on board probably before the normal loading operation began and were escorted by one sergeant and three soldiers. The trucks were belonging to an Estonian Freight Forwarder and the drivers were private but prepared for the job.

- Reportedly at about this time a computer with highly sensitive data disappeared from the headquarters of the Estonian Army. Actually, it had been located in the office of Lieutenant Kitti Jurgens, next door to the office of General Einseln, and was reported missing only about 3 months later by Kitti Jurgens according to the press reports. As this computer was too large to be transported by bag or suitcase and it disappeared towards the end of September 1994, it is not illogical to assume that it was in one of the two trucks.

- Apparently one of the Russian Intelligence officers in Tallinn, Igor Kristopowich, got hold of some information about the above-mentioned, possibly by taping the various communication lines between Einseln and his partners, but it was too late for counter-action while the vessel was in port respectively counter-action in port was not possible due to too close guarding.

- The Russians by all means wanted to avoid that the contents of the 2 trucks got into the hands of the Swedes respectively the USA.

- According to the aforementioned militaries from the Paldiski base, the sender had been active during the night of September 27/28th, 1994, thus at least one of the big nuclear submarines had been out.

- Many of the survivors, in particular crew members with some experience at sea, have testified that the 2 or 3 heavy impacts shortly before the abrupt starboard list were not like having been caused by sea-impact.

- According to at least one of the reliable survivors from the first deck water was splashing up from the deck in the area of the alleyway as if a valve had been opened. This observation was made shortly before the abrupt starboard list occurred. This indicates that the space below the forward part of the 1st deck, the swimming pool and sauna department, was then flooded. The explanation could be an opening in the starboard shellplating, on which the vessel is lying now.

- This would mean that ESTONIA was deliberately sunk by explosives or by a submarine. This was known since the early stage by the Swedish, Finnish and Estonian governments. It is even possible that these governments knew before that the Russians would do something like this (remember the shooting down of the Korean Air Jumbo near Sakhalin Peninsula) and tried to counteract, but in vain. It is even possible that during these attempts the indentation in the visor was caused (at least the upper corroded part). Reference is also made in this respect to the report of one survivor that one cabin window at starboard side was smashed in by some other vessel almost alongside when the list occurred and to the report of some survivors that a vessel had been between the liferafts, picked up some people and disappeared without taking care of others. Also one of the rescue reports mentions an unidentified vessel having been close to ESTONIA at the time of casualty which disappeared into the Uto/Hango archipelago.

- The above would explain the very strange attitude of the Swedish government in many respects, for example

- the very early statement by the International Commission, being clearly under the leadership of the Swedish government Commission, that the disaster was due to the failure of the locking devices of the visor; this statement was made before the visor was found;

- the energy with which the Commission is blocking off all other evidence disturbing that scenario, which includes the use of the military intelligence service to try to throw doubts on a video showing severely damaged visor hinges which every investigation commission would be happy to have, but also the ignorance of the statements of eye witnesses (time of heeling) as well as the laws of physics (water in visor) just to mention a few;

- the obvious fact that the Commission is not interested in the actual condition of the vessel upon departure from Tallinn because they have neither spoken to the BV surveyor Anders Wirstan nor to the relevant members of the relief crew;

- the very passive, if not to say uninterested, way the public prosecutor and the police are handling the maters;

- the eagerness and energy with which the government tried to cover the wreck for ever;

- the very self-confident behaviour of the part owners and technical managers, Nordström & Thulin, demonstrating to the outside word that the are sure that absolutely nothing will happen to them (because they enjoy government protection from the highest level);

- a similar behaviour by Bureau Veritas whose surveyor Anders Wirstan, responsible not only for the classification items but also for the ship safety requirements according to SOLAS, etc., has e.g. never been heard by the criminal police although he together with the inspectors Hobro and Rasmusson as well as the chief engineer Mosaar from the relief crew know the ESTONIA's condition in detail, thus it has to be assumed that also BV enjoys government protection which is probably due to their contract with the Estonian Board of Navigation;

- the apparent fact that at the end of last year the matter was withdrawn from the Ministry of Transport and Communication inside the Swedish government and is now handled by the Ministry of Defence.

- It would also explain the disappearance of Capt. Arvo Piht who, as well as Capt. Andersen, apparently knew about the crucial transports, whilst the other missing crew members were just in bad luck to have been in the same liferaft with Piht.

- As far as the work of the International Commission is concerned it has to be assumed that they are just following instructions to the effect to do anything to make the most simple scenario by means of their report to be the most probable one.

- Unfortunately for the Meyer Werft the most simple and therefore best understandable scenario for the public is to blame the failure of the locking devices, as the primary cause and indicate the impression that if those devices had been strong enough, the casualty presumably would not have taken place.

APPENDIX V: FOIA Responses

NATIONAL SECURITY AGENCY
CENTRAL SECURITY SERVICE
FORT GEORGE G. MEADE, MARYLAND 20755-6000

FOIA Case: 41799A
20 January 2004

Mr. Drew Wilson

Dear Mr. Wilson:

This is a final response to your Freedom of Information Act (FOIA) request of 17 June 2002 for information on the passenger ferry MV Estonia, which sank in the Baltic Sea between Sweden and Estonia on 28 September 1994. A copy of your request is enclosed for your convenience.

Your request has been processed under the provisions of the FOIA. Three documents (7 pages) responsive to your request have been reviewed by this Agency as required by the FOIA and have been found to be currently and properly classified in accordance with Executive Order 12958, as amended. These documents meet the criteria for classification as set forth in Subparagraphs (b), (c), (d) and (g) of Section 1.4 and remain classified SECRET as provided in Section 1.2 of Executive Order 12958, as amended. The documents are classified because their disclosure could reasonably be expected to cause serious damage to the national security. Because the documents are currently and properly classified, they are exempt from disclosure pursuant to the first exemption of the FOIA (5 U.S.C. Section 552(b)(1)).

In addition, this Agency is authorized by various statutes to protect certain information concerning its activities. We have determined that such information exists in these documents. Accordingly, those portions are also exempt from disclosure pursuant to the third exemption of the FOIA which provides for the withholding of information specifically protected from disclosure by statute. The specific statutes applicable in this case are Title 18 U.S. Code 798; Title 50 U.S. Code 403-3(c)(7); and Section 6, Public Law 86-36 (50 U.S. Code 402 note). No portion of the information is reasonably segregable.

NATIONAL SECURITY AGENCY
CENTRAL SECURITY SERVICE
FORT GEORGE G. MEADE, MARYLAND 20755-6000

FOIA Case: 59333
31 August 2009

Mr. Drew Wilson

Dear Mr. Wilson:

    This responds to your Freedom of Information Act (FOIA) request submitted via the Internet on 3 August 2009, which was received by this office on 4 August 2009, for information related to the passenger ferry MV Estonia (sometimes written as passenger ferry M/V Estonia), which sank in the Baltic Sea between Sweden and Estonia on 28 September 1994, including copies of every document related to the matter, regardless of the format in which the information is stored, from the period of 1 September 1994 to 3 August 2009, as well as minutes of meetings, notes, correspondence, faxes, telexes, submissions, reports, memoranda, and electronic mail. Your request has been assigned Case Number 59333. For purposes of this request and based on the information you provided in your letter, you are considered an "all other" requester. As such, you are allowed 2 hours of search and the duplication of 100 pages at no cost. There are no assessable fees for this request.

    This Agency has already complied with the requirements of the FOIA and provided a response to you concerning this subject matter in your FOIA request received 1 March 2005, assigned Case Number 44955. As a courtesy, we conducted another search, and no additional records were located for the period 1 June 2002 (the date we conducted the search for your previous request of 2005) through 3 August 2009. For your convenience, we have enclosed a copy of your previous request and our response letter dated
27 September 2005.

    We have re-reviewed the responsive documents that were located during the processing of your 2005 request and have found them to still be currently and properly classified in accordance with Executive Order 12958, as amended. The responsive documents meet the criteria for classification as set forth in Subparagraphs (b), and (c) of Section 1.4 and remain classified SECRET as provided in Section 1.2 of Executive Order 12958, as amended. The documents are classified because their disclosure could reasonably be expected to cause serious damage to the national security. Because the documents are currently and properly classified, they are exempt from disclosure pursuant to the first exemption of the FOIA (5 U.S.C. Section 552(b)(1)).

FOIA Case: 59333

In addition, this Agency is authorized by various statutes to protect certain information concerning its activities. We have determined that such information exists in these documents. Accordingly, those portions are exempt from disclosure pursuant to the third exemption of the FOIA which provides for the withholding of information specifically protected from disclosure by statute. The specific statutes applicable in this case are Title 18 U.S. Code 798; Title 50 U.S. Code 403-1(i); and Section 6, Public Law 86-36 (50 U.S. Code 402 note). No portion of the information is reasonably segregable.

The Initial Denial Authority for NSA information is the Deputy Associate Director for Policy and Records, Diane M. Janosek. Since your request has been denied, you are hereby advised of this Agency's appeal procedures. Any person notified of an adverse determination may file an appeal to the NSA/CSS Freedom of Information Act Appeal Authority. The appeal must be postmarked no later than 60 calendar days after the date of the initial denial. The appeal shall be in writing addressed to the NSA/CSS FOIA Appeal Authority (DJP4), National Security Agency, 9800 Savage Road STE 6248, Fort George G. Meade, MD 20755-6248. The appeal shall reference the initial denial of access and shall contain, in sufficient detail and particularity, the grounds upon which the requester believes release of the information is required. The NSA/CSS FOIA Appeal Authority will endeavor to respond to the appeal within 20 working days after receipt, absent any unusual circumstances.

The CIA has asked that we protect non-substantive information pursuant to 5 U.S.C. 552 (b)(1) and (b)(3). Any appeal of the denial of CIA information should be directed to that agency.

Sincerely,

PAMELA N. PHILLIPS
Chief
FOIA/PA Office

Encls:
a/s

APPENDIX VI:
Classified request for cargo information

> *Nov.*
> MFR 21 ~~Dec~~ 2006
>
> Subject ESTONIA, September 1994
>
> 1. Border Guard, Customs and ESTLINE records ▓▓▓▓▓▓▓▓ ▓▓▓▓▓▓ differ. Not surprising considering the overall chaotic situation and lack of professionalism in Estonia at the time.
> 2. In response to a request on 28 October 1994, the following info was provided:
>   a. ESTLINE sold 75 tickets, 39 trailer trucks, 32 autos, 4 merchandise vehicles.
>   b. Border Guard claims 61 vehicles boarded Estonia, 14 less than tickets sold.
>   c. Responder reports actually 83 vehicles boarded, 8 without ESTLINE tickets and 22 without Border Guard registration.
> 3. Registered merchandise ranged from textiles, handicraft, fish to furniture and ▓▓▓▓ lumber products. Two trailer trucks were registered as empty and some did not list merchandise.
>   a. NXF 876
>   Blue Volvo
>   Length 18 meters
>   Weight 14 tons
>   Empty
>   No company/sender name
>   Driver "Bernt Egström, accompanied by another Swede"
>   b. 250 AUM
>   White Volvo
>   Length 9 meters
>   Weight 7 tons
>   Empty
>   Company: Hancon LTD, Tallinn, Pikk 42-7
>   Driver Kullo Palvader, Estonian
>   c. DDG 182 (Per ESTLINE ticket) DDG 188 (Per Estonian Border Guard info)
>   Blue SCANIA
>   Length 16 meters
>   Merchandise NOT DECLARED
>   Company SCANSPED AB, Rootsi Barns 50110
>   Driver Eduard Klug (Swede)
> 4. Info requester was interested in vehicle registration no's, owners names, vehicles not registered in customs, type and dimensions of vehicles. Requester also stated that "it is known that auto deck was tightly packed" and "this matter should be handled confidentially as a matter of national security."
> 5. Responder reported that:
>   a. "Only the lower auto deck had vehicles on it."
>   b. "Based on information received by us, one trailer on board had circa 6 tons of cobalt not declared in Customs." Nothing about identifying the vehicle which had the undeclared cobalt as cargo. Of the listed vehicles none showed cobalt as cargo.
>   c. "Thus far concrete facts about smuggling have not been determined by us. Will inform when we find such info."
>   END

The "requester" in the document was Lennart Meri and the "responder" was the Estonian secret police (KAPO). Immediately after the sinking of the Estonia, Meri issued classified orders to investigate the cargo list.

APPENDIX VII: Undersea tracks

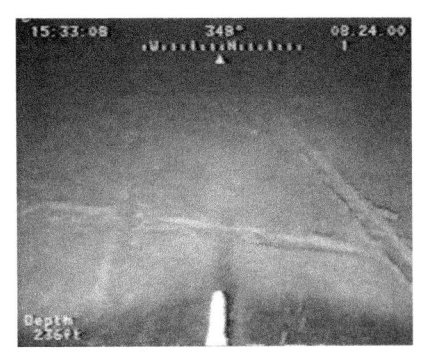

In August 2000, Greg Bemis and Jutta Rabe organized an unauthorized dive to the *Estonia* wreck. The crew had lost a piece of equipment – a sonar fish – and used a remotely operated vehicle (ROV) to look for it near the wreck. The ROV videotaped the search and these stills, clearly showing undersea tracks, are captured from the videotape. The tracks were relatively fresh and deep, supporting assertions that an undersea vehicle visited the wreck just before the dive.

APPENDIX VIII: Timeline of Key Events

Timeline of Key Events

1988
- Estonia officially declares its own laws higher than Soviet laws, becoming the first Soviet state to attempt to break away and the trigger for the collapse of the USSR.

1989

November
- Berlin Wall comes down. Eastern Europe breaks free of USSR domination. Cold War ends.

1990
- Estline, a joint venture ferry line between Sweden and Soviet Estonia, is set up largely through the efforts of Swedish Prime Minister Carl Bildt. A small ferry, the *Nord Estonia*, begins service from Tallinn-Stockholm.

1991

January
- Moscow-directed violence erupts in Lithuania and Latvia.
- Dzhokar Dudayev, Soviet commander of an airbase base in the Estonian city of Tartu, commits treasonous act by refusing to allow his soldiers to take any action against rebellious Estonia.

August
- Coup attempt as Soviet leader Mikhail Gorbachev vacations in Crimea. Speeds collapse of USSR.
- Estonia declares independence from the USSR.

November - December
- Dudayev resigns. Inspired by Estonia's independence, he leaves for his native Chechnya where he declares himself president and the republic independent.
- USSR officially dissolved. Russia assumes role of successor state.

1993
- The *Estonia*, a larger luxury ferry purchased from Finland with a European Bank of Reconstruction and Development loan, replaces the *Nord Estonia* on Estline's Tallinn--Stockholm route.
- Iranian crew manning a purchased secondhand Russian submarine spotted in Baltic Sea.
- Potential for ethnic conflict or worse as Russians living in Narva, Estonia, hold referendum and overwhelmingly vote for turning part of Northeast Estonia into an autonomous region.
- Russian ultra-nationalist Vladimir Zhirinovsky, who vowed to take the Baltic States back by force, gains political power through Russian parliamentary elections.

1994
- Brutal organized criminal groups spread across the former Soviet Union. Russian president Boris Yeltsin calls Russia "Superpower of Crime."
- Frequent smuggling of weapons, drugs and strategic materials through Estonia alarm Washington DC. A major concern in the White House is nuclear smuggling through vulnerable places in the former Soviet Union like Estonia.

August-October
- Russian troops pried out of Estonia after 50 years of occupation, officially ending World War II.
- Two nuclear reactors disassembled by Russian military in a tightly-classified operation at former Soviet submarine base Paldiski in Estonia.
- Russian troops quietly massing in Chechnya.
- Several documented incidents of weapons-grade nuclear material smuggled out of Russia.

September 27
- Estonian Prime Minister Mart Laar resigns from office.
- Swedish Prime Minister Carl Bildt leaving office, attending a farewell dinner.
- Russian President Boris Yeltsin in US.
- *Estonia* ferry sets sail from Tallinn harbor around 19:15 Estonian time. Destination Stockholm.
- Large NATO exercise in Norway's Skaggerak area ramping up.

September 28
The *Estonia* ferry sinks in 35 minutes:

00:30 *Estonia* reaches halfway point between Tallinn and Stockholm.
00:30-01:00 Passengers hear two-three loud, unnatural bangs. Some report a scraping noise on the hull. Crew is changing shifts.
01:15 Ship lists hard to starboard.
01:22-01:24 Mayday message from the *Estonia*.
01:30 Ferry rolls to starboard side at 60-70 degrees.
01:50 Ferry disappears from radar.
07:30-08:00 Last person rescued from the sea.

Afternoon
Bildt makes conclusion that the ferry sank due to technical fault.
Bildt's aide, Commander Emil Svensson, states straight away that the wreck should not be recovered. At the time, search-and-rescue operations still ongoing, the wreck is not yet located and the investigative committee not yet formed.

September 29
- Prime Ministers of Sweden, Estonia and Finland agree to set up the Joint Accident Investigation Commission (JAIC) with representatives from each country. The JAIC will carry out the government's task of investigating the disaster.

- The *Estonia* carried 989 people from 17 countries. Survivors number 134. Many passengers who escaped the sinking ferry died from drowning or hypothermia while awaiting rescue. 757 bodies remain missing, most presumed to still be inside the shipwreck.

September 30
- Wreck position found by sonar.

October 2
- Wreck videotaped by ROV.

October 18
- Visor located.

November 18
- Visor recovered.

December 4-10
- Swedish government-supervised dive to the shipwreck by salvage divers from the company Rockwater. After divers inspect the ferry, the subsequent dive report declares bodies and shipwreck are salvageable.

1995

January
- Swedish officials announce bodies will not be retrieved and shipwreck will be covered in a concrete tomb.
- Sweden lobbies all countries around the Baltic Sea to sign a Gravesite Treaty, which prevents anyone from going near the shipwreck. Wrecksite is monitored 24 hours by military vessels and shore equipment. Violators subject to arrest.
- Due to a mistake in communications, Russia comes within minutes of launching a nuclear strike on the US.

June
- Concrete tomb covering decision revoked after strong public protests.

1996

The Joint Accident Investigation Commission (JAIC) in turmoil:

- Estonian Andi Meister, head of entire commission, resigns, says Sweden withheld evidence.
- Swede Olof Forssberg resigns, ostensibly due to an administrative mistake. Real reason unclear.
- Swede Bengt Schager resigns, says commission falsified information.

1997

December
- Final Report released three years after catastrophe. JAIC blames shipyard for inadequately designed bow visor locking system. But JAIC implies no one holds clear and full responsibility because the design specs were valid at the time the ferry was built.

1998

- Continuous public demands for recovery of victims forces Sweden to appoint a commission to study the issue. Headed by Peter Oern, the group concludes bodies should be recovered.
- Sweden says no to the recommendation, claiming Finland and Estonia objected.

2000

August
- Unauthorized dive to the shipwreck organized by independent investigators, American Gregg Bemis and German journalist Jutta Rabe. Swedish military tries unsuccessfully to stop them. Metal samples brought up by the divers test positive for an explosive force according to three different labs. German government lab does not get the same results and Sweden dismisses the claims. Bemis and Rabe face arrest if they visit Sweden.

2001
- Proposal for a motion to debate, in the Swedish parliament, the reopening of the *Estonia* investigation is rejected.

2004
December
- A Swedish customs official breaks years of silence to admit Soviet military equipment had been transported on the *Estonia* passenger ferry. Sweden launches an inquiry.

2005
January
- Swedish government inquiry reveals the *Estonia* ferry had been used to transport military equipment in the weeks preceding the catastrophe, but was not using it for military transport the night it sank. Authorities refuse to specify what the equipment was or who had authorized the acquisition.

March
- Sweden announces it will conduct a $1.1 million study into why the *Estonia* ferry sank so quickly. Government officials say the study is to improve safety at sea and the findings in the JAIC's Final Report are not in question.

2006
- Court case by a small group of relatives taking legal action against the shipyard and the ship certification agency stalled in France.
- Over 750 bodies remain in the shipwreck 40 kilometers from Finland in 70 meters of water.

APPENDIX IX:
Glossary of Abbreviations and Terms

ESCO -- Estonian Shipping Company. State-run enterprise that owned the Estonian half of Estline.

Estline -- the 50/50 joint venture between Sweden's Nordstrum & Thulin and Estonia's ESCO that was set up to manage ferry lines between Estonia and Sweden.

Final Report - Shorthand for "The Final Report on the Capsizing on 28 September 1994 in the Baltic Sea of the Ro-Ro Passenger Vessel *MV Estonia*" which contains the final conclusions of the JAIC's investigation, released in December 1997.

FSB -- Federal Security Service (*Federalnaya Sluzhba Bezopasnosti*). The domestic security organization in Russia, the main successor to the KGB.

FSK - Federal Counterintelligence Service (*Federalnaya Sluzhba Kontrrazvedki*). Existed from 1991-1995 and was then transformed into the FSB.

FSU -- Former Soviet Union.

GGE -- German Group of Experts. The group of investigators hired by the Meyer Werft Shipyard to investigate the disaster.

Gravesite Treaty -- agreement between the countries bordering the Baltic Sea (except Germany) that declares the site of the *Estonia* ferry shipwreck a grave and prohibits dive expeditions.

GRU -- *Glavnoye Razvedyvatelnoye Upravlenie*, Russia's military intelligence.

JAIC -- Joint Accident Investigation Commission. The trilateral commission made up of representatives from Sweden, Estonia and Finland formed to investigate the reason for the sinking of the *Estonia* ferry.

M/V Estonia -- official designation for the *Estonia* ferry, M/V meaning "Motor Vessel." Could also be written as *M/S Estonia* or "Motor Ship."

OMON -- Acronym for *Otryad Militsii Osobogo Naznacheniya*, special Russian Ministry of Interior troops with a reputation for excessive force usually deployed in crisis situations.

One Eagle -- The vessel hired by Gregg Bemis and Jutta Rabe in August 2000 to carry out an unauthorized research dive on the *Estonia* shipwreck.

Portside -- The lefthand side of a ship as one faces forward.

Riigikogu -- Estonian Parliament.

Rockwater -- Salvage diving company contracted and supervised by the Swedish government to examine the *Estonia* shipwreck in December 1994.

Ro-Ro -- Roll-on, roll-off. A type of ferry that usually opens at both bow and stern, allowing vehicles to drive on and off the cardeck quickly.

ROV -- remotely-operated vehicle for underwater use. Typically used for underwater videotaping.

SMA -- the Swedish Maritime Administration or *Sjöfartsverket*.

Starboard side -- The righthand side of a ship as one faces forward.

Visor scenario -- The JAIC's conclusion that huge waves tore off the ferry's bow visor, which pulled open the cardeck ramp as it fell off, sending seawater onto the cardeck and sinking the ferry.

List of Illustrations

Page 10: Giedre Karsokiene

Page 11: Giedre Karsokiene

Page 13: Aurimas Svedas

Page 16: Aurimas Svedas

Page 20: Aurimas Svedas

Page 22: Aurimas Svedas

Page 27: Giedre Karsokiene

Page 35: JAIC

Page 39: Giedre Karsokiene

Page 47: JAIC

Page 75: Giedre Karsokiene

Page 116: Giedre Karsokiene

Page 132: German Group of Experts

Page 165: Giedre Karsokiene

Page 315: Aurimas Svedas

Page 316: JAIC

Page 318: Giedre Karsokiene

Page 329: Aurimas Svedas

Page 336: JAIC

All other charts and tables: Giedre Karsokiene

Sources

Interviews

Sweden
Akesson, Per, Baltic Sea diver
Angstrom, Lars, Parliamentarian
Björkman, Per, lawyer
Blixt, Tomas, customs official
Calamnius, Bertil, father of *Estonia* victim and head of *Estonia* victims' relatives group AgnEF
Carlqvist, Knut, journalist, author of *Estonia* book
Franson, Johan, head of Swedish Maritime Administration
Freden, Lars, Foreign Ministry official
Hellberg, Anders, journalist, author of *Estonia* book
Heyman, Tom, retired Parliamentarian
Holm, Mats, journalist, author of *Estonia* book
Hugemark, Bo, retired military officer
Jarrel, Henrik, Parliamentarian
Laidwa, Hans, former managing director of Estline
Örn, Peter, head of Örn Commission
Övberg, Carl, survivor
Schager, Bengt, former JAIC member and maritime psychologist
Sörman, Rolf, survivor
Sundelius, Bengt, professor at Uppsala University and the Swedish National Defence College
Tidstrom, Catrin, desk officer, Transport Ministry
Weman, Gunnar, Archbishop of Church of Sweden

Estonia
Andresson, Veronika, wife of the *Estonia's* captain
Arike, Heike, Minster of Interior, 1994
Dresen, Urmas, director of the Estonian Maritime Museum
Einseln, Alexander, former head of Estonia's Armed Forces
Johansen, Johannes, former managing director of Estline, the Estonian

half of the ferry line
Kadak, Hannes, surviving crewmember
Laar, Mart, Prime Minister, 1994
Laur, Uno, former head of Estonian JAIC
Lauristin, Marju, professor, former parliament member
Lee, Aina, survivor
Levald, Heino, professor and maritime engineer and former JAIC member
Lindpere, Heike, maritime law professor, former ESCO board of directors
Moik, Erich, ship captain, friend of both *Estonia* ferry captains
Ninnas, Toivo, former managing director, ESCO
Paeorg, Ander, relative of victim
Piht, Sirje, wife of the *Estonia's* relief captain
Putnik, Henno, former head of ALARA, main environmental agency
Roos, Aarand, former Estonian diplomat
Ruussaar, Ainar, journalist
Same, Siiri, survivor
Sinisoo, Mark, Estonian Ministry of Foreign Affairs
Stern, Jaan, survivor
Tammes, Sigrid, wife of *Estonia* ferry third officer
Treufeldt, Indrek, journalist
Tross, Jaan, head of Estonian Crisis Committee 1994
Vaarik, Daniel, former government press officer
Vare, Raivo, former Estonian Minister of Transport and Communications
Vöösa, Timmo, survivor

Finland
Aho, Esko, prime minister 1992-1995
Alenius, Pekka, senior scientist, Finnish Institute of Marine Research (FIMR)
Jolma, Kalervo, engineer, Finnish Environmental Institute
Karppinen, Tuomo, former JAIC member
Lehtola, Kari, former head of Finnish side of JAIC
Mykkänen, Erkki, engineer, Finnish Environmental Institute
Nuorteva, Jouko, sonar photograph expert

U.K.
Barney, Paul, survivor
Coe, John, Rockwater diver
Mearns, David, marine salvage expert

Ventura, Ken, Rockwater diver

France
Björkman, Anders, nautical engineer
Schmill, Erik, lawyer

U.S.
Bemis, Gregg, co-organizer of dive to the *Estonia* ferry in August 2000
Downs, Jamie, forensics specialist
Ermarth, Fritz, former CIA bureau chief
Garverick, Mickey, director, Naval Submarine League
Polmar, Norman, submarine expert and consultant on intelligence issues to U.S. government
Poteat, Gene, former intelligence professional
Stolorow, Mark, executive director of forensic science at Orchid Cellmark Inc

Russia
Benukh, Oleg, author
Chapkis, David, author
Kuteinikov, Anatoly, head of submarine design firm "Malakhit"
Surikov, Anton, former Russian military intelligence officer
Antsulevich, Alexander, senior scientist, St. Petersburg State University and Baltic Sea expert.

Germany
Hummel, Werner, head of German investigation into the sinking
Rabe, Jutta, journalist, co-organizer of dive to the *Estonia* ferry in August 2000
Rebas, Hain, Estonian Minister of Defense 1992-1993

Netherlands
DeKat, Jan, nautical engineer

Czech Republic
Yasmann, Victor, journalist, Russia research analyst

Books

Benukh, Oless [Oleg], "The Clash of the Triads," ["Udar Triadi"] Moscow: Astrel Publishing, 1999. Russian language.

Beschloss, Michael R. and Talbott, Strobe, "At the Highest Levels: The Inside Story of the End of the Cold War," Little, Brown and Company, 1993.

Björkman, Anders, "Lies and Truths about the M/V Estonia Accident," Monaco: Editions EGC, 1998.

Borjesson, Kristina, editor, "Into the Buzzsaw. Leading journalists expose the myth of a free press," Amherst, New York: Prometheus Books, 2002.

Bynander, Fredrik, "Crisis Analogies, A decision making analysis of the Swedish Harsfjarden Submarine Incident of 1982," Stockholm: The Swedish Institute of International Affairs, 1998.

Carlqvist, Knut, "Tysta Leken. Varför sjonk ESTONIA?" ["Silent Game. Why Did the ESTONIA Sink?"]. Stockholm: Fischer & Co, 2001. Swedish language.

Cockburn, Andrew and Leslie, "One Point Safe," New York: Doubleday, 1997.

Dillon, Patrick, "Lost at Sea," Simon and Schuster, 1998.

Gall, Carlotta and de Waal, Thomas, "Chechnya, Calamity in the Caucasus," New York: New York University Press, 1998.

Holm, Mats and Popova, Susanna, "Protokollet *Estonia*. Darfor Kommer Det Att Handa Igen," ["The Case of the *Estonia*: Why it Will Happen

Again"], Bonnier Fakta, 2003, Swedish language.

Hooke, Norman, "Maritime Casualties, 1963-1996," Lloyd's Press, 1997.

Junger, Sebastian, "The Perfect Storm," Harper Collins Publishers Inc, 1997.

Klebnikov, Paul, "Godfather of the Kremlin, Boris Berezovsky and the Looting of Russia," Orlando, Florida: Harcourt Inc., 2000.

Kulling, Per and Lorin, Henry, eds., "The *Estonia* Disaster. The loss of the *M/S Estonia* in the Baltic on 28th September 1994," Sweden: Socialstyrelsen, KAMEDO (Organizing Committee for Disaster Medicine Studies), 1997.

Lauristin, Marju and Vihalemm, Peeter, editors, "The Disaster in Estonian Media," published by Styrelsen for Psykologiskt Forsvar (Sweden's "Board of Psychological Defense"), 1996.

Lauristin, Marju and Vihalemm, Peeter, editors, "Return to the Western World: Cultural and Political Perspectives on the Estonian Post-Communist Transition," Estonia: Tartu University Press, 1997.

Lieven, Anatol, "The Baltic Revolution," New Haven: Yale University Press, 1994.

Lord, Walter, "A Night to Remember," New York: Bantam Books, from Holt, Rinehart and Winston, 1955.

Meister, Andi, "Lopetamata logiraamat" ["Unfinished Logbook"], Tallinn: Baltic News Service, 1997. Estonian language.

Milton, Pat, "In the Blink of an Eye, The FBI Investigation of TWA Flight 800," Random House, 1999.

Moore, Robert, "A Time To Die, The Untold Story of the *Kursk*," New York: Crown Publishers, 2002.

Negroni, Christine, "Deadly Departure, Why the Experts Failed to Prevent the TWA Flight 800 Disaster and How it Could Happen Again," Harper Collins Publishers, 2000.

Oberg, James E., "Uncovering Soviet Disasters," New York: Random House, 1988.

Piht, Sirje and Kaas, Imre, "Raske Tee Toeni" ["Hard Way to the Truth"], Estonia: Mandala, 2003, in Estonian Language.

Rabe, Jutta, "Die Estonia, Tragödie eines Schiffsuntergangs" ["The *Estonia*: Tragedy of a Ship Disaster"], Germany: Delius Klasing Verlag, 2002, English version.

Ready, Kevin E. and Parlier, Cap, "TWA 800, Accident or Incident?" Ventura, California: Saint Gaudens Press, 1998.

Rüütel, Arnold, "Estonia: Future Returned," Tallinn, Estonia: National Development and Cooperation Institute, English translation, 2001.

Sanders, James D., "Altered Evidence. Flight 800: How the Justice Department Framed a Journalist and his Wife," 1999.

Sellwood, A.V., "The Damned Don't Drown: The Sinking of the Wilhelm Gustloff," Annapolis, Maryland: Naval Institute Press, 1973.

Smith, Graham, ed, "Baltic States: The National Self-Determination of Estonia, Latvia, and Lithuania," Palgrave Macmillan, 1996.

Sontag, Sherry and Drew, Christopher, "Blind Man's Bluff, The Untold Story of American Submarine Espionage," Harper Collins Publishers Inc, 1999.

Stern, Eric K. and Nohrstedt, Daniel, eds. "Crisis Management in Estonia," Stockholm: Crismart, 2001.

Sundelius, Bengt and Nohrstedt, Daniel, eds., "Crisis Management in Estonia: Case Studies and Comparative Perspectives," Volume 3, Stockholm: Forsvarshogskolan, 2001.

Suvorov, Viktor, "*Spetsnaz*. The Story Behind the Soviet SAS," Hamish Hamilton Ltd, 1987. Translated from Russian.

Wedel, Janine R., "Collision and Collusion. The Strange Case of Western Aid to Eastern Europe," Palgrave Publishers Ltd, 2001.

Winocour, Jack, ed., "The Story of the Titanic as Told by its Survivors," New York: Dover Publications, 1960.

Witte, Henning, "*M/S Estonia* Sanktes, Nya Fakta Och Teorier om Estoniagate," [The sinking of the *M/S Estonia*, New Facts and Theories on Estoniagate"], Stockholm, 1999, Swedish language.

Yeltsin, Boris, "Midnight Diaries," New York: Public Affairs, 2000.

Yeltsin, Boris, "The Struggle for Russia," New York: Times Books, 1995.

Reports and other background material

"The Final Report on the Capsizing on 28 September 1994 in the Baltic Sea of the Ro-Ro Passenger Vessel *MV Estonia*," The Joint Accident Investigation Commission of Estonia, Finland and Sweden, Edita Ltd, Helsinki, 1997. English language version.

"Supplement to The Final Report on the Capsizing on 28 September 1994 in the Baltic Sea of the Ro-Ro Passenger Vessel *MV Estonia*," Part I and Part II, The Joint Accident Investigation Commission of Estonia, Finland and Sweden, Preliminary Versions.

"German Group of Experts Investigation Report on the capsizing on 28 September 1994 in the Baltic Sea of the Ro-Ro Passenger Vessel *MV Estonia*," Peter Holtappels and Werner Hummel. CD-ROM, 1999.

"*MV Estonia*, Preliminary Critique of the Joint Accident Investigation Commission Report," Burness Corlett & Partners, U.K., April 1998.

"Report on the diving expedition in the Baltic Sea to the wreck of the passenger ferry *Estonia* from August 19th to August 31st 2000" by Gregg Bemis and Jutta Rabe. Undated.

"Condition Survey of the Vessel `Estonia' for the Swedish National Maritime Administration Survey Report, Rockwater A/S. Undated.

"X-ray microstructure investigations on two specimens of shipbuilding plates," Institut für Materialprüfung und Werkstofftechnik, Report 20130-03, October 16, 2000.

"Examination of Metal Samples for Evidence of Shock Loading," Southwest Research Institute Project No. 18.04042.01.109, Final Report, January 26, 2001.

"Examination Report," Materials Testing Laboratory of the State of Brandenburg, No. 1.1/00/3669 [10/26/00].

"Court of Inquiry into the Circumstances Surrounding the Collision Between USS *Greeneville* (SSN 772) and Japanese *M/V Ehime Maru* that occurred off the coast of Oahu, Hawaii on 9 February 2001," Record of Proceedings. April 13, 2001.

Analysgruppen [Örn Commission Report], SOU 1998:132. Swedish language. En granskning av Estoniakatastrofen och dess följder," [Analysis group report on the Estonia catastrophe]. Swedish language.

"Russia: Mafia in Uniform: The Criminalization of the Russian Armed Forces," Foreign Military Studies Office, Fort Leavenworth, KS, 1995, by Dr. Graham H. Turbiville, Jr.

"Enhancing Security of Lithuania and Other Baltic States in 1992-94 and Future Guidelines," NATO Research Fellowship report, May 1996, by Ceslovas Stankevicius.

"Russia's Military: Corruption in the Higher Ranks" Perspective, Volume IX Number 2, November-December 1998, Hoover Institution and Boston University, by Richard F. Staar.

"International Narcotics Control Strategy Report," U.S. Department of State, Bureau for International Narcotics and Law Enforcement Affairs, March 1995.

"Nuclear Smuggling From The Former Soviet Union: Threats And Responses," Foreign Policy Research Institute, CSIS Global Organized Crime Project, April 27, 2001, by Rensselaer Lee.

"Nuclear Smuggling: How Serious a Threat?" Report from the National Defense University's Center for Counterproliferation Research, January 1996, by James L. Ford.

"Weapons Proliferation and Organized Crime: The Russian Military and Security Force Dimension," USAF Institute for National Security Studies, U.S. Air Force Academy. INSS Occasional Paper 10 in the

Proliferation Series, June 1996, by Graham H. Turbiville, Jr.

Report on the *Estonia*, Norske Veritas, November 22, 1994.

"M/V *Herald of Free Enterprise* Formal Investigation," Report of Court No. 8074, U.K. Department of Transport, September 1987.

"Katastrofutredning" ["Catastrophe Investigation"], English Internet version, dated 28 June and 12 December 2001. http://heiwaco.tripod.com/news.htm, Anders Björkman.

"Crisis for Estonia? Russia, Estonia and a post-Chechen cold war" 1995: 05898, by Graeme Herd, Ene Rôngelep & Anton Surikov, London Defense Studies.

"Patterns of Global Terrorism 1994," U.S. Department of State, April 1995, Department of State Publication 10239, Office of the Secretary, Office of the Coordinator for Counterterrorism, Philip C. Wilcox, Jr.

"Submarine Operations in Taiwan Waters," *The Submarine Review*, January 2003, Royal Swedish Navy Captain Bo Rask.

"International Narcotics Contraband and the Former USSR," Research Group "Felix," Moscow, February 1995, translated from Russian, Ivan Ivanov.

Notes

All U.S. government documents were obtained through the Freedom of Information Act (FOIA) and declassified on release.

All references to the Joint Accident Investigation Commission's Final Report come from the English language version.

Abbreviations for news services: Agence France Presse (AFP); Baltic News Service (BNS); Polish Press Agency (PAP); Radio Free Europe/Radio Liberty (RFE/RL).

FOREWORD

[1] It is commonly estimated 6,500 - 7,500 people perished, making the *Wilhelm Gustloff* the worst sea disaster in recorded history in terms of loss of life from the sinking of a single vessel. Some estimates of deaths are as high as 10,000. About 500 people survived.

PART ONE: ESCAPE
THE LABYRINTH

[1] Interviews with Siiri Same and Jaan Stern. The accounts of escape in this chapter are based on several survivors' accounts. Incidental details have been changed for coherence. None of the author's modifications have fundamentally altered the recollections of Same and Stern.

PART TWO: EXPLANATIONS
GOVERNMENT VERSION OF THE DISASTER

[1] Excerpted and condensed from "The Final Report on the Capsizing on 28 September 1994 in the Baltic Sea of the Ro-Ro Passenger Vessel *M/V Estonia*," The Joint Accident Investigation Commission of Estonia, Finland and Sweden, Edita Ltd, Helsinki, 1997, Part 1, Chapter 1, "The Accident," p.9.

THE LOGIC OF THE HOLE

[1] Times are according to the JAIC. See Appendix I, the "Kalmar Chart."

[2] Interview, Schager.

"There were lots of debris and if the cabin turned, debris fell on the door and you couldn't open the cabin door. We calculated there was 10 minutes to escape the ship. After that, the list was more than 45 degrees. The generators stopped at 45 degrees because of the lack of lubrication, so we know the timing. When the main lights went out and emergency generator started, that could be seen from other ships [in the area] as well. When it is 45 degrees, only the well-trained could escape. We estimate that around 250 people made it out on decks. [There were] 134 survivors, and 90 bodies were found. The majority stayed on the ship."

[3] Interview, Hummel.

[4] Interview, Björkman.

[5] A Swedish diver named Hakan Bergmark also mentioned a "five meter hole." According to the Swedish daily newspaper *Expressen*, August 22, 2000, p. 13, in an article by Fredrick Engstrom, Bergmark claimed to be:

"--one of the first who dived down to the *Estonia*. He says he found a big hole in the side of the ship. He did not give it great attention then. 'It was not my job to find the cause of the accident. But when the Final Report of the commission was issued several years later I was very surprised,' Bergmark says, who today wants to forget everything about the *Estonia*. Two of the other four divers who were down together with Bergmark do not want to comment upon the *Estonia* at all."

NOTE: Bergmark's story could not be corroborated.

[6] "Swedish expert believes in large hole in ferry *Estonia* hull," BNS, May, 31 2000; Interview, Rolf Sörman. Sörman added that the investigating commission altered his testimony.

[7] German Group of Experts Investigation Report on the capsizing on 28 September 1994 in the Baltic Sea of the Ro-Ro Passenger Vessel *M/V Estonia*, Peter Holtappels and Werner Hummel, 36.3, "The Hole in the Starboard Side"; Interview, Sörman.

Further evidence about a hole in hull comes from the Rockwater dive to the shipwreck. During the dive, a remotely operated vehicle (ROV) was maneuvered onto the cardeck. That would not be possible unless there was a hole through which the vehicle could pass.

According to "The *Estonia*: Tragedy of a Ship Disaster" ("Die *Estonia*, Tragodie eines Schiffsuntergangs") (Delius Klasing Verlag), 2002, Jutta Rabe, English version, p.150, on a videotape of the dive, "...all at once very excited voices can be heard in the background talking about the ROV being on the car deck...Even David Becket, director of operations for the Rockwater divers, remarked on an episode of the [German TV news magazine] *Spiegel* broadcast on January 2, 2000 that it was very easy to get onto the car deck, and not by going over the car ramp either. But as to how that would have been possible, [he replied] 'I can't recall.'...the official Rockwater protocol includes an entry about the cardeck activity and it's thus officially on record."

[8] In an interview with the author, Franson claimed his twice mentioned "hole in the

hull" was actually a shorthand description of the open area where the visor tore off. The best way to describe this explanation is disingenuous. A broken off bow visor is just as prominent as a missing tail section of a plane. No one in his position, with a precise legal mind, would carelessly mislabel such an obvious missing part a "hole" at a public conference.

Franson is perhaps the only person who had unlimited access to real-time information from divers as they inspected areas of the shipwreck, often according to his instructions, making his statements about an actual hole credible. Unfortunately, Franson has not been challenged by authorities to clarify what he said.

[9] Interview, de Kat.

[10] In the final, double breach simulation, three contexts were run: The ferry drifting, bow quartering, engine room flooded; ferry drifting, beam seas, engine room dry; ferry drifting, bow quartering, engine room dry.

PART THREE: THREE EVENTS THAT SHAPED THE DISASTER
THE CULT OF THE VISOR

[1] Report: "Preliminary Critique of the Joint Accident Investigation Commission Report" by Burness, Corlett & Partners, maritime consultants, commissioned by the ITF. April 1998 [5.10.1]:

"The Joint Commission have expended a considerable amount of effort on various analyses to try and determine which component of the visor system failed first and what the sequence of events was thereafter. We would regard much of this work as of being only academic interest, because of the way that the visor system was designed. Once one of the attachment devices failed, complete failure would be almost inevitable, because loading on the other devices would be greatly increased; the `domino effect' would take over. Uncertainties in the actual loads at the time mean that no definite conclusions could be drawn."

[2] Örn Commission Report (Analysgruppen, SOU 1998:132), pp. 28-30.

[3] "Crucial half hour 'was wasted' as ferry sank," by Leonard Doyle and Annika Savill, *The Independent*, September 30, 1994.

[4] Press release from Rabe, "The *Estonia*," p.108.

THE DIVE TO THE SHIPWRECK

[1] The wreck was examined by divers from Rockwater A/S Stavanger (Norway), contracted by the Swedish Maritime Administration (*Sjöfartsverket*), the government organization headed by Johan Franson. Rockwater is part of Halliburton Co. In 1994 it was owned by Brown & Root Energy Services, which was owned by Halliburton.

Out of several tenders from companies bidding for the dive survey on the *Estonia* ferry, Franson chose Rockwater. Halliburton has a reputation for doing politically-sensitive work. Halliburton's underwater salvage division assisted Russian divers in recovering bodies from the sunken *Kursk* submarine, a vessel Russia classified as top secret.

[2] "Lopetamata logiraamat" ("Unfinished Logbook"), (Baltic News Service), Tallinn 1997, by Andi Meister, p. 109, translated from Estonian language.

Meister describes the tattoo sighting in his book, but gives no source. Meister was not on the SEMI platform, so someone had told him the information. There is no corroboration, but his comments are plausible because he was the head of the entire commission and therefore in a position to know inside information.

Meister refused three requests for an interview for this book and added that he wants to forget about the *Estonia* ferry disaster.

Additionally, according to Rabe, p. 140: "Two sources from the Finnish armed forces assured me that they saw the original videos and that clearly recognizable on these videos is the body of Captain Andresson, shot through the head."

Rabe explained that after the *Estonia* disaster, the Finnish navy intensified their sea rescue training. Part of the training involved special operations and included watching the videotape of the *Estonia* dive. Finnish sources told her in detail what they viewed. Because the sources are active duty military personnel, she cannot disclose their names. Therefore, the story could not be corroborated.

[3] Rockwater dive videotape number 18.

NOTE: Alexander Voronin, a Russian who lived in Kohtla-Järve, Estonia, was a passenger on the ferry. He survived with his uncle and nephew.

The diver goes on to suggest that the briefcase may have belonged to the victim just outside the cabin door. He obviously didn't know the name "Voronin." But did he have instructions to go into certain cabins? Why did he read a name and why was it cross-checked by the supervisor? The incident is all the more weird because by identifying a victim through personal belongings, the diver broke a cardinal rule of dive organizer Franson. No specific bodies were to be identified in any way. That would create an outburst from the relatives who would want their loved ones identified as well. Franson wanted to avoid that at all costs.

According to the GGE Report, Chapter 27, "The Diving Investigation": "--[T]he diver carried the suitcase out of the accommodation and it was apparently hoisted up to the diving platform." Yet on the videotape, there is no indication that the briefcase (suitcase) was actually taken out of the cabin. (NOTE: "Voronin" is mistakenly written as "Vorodin" in the German Report).

Diver John Coe, who did not participate in the briefcase incident, said Rockwater divers were split into three teams and the divers who found the briefcase were from a different team than Coe's. He gave a slightly different version of what happened: "From what I understand," Coe said, "they found this guy in his cabin and handcuffed to his wrist was his briefcase. That indicated that whatever he had within the briefcase, documents, whatever, was obviously quite important for him to be in that situation with the attaché case handcuffed. I can't shed any light on that. The rumor was that Swedish police connected [the briefcase] to the Russian mafia." Interview Coe.

Since 1994, the briefcase incident has caused terrific confusion and suspicion. No Swedish official who could clarify it has taken the time to do so.

[4] "Approximately 35 Estonians are among the survivors, including, at last report, Avo Piht, one of the two captains of the ship…" U.S. Embassy in Tallinn Memo, September 28, 1994, Subject: "Update on the *Estonia* Ferry Tragedy," Unclassified, Keith Smith, Charge d' Affaires.

See also: "Jail warning for the guilty as key witness is found alive," Colin Adamson, *Evening Standard* (London), September 29, 1994.

NOTE: Today, deep suspicion still surrounds the fate of Piht and several other crew members. Jutta Rabe has done extensive research that she believes shows Piht and several crew members survived the sinking only to disappear later. See Rabe, "The *Estonia*," for example, p.78 -81. Moreover, she found a search-and-rescue helicopter logbook showing that Piht and other crew members were flown to a hospital after the ferry sunk.

Here is another area where Swedish and Finnish authorities could take relatively simple administrative steps to publicly clarify recorded inconsistencies concerning the search-and-rescue operation. Yet no one has done so.

[5] GGE, Chapter 14, "The Day in Tallinn."

[6] Interview, Coe.
Coe is speaking strictly about cabins on the accommodation decks. He said he does not know if the diver examining the briefcase received instructions directing him there.

The Rockwater divers signed an agreement stating that they would not talk about what they saw down at the shipwreck. Franson maintains that the requirement was to prevent them from talking to the media about victims. But why they would be legally prevented from openly discussing technical and operational aspects of the shipwreck more than a decade later is unknown. Presumably the agreement is not a lifetime confidentiality oath, which would equate it with allegiance to national security.

Another Rockwater diver, Dave Mawston, was contacted by the author. Mawston, citing the SMA contract, did not want to talk about the *Estonia* dive. He added that it is not a typical practice to sign secrecy contracts on survey dives.

[7] Interview, Franson.

[8] "Unfinished Logbook," Meister, p. 102.

[9] Ibid., p.102, pp. 109-110.

[10] "The wreck was examined…" see GGE, Chapter 24 "Locating the Wreck and Visor."
"Videos of the wreck…" see GGE, 41.2 "Difference in Methodologies."
"…the *Estonia's* logbook…" see GGE, Chapter 37.2, "Activities to the end of 1994."

[11] Interviews, Tidstrom and Coe.
Coe said that when the Rockwater divers arrived at the wrecksite, they weren't put down on the actual wreck itself but specifically near the bow doors. Therefore he believes ROVs had been on the jobsite, but said he saw no signs of previous diver intervention.

340 NOTES

[12] "Estonian Observer Claims Did Not See Whole *Estonia* Ferry Divers' Mission," BNS, November 13, 1997.

[13] GGE, 34.6 "Investigation Report of Video Tapes Featuring the Car/Passenger Ferry 'Estonia' by Disengage, Axminster/U.K.."

[14] "diver activity had been written and cut out..." see GGE Chapter 27, "The Diving Investigation" Video tape log RW/SEMiI/EST/D/011 dated December 3, 1994.
"JAIC did not desire..." see GGE, Chapter 27 "The Diving Investigation."
The German investigators also speculated that the Rockwater divers had two sets of earphones, one for instructions from the dive supervisor that were heard on the videotapes and another for instructions that would not be recorded on the video but the divers could hear nonetheless.
Rockwater diver Coe said that there was only the dive supervisor giving divers instructions and everything that is said in supervisor-to-diver communications is heard elsewhere. "A dive super talks to you direct. There is no other communication. Swedish police would've been in dive control and could've been listening in the dive office or client's office they have on board, but they would have no direct communication with divers. Only the dive supervisor does. That's the way saturation diving is."

[15] Lars Angstrom, a member of Sweden's Green Party in Parliament, for example, said he has no clear answer as to where the uncut videotapes are.

16 Interview, Franson.

[17] "Sweden's top ferry disaster investigator says filming of bridge not important," BNS, July 22, 1998.

[18] Meister, p. 107.
Meister refers to the contentious cost issue in his book:
"--Forssberg accused me of not proposing to organize a new expedition to film the command deck. I would never have done that. Perhaps my heart would have been bothered by the costs of the diving works, although Sweden paid for it."
In an interview with the author, Finnish JAIC member Tuomo Karppinen estimated that the JAIC investigation cost Sweden about $1.4 million, Finland $1.2 million. He wouldn't say how much Estonia paid, except that it was "much less." The cost issue is relevant because it reveals the serious tensions inside what was a supposedly harmonious, objective and open government commission.

[19] Interview, Karppinen and Lehtola.

[20] "Estonian Observer Claims Did Not See Whole *Estonia* Ferry Diver's Mission" BNS, November 13, 1997.
Meister's resignation was one of several that would damage the JAIC's reputation. But because he was head of the entire three-country commission and not just the Estonian side, his departure was a powerful sign that something unacknowledged

was tearing the commission apart.

CONCRETE BLANKET

[1] "Condition Survey of the Vessel *Estonia*" for the Swedish National Maritime Administration,
Survey Report, Rockwater A/S, Section 5.2 "Internal Intervention."

[2] Interview, Franson.

[3] GGE, 36.3 "Hole in the Starboard Side."

[4] "Sweden in new 'Estonia' row: TV debate sees angry exchange between minister and relatives" *Lloyd's List*, James Brewer, February 6, 1996. See also: "Consortium to encase 'Estonia'," *Lloyd's List*, January 12, 1996, by John Prescott.

[5] "Estonia concrete burial opposed," *Lloyd's List*, Gordon Mackenzie, January 15, 1996.

[6] "Relatives of *M/S Estonia* Victims Say Intend to Retrieve Bodies, BNS, March 15, 1996.

[7] Interview, Aina Lee.

[8] Interview, Paeorg.

[9] Interviews, Mykkänen and Jolma.

[10] Interviews, Mykkänen and Jolma.

[11] From a surface platform some 60 meters above the wreck, engineers from the Finnish Environmental Institute (SYKE in Finnish language) maneuvered ROVs to deposit magnets on the *Estonia's* hull. In this way, they mapped the hull for drilling points. Then robot drills were steered to the magnets, securing themselves to the hull by self-drilling bolts. Next, equipment heated the heavy fuel oil--the Baltic Sea at 50-80 meters deep is near the freezing point of water--and the robots attached a vacuum hose to extract the liquids to the surface, where it was disposed of as waste material. Engineers removed 250 cubic meters of fuel and oil together weighing about 400 tons in total. They accessed 14 tanks in the *Estonia* ferry. The operation lasted six weeks and was repeatedly delayed by the covering operation.

[12] Rabe added further detail about the unusual accumulation of sand near the starboard side area, suggesting that unknown divers visited the wreck a few weeks prior to Greg Bemis' *One Eagle* expedition (which had been publicly announced months in advance):
"--[T]he [*One Eagle*] divers had noticed something…There was a band of sand approxi-

mately one hundred feet wide covering the first third of the ship. Why was the sand only there and not over the rest of the wreck?...In addition, strange vertical scratch marks were sighted along the ESTONIA's bottom side, now lying facing upward, down to the starboard side. The divers described this discovery as looking like cable or hoses had slid up and down this section. That kind of activity would not have taken place too long ago because the experienced divers knew that a hull would quickly become covered with sediment again and the ship's paint was still distinct at this section. Therefore, the divers estimated these marks to be four-to-six weeks old at the most."
Rabe, The *Estonia*, p. 176.

PART FOUR: THE BACKDROP
1994: CHAOS UNLEASHED

[1] The 1986 Chernobyl nuclear reactor accident was a fitting metaphor for the internal decay and collapse of the Soviet empire. A shining symbol of Communist scientific progress, Chernobyl's poor design, shoddy management and ill-disciplined practices resulted in a catastrophic collapse that threatened a broad geographic region. The disaster was kept secret by the Soviet government until pressure from neighboring countries forced more openness.

[2] "Midnight Diaries," (Public Affairs, New York), 2000, by Boris Yeltsin, p.254.

[3] Nikita Khrushchev transferred the Crimea to Soviet Ukraine in 1954. After Ukraine broke off from the Soviet Union in 1991, it required the former Soviet Black Sea Fleet in Crimea to take an oath of allegiance to Ukraine. Moscow retaliated by invoking the illegality of Khrushchev's transfer of the region, making the Crimea another potential serious flashpoint. The Black Sea Fleet was armed with nuclear weapons. See: "The Struggle for Russia," (Times Books, New York), 1995, by Boris Yeltsin, p. 152-3.

[4] Statistics from Graham Smith, ed, "Baltic States: The National Self-Determination of Estonia, Latvia, and Lithuania" (Palgrave Macmillan), 1996. p. 182. Latvia fared worse, going from 75.5 percent Latvians to about 52 percent. Lithuania remained the same in both periods at about 80 percent.

From 1939 to 1989, the number of Russians living in Estonia had multiplied 23 times to 600,000. Part by design, part by desire, Russians over the decades packed up and moved to Estonia. A factory worker or engineer could readily find work in the industrial region of Northeastern Estonia, where Moscow was pushing the development of strategic industries. Estonia's living standard was higher than Russia's. For Soviet Russians, Estonia was the West. Moscow also installed an ample military in the country. At the end of 1991, Estonia held 25,000 Soviet troops, a force that included air bases, special forces units, a submarine base and nuclear submarine training center at Paldiski Naval Base.

[5] "Estonians struggle with the question of how to deal with Russians," Knight Ridder/Tribune News Service, August 2, 1993, by Zeke Wigglesworth.

[6] Estonian journalist Ainar Ruussaar recalled an incident that illustrates Dudayev's respect for Estonians. In 1992, Ruussaar said he went to Grozny along with the rest of the world's media to report on Dudayev's return to Chechnya and the declaration of independence from Russia. Journalists from the leading international newspapers along with CNN and BBC were clamoring for an interview with Dudayev. Ruussaar tried a different approach. He gave an Estonian business card to one of Dudayev's security guards, said he was from Estonia, and requested an interview. A short while later he was selected from the journalistic pool for an exclusive interview with Dudayev. The next day Dudayev invited Ruussaar back for dinner and gave him a tour of Chechnya in his own personal helicopter, which Dudayev himself piloted.

Dudayev showed sympathy for Estonia in various ways. He offered weapons to the *Kaitseliit*, an Estonian paramilitary group. When Russia cut off gas supplies to Estonia, he suggested a plan for sending fuel oil from Chechnya. Later, as Chechen president, during several days of armed conflict with Moscow-backed opposition forces, he managed to send condolences to President Meri when the *Estonia* ferry sank on September 28, 1994.

Today, the Estonian respect for Dudayev is evident at Tartu's Barclay Hotel, which displays a marble plaque at the entrance: "The first president of the Chechen republic Ichkeriya, General Dzhokhar Dudayev, worked in this house from 1987 to 1991." Translations of the sentence are in Estonian, Chechen and English but not Russian. Additionally, the plaque uses the name "Ichkeriya," the Chechen name for a sovereign Chechnya.

[7] The story has been restated several times in slightly different versions by various people, including Marju Lauristin who was in Tartu city administration at the time and knew Dudayev. By some accounts, Dudayev actually refused an order from Moscow to attack Estonia. In the Carlotta Gall and Thomas de Waal book, "Chechnya, Calamity in the Caucasus," (New York University Press), 1998, "Dudayev declared that he would not let Soviet planes land on Estonian soil." Another detail sometimes mentioned is that Dudayev had the Estonian flag hoisted over the air base. However, I've never been able to find documentation supporting Dudayev's declaration and Estonian officials claim no public record exists.

A book by former Estonian president Arnold Rüütel corroborates the anecdote, which has always seemed to be mythical. On January 12, 1991, in Lithuania, when the Soviet armed forces turned their weapons against the people, "head of the Tartu garrison [Dzhokhar] Dudayev called me and promised that the armed forces would not resort to force in Tartu and that he would do his best to prevent any soldier from leaving the [military base]." Arnold Rüütel, "Estonia: Future Returned" (National Development and Cooperation Institute), English translation, 2001, p. 162.

Dudayev was killed in Chechnya in 1996 in the war against Russia. The Russians sent a smart bomb that targeted his satellite telephone while he was engaged in conversation with an aide to the King of Morocco, whom the U.S. had tried to recruit as an intermediary in the conflict. Some speculate that the U.S. and Russia collaborated in the killing of Dudayev, as Russia at the time lacked the technology to pinpoint a target with such accuracy.

[8] Interview, Laar.
"a link in supplying arms..." "Chechnya, Calamity in the Caucasus," New York University Press, 1998, Carlotta Gall and Thomas de Waal, p. 129.

[9] Arnold Rüütel argues that Estonia was the first to pull the plug on the U.S.S.R. Though resistance in Hungary, Czechoslovakia and Poland came earlier, these countries were in the East Bloc, not in the U.S.S.R. Rüütel writes that Estonia, out of all countries forced into the Soviet Union, was the earliest to take action that would help cripple the U.S.S.R. and lead to independence: "[Estonia in 1988 declared its own laws have supremacy over Soviet laws]...To characterize the importance of [that declaration] we first have to recall that nearly one year still remained until the fall of the Berlin Wall... on November 16, 1988 we set in motion a process for the democratic restructuring of the Soviet Union and for Estonia's secession from the union...later other republics followed our example, it was pertinent to say that a virus caught from Estonia destroyed the empire." Rüütel, p. 75.

"--We can be proud that it was our small Estonia to trigger the great opposition to the totalitarian system that came to involve ten countries." Rüütel, p. 192.

[10] Einseln served in the Korean War and in Vietnam in a Special Forces unit. He later worked for the U.S. Joint Chiefs of Staff as a specialist on Japan and Eastern Europe and served in the U.S. Pacific Command before retiring in 1985. In 1991, when Estonia broke free of the Soviet Union, U.S. officials informally recommended Einseln and other Estonian-Americans to the Estonian government for assistance in rebuilding the country. Estonian President Lennart Meri soon asked Einseln to become Chief of the Estonian Armed Forces, which carried the rank of Lieutenant General. The U.S. State Department was dead set against it, fearing Russian reaction (see Chapter 12).

While de-Sovietizing the Estonian army, Einseln was under critical attack from all sides. Besides the U.S. State Department, Moscow politicians, the Russian high command, former Soviet military officers he now commanded, Estonian politicians and others all had their own reasons to retaliate against him. He managed to stay the course longer than other expatriates, but gave his resignation in late 1995.

[11] Yeltsin's comment: *Reuters*, September 8, 1995.
Grachev's comment: Associated Press, September 25, 1995.
Several Russian newspapers also quoted high-level government officials threatening military action if the Baltic States joined NATO. 1996 was an election year in Russia and political factions were positioning themselves with voters. Nonetheless, the comments were not without foundation.

[12] For example, Chairman of the NATO Military Committee, Field Marshal Sir Richard Vincent arrived in Estonia, the first NATO officer of his rank to drop in for a high level visit. "The Field Marshal brought good news to Estonia," Einseln told the press. "Our co-operation with NATO has gone beyond just talk." "Regional Cooperation NATO Representative's Visit to Estonia," RFE/RL, March 16, 1994.

[13] Rüütel, p. 189.

[14] "Crisis Management in Estonia," (Crismart), 2001, Eric K. Stern and Daniel Nohrstedt, Eds., p.51.
"declaring war against the Russian-speaking population" "Estonian law bill may trigger ethnic cleansing," Itar-Tass, June 21, 1993, by Albert Maloveryan.

NOTE: Ethnic Russians living in Estonia have three levels of citizenship to choose from. The top notch is a dark blue passport that denotes Estonian citizenship. Next is the red passport issued to those who chose Russian citizenship but reside in Estonia. The other level of citizenship is the gray non-citizen passport. Anyone who did not apply for or meet Estonian citizenship requirements, and has not chosen to take citizenship of another country, is in the non-citizen category. In 1994, most Russians in the Narva region were non-citizens.

Yeltsin's rants about ethnic cleansing and apartheid invigorated Russians living in Estonia, despite the fresh historical memories of ruthless brutality heaped on the Baltic States in Soviet times. In some cases, local Russians who equated an obligatory Estonian language test with a violation of human rights were living on the same street as Estonians who in Soviet times had family members executed or deported to death camps on Moscow's orders. The Russians apparently never saw the cruel irony of their comparative statements. Given this emotionally-charged situation, it is remarkable that armed conflict didn't break out. Much credit is due to the Estonians, who ultimately kept their composure and rose above revenge.

[15] "Will The "Narva Powder Keg" Explode?" Russian Press Digest, July 1, 1993, sourced from *Nezavisimaya Gazeta*, p. 3, by Ilya Nikiforov and Vladislav Kuzmichev.

[16] The Clinton administration used a similar show of force tactic during heightened tensions between China and Taiwan in 1996. A U.S. aircraft carrier unexpectedly sailed through the Taiwan Straits, with the explanation that it was taking a short cut due to engine trouble.

[17] Stern and Nohrstedt, eds., p. 69.
Also, Interview, Laar: "--[W]hen necessary, Bildt was always ready to come to Estonia, even for just a couple of hours, to demonstrate his clear support for Estonia."

[18] "Will The "Narva Powder Keg" Explode?" Nikiforov and Kuzmichev.

[19] Events in Moldova exemplified Russia's strategy to keep former Soviet vassal states under the influence of Moscow. During the 1991 Soviet putsch, a group of Russian citizens resident in Moldova seized the Trans-Dniester region. A short war in which Russian troops were involved followed in 1992 and after relative calm returned, Russian troops remained. Although Trans-Dniester is not recognized internationally, locals control the province with the support of Russian soldiers. They installed a Soviet-style police apparatus, a ban on all opposition and continually call for a Greater Russia. Russia failed to honor an agreement with the Organization for Security and Cooperation in Europe to withdraw its troops as well as thousands of tons of weapons and ammunition from Trans-Dniester by 2003. As of this writing, Russian troops are still in Trans-Dniester militarily supporting the breakaway region. In 1994, Moscow appeared to be using the

same strategy in Estonia's Northwest region.

Also, Stern and Nohrstedt, eds., p. 44: "Claims were soon made that Narva, Kohtla-Järve and Sillamäe--three cities whose industrial enterprises were principally dependent on the Soviet market--represented a common economic area and therefore were entitled to special status. It was evident that ambitions to bring [the region called] Ida-Virumaa closer to Soviet rule were behind these claims. The eventual goal behind these claims was seeing the Ida-Virumaa territory permanently divided from the existing Estonian territory, as in Moldova."

Apparently Moscow had designs on Northeast Estonia as far back as the 1980s. According to Rüütel, in the late 1980s, a Soviet delegation had visited China and came back with ideas for the rebellious republics clamoring for more autonomy. "--Referring to the free economic zones successfully operating in China, Moscow suggested that we, too, should set one up [in Estonia]. But as the idea was to create it in the Northeast, where the population of the big industrial centers of Narva, Sillamäe and Kohtla-Järve was mainly Russian speaking, it was clear it was an attempt to bring the area directly under central control." Rüütel, p 83-84.

However, not all people who were close to Estonia in the early 1990s agree that the Narva situation was a potential flashpoint for violence. Paul Goble, an American who worked with the team negotiating the Russian troop withdrawal, says that the secession of Northeast Estonia was not a unanimous desire among Russian politicians. "They knew that if Tallinn did [allow the Northeast to secede], the percentage of ethnic Russians in the remaining [Estonian] state would be so low that [Russia's] influence would be minimal. Moreover, people in Moscow were very allergic to any border changes, lest they be played back on them."

[20] Zhirinovsky's quote is from *Postimees*, April 26, 1996, sourced from a list of Zhirinovskyisms. http://www.russia-channel.com/forums/showthread.php?t=13721
See also: "The Baltic Revolution" (Yale University Press, New Haven), 1994, Anatol Lieven, p. xxi:
"Like many Russian nationalist extremists, Zhirinovsky has a particular hatred for the Balts, whom he has on occasions threatened to reconquer and even exterminate...[M]embers of the Baltic Russian population (numbering 42,000 in Estonia) who had by December 1993 taken Russian citizenship, tended to use [the citizen's right to vote] to support the communists or Zhirinovsky."

NOTE: Zhirinovsky in 2006 was still serving in the Russian parliament, but has lost much of his influence and is categorized as an entertainer. In 1994, however, Zhirinovsky's threats carried weight and he was regarded cautiously by the highest levels of state in the West. For some, the mention of Zhirinovsky as a potential danger in the early 1990s is hard to accept because hindsight interferes.

In Estonia, threat perception was low, adding another dangerous dimension to the potential conflict in Narva. For example, Laar insisted he knew at the time that Zhirinovsky's threat could be dismissed as simple bluster, even though in 1994 no one understood the extent of Zhirinovsky's influence in Moscow, and in which direction Russia was moving. The stratagems behind the dangerous rhetoric were at the time unknown.

Lieven, page xxi, also mentions the lack of awareness among Estonians: "--[M] any Balts, including as intelligent a statesman as Mart Laar, profess to see no difference between the attitudes of Boris Yeltsin and of Zhirinovsky towards the Baltic States."

[21] US State Department correspondence, February 1994, From: American Embassy Tallinn, To: US Secretary of State, Classification: "Confidential," Subject: "Russian politics in Estonia--tension, divisions and a cold wind from the East."

[22] Report: "Crisis for Estonia? Russia, Estonia and a post-Chechen cold war" 1995: 05898, by Graeme Herd, Ene Rôngelep & Anton Surikov, London Defense Studies.

[23] "Crime but no punishment: Russian troops in Estonia" Press Release, Estonian Ministry of Foreign Affairs, March 1, 1994.

[24] Larger conflict could not be ruled out. The Communist Party had evaporated. Russia's Baltic commanders held a loosening allegiance to the drifting authority in Moscow. Moreover, by 1994 a corrupt core had formed in the Kremlin, effectively usurping Yeltsin's authority. No one was clearly in command of Russia, much less troops scattered in foreign countries.

According to "Constructing Threat in Russian Foreign Policy: Ethnicity, Apocalypse, and Baltic Warriors," Martha Merritt, Woodrow Wilson International Center for Scholars, in 1994, a poll of the Russian public would reveal that Estonia was considered to be Russia's greatest enemy.

See also: "'Bosnias' on Russia's Borders?" Perspective, Uri Ra'anan, Institute for the Study of Conflict, Ideology & Policy, Volume III, No 4, April-May 1993.

Heightened tensions were partly influenced by political posturing before the 1996 presidential elections. However, the rhetoric had substance. In 1995, Russian Foreign Minister Andrei Kozyrev spelled out a new foreign policy doctrine that explicitly sanctioned the use of military force to protect ethnic Russians living in former Soviet republics. See: "Kozyrev won't Retract his Disquieting Statement," BNS, April 20, 1995: "Estonian President Lennart Meri also sharply condemned the Kremlin's threat to use force to protect the rights of Russians in neighboring countries as the same kind of mistake that led to World War II..."

Some analysts even saw a more extreme "Weimar-Russia" scenario, with the remnants of a humiliated empire re-establishing a dictatorship based on nationalism. In a country with virtually no legacy of democratic institutions, some totalitarian hybrid could logically replace the old one.

[25] "Russia: Mafia in Uniform: The Criminalization of the Russian Armed Forces," Foreign Military Studies Office, Fort Leavenworth, KS, 1995, by Dr. Graham H. Turbiville, Jr: "--poorly paid, badly housed, and demoralized Russian military forces at home and abroad are deeply immersed in criminal activities conducted for personal and group profit. Smuggling crimes of all types (particularly drug and arms trafficking), the massive diversion of equipment and materials, illegal business ventures, and coercion and criminal violence, all fall under the umbrella of military organized crime. ...the criminal legacy left by Russia's departed garrison forces in Eastern Europe and the Baltic states has proven substantial as well."

[26] "much of it involving organized crime…" is from US State Department correspondence, August 1994, From: American Embassy Tallinn, Charge d' Affaires Smith, To: US Secretary of State, Classification: "Confidential," Subject: "Securing Estonian Sovereignty Through Assistance."

NOTE: Brash criminals infiltrated state enterprises in the former Soviet Union with ease during the 1990s. According to Alfred Malinovsky, President of the Russian Federation Flight Crews Trade Union: "One evening the captain of an airliner scheduled to fly out of [St Petersburg's] Pulkovo Airport the next day got a telephone call at home. Without identifying himself, a man said: 'A car is going to drive up to your plane--take the cargo it's carrying.'

The captain was outraged: 'I will do no such thing,' he replied.

Then he heard: 'Have you thought about your little girl? She's a pupil at such-and-such school and walks there on such-and-such streets. Moreover, we know that your pilot's license will be up for renewal in six months. Do you want it not to be renewed?'

The next morning, as if there were no rules governing procedures at the airport, not one but two cars drove up to the plane. They seemed to belong to different 'departments.' The drivers began to argue with each other and pulled out pistols. In the end, they came to an agreement and ordered the captain to take cargo from both cars. Begging off with a plausible excuse, the pilot went to the medical unit and said he was ill. But the plane departed on its flight--with a reserve crew." "Does the Mafia Give the Go-Ahead for Takeoff?" *Izvestia*, Igor Andreyev, April 15, 1994, p. 5.

[27] "Godfather of the Kremlin, Boris Berezovsky and the Looting of Russia" (Harcourt Inc, Orlando Florida), 2000, Paul Klebnikov, p. 21 and p. 29. In 1994, Russia's Interior Ministry estimated that 40 percent of all private businesses, 60 percent of all state owned companies and 85 percent of all banks had links to organized crime.

Klebnikov, who later set up the Russian language *Forbes* magazine, was murdered leaving his Moscow office in July 2004. As of this writing, no one has been convicted for his murder.

[28] In 1992, the official number of reported murders or attempted murders in Estonia climbed 75 percent from the previous year to 239. By 1994, the total reached 365. Statistics for 1994 are from the Statistical Office of Estonia. For 1992, they are from the website: http://www.1upinfo.com/country-guide-study/estonia/estonia27.html which cites as its source the Library of Congress country studies.

The Estonian Police Board supplied the following statistics for murder only. 1994 was the peak year, more than three times higher than in 2004:

1993 - 259 murders
1994 - 295 murders
1995 - 242 murders
1996 - 206 murders
1997 - 177 murders
2004 - 91 murders

"…one of the world's most violent capitals…" from "Russian Organised Crime and the Baltic States: Assessing the Threat" Working Paper 38/01, published in 2001 by the ESRC "One Europe or Several?" Programme, by Paddy Rawlinson, Sussex European

Institute, University of Sussex, p. 12. "The brutality of the underworld was exacerbated by the availability of illegal weapons. As in the other two Baltic States, Estonia had become a haven for the black trade in armaments." Ibid, p. 12.

"commonly arriving in Stockholm with cans of mace or sometimes even knives…" from Swedish port customs incident reports from 1993-1994. These reports tell a story by listing the increasing confiscations of personal weapons from residents of Estonia arriving on the Estonia ferry in Stockholm.

[29] "Between 1992 and 1995 authorities in the [Baltic] region discovered at least 1600 people in 23 separate incidents attempting to make the long and torturous journey to Western Europe. How many failed to make it across the Baltic Sea is anyone's guess." Stern and Nohrstedt, eds., p. 114. When 85 asylum seekers went on a hunger strike in Estonia, Tallinn finally admitted the country was in crisis. Ibid, p. 123

According to "Iraqi Kurds risk death as stowaways to Sweden" *The Independent* (London), February 21, 1994, by Jan Dungren (Associated Press), p. 9: "Before being taken to refugee centers, where they were expected to seek asylum, the group of mostly Iraqi Kurds told police they had paid $ 2,500 each to be smuggled to Sweden…Since the collapse of the Soviet Union and relaxation of border controls, hundreds of refugees from North Africa and the Middle East have made their way to Russia and then to the Baltics, where they pay smugglers to transport them by boat to Sweden."

See also: "From Iraq To Sweden Via Tallinn" Russian Press Digest, January 15, 1993, sourced from *Nezavisimaya Gazeta*, by Ilya Nikiforov, p. 3; "Iraqi Kurds bribed their way into Estonia: border guards official" AFP, January 5, 1993.

NOTE: The emergency of displaced persons and Tallinn's reluctance to admit a crisis situation highlighted the tiny country's obsession with its international image. The fear of appearing inadequate would consistently shape Estonia's political character and institutional response.

Estonia alone simply did not have the institutional capability to overcome continuous crises in the 1990s. The Estonian government often turned to Finland for help. Finland, with cultural ties, a similar language and close proximity, is often referred to as Estonia's big brother. In the refugee crisis, Finland accepted some of the asylum seekers. Estonia also appealed to Finland to take over the burden of medical rescue and investigatory expertise after the *Estonia* ferry disaster; for emergency winter heating oil after Russia cut off supplies in 1992; to allow a hijacked Aeroflot jet land in Helsinki and not Tallinn in 1994; for helicopter rescue assistance after a 1997 multiple drowning during a military training accident.

[30] "Estonian Wanted To Smuggle Uranium To West," *Berlingske Tidende*, August 27, 1994. See also: "Uranium Seized By Estonian Police," *The Washington Times*, August 27, 1994, p. A7; "The Preventing of Illicit Trafficking in Estonia," September 14, 1998; "Safety of Radiation Sources and Security of Radioactive Materials," IAEA-TECDOC-1045, September 14-18, 1998, pp. 224-227, by Tuuli Velbri and Lauri Aasmann.

[31] "[Alexander Einseln] related that in a recent sting operation, every border guard and customs official who was offered a bribe accepted it. He attributed part of the problem to the five US [dollars] per month salary of servicemen and border guards." US

Embassy correspondence, July 1994, Classification: "Confidential," From: American Embassy Tallinn, Charge d' Affaires Smith, To: Secretary of State, Washington DC, Subject: "Building a new military on post-Soviet Rubble."

[32] "One Point Safe" (Doubleday, New York), 1997, Andrew and Leslie Cockburn, pp. 100-101.

[33] "Latvians, Estonians Cheer As Russian Troops Leave; Withdrawal Hailed as Start of Independence," *Washington Post*, September 1, 1994, Fred Hiatt.
   The positive voices were offset by Juri Luik, Estonia's Foreign Minister, who said the pullout was "only a first step. I do not believe that we have solved all of the security problems of the Baltic states...there are political forces in Russia seeking to restore the Soviet Union." "The Baltic republics become masters of their fate" *The Times*, September 1, 1994, by Richard Beeston.

[34] "Latvians, Estonians Cheer As Russian Troops Leave; Withdrawal Hailed as Start of Independence," *Washington Post*, September 1, 1994, Fred Hiatt.

[35] Figures are from the NATO Research Fellowship report "Enhancing Security of Lithuania and Other Baltic States in 1992-94 and Future Guidelines" May 1996, Ceslovas Stankevicius. The Baltic States in total in 1995 hosted approximately 42 000 retired military officers.
   See also: "Russian Exodus is a Tooth Pull," *Cleveland Plain Dealer*, September 10, 1994, by Holger Jensen, p. 11B.

36 US Embassy correspondence, March 1994, Classification: "Secret," From: American Embassy Tallinn, Ambassador Frasure, To: Secretary of State, Washington DC.

[37] "[Einseln] believes that the GRU [Russian military intelligence] has succeeded in penetrating the [Estonian] defense ministry; two of the ministry's most talented officials are on Moscow's payroll. Unfortunately he has only the thinnest evidence of their GRU connection and cannot have them fired." US Embassy correspondence, July 1994, Classification: "Confidential," From: American Embassy Tallinn, Keith Smith, To: Secretary of State, Washington DC, Subject: "Building a new military on post-Soviet Rubble."
   See also: "Sweden gives financial support to Estonia for surveys on security," BNS, April 15, 1994.

[38] The 1992 re-phrasing of Sweden's security policy, under Carl Bildt, introduced a vagueness that could technically allow the Swedes to get involved militarily in the Baltics, if necessary.

[39] *Foreign Affairs*, September - October, 1994 "The Baltic Litmus Test" by Carl Bildt. The general theme of Bildt's "Litmus Test" was probably first introduced by William C. Bodie in a 1993 article entitled "Anarchy and Cold War in Moscow's 'Near Abroad'" in the journal *Strategic Review*: "Russian policy towards the belt of 'blizhniye zarubezhniya' countries (Ukraine, Belarus, Moldova and the Baltic republics) will indicate what

kind of Russia--nation, empire or anarchic battleground--the West will face in the 21st century."

NOTE: In Soviet times, Sweden recognized Soviet authority over the Baltic States, turning over the Baltic embassies as well as bank assets that had been transferred to Sweden for safe keeping. The U.S. and the majority of Western countries never recognized the forcible incorporation of the Baltic States into the U.S.S.R. and view the present Government of Estonia as a legal continuation of the interwar republic.

"gold deposits," Rüütel, p. 153.

"70,000 Estonians escaped [Estonia] by the end of World War II. Some of the refugees had army clothes, maybe a t-shirt. 140-150 of them had remnants of German uniforms and that was enough to accuse them of being Nazis. Stalin ordered 30,000 Estonians in Sweden back to the U.S.S.R. Even if they had nothing that could create suspicions that they were Nazis, they were rounded up and sent back. On the ship that went to the U.S.S.R., many on board tried to kill themselves. [When they returned to Soviet Russia] most were then killed. Swedes have said for 50 years it was their most shameful dot on post war history. There has been no apology." Interview, Roos.

See also: *Irish Times*, February 23, 1995, "Stockholm Firmly Restates Neutrality," by Hugh Carnegy: "After Bildt left office, Swedish foreign minister Ms Lena Hjelm-Wallen reprimanded him for his comments as prime minister suggesting that Sweden would not remain neutral in the event of a threat to the independence of the three Baltic states which won their freedom from Moscow in 1991...Mr Bildt replied by invoking Sweden's controversial neutrality during the Second World War when Norway was occupied by Nazi Germany. 'If a threat should arise to the Baltic States, I say never again 1940, never again to accept in silence the occupation of a neighboring state.'"

"Northern pillar," see also: "Sea change in Sweden's political tide brings opposition leader to London," *Financial Times* (London) April 12, 1991, Section 1, p. 2, by Robert Taylor.

[40] NOTE: The first Estline ferry after the fall of the U.S.S.R. to serve the Tallinn-Stockholm route was a ship called the *Nord Estonia* until she was replaced by the larger *Estonia* in February 1993.

Hans Laidwa had worked as managing director for Nordström and Thulin. He was born in Estonia and his family soon immigrated to Sweden. In late 1988, Laidwa had read in the newspaper that Bildt had been in Estonia. "Bildt was a friend of mine. I called him and asked about opening a [ferry] line to Estonia, asked if he knew any partners. He said 'sure, it's possible'. He gave a name in the Estonian transport ministry. In February 1989, they had just raised the Estonian flag and I felt the time was right. I asked [the Estonians] in May 1989, 'When do you want to open the line?' They said it's a good idea but it will take five years. I told them next summer. They said it was impossible. But we opened it on June 17, 1990, exactly 50 years after the U.S.S.R. came to Estonia and occupied it." Interview, Laidwa.

[41] Interview, Laidwa.

[42] "The *Estonia* was symbolic. It was in the political sphere. They kept it going even though it was losing money. They put money into it. After World War II, Sweden had handed over Baltic [refugees] to the Soviets, so in the last years of the 1980s there was

a strong political force to liberate the Baltic States. It came from the conservative party, which hated Soviets. The Baltics became independent and [the Swedish government was] pushed to give them aid. And assistance and this ship was part of it. It was named after the republic. The whole ship itself is part of a political game here." Interview, Hellberg.

"--[S]omeone in ESCO [the Estonian state-owned shipping company and co-owner of the ship with Sweden] proposed the name *Estonia* for the ferry. Today you need government approval to use the name. The name was chosen because the ship was the crown of the fleet. The board of directors felt the ship was reconnecting Estonia to the West. It was symbolism. Interview, Lindpere.

[43] "Sweden Returns to Baltic Region--Russia Pays No Attention Yet," Current Digest of the Post-Soviet Press, June 9, 1993, No. 19, Pg. 19. Sourced from *Sevodnya*, May 14, 1993, by Aleksandr Polyukhov, p. 5.

[44] "Power Switched Off At Nuclear Submarine Plants" AP Worldstream, September 24, 1994.

Russia spent most of the 1990s on the brink of economic catastrophe: "[Russian State firms] outstanding debts total $45 billion and the national average for payroll arrears is 1 1/2 months. Unemployment has crept up to 12% and will reach 20% to 30% in another year if industrial production keeps falling…25% unemployment could trigger another revolution."

"Russians, U.S. fight fierce war of policies: Former Sen. Gary Hart warns disintegration of Russia into warring tribes, clans possible," *Rocky Mountain News*, (Denver) September 9, 1994, by Holger Jensen.

PART FIVE
ALTERNATIVE SCENARIOS

[1] "Meister said the commission at the current stage was ruling out the possibility of explosion on the *Estonia* or that the ferry collided with an object." "Investigators of Ferry Disaster Remain Cautious in Their Comments on Claims by Shipmaker," BNS, March 17, 1995.

[2] Cockburn, pp. 241-243.
In addition: "On the other side of the world, this terrifying brush with nuclear disaster went almost unnoticed. The giant antennae of the National Security Agency picked up the frantic commands and discussions that flashed over the Kazbek network that morning, but such intelligence is considered so sensitive that very few people, even in the intelligence agencies, were allowed to see the "blue border" reports describing the Russian alert. SAFE, the main classified database at the CIA Intelligence Directorate, contained no mention of the affair."

HIT AND RUN

[1] Interview, Einseln.

[2] Interview, Dresen; Interview, Mykkänen. Mykkänen believes more mines set by Soviet submarines remain in Finnish waters.

[3] The Treaty of Paris in 1947, part of the formal conclusion to World War II, prohibited Finland from owning military submarines. However, according to "Swedish submarine in tests with Finnish Navy in 1994," *Helsingin Sanomat*, March 31, 2000, the Finnish Navy tested a Swedish submarine in the Baltic Sea area between the two countries in November of 1994.

[4] NOTE: The submarine in the 1981 "Whiskey on the Rocks" incident was carrying nuclear-armed torpedoes.
In reference to "schools of swimming minks," media had fun with the revelation. "Furry clue in mystery of Baltic prowlers" wrote *The Independent* of London. The Russian press referred in its tongue-in-cheek style to "sea polecats" and "weasels" "emitting suspicious sounds."
According to "The Swedes and Soviet Subs" *The Nation*, April 3, 1995, Richard Lingeman: "The navy noted that only 20 percent of the reported incursions had been detected by listening devices; the remaining 80 percent were based on photos of tracks on the sea bottom, eyewitness reports and other evidence."
See also: "Russia ready to re-examine the submarine problem with Sweden," Itar-Tass, September 14, 1994, by Tamara Zamyatina; "Russia ready for dialogue on foreign submarines off Sweden," Itar-Tass, February 14, 1995 by Nikolai Vukolov and Yuri Kozlov; "Furry clue in mystery of Baltic prowlers," *The Independent* (London), December 23, 1995, by Christopher Bellamy.
On www.bildt.net, Bildt's website, he refers to the minks as "biological phenomenon."

[5] Interview, Aho. "--[B]ut [incursions in Finland were] nothing on the scale of what Sweden had."

[6] Lithuania, which for several centuries was united with Poland, came under Russia's rule in 1795.

[7] "The Soviet Baltic Fleet and the Grand Strategy Against NATO," *Defense & Foreign Affairs*, November, 1986, by Frederic N. Smith.

[8] "Sunk Russian Ships Hinder Navigation in Latvia," Itar-Tass, September 23, 1994, by Galina Kuchina.
See also: "In Latvian Harbor, a Nautical Nightmare" *The Moscow Times*, June 9, 1994.

[9] See, for example, http://www.spb.org.ru/bellona/ehome/russia/nfl/nfl1.htm 1.3.1 "Economic conditions."

[10] "More Debate Over the Future of Nuclear-Powered Submarines," *The Monitor*, Center for International Trade and Security, Summer 1995, p. 39.
See also: "Russia Seeks New Uses For Old Submarines," *The Monitor*, September 1995.

[11] "Russian Submarine Breaks Western Barrier," PR Newswire Europe, August 25, 1994.

[12] "Viewpoint: A Submarine Isn't a Needle. You Can't Hide One In The Persian Gulf--Why the West Doesn't Want Russia to Sell Arms to Iran," Current Digest of the Post-Soviet Press, February 17, 1993, page 15. Original source *Rossiiskaya Gazeta*, January 19, 1993, by Aleksei Bausin, p.7.

See also: Jane's Intelligence Review, September 1994, by Dr. Taeho Kim, pp.421-424.

According to "Russian arms sales to Iran," *Navy News & Undersea Technology*, October 3, 1994: "--Yeltsin confirmed that Russia will sell at least a third Kilo-class diesel submarine to Iran, in addition to the two already sold."

Presumably, the subs sold to Iran were Type-877EKM "Kilo" class submarines. See *Jane's Defense Weekly*, October 8, 1994.

[13] Yonhap News Agency (Seoul), January 18, 1994. The number of Russian Golf II-class submarines sold to North Korea was later changed to 12.

[14] Xinhua News Agency, April 27, 1994.

Defense & Foreign Affairs' Strategic Policy, November/December, 1995, Section on Arms Transfer Tables, p. 24.

Kyodo News Service, January 21, 1994.

"99 vessels from 186..." is from "New Russian Submarine Hunts Export Market" *International Defense Review* 27:52+ September 1994, by David Miller.

[15] Cockburn, pp. 179-180.

[16] "Third World Submarines" *Scientific American*, August 1994, pp. 16-21.

[17] "Iranian submarine appears in the Baltic," BBC Summary of World Broadcasts/The Monitoring Report, June 10, 1993.

[18] The Cooperative Venture 94 training exercise press release was dated September 16, 1994, but the general announcement about Partnership for Peace (PfP) sea exercises as well as previous PfP naval exercises, came earlier in 1994. Moreover, Russia itself was asked to participate in the exercise and therefore knew the training exercise dates well in advance.

[19] NATO nations participating were Belgium, Canada, Denmark, Germany, Italy, the Netherlands, Norway, Spain, United Kingdom and United States. Partner nations participating are Lithuania, Poland, Russia and Sweden.
"--Many other Allies and Partners will send observers to the exercise...The 10-day maritime exercise was designed to familiarize maritime forces of NATO and Co-operation Partners with each other and to enhance their capability to work together in future peace-keeping operations." Press Release (94)82, September 16, 1994, "Exercise Cooperative Venture 94," issued by Chief Public Information SACLANT, Norfolk, Virginia, U.S. and Chief Public Information CINCEASTLANT, Northwood, U.K..

[20] Using a training exercise and surface vessels as a smokescreen for submarine movements seems to be a Soviet tradition. In his book about the *Kursk* submarine tragedy, Robert Moore describes the cagey strategy behind the sea exercises in 2000 when the *Kursk* exploded:

"Under the disguise of war games, one of the Northern Fleet missile submarines--a boomer, fully armed with her nuclear missiles--would attempt to sneak out of her home port and slip under the summer ice, undetected by the Americans...the American spy submarines would be drawn to the exercise like bees to honey. If the Americans fell for the trick and decided to monitor the missile and torpedo firings, that would leave a crucial gap in their surveillance of the route up to the icepack. The routine August naval maneuvers were important in their own right, but of much greater strategic significance was this question of whether Russia could deploy its missile submarine without being trailed. Many ruses had been used in the past, such as Russian submarines following in the wake of a large merchant ship, hoping the acoustic disturbance would disguise the submarine's presence, and the stakes behind such diversionary games have always been high." Robert Moore, "A Time To Die, The Untold Story of the *Kursk*" (Crown Publishers), New York 2002, pp. 23-24.

[21] Final Report, p. 63.

[22] Final Report, p. 64.

[23] Siegel statement: GGE, 21.5, "Summary of Observations and Noises Heard Before the Abrupt Heel"

NOTE: Swedish journalist Knut Carlqvist has suggested the *Estonia* could even have hit a floating platform. A few years prior to the *Estonia* accident, a lighthouse foundation broke loose in a storm and waves pushed it around the Finnish Gulf, causing an accidental collision at sea.

[24] Testimonies from GGE Report, 21.2.6 "Further Evidence," also 21.3.2 "Reports from Deck 4."

[25] Final Report, p. 73.

[26] Interview, Barney.

[27] Interview, Sörman. Later, after tumbling into the sea, Sörman grasped onto an upside down lifeboat and drifted underneath the bulbous bow of the upside-down ship, where he could smell oil.

[28] GGE, 21.3.1, "Reports from Deck 1 - Passenger Area," Nikolajs Andrejev - cabin 1016, Carl Övberg - cabin 1049

[29] Compelling patterns found in testimonies of dispersed witnesses have been downplayed or dismissed in other catastrophes as well. In the aftermath of the TWA flight 800 crash in 1996, 34 eyewitnesses in different locations along the east coast of the U.S. saw

a flare rise from the west toward the jet, which traveled east from New York to Paris. Eventually, the descriptions were dismissed because the U.S. government told the witnesses what they saw: The rising streak didn't rise, but was actually falling pieces of the jet as it disintegrated during the explosion. The government interpretation was imposed on nearly three dozen witnesses who did not know each other and only by chance happened to see the catastrophe unfold.

[30] In 1974, the U.S. government spent $500 million in attempt to secretly retrieve a military cache from a sunken Soviet sub for intelligence gains. They examined the boat's construction. James E. Oberg, "Uncovering Soviet Disasters" (Random House) New York, 1988, p. 243-244.

[31] Authorities discovered the wreck and saw the stripped threads of the wheel mechanism. They also found out that the sailor had previously served on another submarine with a hatch wheel that closed the opposite way from the S-80. Moore, p. 80.

[32] "--The three-inch deep, 15ft by 4ft gouge caused by the collision was only discovered six weeks later when the *Valiant* went in for a 125 million [Pounds Sterling] refit. The accident happened because the hunter-killer submarine was eight-and-a-half miles off course. The court martial at Greenwich heard that [submarine] Commander Burston was not on the bridge when the collision happened, but was not told why. For security reasons, no details were given of why the *Valiant* was off Norway." "Nuclear sub on rocks sinks officer's career" *Daily Mail* (London), October 27, 1993.

[33] "Submarine safety shake-up after sinking," *The Herald* (Glasgow), December 27, 1994. Moreover, the Irish trawler *Lupina C* in September 1992 had its nets snagged by the *USS Sturgeon*, a nuclear attack boat, halfway between Northern Ireland and Scotland. In November 1993, the nets of the trawler *Audacious* were apparently snagged off the Butt of Lewis by the British hunter-killer submarine *HMS Valiant*.
In 1994, a Russian fishing trawler netted a Russian nuclear sub off the Kamchatka Peninsula in the Far East, narrowly avoiding a collision. "Russian Fishermen Net Russian Nuclear Submarine," Itar-Tass, February 23, 1994.

[34] "Sailboat ripped apart by submarine" *Calgary Herald*, September 13, 1994, by Michael Roberts.

[35] "Russian navy denies reports of Russian submarine caught in Polish fishing nets," BBC Summary of World Broadcasts, February 25, 1994, quoting source Itar-Tass February 22, 1994.

[36] "Submarine safety shake-up after sinking" *The Herald* (Glasgow), December 27, 1994, by Ian Bruce.

[37] "Crash sub on anti-collision practice run," *Lloyd's List*, August 20, 1993, by James Brewer.

[38] Report: Court of Inquiry into the circumstances surrounding the collision between the *USS Greeneville* (SSN 772) and Japanese *M/V Ehime Maru* that occurred off the coast of Oahu, Hawaii on 9 February 2001.

[39] Anders Björkman, among others, had speculated that the starboard stabilizer fin might have broken off due to equipment failure or collision. Stabilizer fins are on each side of the vessel about amidships. They extend like jackknife blades to provide better stability in rough seas. When speed falls to four knots, they fold back in automatically. A snapped starboard stabilizer fin could open a hole that admits water from belowdecks. But the *One Eagle* expedition in August 2000 proved that the starboard stabilizer fin was in its pocket, according to Bemis.

[40] "*Greeneville* repair update," *Pacific Fleet Public Affairs*, Pearl Harbor, Hawaii, March 9, 2001.

[41] "Submarine Collision off Murmansk: A Look from Afar" *The Submarine Review*, April, 1993, by Eugene Miasnikov, pp. 6-14.

[42] *The Financial Post* (Toronto), September 10, 1993, Diane Francis.
"Kaliningrad Region To Become Special Defense Region," Russian Press Digest, March 26, 1994, by Ilya Bulavinov.
"Russians hold three men over plutonium smuggling," *Financial Times* (London), August 19, 1994, by Christopher Parkes and John Thornhill.

[43] Örn Commission Report (Analysgruppen, SOU 1998:132), p. 17.
See also: Working Papers of the Örn Commission, section with Alf Svensson, chairman of Christian Democrats interview.
Interview, Aho; Interview, Carlqvist.
NOTE: It does seem odd that Bildt was thrust into the vortex of Scandinavia's worst peacetime catastrophe in the 20th century and he can't remember who initially notified him. Certainly there are chain of command procedures that are followed and documented.
Finnish Prime Minister Esko Aho recalls in some detail how he was woken up by a phone call from his secretary around 4:00 a.m.: "It was dark and I took the phone. He said his name and I said, 'You don't have anything positive to tell me.' That was my feeling. That something has happened. And then he told me that an Estonian ferry has turned over. I didn't know [then] that it had sunk."
According to the Bildt interview in the Örn Report, Bildt forgot who notified him initially, but recalls he was notified when he and an aide, Peter Egardt, were leaving the restaurant. He does not give a time. It might be anywhere between 01.40 and 02.31 Estonian time. The Örn Report states they were leaving the restaurant when notified.
The first contact between Finnish and Swedish rescue organizations was a request for helicopters at 01.52 Estonian time. Eight minutes later, Sweden confirmed the request. Swedish Marine Rescue always alerts military headquarters when big accidents happen, so by procedure Swedish military headquarters knew at 02.00 Estonian time that a sea disaster required helicopter assistance.

Military headquarters knew the core of the Swedish government was at the moment sitting in one place, the Rosenbad restaurant. Swedish helicopters, in order to reach Finland, would have to fly over the Aland Islands in the Bothnian Sea between the two countries. By international agreement, only Sweden's highest levels could grant them flyover permission. Thus, following alert notification procedures, military headquarters would call the officer on duty at Rosenbad, who would notify Bildt.

Certainly, military men relaying the news would document the time and steps taken. But because Bildt and his close aides do not recall who first notified them, established procedures apparently weren't followed. Most noteworthy, they did not want to give the notification time. If it was before 02:00 Estonian time, intelligence services were almost certainly tracking the *Estonia* that night.

Knut Carlqvist makes the point that if Swedish intelligence services had merely overheard the *Estonia's* Mayday and buzzed Bildt (pagers were used by the government in 1994), that would have been acknowledged as standard operating procedure. In the Örn Commission report, Bildt makes no mention of intelligence services.

[44] Interview, Aho.

[45] GGE, 12.4.4, "Water in the visor and on the car deck."

The GGE believes the frequent seawater on the cardeck resulted from a misaligned bow visor that couldn't shut properly, as well as from pre-existing damage to the cardeck ramp at portside.

[46] Örn Commission Report (Analysgruppen, SOU 1998:132), P. 28-29.

Precisely where Bildt got the visor-as-cause idea just hours after the accident is unknown. According to the Örn Report, during Bildt's flight to Turku, before meeting the other prime ministers there, he was reached by a pager message from TT, a Swedish news agency, saying a crew member had seen the bow door open. This is one possible explanation. The central point is not where he got the visor-as-cause idea, but that he fixated and acted on it, influencing the subsequent investigation well before anyone even knew the sunken ship's location.

Carl Bildt received but did not respond to three requests by the author for an interview about the *Estonia* ferry disaster.

[47] GGE, 29.3, "The Car Deck"

The Germans have proposed that the water spray was not from the sea, but was actually from the fire protection sprinkler system mounted on the cardeck roof. In this interpretation, sprinklers had been activated. A jet of water sprayed the videocamera lens and made it appear on the monitor (which continually changed to different views of the ship every few seconds) as if water was spraying onto the cardeck. Moreover, a crew member issued the fire alarm warning over the ferry's loudspeaker system as it listed. Together, these two incidents suggest a fire onboard.

[48] "That was the feeling," Aho said. "When we left we had the impression that something had happened with the front visor or door and the water had come in and the amount of water was huge. That was the impression the guys [Treu and Sillaste] gave us. They

sounded so clear and so reliable because they said they were standing where it was possible to monitor the cardeck. They couldn't speak anything else but the truth." Interview, Aho.

[49] Örn Commission Report (Analysgruppen, SOU 1998:132), pp. 28-30.

[50] Some passengers may have died after the ship settled on the bottom. The speed of the sinking would have created sizeable air-pockets, according to doctors on the scene, but the cold and the pressure would still have killed them within minutes. "Ferry Sank After Its Bow Came Open, Experts Say; Tougher Inspections Ordered Amid Reports About Near-Disasters" *International Herald Tribune*, October 01, 1994, by Erik Ipsen.

[51] Örn Commission Report, p. 28-29.

[52] Translating the actions of Bildt and Svensson to the TWA Flight 800 catastrophe make them sound even more outlandish. An analogous situation in the US in 1996 would see President Clinton discreetly telling Boeing Co. and the National Transportation and Safety Board that TWA Flight 800 crashed due to a technical fault and adviser Gen. John Shalikashvili, Chairman of the Joint Chiefs of Staff, declaring that neither the jet nor the bodies will be recovered--all on the same day the flight went down.

[53] Interview, Laar. "What was very clear was understanding at the beginning that there is no limit to finding the truth [behind the disaster]. The Commission worked out all possibilities, our institutions worked with all those scenarios. Maybe it would have been even better for Estonians to have such scenarios and then to point the finger at the Russians and say 'See, those people are guilty'. But the truth is more simple, more tragic. There were human mistakes, mistakes that the ship should not have been allowed to go to open sea at all. All such human, simple things and an enormous tragedy." NOTE: Laar believes the JAIC's findings in the Final Report.

[54] "Are Russians Again To Blame For The 'Estonia' Tragedy?" Russian Press Digest, October 6, 1994, original source *Komsomolskaya Pravda*, October 6, 1994, by Galina Sapozhnikova, p. 1, 7.

Emotions ran high also due to maritime history. Urmas Dresen, director of the Estonian Maritime Museum in Tallinn can recall deliberate and unprovoked Soviet attacks on Estonian ships. During the war with Finland in 1939, a Soviet submarine sank the Estonian ship *Kassari* halfway between Tallinn and Helsinki. Estonia was not at war with Russia and the ship was flying an Estonian flag. At the time, Soviet subs used 40mm rapid fire guns. The sub surfaced, circled and fired repeatedly at the *Kassari*, killing two crew members. The rest managed to escape unseen in a lifeboat on the opposite side of the ship. To this day, Russians do not admit responsibility or even involvement in the sinking, Dresen said. The wreck of the *Kassari* is still at the bottom of the Gulf of Finland at about 60 meters depth.

[55] "Russia Says No Navy Ships Were Present In Area Of Ferry Disaster," BNS, Sept 29, 1994.

NOTE: The vessels Gorbachuk mentions in the North Sea were likely at the Cooperative Venture 94 NATO exercise, participating in the Partnership for Peace program.

[56] "Russian Rescue Service Received No May Day From Capsized Ferry," Itar-Tass, September 28, 1994, by Anatoly Krasnov.

[57] GGE, 22.3, "The Rescue Operation." "The ship passed the lighthouse, averted the first rocks by sheer luck, then turned sharply to [the] south and safety. After this, radio contact was established and the captain of the "Leonid Bykov" explained that the fresh First Officer keeping watch didn't know any English but when radio messages continued [he] had figured out that maybe he needed to wake up the captain (who had made the safety move)."

See also: "Study says Russian merchant ships spy on U.S.," By Bill Gertz, *The Washington Times*, July 24, 2001. According to classified documents obtained by *The Washington Times*, a U.S. State Department monitoring program provided "confirmation of ongoing hostile intel collection by Russian merchant vessels...The document said that it is unknown whether Kremlin intelligence 'directed' the spying or was 'unsolicited' activity by government-linked commercial firms that run the merchant fleet..."

[58] "*Estonia's* Capsizing Resulted From Wild Business," Russian Press Digest, quoting *Krasnaya Zvezda*, by Vladimir Maryukha, October 7, 1994.

NOTE: Selivanov's phrase "Any intelligence service in the world" looks like a jab at Finland and Sweden who are widely assumed to monitor Russian subs with underwater acoustic equipment. Russian minisub operations on the seafloor have even pinpointed some of these listening posts.

According to the article, Admiral Selivanov has his own theory for the tragedy. The ferry was running on water-diluted fuel because some had been siphoned off for sale on the black market. The impure fuel stopped the engines, unsecured vehicles fell, the ship listed and sank.

[59] GGE, 21.3.3 "Reports from deck 5." Police are trained to observe precise details and report facts while under stress. Policewoman Fägersten added that after the collision, "the vessel started to shake/vibrate; at 00.45 hours the casualty sequence-of-events began."

[60] Interview, Aho.

[61] "The Navy is on the Verge of Collapse," *Moscow News*, March 18, 1994, by Viktor Starikov.

[62] Interview, Laar. "Carl Bildt was enormously important to Estonian independence. Because Carl Bildt from the early stages developed from the Western side the structures [such as] an ad *hoc* committee, which dealt with Baltic questions and supported very clearly the development in the Baltic region. This was something that was missing in the Baltics and is one of the reasons the Baltics have been so successful.

"--We can say Carl Bildt was one of the first Swedish politicians who gave his clear support to Estonian independence. We knew each other from 1990 before the official independence as he had visited Estonia then. There were important Western countries that were following his advice and questions. That was the power the Russians understood. Because if you're speaking with Russians, you can only rely on power. If you're weak, if you're nice, then you're nobody. Mostly we made it clear we we're going forward. Only nations themselves can do this convincingly, but Bildt was an enormous help because the more power you can put to this, the less trouble you will have."

[63] "The Baltic Litmus Test: Revealing Russia's True Colors," *Foreign Affairs*, September/October 1994, by Carl Bildt.
"Personal View: Importance of Nordic influence in EU," *Financial Times* (London), November 22, 1994, by Carl Bildt.

Bildt saw the Baltic States as the key to a post-Cold War stability that would extend into Europe:
"The revanchists of the extreme right and left are far from dominating Russia's political scene," Bildt wrote two months after the disaster. "Yet any sign that their influence is growing will send shock waves into the Baltic region and then the entire European system."

[64] "Russia-Sweden: no more reefs ahead?" *Moscow News*, February 13, 1993, Dmitry Yakushkin.
"Q: Do you believe that those [trespassing submarines in Swedish waters] could be Russian submarines?
[Carl Bildt]: I wouldn't rule out this likelihood since we have not yet established whom they belong to. Possibly, it is the structures remaining intact since the U.S.S.R.'s disintegration that carry on this kind of activity. But this still has to be specified."

According to "The Swedes and Soviet Subs," *The Nation*, April 3, 1995, Richard Lingeman: "In February 1993, Prime Minister Bildt traveled to Moscow bearing what was termed definitive electronic evidence that the incursions were real and were continuing. President Yeltsin obligingly agreed there was something out there but insisted it wasn't Russian. Bildt, not wanting to undermine Russia's first democratic leader, pointedly played up Yeltsin's assertion that he had never ordered any incursions. Bildt apparently accepted the theory that an anti-Yeltsin cabal was behind it all. When he later wrote Yeltsin to this effect, Yeltsin was reportedly outraged at the implication that he wasn't in control of his own government."

NOTE: Bildt has been described as a submarine expert. He had access to signal intelligence from Sweden, Finland, the U.S. and probably NATO. His tactic of prejudging the accident's cause as a technical fault effectively stopped the JAIC inquiry from looking into other possible explanations and suggests he held suspicions about the circumstances surrounding the ferry sinking.

There were other factors for keeping submarine involvement out of the investigation. Bildt was about to become a UN negotiator in the Balkans. If the investigation led to indications of a collision and Russian-Estonian relations unraveled as a result, his credibility as an effective negotiator would be in question. Second, there was personal embarrassment. Sweden had recorded sounds of what Bildt believed were Russian submarines in Swedish waters. Bildt had confronted Yeltsin with the evidence. Later, a portion of these sounds turned out to be swimming minks. Andrei Kozyrev, the Russian foreign minister, spoke publicly about Bildt with stinging humor: "The minks have taught us not to jump at conclusions..." Therefore, another reason Bildt kept his suspicions to himself may have been to avoid media comparisons that implied he was again confusing submarines and swimming minks.

See also: "Russia ready for dialogue on foreign submarines off Sweden," Itar-Tass, February 14, 1995, by Nikolai Vukolov and Yuri Kozlov.

[65] "Mine Could Have Sunk Ferry Claim," *The Guardian*, October 3, 1994, by James Meek In Tallinn and Greg Mcivor In Stockholm.

"Doubt Cast On Suggestions People Could Still Be Alive In Air Pockets," Associated Press, September 29, 1994, by Frank Bajak.

GGE 37.2, sourced from "'Estonia' Visor Broken Away Evidence of Catastrophic Failure as Submersible Finds Bow Visor 15m From Sunken Ferry," *Lloyd's List*, By Jim Muluran, October 3, 1994.

Rabe adds: "--One also needs to know in this context that the JAIC gathered the next day [after the October 3, 1994 *Lloyd's List* article] in Turku to watch the ROV-produced video material. Based on the temporal sequence of events, I thus assume it was during this meeting that the decision was made to consider the visor as "still not found," even though one of the JAIC members had already informed the *Lloyd's List* reporter that the visor had been found just fifty feet from the wreck." Rabe, p. 116.

NOTE: The bow visor was officially found weeks later on October 18 almost 1.5 kilometers from the wreck. Therefore, the object sighted by the ROV about fifty feet or 15 meters from the ferry was not the visor. What was it?

[66] "Russian Scientists Offer Plan to Rescue People Out of Ferry," Itar-Tass, September 29, 1994, by Lev Rumyantsev. "Russian submarine designers Igor Spassky and Sergei Kovalyov believe there are still some survivors on the ferry *Estonia*...Stressing that 'delay may mean death', they offer a plan for rescuing these people out of the sunken ferry. 'With highly experienced divers, we can apply a pipe down to the *Estonia*, cut the bilge with due regard for the position of the ferry and pull the surviving passengers and crew up to the surface,' Spassky said."

[67] Interview, Nuorteva.

[68] "Mine Could Have Sunk Ferry Claim," *The Guardian*, October 3, 1994, by James Meek In Tallinn And Greg Mcivor In Stockholm.

NOTE: The sonar pictures were transmitted to the Finnish government vessel *Halli* from an unmanned submersible. Nuorteva also wrote a report on October 3, 1994, in which he explains that the object was probably a misinterpretation.

[69] The group of German investigators believes these ROV videotapes have been edited. GGE, 25.4 "Further Evidence": "--the first ROV inspection [of] the wreck was carried out from the "HALLI" on 2 October 1994. The respective logbook pages have recently been received, although the name "HALLI" is nowhere written on the available pages... Video recordings by ROV were performed between 12.17 hours - 20.45 hours. The three tapes received from the Finnish JAIC in March 1995 do fall into this time frame,

however, substantial parts were cut out in a rather unprofessional way." NOTE: Today, the video of the purported object is unavailable.

Faxes are from GGE, Chapter 24, "Locating the Wreck and Visor"

[70] There's much confusion surrounding the object and the reader can easily get confused. A steel object seen on *video* by Lehtola later disappeared. The main idea to keep in mind is the difference between the possible misreading of cryptic sonar photographs, and the certainty of seeing an object on videotape. The rough analogy is the difference between an abstract painting and a photograph.

In an interview with the author, Lehtola explained that the mysterious object mentioned in the fax with its specified depth and dimensions resulted from a misinterpretation of sonar photographs. He does not recall the ROV videotapes from eight years prior. But his fax of 09.10.94 stated (italics are mine):

"Karppinen, Aarnio and the ROV I team go onboard of "Tursas" at Nagu at 11.00 (Finnish time) and the work starts at ca. 13.00 hrs. *They shall video film at first the "large object"*. Attached please find a sonar picture including an enlargement of it." GGE, Chapter 24, item j.

Nuorteva said in an interview with the author that the object was a 5x7 meter piece of detached sundeck roofing from the ferry. He confirmed the object had been videotaped by the ROV and *he'd seen the footage on the ship's video monitor*. The object was not recovered from the seabed, he added.

Yet another description comes from Tuomo Karppinen. He recalled the object as a "corrugated steel roof that was crumbled like a wad of paper." It was "not so rusted, painted white, appeared to be freshly fallen on the bottom." He emphasized that he wasn't sure if it was from the ferry.

Karppinen then contradicted Nuorteva by adding that the object lay a "few hundred meters" from the wreck, not 15 meters, and said it was not videotaped, but only seen through sonar images. "[The object] might have been just a disturbance on the sonar picture," he said. "It is very possible it is echoes." Karppinen speculated that the object could have been crumbled sundeck roofing made from aluminum, which reflects radar well. "The [sonar] reflection was from all angles because it was crumpled."

But sundeck roofing on the Estonia's sister ship, now called *Meloodia*, is tightly secured to a framework by rivets or screws. The panels are relatively small, perhaps a meter square, and are hardened plastic. An inside and outside search of the *Meloodia* during the summer months revealed nothing remotely the size or shape of the described corrugated sunroof. Moreover, autumn in the Northern Baltic area is notoriously rainy and windy and everything on the *Estonia*, if it hadn't been bolted down or stored away, would've been blown overboard well before the chain of events began.

What to make of all this? In summary, documents show that a large object near the shipwreck was recorded on both sonar photographs and on videotape. The sonar image could possibly be explained as a misreading. However, a video image cannot. The German investigators saw these specific videotapes in 1995 and said they had been edited. Today these videotapes are no longer available.

Speculation is that an object was sighted on video. The object was not directly related to the ship disaster, but public disclosure of the object was not authorized.

[71] Ferries have sailed without bow visors before.

[72] Fax about the security scale of the requested vessels is from GGE, Chapter 24, "Locating the Wreck and Visor," item h.

NOTE: Nuorteva initially told the author that Swedish mine hunting ships helped to search for the visor. He explained that the Swedish ships were crisscrossing the grid square search area and their sensitive equipment reacted to every tin can, slowing them down. Later he retracted his statement and said that Swedish mine ships were not involved in the visor search.

[73] Interview, Lehtola. See also: GGE, 24.1, item d.

[74] "Navy Diving for 'the Truth'," *Moscow Times*, by Pavel Felgenhauer. Admiral Vladimir Valuyev, first deputy commander of the Baltic Fleet: "In the opinion of the navy command, these fragments should include parts of the hull of the foreign submarine that caused the accident."

The Mir subs scanned four square kilometers of the seabed around the *Kursk*, but did not find any U.S. or British submarine debris.

[75] "Sweden warns against submarine intrusions," UPI, December 21, 1987, By Rolf Soderlind.

[76] Interview, Johansen.

[77] On October 18, 1994, officials announced the visor was found in position 59°23,0'N; 21°39,2'E, which is 0.85 nm (about 1400 meters) in direction 272° from the actual wreck position.

For the theory about the visor being moved away from the wreck, see: GGE, Chapter 24, "Locating the Wreck and Visor"; Independent Fact Group website: http://est.jbn.nu/factgroup/est/reports.html; Anders Björkman website: http://heiwaco.tripod.com/disasterinvestigation.htm

[78] GGE, 25.4, "Further Evidence." The German investigators believe debris was filmed by the ROV, but the videotapes were edited by the commission. The JAIC denies the claims.

[79] "Nuorteva called me with a mobile telephone from [the ship] *Tursas* [and read the coordinates]. I had written this position in my book. It is very possible that I had heard wrong. Because the mobile telephone connection to this accident site was very bad. I had given to many people this wrong position but this wrong position is also in my book... The correct position can be found in several logbooks of vessels that participated in the ROV surveys... For example, when we first went with the *Halli* on 2 October, we went to the wreck and started the ROV survey. We had no problems finding the wreck. *Halli* just went directly above the wreck and could confirm that the wreckage was underneath it. The correct position had been in the *Halli* logbook." Interview, Lehtola.

[80] GGE, Chapter 24, "Locating the Wreck and Visor."

[81] Interview, Lehtola.

[82] EPIRB buoys, mounted inside the ship, are designed to detach, float and give off a distress signal when a ship sinks.
"The last check of the radio beacons [EPIRBs] was reported to have been made about one week prior to the disaster by the radio operator. The check confirmed that the EPIRBs were in full working order and it has to be assumed that both were left in "switched-on" condition after the test. Nevertheless, no signals from the two buoys were received in the course of the rescue operation." GGE, 22.2 "The EPIRB Buoys."

[83] About communications malfunctions on the night of the disaster, see also Rabe, p. 69.
NOTE: It's a curious coincidence that during the *One Eagle* dive in August 2000, both Bemis and Rabe reported communications anomalies similar to the breakdown during the time of the disaster in 1994. Both suspected the Swedish navy. Rabe, p.176-177: "We also quickly noted problems when navigating. Our GPS was indicating the wrong position...Craig, one of the ROV pilots who had worked for the [U.S.] Navy during the first Gulf war, drew on his military experience and announced he suspected the Swedes and the Finns were disrupting our position measurements. This seemed to be quickly confirmed because while I had received numerous telephone calls from interested journalists on my satellite telephone the day before, it hadn't rung once this entire morning. There was no signal; I couldn't get any connection."
Bemis also believes the Swedish forces were jamming the *One Eagle's* ship-to-shore communications, which he said worked intermittently. Yet all equipment had been tested before leaving port and worked fine.

[84] "Russian naval sender damped *Estonia's* emergency call, commission member tells newspaper," BNS, October 18, 1994. "Difficulties in hearing the *Estonia's* 'Mayday' signal in the early hours of September 28 were traced back to the Hoaglund transmitter, which some technical experts said had been disturbing radio communications in the area for a month."

[85] NATO Press Release (94)82, 16 September 1994, "Exercise Cooperative Venture 94."
NOTE: NATO has refused repeated requests by the author for additional information on the "Cooperative Venture 94" exercise.

[86] My request for more information was denied because it could "compromise [Sweden's national] security."

[87] "They tracked the killer of the *Kursk*," *Versiya*, No 48, December 12 - 18, 2000, p. 2.

[88] Report: "Enhancing Security of Lithuania and Other Baltic States in 1992-94 and Future Guidelines" by Ceslovas Stankevicius. The Kaliningrad military enclave shares a border with Lithuania.

[89] Oberg, p. 40. "The Soviets...officially denied that any such thing had happened and claimed the jet was fifty miles from where the Swedish radar showed it...They provided carefully labeled maps to demonstrate this and even had testimony from another pilot, who swore he was looking at the jet in question on maneuvers over the Baltic when the Swedes claimed it was over their territory."

[90] The standard logbooks of the Swedish submarines *Sjolojonet, Sjobjorner, Sjohunden* and *Nacken* are verified as docked during dates September 27-September 29, 1994. The standard logbooks of the *Sjohasten, Neptun, Najad, Vastergotland, Sjoormen* and *Halsingland* are supposedly available for public inspection.

A scenario that would put a Swedish sub near the *Estonia* ferry unfolds naturally. Bildt believed that renegade groups within the Russian military could have been responsible for submarine incursions in Sweden's territorial waters. If Swedish intelligence had picked up information that constituted a threat to the *Estonia* ferry, a submarine escort could be authorized. Something goes wrong and the two vessels collide. The crew would be under military secrecy laws and advised that country's national security was at stake. Logbooks and repair records would have to be doctored or classified. Clandestine work would begin on the shipwreck. Identifiable debris would be collected. Sweden never issued a public statement that categorically states none of its submarines were in the area of the *Estonia* the night it sank, yet Russia did.

But perhaps in Sweden, responsibility for the accidental death of 1000 civilians would not fade away after signing an oath of secrecy. Someone should talk, or at least through silence circulate rumors or anonymous tips, and that hasn't happened.

[91] A request for documents concerning sounds detected by SOSUS, or any other underwater acoustic equipment under the command of the U.S. Navy, in several specified grid squares that corralled the *Estonia* ferry sinking site, for September and October 1994, came back with the standard "No documents relevant to your request." The Navy, of course, reserves the right under the Freedom of Information Act (FOIA) to deny certain documents exist, even though they do exist, in order to protect national security.

The highly sensitive area of the Baltic where the *Estonia* went down, with St Petersburg sub bases, design and construction yards nearby, would preclude any disclosure that may suggest the U.S. is listening in those waters.

[92] "Scientists Fight Navy Plan to Shut Far-Flung Undersea Spy System," *The New York Times*, June 12, 1994 by William J. Broad. "For decades the SOSUS system was so secret the Government refused to acknowledge its existence. The network was begun in the 1950's as a way to strip the cloak of secrecy from enemy submarines. It turned out to work better than expected, prompting the Navy to vastly expand its size in step with expanding Soviet threat."

DARK SIGNATURE

[1] Report: "Patterns of Global Terrorism 1994," U.S. Department of State, April 1995, Department of State Publication 10239, Office of the Secretary, Office of the Coordinator for Counterterrorism, Philip C. Wilcox, Jr.

[2] "In Estonia, there were no bomb explosions reported in 1991, but 63 occurred in 1993 (along with 50 car bombings)" from "Image of Lawlessness Distorts Moscow's Reality" *Crime and Justice International* (Europe) March/April 1996, Steven Erlanger. NOTE: All of the 63 bombings did not necessarily result in deaths. The point is that bold criminal/political elements were behind a startling increase in bombing incidents during the early 1990s.

"The incident was strangely underplayed in the newspaper": from The *Financial Post* (Toronto), September 10, 1993, by Diane Francis.

[3] Lieven, p. xvi.

[4] Stern and Nohrstedt, ed. p. 19.

[5] "Government interprets weekend bomb blast as direct attack against Estonia," RFE/RL, August 30, 1994.

"Three 'underworld figures' arrested in wake of Narva bomb," BBC Summary of World Broadcasts, September 20, 1994.

[6] GGE, 7.3.4 "Training and drills":
"The threat that a bomb might explode in the sauna and swimming pool compartments half way between the Estonian and the Swedish coasts, i.e. approximately in the actual casualty position, was simulated. The purpose of this exercise was to train [for] co-operation between the shore-based, helicopter landed anti-terrorists experts with bomb dogs, etc. and the vessel's safety organization."

NOTE: Several bombs threats had been made against the *Estonia* ferry as well as the Finnish shipping company Silja Line. According to Rabe, p. 203: "Lennart Alberg of Sweden's RITS [Räddning Insatser Till Sjöss – Maritime Fire and Rescue Operations] organization, one of the officials responsible in such cases, cited extortion as the main motive. 'Pay up or we plant a bomb on the ship,' as Lennart Alberg categorized most of these threats…During 1993 and 1994, RITS conducted four mock bomb drills on different ships [worked on] all conceivable scenarios. One of the larger exercises had even taken place aboard the *Estonia* herself..."

See also: GGE, 36.2, "Early Indications of Something Unusual."

[7] "Ferry disaster investigators view video of wreck" AFP, October 03, 1994 by Antoine Jacob.

NOTE: Johansen at the time also speculated that the ship might have hit a World War II floating sea mine (the Baltic Sea still contains ordnance from 20th century conflicts).

In an interview for this book, Johansen denied that he had suggested a bomb was involved in the disaster. However, his comments at the time in 1994 were made at a news conference and reported by several media outlets.

See, for example, Lauristin and Vihalemm, p.84: "On the first day following the disaster [Johansen] told the press that a ship like the *Estonia* could not sink unless there was some kind of external cause, like a collision or a bomb blast…"

[8] Lauristin and Vihalemm, p. 46.

[9] "Who benefited from this?" *Post* [Estonia], October 28, 1994, by Toomas Liiva, translated from Estonian language. Also from the same article, another theory proposes that gangsters wanted to kill the 70 Swedish policemen onboard the ferry that night to gut Sweden's anti-organized crime efforts. (Of the 70 Swedish policemen, only 7 survived). As mentioned earlier, by sheer coincidence the Swedish policemen had been in Estonia conducting training involving a mock bomb threat on the ferry and were returning home.

[10] "Swedish prosecutor closes inquiry in *Estonia* ferry disaster criminal case," BNS, September 19, 1998.
"Sweden Ends *Estonia* Ferry Probe But Suit Continues," *Reuters*, February 19, 1998, by Belinda Goldsmith.

[11] Swedish authorities claim that the only editing done was on footage that showed human remains. No member of the public has access to the unedited videos. The location of the original tapes is unclear.

[12] "high degree of probability as an 'explosive charge'" see GGE, 32.1, "Introduction," Unexplained Damage/Unexplained Evidence.
"The suspect package could have been..." see GGE, 34.7, "Investigation Report on Possible Explosion Damage on the Ferry 'Estonia' by Brian H.L. Braidwood, MBIM, MIExpE, Weymouth/U.K., "c. Damage to the car deck port side forward."
In one specific damage area on the port side bulkhead, Braidwood's analysis found metal even pushed *inward* toward the cardeck space, an opposite direction of force that is not possible to reconcile with the JAIC explanation of the immense *outward* force of the falling bow visor: "--The [portside forward] damage hole itself is fairly round and about 300 mm across. The hole is bordered by petals of split metal which have split in all directions away from the centre of the hole. The photos are taken looking at the bulkhead from inside the car deck space and it can be seen how the petals cast strong shadows onto the bulkhead. This clearly shows that the metal has been pushed away from the bulkhead into the car deck space [i.e. turned inward]." Ibid.

[13] GGE, 32.1, "Introduction," Unexplained Damage/Unexplained Evidence; GGE, Chapter 36, "Other Activities"

[14] "*Estonia* probe team defends its findings," Lloyd's List, September 27, 1999.

[15] Interview, Bemis. Human remains were found by the ROV, not the divers.

[16] "bubble making equipment..." from US Embassy correspondence, July 14, 2000, Classification: "Sensitive," From: American Embassy Stockholm "Olson," To: Secretary of State, Washington DC, Subject: "Objection to 'Estonia' shipwreck dive."
Regarding "the loss of this essential and costly locating tool," Bemis added: "A search for the [sonar] fish was launched due to the known location from the GPS naviga-

tion system on board. Eventually it was located along with the 200 feet of yellow cable attached, and an initial attempt to raise it with the ROV was tried. The equipment wasn't sturdy enough and by the time other better arrangements were devised for the lift and recovery, the fish and cable just disappeared... [I suspect] the Swedish marine forces were involved in the disappearance of the equipment with a nighttime recovery while the *One Eagle* was away from the site."

Rabe details Sweden's crude harassment during the *One Eagle* dive in her book, p. 181:

"Our work proceeded well on the following days, even if we were continually pestered by low-flying airplanes and helicopters from the Swedish Coast Guard. One day, Swedish frogmen even piled out of a helicopter. Of course, we were not privy to their orders or what they actually did. Swedish warships also cruised by repeatedly. It was apparently absolutely imperative that one of them clean their gun barrels right there on the spot, although we only found out about this over the radio after they had pointed one of the barrels straight at us. Another warship felt it critical to test their water cannon for hours. While not aimed in our direction but off to the other side, it still came across as a threatening and demonstrative gesture. Finally, the day before our last, at the same time we got the weather report, we also learned that the Estonian Navy would be holding a mine sweeping exercise quite nearby. But we didn't let any of these actions ruffle us."

[17] Southwest Research Institute Project No 18.04042.01.109, "Examination of Metal Samples for Evidence of Shock Loading" Final Report, January 26, 2001.

[18] Materials Testing Laboratory of the State of Brandenburg, "Examination Report" No. 1.1/00/3669 [10/26/00].

[19] "Did a Semtex bomb sink the 'Estonia'?" *The Independent*, December 17, 2000, by Paul Lashmar, Arlen Harris and Nick Savvides.

[20] "New bombshell as *Estonia* row goes on," *Lloyd's List*, December 16, 2000, by Nick Savvides.
NOTE: Sweden has had several different government ministers responsible for transportation since the catastrophe. The officials relevant to this book are:
Mats Odell, outgoing minister when the ferry sank on September 28, 1994
Ines Uusmann, 1994-1998
Mona Sahlin, 1998-2002
The Ministry for Transport and Communication was also was dissolved on 31 December 1998. Transport was brought under the Ministry of Industry, Employment and Communication.

[21] Interview, Bemis.

[22] "New bombshell as *Estonia* row goes on," *Lloyd's List*, Saturday December 16 2000, by Nick Savvides.

[23] Institut für Materialprüfung und Werkstofftechnik, Report, "X-ray microstructure in-

vestigations on two specimens of shipbuilding plates," Report 20130-03, Date of report: October 16, 2000.

[24] Interviews, Bemis and Rabe. According to Bemis, the BAM laboratory admitted that this had been the first time the lab had ever performed the comparative type of metal analysis.

In reference to "Researchers applied explosive forces by various means directly on the metal..." Rabe said that intermediary material (such as plastic or cloth) sandwiched between explosive force and metal, as well as testing metal in seawater, would affect the structural damage pattern. Because BAM did not conduct metal tests using either of these variations in conditions, nor did it test the actual metal samples that had been analyzed by other labs, their report does not accurately reflect the test objective.

Rabe also brought the metal samples that had tested positive to Michael Edwards, a researcher and lecturer at the Royal Military College of Science at Cranfield University in England. Edwards specializes in the behavior of materials at high rates of strain, especially in relation to explosions. Edwards did not write a report, but concluded that "most probably there had been an explosion, but that something like textile or plastic or wood had been between the explosives and the hull of the ship," Rabe said.

Rabe, p. 194-195: "--The fact that neither the Meyer shipyard nor the steel manufacturing company even had facilities for shot peening at the time did not sway the designated experts from their assertion."

[25] "New *Estonia* blast claim rejected," *Lloyd's List*, January 2, 2001.

[26] "Retrial Ordered in Kholodov Killing," Itar-Tass, May 28, 2003, by Oksana Yablokova: "A group of paratroop officers close to [Russian Defense Minister Pavel] Grachev was arrested in the Kholodov case. The group was led by Pavel Popovskikh, head of military intelligence in the airborne forces. Popovskikh was suspected of forming a 'death squad' that eliminated Grachev's enemies 'without his knowledge.'"

Report: "Russia: Mafia in Uniform: The Criminalization of the Russian Armed Forces" by Dr. Graham H. Turbiville, Jr., Foreign Military Studies Office, Fort Leavenworth, KS, 1995: "The murder of Kholodov makes the participation of military personnel in such crimes seem at least plausible and also further fuels suspicions about the existence of 'military assassins' or even some form of military 'death squads.'"

Report: "Russia's Military: Corruption in the Higher Ranks" Perspective, Volume IX Number 2 (November-December 1998) by Richard F. Staar, Hoover Institution and Boston University: "More evidence of renegade death squads emerged in 1998 when General Lev Ya Rokhlin [who openly criticized the military-criminal connection] was murdered by three men at his home near Moscow...[the men] warned his wife to tell police she was the one who killed her husband ...The apparent contract murder could have been the work of a joint government-mob conspiracy, consummation of which obviously benefited both."

NOTE: Rokhlin's wife initially confessed to the killing, but later said she made the confession under duress. She was convicted of the crime and sentenced to prison.

[27] "Submarine Mystery," Swedish Press (Digest), January 31, 2001, Vol. 73, No. 1, Pg. 11.

"The Swedes and the Soviet Subs," *The Nation*, April 3, 1995, by Richard Lingeman.

[28] "about 2500 such illegal residents in Estonia," Stern and Nohrstedt, eds, p. 123.

Also in Soviet times, sleeper cells had been awakened by Moscow's trumpet. Estonian president Arnold Rüütel tells about legal Russian "political groups" in Estonia who were responsible for a sudden attack on Toompea Castle (now the seat of the Estonia parliament), in May 1990. They'd been activated by Moscow: "--the Kremlin felt secure enough thanks to the activity of its 'Fifth Column' in the Baltic Countries." Rüütel, p. 150.

[29] In "The Struggle for Russia," Yeltsin mentions Viktor Anpilov, the leader of an extremist neo-communist movement called Working Moscow, who tried to take Ostankino by force in 1992. Anpilov was a typical example of the dangerous spirit of the times. Yeltsin writes, "Anpilov's militants were out for blood. Violence would prove that the authorities were incapable of handling the situation, and would be a sign of trouble and anarchy. So they strove to shed blood at any cost." Pp. 177-8.

[30] Michael R. Beschloss and Strobe Talbott, "At the Highest Levels: The Inside Story of the End of the Cold War," (Little, Brown and Company), 1993, p. 197.

[31] "Grachev Finds Ranks Restive," radio report from RFE/RL by Vladimir Socor quoting *Nezavisimaya Gazeta*, September 20, 1994.

[32] Lieven, p. 203.

[33] Interviews, Rebas and Einseln.

[34] Stern and Nohrstedt, eds, pp. 174-5.

NOTE: Historically the *Kaitseliit* was apolitical with the clear aim of defending territory. Largely supported by farmers, the *Kaitseliit* kept their weapons at home, ready to defend their farms from the occupying powers of the moment. The post-Soviet *Kaitseliit* were different. The Russian press has claimed the *Kaitseliit* were involved in illicit arms sales to Chechnya and the IRA.

[35] Fortunately, the incident ended without bloodshed.

"There was a provocation and it looked like there was going to be a shootout. [The militia group] caused unnecessary friction with the Russian military," Einseln added.

The Estonian government's inaction over the *Jaagrikriis* prompted Defense Minister Rebas to resign. Now a professor at the University of Kiel in Germany, Rebas added that difficulties in working with some of the army's Soviet-trained commanders had also been an ongoing source of tension: "I was on vacation, and I was [called] back a bit late [in the crisis] and the government didn't act as they should have done, directly taking initiative. They didn't accept my suggestions. The education of the decisive members of the Estonian government was a Soviet education. They were quite young. Their experience, education and training in no way responded to what was needed at those times and what Einseln clearly understood. So he spoke to deaf ears and so did I." Interview, Rebas.

See also: "Estonian Forces Operation to take over Russian Base," BBC Summary of World Broadcasts, March 18, 1993: "Estonian authorities began an extensive operation...at Paldiski, a closed town under Russian naval control, in order to combat crime and ensure security and order. The operation's final aim is to subordinate the town to the Estonian authorities...The Estonian authorities have been concerned about the illegal arms trade and thefts taking place in Russian military units. In January, 261 guns and 43 sub machine guns went missing from a military unit at Paldiski, amounting to one of the biggest arms thefts in Estonia in recent times."

See also: Stern and Nohrstedt, eds, p. 18.

[36] US State Department correspondence, February 1994, From: American Embassy Tallinn [Frasure], To: US Secretary of State, Classification: "Confidential," Subject: "Russian politics in Estonia – tension, divisions and a cold wind from the East":

"[NAME DELETED] explained to us that there are still two basic attitudes among Russians toward Estonia. The first, represented by the Russian democratic movement and then by the RRA, advocated 'cooperation and integration' while the second, represented by the Interfront movement and then by the 'Russian community' championed 'Conflict and Russian Chauvinism.'

"In this uncertain context and following on Zhirinovsky's success in the Duma elections, Russian hardliners have gleefully arisen from their shallow political graves... Piotr Rozhok, previously just one of a crowd of chauvinistic Russian nationalists... rocketed from relative obscurity to instant notoriety as the self-proclaimed leader of the unregistered liberal-democratic party in Estonia. Trumpeting assurances from Vladimir Volfovich [Zhirinovsky] that economic sanctions would be imposed on Estonia if human rights violations were not stopped, he took the line that Estonia is ancient Russian land and called for retired Soviet military officers in Estonia to resist with arms any attempt to throw them out of their apartments...[NAME DELETED] also remarked that, while the leaders of the veteran's groups are appropriately aware of Rozhok's inflammatory remarks, there are a lot of hotheads just below them...Not surprisingly, Russian moderates here are alarmed by all of this rhetoric. [NAME DELETED] told us with horror and disgust that with this "dangerous provocation" Rozhok was playing on fears that Russians wouldn't be issued residence permits."

Holbrooke memo: US State Department correspondence, August 1995, From: Richard Holbrooke [Assistant Secretary of State], To: The Deputy Secretary, Classification: "Confidential," Subject: "Expulsion from Estonia of Russian nationalist and Zhirinovsky representative Pytor Rozhok."

"brink of civil war...": "Ethnic Russians protest actions by Estonian government," Itar-Tass, August 12, 1997.

NOTE: Rozhok in 1995 was expelled under armed guard from Estonia for urging non-citizens to disobey Estonian law. Russia claimed his rights were violated. The Estonian court later overturned their previous decision, allowing Rozhok to return to Estonia. In 2000, he was held in custody in Tallinn and charged with extortion that involved a bomb and physical violence, but was later released.

See also: "Estonian proceedings against Russian nationalist," Keesing's Record of World Events, February 4, 1994.

[37] Moreover, "--democracy and the rule of law is not yet firmly rooted in Estonia, nor has the threat from Russia disappeared." US Embassy correspondence, November 1994, Classification: "Limited Official Use," From: American Embassy Tallinn, Keith Smith, Charge d'Affaires, To: Secretary of State, Washington DC, Subject: "Future Assistance to Estonia"

NOTE: Throughout Soviet history, intelligence and security services held ties with criminal clans. Gangster groups in the 1990s were to some extent created and nurtured by the Russian security services in order to squirrel away money and state assets from the disintegrating U.S.S.R.

"[The Russian mob] is not so much organized crime as authorized crime..." "Understanding the Russian Mafia," Testimony of [former CIA chief and Russian analyst] Fritz W. Ermarth Before the House Committee on Banking and Finance September 21, 1999.

[38] "Mafia in Uniform: The Criminalization of the Russian Armed Forces" by Dr. Graham H. Turbiville, Jr., Foreign Military Studies Office, Fort Leavenworth, KS, 1995.

NOTE: Splinter units were common in the unruly 1990s. They were active in the violent events of October 1993 in Moscow. The rebellious Russian Parliament was defended by a patchwork of soldiers: Special assignment battalions from the breakaway Trans-Dniester region of Moldova, OMON troops brought in from Vilnius and Riga, several hundred officers of the Supreme Soviet's security department and combat troops from the fascist parties. See: "The Struggle for Russia," Yeltsin, p. 268.

Spetsnaz troops have a history of cross-border clandestine operations under the Soviet government. In May 1968, a small *Spetsnaz* team posing as tourists arrived on an Aeroflot flight in Prague and seized the airport as a prelude to the Soviet tanks rolling into Czechoslovakia. In December 1979, a *Spetsnaz* unit dressed as Afghanis and carrying guns with silencers executed Afghanistan President Hafizullah Amin at his palace in Kabul. See: "Spetsnaz, Soviet Innovation in Special Forces," Air & Space; Power Chronicles November/December 1986 by Robert S. Boyd, an Intelligence Research Specialist for the General Threat Division, Directorate of Estimates, Hq USAF.

In the early 1990s, *Spetsnaz*, like the rest of the Russian military, were thrust into poverty, disillusioned and freed from the strong central controls of Soviet times. In Estonia, *Spetsnaz* units were stationed in the cities of Tallinn and Viljandi.

[39] "Withdrawal of Russian troops from the Baltics," USIA Foreign Press Center Briefing, Federal News Service Transcript, Guest: Robert Frasure, Deputy Assistant Secretary of State for European and Canadian Affairs, Moderator: Susan Robinson, August 31, 1994. "--*Spetsnaz* veterans no longer shun contact with these [criminal] structures and groups, where the pay for one day's work is higher than the monthly pay of a professional officer on active service. The ideological and moral reasons for not doing so no longer exist in today's Russia, and the `wild capitalism' fostered by the Russian authorities implies the simple principle that everything can be bought and sold."

"The Degradation of Russia's Special Forces," *Prism*, a publication of the Jamestown Foundation, Volume 2, Issue 10, May 17, 1996, by Stanislav Lunev, formerly a colonel in Soviet Military Intelligence [GRU].

The $800 street price for contract killings comes from interviews with criminal groups by the author in 1994 in St Petersburg. Hundreds of business disputes were settled by contract killings in the early 1990s in the former Soviet Union. Almost all remain unsolved.

[40] Historically, rogue forces have acted when the head of state travels outside Russia. In 1957, Nikita Khrushchev was overthrown by hardliners while on a visit to Helsinki. In 1991, coup plotters waited until Mikhail Gorbachev was vacationing in Crimea before seizing power.

[41] "Estonian Prime Minister not to Resign" RFE/RL, by Dzintra Bungs, quoting BNS, September 22, 1994.
"Renewed calls for Estonian Prime Minister to Resign," RFE/RL, by Saulius Girnius quoting BNS, September 6, 1994.

[42] In 1994, Baltic ferries did not keep records of last-minute leavers. If a crew member or port security man was stationed at the entrance door, he did not monitor exiting passengers before departure. Passport registration of ticket buyers was not mandatory at the time. Moreover, Tallinn port security and customs in the early 1990s was highly susceptible to bribery and corruption.

[43] Interview, Arike. He added: "I'm personally not excluding anything, but I think most probably the cause was technical failure and bad weather conditions and also some mistakes crew members made. But I don't believe in any plot. If someone is hiding something it has to be something that never reached Estonia. I was in the government at the time and I was convinced the Estonian government was not hiding anything."

[44] The Lieven book mentions a precedent for lethal groups acting on their own (italics are mine): Latvia's OMON, special security troops installed by Moscow, "are also held by the Lithuanian Procurator's office to have been responsible for the cold-blooded murder of Lithuanian police and border guards at Medininkai on 30 July 1991. The incident followed several months of OMON attacks on Baltic border posts *in attempt to destroy an obvious symbol of Baltic independence*...the Medininkai killings gave reason to fear that the hardline Soviet campaign of provocation was moving onto a new level...*the thought, however, that those responsible may still be present in the Baltic, waiting for an opportunity to restart the campaign, is obviously of deep concern to many Balts.* Lieven, p. 199.

"The Degradation of Russia's Special Forces," *Prism*, a publication of the Jamestown Foundation, Volume 2, Issue 10, May 17, 1996, by Stanislav Lunev: At the beginning of the 1990s, during "the storming of the television center in Vilnius [Lithuania], one member of Alpha was killed under mysterious circumstances. At that time, rumors circulated in the Soviet *Spetsnaz* that he had refused to obey the order to attack and had been shot on the orders of the unit's commander, after which his corpse had been thrown into the television center captured by the Alpha men...It is difficult to judge the truth of such rumors, but after the storming of the Vilnius television center, President Gorbachev, KGB Chairman Kryuchkov and other former Soviet leaders all denied having anything to do with Alpha's actions. So it turned out that Alpha had undertaken the storm of the television center without orders from anyone, that is, on their own authority…"

Moreover, crack military units are expert at covering their tracks. "--[O]nce he has carried out his act of terrorism, the *Spetsnaz* commando will destroy all traces of its work and any witnesses, including the agent who protected or helped the group in the first place. A man who is recruited as an agent to back up a commando group very rarely realizes what will happen to him afterwards." From "*Spetsnaz*. The Story Behind the Soviet SAS," (Hamish Hamilton Ltd), 1987, Chapter 8, "The Agent Network," by Viktor Suvorov, translated from Russian.

NOTE: Lack of information about foul play in the ferry disaster could also be attributed to the woeful lack of resources and experience of Estonian law enforcement in the early 1990s, as well as the corruption and apathy that infected many insitutions.

[45] Cockburn, p. 246-7, quoting *Komsomolsky Pravda*, "We Could Launch an Accidental Nuclear Strike at the Enemy," March 15, 1997.

BALTIC DRAINPIPE

[1] "The Baltic region [and Russia], within the last few years, have turned into major transshipment points for the flow of drugs from the cultivation and production areas of Central Asia, and Southeast and Southwest Asia to the markets in Scandinavia and Western Europe." "Crime and Security in the Post-Soviet Era," *Crime and Justice International* (Europe), January/February 1996, Christopher J. Ulrich.

See also: "The Growth of Crime in Russia and the Baltic Region," RFE/RL Research Report, 3, 23, 10 June: 24-32 (1994), Christopher J. Ulrich.

[2] "Guns and drugs: Estonia's growth industries--Pelle Neroth meets smugglers, KGB soldiers and CIA agents in Tallinn," *Financial Times* (London), September 5, 1992, by Pelle Neroth.

[3] "400 tons of heroin…" Ibid.
"South American drug runners…" "Police Chief in `Jaws of Crime' Warning," Press Association, September 10, 1993, by Grania Langdon-Down.

[4] Report: U.S. Department of State, International Narcotics Control Strategy Report, Bureau for International Narcotics and Law Enforcement Affairs, March 1995.
"Most of the drugs transiting through or brought to Estonia originate in Russia, Transcaucus, Ukraine, Lithuania, Latvia, Afghanistan and the Middle East. Various organized crime groups, primarily from Russia and Central Asia, are involved in illicit drug trafficking. Estonian authorities report that drug groups from Afghanistan, Pakistan and Turkey have also been active in their country."

See also: "Redfellas: The growing power of Russia's mob," *New Republic*, April 11, 1994, by Claire Sterling: "The start of large-scale drug smuggling in the Central Asia region goes back to the early 1980s, when Soviet soldiers fighting in Afghanistan first established business relations with local heroin producers."

See also: Lieven, p. 325: "Scandinavian police are also worried by the threat of a major heroin trade extending from Soviet Central Asia…Large scale cooperation exists between organized crime and parts of the Russian armed forces--which have all the transport and weapons that any mafia could desire...Organized crime in the Baltic [region] has the potential to make from drugs many times the profits of legitimate business and thereby become a major power in the land...the Baltic authorities are as yet in no condition to prevent such trade..."

[5] Interview, Benukh. NOTE: Because Benukh was former editor of *Soviet Life* in Washington D.C. during the Cold War, his sensitive position certainly put him in close contact with the KGB, if he wasn't a KGB officer himself. Presumably when he returned to Russia he kept contact with the former security service network, some of whom lived in Estonia. With Estonian officials debating war crimes trials for former KGB agents, these ex-spies had every reason to create a scandalous smuggling story in order to discredit their enemies in the *Riigikogu*, the Estonian Parliament.

[6] Two years after the sinking, Silver Linde, an *Estonia* crewmember who survived the catastrophe, served time in a Finnish prison for a drug smuggling conviction unrelated to the *Estonia* ferry.

[7] Little is known about Andresson, but it can be inferred that he was an Estonian patriot. Neither Andresson, his parents nor sister had been Communist Party members during Soviet times. Andresson, however, joined in 1976, probably in order to be allowed to sail internationally. "I did not serve in the Soviet Army. I have no state awards," Andresson wrote in a short biography for the Leningrad Maritime Academy (now the Makarov Institute), the prestigious Soviet maritime academy in St Petersburg, Russia, where he had continued his studies from 1977-1982.

Soviet Moscow considered Estonians a risk for international travel and an even higher risk if the Estonian was not a Communist Party member. For example, Andresson's friend, Estonian Erich Moik, was denied a position as a long-distance captain during Soviet times because a background check revealed his wife's distant relatives were from Sweden. Interview, Moik.

"Andresson also had an unlimited contract with ESCO..." Interview, Lindpere.

[8] US Embassy correspondence, November 1994, Classification: "Limited Official Use," From: American Embassy Tallinn Keith Smith, To: Secretary of State, Washington DC, Subject: "Estonia: Migration Update":

"--Juri Ruus, [Estonian] interior ministry chancellor...said that the movement of prospective refugees is well-organized mostly by Russian mafia groups. 85 detainees--eighty-two Kurds and three Afghanis--that had illegally come from Russia want to go on to Sweden...likewise the Afghanis have refused airline tickets to Afghanistan via Belarus, but insist on going to Sweden.

"Iraqi Kurds risk death as stowaways to Sweden," *The Independent* (London), February 21, 1994, by Jan Dungren: "--[T]he group of mostly Iraqi Kurds told police they had paid $ 2,500 each to be smuggled to Sweden...Since the collapse of the Soviet Union and relaxation of border controls, hundreds of refugees from North Africa and the Middle East have made their way to Russia and then to the Baltics, where they pay smugglers to transport them by boat to Sweden."

[9] GGE, 17.1 "Loading." "It is also evident from the customs list that the truck or trailer no. 46 with the number plate 417 EEE had no driver registered. It is thus possible that this was the truck or trailer which had been shipped on board the *Estonia* on the basis of incorrect documents and which contained between 148 and 174 Iraqi Kurds, according to information from the files of the public prosecutor Tomas Lindstrand, Stockholm."

[10] "Military Planes Used by Smugglers," Severo-Zapad News Service, St Petersburg, April 19, 1994.

[11] US Embassy correspondence, July 24, 1994, Classification: "Confidential," From: Charge d' Affaires Smith in charge of the US Embassy in Tallinn, To: US Secretary of State, Subject: "Building a new military on post-Soviet rubble."
Additionally, "[Einseln] mentioned several times that coming to Estonia had been a culture shock, particularly the prevalence of Soviet-inspired corruption pervading the country's political and economic class. Einseln said that his goal is to make the armed forces and the defense ministry an ethical model for the rest of Estonia's society; he believes he is 70% of the way there with the officer corps, but not as far along with the NCOs and defense ministry officials."

[12] "Guns and drugs: Estonia's growth industries--Pelle Neroth meets smugglers, KGB soldiers and CIA agents in Tallinn," *Financial Times* (London), September 5, 1992, by Pelle Neroth.

[13] Report: "Mafia in Uniform: The Criminalization of the Russian Armed Forces," Turbiville.

[14] "21 Soviet armored personnel carriers..." Lieven, p. 321.

[15] "Pistols smuggled into Moscow," *Moscow News*, March 11, 1994, by Igor Baranovsky.
See also: "Russian Organised Crime and the Baltic States: Assessing the Threat," Working Paper 38/01, published in 2001 by the ESRC "One Europe or Several?" Programme, by Paddy Rawlinson, Sussex European Institute, University of Sussex, page 13: "The impact of the illegal arms trade was not just a Western problem. In 1994 the killing of Otari Kvantrishvili, reputedly one of Moscow's most notorious crime bosses, was allegedly carried out using a weapon from Estonian arms smugglers linked to the renegade Estonian Defence League's Laanermaa Unit."

[16] *The Financial Post* (Toronto), September 10, 1993, by Diane Francis.
See also: "Gun-runners target old Soviet borders: Financial Times reporters investigate a disturbing story of arms and the Isle of Man," *Financial Times* (London), by David White, Jimmy Burns, Neil Buckley, Sara Webb and Sue Stuart, April 29, 1992.

[17] "Eastern Europe: Rare Metals Traffic," *Intelligence Newsletter*, January 21, 1993.
Silves was also the subject of 1996 documentary, "The Cinderella of Tallinn."

[18] "Comrade criminal: Russia's new mafiya," Yale University Press, 1995, by Stephen Handelman.

[19] Testimony to the Senate Committee on Foreign Relations Subcommittee on European Affairs
August 23, 1995, by Graham Allison.

[20] "Firm Illegally Exports Rare-Earth Metals," *Molod Ukrainy*, August 11, 1992. Measured by the kilogram, zirconium is worth $1,000 and hafnium $25,000.
"Nuclear Exports from the Former Soviet Union: What's New, What's True," Arms Control Today, January-February 1993, pp. 3-10, by William C. Potter: "The shipment was ostensibly meant for the jewelry-manufacturing industry, but the amount and grade of zirconium were incompatible with such purposes."
See also: "Crime and Security in the Post-Soviet Era" January/February 1996, *Crime and Justice International* (Europe), Christopher J. Ulrich.

[21] "Russia's Yard Sale," *Time* Magazine, April 18, 1994, p. 52.

[22] "export licenses..." "Estonian Strategic Goods Export Control Commission Begins Work," Press Release, 1 November 1994, Press and Information Office, Estonian Ministry of Foreign Affairs.
"smugglers with radioactive Californium..." The californium 235 is believed to have originated at the Tomsk-7 nuclear complex in Siberia. "Soviet Isotope Smugglers Arrested in Germany, Finland," Nucleonics Week, September 2, 1993.
Also in 1993, the dual-use material beryllium had been found in a Lithuanian bank vault, intended for a buyer in Switzerland. "--[I]f the plutonium core of a weapon is surrounded by a shell of beryllium, neutrons created during the fission reaction are reflected back into the sphere, enhancing the chain reaction. A bomb designer can produce a satisfactory explosion with far less plutonium--or uranium 235--than he would otherwise need...the beryllium hoard in the bank vault had originally come from a Russian nuclear research institute in Obninsk, 60 miles south of Moscow." Cockburn 114-116.
"radionuclides and cesium-137..." "Kontrabanda smerti" November 19, 1992, *Izvestiya*, p. 7.
"28-kilogram lead container of cesium-137 onto a ferry..." "Estonia Arrests Swedes Who Had Radioactive Material," *Reuters*, July 9, 1993.

[23] "Estonia Nuclear Waste" Trade & Environment Database (TED) Case study number 244, Volume 5, Number 1, January, 1996, by Christopher A. Corpora.

[24] "Border with Russia to be closed to stop crime," BBC Summary of World Broadcasts, September 9, 1994.

[25] Of these incidents, eight cases involved cesium-137, one involved radium, and two involved uranium. "The Preventing of Illicit Trafficking in Estonia," September 14, 1998 and "Safety of Radiation Sources and Security of Radioactive Materials," IAEA-TECDOC-1045, September 14-18, 1998, pp. 224-227, by Tuuli Velbri and Lauri Aasmann.

[26] "responsible officials worldwide braced themselves..." On his 10-day trip to Russia and other East European nations in summer 1994, FBI Director Louis Freeh declared that the greatest long-term threat to the security of the United States "is the possibility that organized criminals will steal a nuclear weapon or materials to make one from the former Soviet Union and sell it to terrorists." "World Fears Spread of Nukes," Associate Press, March 28, 1995, by Charles J. Hanley.

"Russia acknowledged 700 incidents..." from Cockburn p. 76. "Reportedly, one of the perpetrators obtained the uranium, enriched to 20 percent, by simply climbing through a hole in the compound's fence and, with the use of a hacksaw, breaking the padlock on the storage shed. There were no guards present and the alarm system was too corroded to function properly."

"After officials caught two workers..." from Cockburn 79-80. "--[T]hese men had enough firepower bouncing around in the back of the truck to wipe out half the eastern seaboard. Officially, the incident never happened."

[27] "the belief was that the lethal cargo could be following..." see "UN in crackdown on smugglers--A global intelligence clearing house and database aimed at arresting the illicit trade in fissile materials is being set up at the UN," *Lloyd's List*, April 8, 1995, by Thomas Land.

"Sweden Braces for Nightmare of Nuclear Smuggling," Reuters, November 7, 1993, by Vibeke Laroi. NOTE: Olsson was at the time of writing working on behalf of the Swedish government in Kosovo. He was contacted by the author but refused to comment on criminal activity involving the *Estonia* ferry.

[28] Report: "Nuclear Smuggling From the Former Soviet Union: Threats and Responses," Rensselaer Lee, Foreign Policy Research Institute, CSIS Global Organized Crime Project, April 27, 2001.

Weapons-ready material actually seized in 1994 included:
--350 grams of 87 percent pure plutonium-239 nabbed from a Moscow flight that landed at the Munich airport;
--5.6 grams of 99.75 percent pure plutonium-239 intercepted in Tengen, Germany;
--0.8 grams of 88 percent enriched uranium-235 in Landshut, Germany;
--slightly more than 1 gram of plutonium, said to be fit for military use, in Verona, Italy;
--2.7kg of 88 percent enriched uranium-235 in Prague, the Czech Republic.
Source: Report from the National Defense University's Center for Counterproliferation Research: "Nuclear Smuggling: How Serious a Threat?" January 1996, by James L. Ford.

[29] "Opening statement Rep. Curt Weldon (R PA), Chairman Research and Development Subcommittee Hearing on Nuclear Terrorism and Countermeasures," October 1, 1997.

Later Lebed was interviewed on the *60 Minutes* TV program and he repeated his claim, increasing the number gone missing to 100. The Kremlin stridently denied Lebed's claims and in October 1996 Lebed was fired by Yeltsin for unrelated reasons. But Alexei Yablokov, a former environmental advisor to Yeltsin, confirmed that suitcase-sized nuclear weapons were developed for the Russian KGB in the 1970s.

According to public statements by U.S. Congressman Curt Weldon, Moscow's assertion "that nuclear weapons of the kind described by Lebed never existed, [is] an erroneous claim that does not help the credibility of Moscow's denials. Russian special forces are known to possess atomic demolition munitions (ADMs) small, man-portable nuclear weapons that could be concealed in a backpack or suitcase."

Although Lebed subsequently retracted the claim, the case of the missing nuclear suitcase bombs has never been conclusively resolved. In 2002, Lebed died in a helicopter crash in Russia.

[30] "Uranium Seized By Estonian Police," *The Washington Times*, August 27, 1994.
See also: "Estonian Wanted To Smuggle Uranium To West," *Berlingske Tidende*, August 27, 1994.

"five kilograms of U238..." see "Police Seize Five Kilograms Uranium in Haapsalu," FBIS- SOV, originally from Radio Tallinn Network, 10 May 1995.

See also: "Estoniya," *Yaderniy Kontrol*, June 1995, p. 13; "Estonian Police Foil Sale of Uranium," OMRI Daily Digest, May 11, 1995, by Saulius Girnius; "In Tallinn yesterday..." *The Guardian*, November 5, 1995;

"Estonskiye Syshyki Vyshli Na Torgovtsev Uranom," *Sevodnya*, May 11, 1995.

The Estonian city of Sillamäe, near the Russian border, hosted one of the biggest nuclear fuel processing plants in the former Soviet Union. Sillamäe Metallurgical Plant (Silmet) developed the process for extracting uranium from black shale, which is widely available in Estonia. It produced over 100,000 tons of uranium for almost 70,000 nuclear weapons and operated in complete secrecy for several decades. It refined the uranium for the U.S.S.R.'s first nuke. During a five-year period under the Soviet Union, the plant handled very-low enriched uranium for fuel processing and some weapons-grade uranium. In 1990, Silmet stopped refining uranium ore.

In 1994, the Estonian Foreign Ministry made a breathtaking claim. Over a two-year period, 1,700 kilograms of uranium enriched to 2 percent had gone missing. Soviet-era documents, which a senior official at the Estonian Ministry of Foreign Affairs characterized as being "trustworthy," provided the accounting.

But theft was never confirmed. Today, the general belief among Estonian officials is that confusion surrounding Soviet inventory records created the impression that uranium was unaccounted for.
See: "Russian Records Send Estonians On Search For Missing Uranium," *Nucleonics Week*, November 3, 1994, pp. 16-17, by Ariane Sains; "Estonia in Nuclear Export Controls in Europe, Harald Mueller, ed., European Interuniversity Press (Brussels), 1995, by Indrek Tarand, p. 263.

[31] "Nuclear Smuggling: How Serious a Threat?" Ford.

Nuclear smuggling scenarios were not paranoia: "The Japanese Aum Shirinkyo cult, the architects of a deadly nerve gas attack in the Tokyo subway in 1995, reportedly explored different pricing operations for buying a nuclear warhead from Russia. A Moscow news report claimed that the Islamic Jihad organization, shortly following the U.S.S.R.'s collapse, sent a faxed letter to the Federal Nuclear Research Center at Arzamas-16 offering to buy a single atomic weapon and specifying the 'parameters, the sum of the transaction and the mode of shipment.'"

"Nuclear Smuggling From The Former Soviet Union: Threats And Responses," Lee.

[32] Dangerous smuggling incidents peaked in 1994, which became the year several practical measures to stem nuclear material smuggling were finally taken at the government level. In August, Germany and Russia inked a mutual cooperation agreement that included a hotline. In Washington, on the day the *Estonia* sank, the White House was detailing a $30 million crime assistance package for Russia, because "the rise of crime and corruption in Russia carries potentially dangerous international consequences." The money was aimed at helping Eastern Europe and the newly independent states fight organized crime, including the flow of narcotics and nuclear smuggling.
"Crime Assistance Package for the Russian Federation" Office of the Press Secretary, The White House, September 28, 1994.

Yeltsin called for stricter control and accounting of nuclear stockpiles and appointed a control commission that answered directly to him. In September, the IAEA expressed "deep concern" over the control of nuclear weapons in Russia and called on Agency Director General Hans Blix to strengthen the IAEA's role in this area. "Smuggling Special Nuclear Materials" a Canadian Security Intelligence Service (CSIS) publication, May 1995.

THE CONSIGNMENT

[33] The *Financial Post* (Toronto), September 10, 1993, Diane Francis.

[34] "Crime but no punishment: Russian troops in Estonia," Press Release, Estonian Ministry of Foreign Affairs, March 1, 1994.

[35] Interview, Putnik.
See also: "Baltic states cleaning up to impress EU," *Globe and Mail* (Toronto), August 14, 2002, by Mark MacKinnon.

[36] According to Putnik, a fuel rod is essentially a long rod with uranium pellets inside.
"The Swedes have offered to monitor the site and to act as neutral observers when the removal of the nuclear fuel rods starts this spring, but the Russians, worried about protecting secret information, have refused," from "Dismantling Of Reactors In Paldiski," RFE/RL News Brief, 30 May 1994, pp. 13-14, Saulius Girnius; "Russia's Toxic Retreat," *The Guardian* (London), April 8, 1994, by Isobel Montgomery.

[37] "Specialists at the Paldiski site planned to pack the fuel rods in a 'special container' and transfer them to Russia by train. The date for the transfer of fuel from Estonia to Russia was not publicized, in order to prevent possible attacks by terrorists...
"On 24 August 1994, the first reactor was opened without increasing radiation above normal levels. A special security 'regime' of checkposts in the Paldiski area was instituted by the Estonian government before 24 August 1994 to ensure that only approved personnel would be at the site." "Russians Start Dismantling Second Estonia Reactor," *Reuters*, September 20, 1994.
See also: "Dismantlement Of Nuclear Reactor Has Successfully Begun In Esto-

nia," August 24, 1994, Russia & CIS Today, sourcing *Novosti* (Moscow), 24 August 1994.

[38] "Not one document..." Interview, Putnik.
See also: "Nuclear Fuel Rods Leave Estonia," RFE/RL Daily Report, October 17, 1994, by Saulius Girnius.
NOTE: An inquiry by the author to the Estonian Ministry of Defense about Paldiski fuel rod documentation went unanswered.

During the disassembly of the reactors, Estonians Mark Sinisoo, senior counselor for the Estonian Ministry of Foreign Affairs and Ants Vist, Estonian documentary filmmaker, were allowed by Admiral Olkovikhov to film highlights of the reactor lid and fuel rod removal. Vist made a short film of the process. They were the only known outsiders permitted near the reactors during the decommissioning. Juri Tikk, an Estonian who served as a spokesman for Paldiski base, was probably in contact with the specialists, though it is unknown whether he was ever allowed on the premises while they worked. In any case, no individuals were allowed to supervise the operation or verify that all the fuel rods had been on the train.

Inventory accountability for the nuclear material removal operation was suspect at the high levels of Estonian government. The Russian team had tossed the reactor control rods--rods without uranium that serve to regulate the reactor--into a radioactive waste dump. But they had pledged to load them on the specially-sealed train with the fuel rods. Estonian Eurominister Endel Lipmaa voiced concern that the Russian dismantling team did not do as they had promised. See: US Embassy correspondence, April 1995, From: American Embassy Tallinn, To: Secretary of State Washington DC, Subject: "Codel Bereuter/Solomon visit Estonia on Eve of Government Changeover."

[39] In an interesting side note, a classified 1996 nuclear smuggling exercise staged by U.S. intelligence and military agencies found that a ship would be the best way to transport a nuclear bomb. The device could be enclosed in a container to shield the radiation detectors, then loaded onto the common long-haul truck that typically parks on a ferry, the exercise report says. To narrow the search for the suspect ship, authorities would first eliminate vessels on their way from countries considered low risk, for example Western European and Scandinavian states. Cockburn, p. 263.

[40] The idea that the Yeltsin government in 1994 would be unaware of illegal procurement of state nuclear material comes as no surprise. The Cockburn book is full of startling examples that underline the 1990s lack of security and accountability for doomsday material. One example is when in September 1994, an American team of scientists arrived in Moscow at the Kurchatov Institute. "They were appalled by what they found...the White House physicists found themselves in a room that housed a zero power space reactor with fuel that was 97% enriched uranium, enough for several bombs...150 pounds of weapons grade uranium was guarded with a padlock. The senior Russian scientists who held the keys earned $30 a month....it turned out at Kurchatov nobody had ever taken inventory." Cockburn, p. 123.

[41] Rabe's ideas formed the general outline of the 2003 commercial film her company

produced based on the ferry disaster entitled "Baltic Storm."

Regarding the "two trucks scenario," see GGE, enclosure 12.4.2.151, statement of Carl Övberg.

NOTE: Werner Hummel, the chief German investigator, has told the author that he has the names of the soldiers who escorted the two trucks on board the night of September 27, but the information is kept confidential unless and until it is needed in the legal defense of the Meyer Werft shipyard.

[42] "Secret Funding for Intelligence Agencies," *Intelligence Newsletter*, October 26, 2000.

[43] Russia was the world's third largest arms exporter in 1994, with varying estimates of sales. The U.S. claims Russia sold $1.5 billion of delivered goods in 1994. (U.S. Arms Control and Disarmament Agency ACDA figures). Deputy director-general of the state-owned Rosvooruzhenie arms exporting company, Valerii Tretyak, said at a Moscow news conference in September 1994 that Russia would have $4 billion in 1994 arms sales.

Terrorist groups also appraised Russia's goods. See report: "Weapons Proliferation and Organized Crime: The Russian Military and Security Force Dimension," USAF Institute for National Security Studies, U.S. Air Force Academy. INSS Occasional Paper 10 in the Proliferation Series, June 1996, by Graham H. Turbiville, Jr.

[44] "Six Topaz-2 reactors and supporting equipment were flown from Russia to the United States, where several of the reactors were extensively ground tested by a joint team of U.S., British, French, and Russian engineers...Topaz utilized a thermionic design for directly converting heat energy into electricity without using a circulating heat transfer fluid or turbine. Although the test program was considered highly successful and the United States retained several flight-capable reactors, no plans were pursued to actually use the equipment in any flight programs."
National Research Council (2006). "Priorities in Space Science Enabled by Nuclear Power and Propulsion." National Academies. p. 114.

See also: "Congratulations on Your Acquisition, Pentagon! Who Delivered the Air Defense System from the CIS to the United States, and Why" Moscow *TRUD*, December 29, 1994. p 4.

"S-300" Cockburn, p.121.

Interview, Ermarth.

[45] "...the [Swedish] Armed Forces on two occasions during the month of September 1994 had transported defense equipment on the M/S *Estonia*, namely on 14 and 20 September. The equipment consisted of electronic equipment without any connection to weapons systems. The equipment was not in any way of an explosive nature." Translated from Swedish.
Memorandum to the [Swedish] Government, "The study on the transport of military equipment on the M / S Estonia," dated 2005-01-21. In Swedish language.

See also: "Report: No military shipment aboard ferry Estonia when it sank," AP Worldstream, January 21, 2005, by Mattias Karen.

"Sweden to launch fresh probe into *Estonia* ferry tragedy," AFP, December 2, 2004; "*Estonia* to cooperate with Sweden on investigation into ferry sinking," AFP, December 9, 2004.

[46] The scene is drawn from the daily logbook of Erkki Mykkänen, engineer at the Finnish Environmental Institute (SYKE), which he kept during the oil and fuel removal operation. A copy was obtained by the author.
Interviews, Mykkänen and Jolma.

NOTE: It is important to emphasize that Kari Lehtola was the head of the Finnish side of the JAIC. He had publicly scoffed at alternative theories and categorically dismissed the idea that factors other than those in the government's conclusions had influenced the accident. In fact, the Preface on page 7 of the Final Report reads: "This final report covers all factors and circumstances considered to have contributed to the development and outcome of the accident."

Yet the documented events in the SYKE diary show that the very same Finnish officials in the JAIC held such intense suspicions that they were attempting to break into the ship, measure radioactivity and interfere with the arrival of other ships.

[47] GGE, Chapter 28, "The ROV inspections in 1996."
See also: "The *Estonia* ferry is reported to have been vandalized by divers," ETA, November 17, 1996.

[48] Meister, page 104. "In their report, the [Rockwater] diving company explained that the openings made to the ship's body were later closed up either with metal plates or [steel] grates. The...covers were lying there on their own weight but to avoid possible movement, bars were welded to their lower parts or extra weight was added. This point was indicated in the [Rockwater] employment contract."

[49] Meister, p. 110.
"Unfortunately it is not possible to verify where the glass pieces had fallen. The possible intruder had not put them on to the deck when cleaning the edges of the window hole...And a window pushed in due to water pressure would have fallen inward with all its pieces."

[50] GGE, Chapter 27, "The Diving Investigation 01.-04.12.94"
"It is quite obvious that part of the damage did exist already on 02.10.94, i.e. 4 days after the casualty when the first (official) ROV went down and that the damage was enlarged during the time until the diving investigation of 01.-04.12.94. The damage is not mentioned in either the Smit-Tak/Rockwater Reports nor in the *Sjöfartsverket* or JAIC Reports and has also not been discussed by the media...This damage cannot be attributed to the casualty and also does not look as having been caused by fire or explosion. It is, however, obvious that there is heavy impact damage at the aft lower part of the bulkhead which together with the vertical stanchion supporting the wing was pushed forward. It therefore has to be assumed that this was caused by interested parties searching for something particular hidden inside the void space between the bridge floor and wing underside, prior to and again after 02.10.94."

See also: GGE, 34.6, "Investigation Report of Video Tapes Featuring the Car/Passenger Ferry "Estonia" by Disengage, Axminster/U.K..

"It can be assumed that those who removed the heavy steel covers from the openings are probably identical with those who broke off the steel sheeting underneath the port bridge wing…Needless to say that these facts are not mentioned in the Report of the JAIC." GGE, Chapter 28, "The ROV inspections in 1996."

Also, Rabe, p. 140: Concerning the Disengage Report about paneling on the underside of the port bridge wing broken open and torn off: "The evaluation of the ROV videos…as well as the diver videos…first shows that on October 2, 1994, a part of the paneling was off; an open hatch up to the bridge visible behind it. This is where the smuggled goods would have been stowed. On October 9, additional parts have been torn off. By December, all the underside paneling has disappeared completely…"

[51] In St Petersburg, Russia, the author spoke to a member of a Russian naval unit equivalent to the U.S. Navy's SEALs. He'd been saturation diving in the Baltic Sea for special training and was asked him about the *Estonia*. He himself hadn't been to the shipwreck, but he said the Russian navy often videotapes their operations for training purposes. He would ask about a video of the *Estonia* wreck. After two weeks, he was contacted him again. He did not specifically say *Estonia* videos existed, nor did he say they didn't. He would only say military videos are classified. That the ferry wreck could be a target of opportunity for underwater training, 10 years after it sank, is unsurprising.

Information about the underwater vehicle tracks near the *Estonia* wreck is from the German group, which had sighted them on ROV videos taken during the vessel's fuel and oil extraction operation in 1996, according to Hummel.

[52] Officially, no Swedish divers went to the wreck. However, as mentioned earlier, the Swedish press interviewed a man named Hakan Bergmark from Stockholm, who said he was one of the first divers down to the *Estonia* wreck. Bergmark didn't give a date of the dive, but said he saw a "five meter hole" in the side of the ship.

See also: "New bombshell as *Estonia* row goes on," *Lloyd's List*, December 16 2000, by Nick Savvides.

Spiggen II, URF: "Jane's Fighting Ships," Jane's Information Group; 98th edition (June 1, 1995).

According to "Tomb Beneath the Sea: Disaster ship salvage may be impossible; The Estonia may have to be left at the bottom of the sea-bed," *Daily Record* (Glasgow), September 30, 1994, by Bill Akass: "Dutch-based salvage company Wijsmuller has been asked by the Estonian Government to conduct the search for the rest of the victims. The firm's experts will decide whether they can raise the wreck once they have analysed underwater photos taken by a Swedish mini-submarine. Sweden has used the robot for underwater search and salvage operations before…Its grasping devices are capable of attaching a cable to bodies, so they can be raised to the surface."

[53] Interview, Franson.

THE COCKTAIL EFFECT

[1] See "Uncovering Soviet Disasters," Oberg, for details on these covered-up tragedies.

386 NOTES

A cavalier attitude toward safety dates back decades. According to Oberg, President Nixon was warned about flying on Soviet made aircraft during a China trip in the 1970s. A report prepared by Americans who'd flown with Soviet VIP pilots warned: "--Soviet pilots were observed using commercial road maps and hand-drawn charts, not proper aeronautical charts. They wandered from approach paths, often too low. Poor fuel management resulted in emergency landings...All these incidents were observed among what must have been regarded as the best, safest Soviet aircrews, and they certainly must raise some concern over general flight safety standards." Oberg, p. 121.

[2] "Accidents at Russian nuclear installations increased 45 percent [in 1992], to a total of 205. None of the former Soviet Union's 45 civilian nuclear reactors meet Western safety standards; 15 are similar to the Chernobyl reactor, a design considered inherently unsafe."
"Radiation in Russia," *U.S. News & World Report*, August 9, 1993, by Victoria Pope and Julie Corwin.

[3] "Tapes recorded teen at controls," Associated Press, September 28, 1994, by Julia Rubin.

[4] "Irkutsk Journal; A Wing and a Prayer: Tragedy Flies With Aeroflot," *The New York Times*, May 12, 1994, by Michael Specter.

[5] Final Report, p. 55.

[6] Ibid, p. 225.

[7] Interview, Schager.

[8] ITF, 2.4 and 5.9.4.
"There is no reference at all to these and various other incidents raised by the German Experts in the Joint Commission report. They only refer to a relatively limited range of maintenance or repair items and conclude that the system was well maintained and in good condition. They effectively say that the in-service management and inspection of the system had been adequate." ITF 5.9.3

At the same time, the Final Report dilutes the issue of accountability: "The locks were designed according to the standards of the time. The Bureau Veritas, which certified the ferry, at the time had no detailed rules regarding procedures for calculating sea loads on the bow visor installation." Final Report, Section 3.3.1, "Bow visor and ramp installation."

Thus, weakly-designed locks were innocently installed and permitted for 14 years because no one made any calculations to see if they were strong enough, even when the ferry changed ownership.

[9] GGE, Chapter 15.

[10] Interview, Holm.

[11] Interview, Tidstrom.

[12] GGE, Chapter 15.

[13] Schager believes the JAIC suffered an organizational management breakdown. "It was a case of being ill prepared and ill trained for such a big investigation," he said. "I was so frustrated with the incompetence of the whole bunch."
   After he resigned, Schager wrote an article," The Mistakes by the Crew are Suppressed," in *Dagens Nyheter*, December 3, 1997 (translated from Swedish) that summed up human factor issues: "Attitudes, risk awareness and safety culture are influenced from the top. The responsibility must be split between both the management of the shipping company and the officers on board…During the night of the accident the crew made the following mistakes:
--*Estonia* was maneuvered without feeling and respect for the forces of nature
--the speed was maintained in spite of metallic sounds and an activated investigation
--the deck officers suspected a problem with the ramp and the visor but did not react
--the AB seaman did not follow given orders
--the engineer never informed the bridge of water entering the cardeck
--the deck officers never looked at their monitor
--the bridge officer steered the wrong way
--a coded fire alarm was sent when the vessel had a list
--alarm was not activated on time
--the emergency signaling was incomplete

[14] Interview, Hellberg.

[15] Final Report, p. 59.

[16] Interview Lindpere. He added: "The financially important aspect was average passenger spending. It was about 1000 SEK (roughly $100 at the time), one way for each Swedish passenger. The *Estonia* [on average] had 70 percent Swedish passengers and 30 percent other. Occupancy on average was over 50 percent of capacity. Conference tourism was profitable for ships. [Groups] pay for tickets and food, really spending a lot. Cargo was also very important and the cargo deck was almost always very full. To get big trading companies interested in our line we needed to have a second vessel. Demand was there. Two weeks before the disaster, we celebrated in Stockholm the acquisition of the new vessel *Mare Balticum*."
   NOTE: The captain apparently wasn't very sensitive to the company's bottom line, as some have suggested. Ferries generally earn 40 percent of turnover from duty-free sales. Estline held a monopoly on the Tallinn-Stockholm route and sold alcohol not subject to the high Swedish alcohol tax. Many Swedish passengers eagerly bought the discounted alcohol. Had Andresson's actions been profit-motivated, his first concern would have been speed reduction to encourage more shopping and prevent broken glass. A one liter bottle of cognac could run $80. Rough seas send shoppers to their cabins and could topple a whole shelf, something the captain would hear about at the next board meeting.

388   NOTES

[17] "Storm may not be the only reason of *Heweliusz* capsize," PAP News Wire, January 15, 1993.

[18] Report: "Court of Inquiry into the Circumstances Surrounding the Collision Between USS Greeneville (SSN 772) and Japanese *M/V Ehime Maru* that occurred off the coast of Oahu, Hawaii on 9 February 2001" Record of Proceedings. April 13, 2001.

[19] Interview, Lindpere.

[20] "Katastrofen Kurs," by Anders Jorle and Anders Hellberg. Excerpts in English translation in GGE Chapter 7.

NOTE: Andresson and relief Captain Piht did have a transition period when they both served on the *George Ots* passenger ferry before taking over the *Estonia*. The *George Ots* was built in Poland during Soviet times. It sailed from Tallinn to Helsinki, often with Westerners--Finns--on board. But neither the *George Ots* nor other Soviet ships had cardecks or modern locking systems that compared to the German-built *Estonia* ferry. Soviet ships were built for military use and constructed for strength. The *Estonia* ferry was built by a private company to civilian passenger standards, full of nuances and trimmings.

The *Estonia* ferry was Western technology--German on top of that, resilient and precision-built like their BMWs and Mercedes Benz were at the time. Therefore, Captain Andresson perhaps thought his stewardship involved an ordinary risk and it turned out to be an extraordinary one. Andresson may have been less sensitive to the *Estonia* ferry's vulnerabilities than his Western counterparts. That played a role in the disaster, but to what extent is a subject for endless debate.

PART SIX: HIDDEN AGENDAS
DETOURS

[1] "KAL 007: The Real Story," *American Spectator*, October 1993, by James Oberg.

[2] Itar Tass, January 14, 1995.

Variations of the White Tights fighters followed. For example, Sergei Stepashin, chief of the FSK, the [first] successor organization to the KGB, noted that "Afghanis, Banderas from Ukraine, the Baltic republics, Tajikistan, Jordan and some Russians are fighting against Russian forces; salary is $800 a day." From broadcast on Ostankino TV, December 29, 1994, as reported in FBIS-SOV-94-251, December 30, 1994, p 11-14.

Also: "--[O]n 10 January competition marksmen from the Baltics were confirmed to be in Chechnya."
"Fighting in Grozny--Russian Troops Facing Experienced, Well-Trained Gunmen," *Krasnaya Zvezda*, 10 January 1995, p 1, by Oleg Falichev.

[3] "*Estonia's* Capsizing Resulted From Wild Business," Russian Press Digest, October 7, 1994, by Vladimir Maryukha, citing *Krasnaya Zvezda*, same date, p. 3. No sources are cited for his evidence, which is designed to appear objective. The Admiral's final sentences in the article betray the bias: "Small Estonia has become known to the whole

world after the worst maritime tragedy. And the whole world feels sympathy for her. But it is no good to cast even a patriotic-motivated shadow on those who were among the first to have offered help."

[4] "Smuggling operation causes ferry boat sinking: report," Xinhua News Agency, June 21, 1995; Interview, Lehtola.

[5] "Mystery of the Baltic 'Titanic'" ("Zagadka Baltiskogo 'Titanika'"), *Itogi*, by Alexander Zheglov and Xenia Pankratova, September 25, 2001.

[6] "Ship Sinks, Mafia Swims," *Moscow News*, April 25, 1996; "Did drug mafia cause the *Estonia* disaster?" The *Evening Standard* (London), September 3, 1996, by Colin Adamson and Simon Young.

[7] "The *Lucona* Affair," *Chicago Tribune*, March 15, 1989, by R.C. Longworth. The *Lucona* carried some cargo containing military explosives, which bypassed customs officials. The ship also hauled repainted scrap machinery that had been falsely declared as uranium processing equipment and insured for around $20 million. Bound for Hong Kong, the *Lucona* blew up near the Maldives in deep water. The ship sank in two minutes, but six out of 12 crew members survived to report the explosion. An investigation began in 1983 but was blocked by Proksch's high-level friends in the Austrian government. Proksch was eventually apprehended. He died in prison in 2001.

[8] Yeltsin, "Midnight Diaries," pp. 201-202. "[Prime Minister Yevgeny] Primakov had an anonymous memo that declared that [Deputy Minister of Health Mikhail] Zurabov was a bandit, that he had ties with a criminal gang from the Caucasus, and so on. In fact, it was later discovered that this young deputy minister had the imprudence to step on the tail of some pharmaceutical mafia. Primakov had summoned Valentina Matvienko, the vice premier, and demanded that Zurabov be fired immediately. But first I asked [then-head of security services Vladimir] Putin to check these reports.

"Soon Putin brought me a real report on Zurabov from the economic security database of the Federal Security Service [the FSB, successor agency to the KGB]. The difference was amazing. Everything in Primakov's anonymous report had been distorted. For example, while the anonymous tipster had said that Zurabov had connections to a Dagestani gang, the document from the FSB said that Zurabov's ties to criminal gangs of 'persons of the Caucasus nationality' had not been established. In the anonymous report, Zurabov had been accused of graft. The FSB report said that no evidence of taking bribes from pharmaceutical companies had been found. These were the kinds of discrepancies between the two reports...That was how I became familiar with the technique known as *kompromat*.

"At that time some commercial firms had found their way to disgruntled FSB agents and other special services. They capitalized on officials who had been fired from the agencies. It was easy for them to put together a 'report' on a competitor or a disliked bureaucrat. Apparently there were quite a few former officers of the FSB or officials from the prosecutor's office who brought Primakov such accusations and didn't bother to provide any proof. These compromising materials piled up on Primakov's desk...he couldn't help believe all these accusations, never thinking that someone might very well pay for such 'exposures.'"

[9] It is curious that Mart Laar, Alexander Einseln, Yuri Toomepuu, Estonian Interior Minister Heike Arike and others from the Estonian government get flayed in the Felix Report, but Lennart Meri, the president of Estonia at the time and the most visible, politically powerful and internationally-known Estonian, is left unscathed.

[10] Lieven, p. xix.

[11] Ibid, p. 284. Also: "--[I]n the elections of September 1992, the "Estonian Citizen" group…led by a retired U.S. colonel of Estonian origin, Juri Toomepuu, won 8% of the parliamentary seats. The group was backed by a small armed volunteer force which rejected the authority of the Estonian government in favor of a self appointed 'government in exile' of which Toomepuu was the 'Defense Minister.' These elements are also of course bitterly hostile to the Russian minority, much of which they hope to pressure into leaving." Lieven, p. 73.

[12] Interview, Einseln. Through the intervention of Senator John McCain (R, AZ), Einseln's pension was reinstated.
See also: "Alexandria soldier vindicated; Retired U.S. colonel got in trouble trying to bring reform to Estonian Defense Forces," *The Washington Times*, July 6, 2003 by Drew Wilson.

[13] Interview, Einseln. In regard to non-Estonian officers, Einseln explained that Estonia had a Soviet military, not a national one like Poland or Hungary, for example. The Kremlin did not trust Estonians in officer positions, leaving many of the higher ranks to Russians. Duty stations for ethnic Estonians were typically at bases in remote areas of Soviet Russia.

In regard to the weapons purchase, Einseln said it was done without his knowledge and that Laar had not mentioned it, which was a breach of governmental procedure. Laar also met with representatives from the Israeli weapons company, but didn't inform Einseln about the meeting. Einseln alleged that Laar received compensation for the Israeli arms deal, but had no evidence.

Soon after Einseln condemned the first batch of weapons, a shadowy figure promised to cut him in on future weapons purchases. Infuriated, he submitted his resignation. President Lennart Meri refused it. Einseln stayed, but he stepped up public criticism of corruption in Estonia's institutions, which eventually led to his firing.

NOTE: Einseln and Laar began in cooperation and ended in conflict. Both distrusted each other, and the rift was ripe for exploitation. The Felix Report latched onto it, using the real life personal conflict to lay a veil of credibility over an invented scenario.

The nature of their disagreements seemed to be cultural. Both men had Estonia's best interests in mind but used starkly different approaches in practice. The two were often at odds in method and tactics. Einseln, for example, believed Russian threats should be met with confident assertions that Estonia was not vulnerable and preparations should be made to back that up. Laar believed Russian threats were better dealt with by ignoring or dismissing them because the Russians typically used threats as a psychological weapon. Einseln, as a returning émigré, believed he was asked to help de-Sovietize the Estonian forces, not adapt to it. Laar, an Estonian who lived under Soviet occupation, believed in a less overt approach. Einseln maybe saw Laar as the naiive and tainted insider; Laar probably saw Einseln as the naiive and interfering outsider.

See also: US Embassy correspondence, July 1994, Classification: "Confidential," From: American Embassy Tallinn, Keith Smith, To: Secretary of State, Washington DC, Subject: "Building a new military on post-Soviet Rubble": "--[A]ccording to Einseln, the Russian army is currently less of a threat to Estonia than is domestic corruption…although Einseln is obviously not a politician, and his outspokenness frequently gets him into hot water with many Estonians, his personal integrity and dedication are welcome qualities in a society suffering from a 50-year Soviet hangover."

[14] Moscow politicians were spouting election rhetoric in 1996, hurling threats at Estonia. Einseln said he was aware of the game, but believed the deployment readiness order was symbolic and necessary. "'Someone here in Estonia had to show confidence that some resistance would take place,' Einseln recalled. 'The Estonian army had never fought when the Soviets walked in 1939. I didn't want anyone to think that would happen again.'"

"Alexandria soldier vindicated; Retired U.S. colonel got in trouble trying to bring reform to Estonian Defense Forces," *The Washington Times*, July 6, 2003 by Drew Wilson.

[15] Interview, Yasmann.

See also: "Russia's Great Criminal Revolution: The Role of the Security Services," *Journal of Contemporary Criminal Justice*, Vol. 11, No. 4, December 1995 by J. Michael Waller and Victor J. Yasmann; "The mysterious Felix Group raises its profile," *Prism*, Volume 1 Issue 11, July 14, 1995, by Victor Yasmann.

[16] Interviews, Ermarth and Einseln.

[17] "President Putin [who is a former KGB officer and former chief of the FSB, the KGB's successor] was never involved. It was only me." Interview, Surikov.

NOTE: At the time of the disaster, Putin was a first deputy mayor of St Petersburg, the chairman of the St Petersburg External Relations Committee and the head of the Inter-Department Commission for Enterprises with Foreign Investments. He often worked in the sphere of encouraging foreign investment.

Although Surikov admitted he personally knew the Chechen leader Dzhokhar Dudayev "and others," he denied he was ever a member of the KGB. He is now in private business in Moscow, and said he is no longer interested in politics. When asked if he himself believes the Felix Report ferry scenario, Surikov said, "I don't know."

[18] "Charges Link Russian Military To Drug Trade," RFE/RL, June 8, 2001, Jean-Christophe Peuch.

[19] "Russian Troops Will Immediately Invade Estonia If Estonia Joins NATO; Interview with Russian Military Analyst Anton Surikov," *Postimees*, April 27, 1996, by Marko

Mihkelson in Moscow. Translation from the Estonian by the Press Spokesman's Office, Estonian Foreign Ministry.

Excerpts from the interview with Anton Surikov give an idea of the tensions existing between Russia and Estonia, as well as Surikov's political views:

MM: What could threaten Russia's security?

AS: First, if, for example, there were to develop a serious conflict between Estonians and Russians. That is very dangerous. Many Russians have developed an understanding of Estonia as a kind of a South African-style small fascist state which implements apartheid policies. Thank God, it has been possible to avoid conflicts. The other problem is connected without a doubt to NATO expansion. There are no other problems.

MM: But you don't really believe that a Russian invasion would occur without any resistance?

AS: Yes, of course. There will be a war in which individual armed groups will offer resistance. But all this will be limited to partisan activities. When it comes to the defense of Tallinn, for example, then you simply are not capable of organizing a Grozny type of defense.

Your problem is that, when the Russian troops come in, instantly society will divide between the two larger ethnic groups. Russians simply do not have anywhere to go other than to pick up a weapon and to fight against you.

MM: Are you speaking here as a private person or do you represent official positions as well?

AS: I'm speaking as a private person. At the same time, I know a number of people who work in high positions in various structures who think exactly the same way. After the collapse of the Warsaw Pact, we have fallen behind the West in conventional weapons. Therefore, our only means of balancing are nuclear weapons. By the way, during the Cold War, NATO used that tactic. Now that move is in the opposite direction. What could they do for you militarily? They could send a naval fleet, land some troops, but the most important is air support. What will we do? Give a nuclear counterstrike to NATO air force bases in Poland, Germany. To stop the navy we would strike the Danish straits. To stop the landing we could use miniature nuclear bombs. And in this connection the strike would come directly at Estonia or the bases of the landing force. But I hope that all this will not happen. If we are provoked and forced into a corner, then we have no other path but this.

[NOTE: Surikov would not say who contracted the Felix Group to write the reports. Presumably it was government authorities who wanted to paint Chechnya as a criminal state to support the unpopular war. The folllowing question from the interview suggests his clients were just such people. When the interview took place, Surikov was connected to a think tank called the Russian Defense Research Institute]:

MM: Who contracts studies from your institute and who, specifically ordered the one on military reform?

AS: Our private institute usually gets contracts from the Ministry of Defense, the State Defense Industry Committee and the Ministry of Atomic Energy. We also offer our work and studies to potential clients. The study on military reform was formally our own institute's initiative. No one paid a penny for it. At the same time it would be naive to say that we just did it. I cannot name specific names, but we were asked to deal with that subject. Those people work in the Ministry of Defense and other organizations. People who work in official positions cannot state such thoughts, because this would create an international scandal. We, however, are an independent institute and can proclaim whatever we want. We sent this concept as well as the defense doctrine published last fall to various ministries, the presidential and parliamentary structures. They were published in all the military newspapers. I can confirm that most of the representatives of the power structures are in agreement with our ideas.

[20] "a graph entitled *Folklore…*" *Fabula*, Journal of Folktale Studies. Issue 39, April 3, 1998.

See also: "Legends Connected with the Sinking of the Ferry *Estonia* on September 28, 1994." Eda Kalmre, Tartu.

For Kristapovich murder in the press, see Lauristin and Vihalemm, eds, p. 96. NOTE: As of 2006, the Kristapovich murder is still unsolved and the investigation is still ongoing, according to the Estonian Police Board.

[21] "The only item in the attachment that I am personally knowledgeable about is the disappearance of the computer. In this regard the anonymous fax is a total fabrication. Kitti Jurgens was away for a week on official business with [Estonian] Captain Germon Kesa. When she returned she found her laptop missing and reported it within 24 hours. She initially thought that someone may have borrowed it during her absence but that turned [out] not to be so. There was no sensitive info in the computer. In fact there was no classified info in the HQ at that time at all. The computer never turned up. My speculation is that it was probably sent directly to Moscow via the Russian embassy in Tallinn." Interview, Einseln.

Einseln said the submarine fax came to him through a friend, an Estonian-Swedish lawyer named Ago Kriisa. He had made several requests to meet Einseln in 1996 because he "had some information." When the two finally met in Estonia, Kriisa admitted he had worked for the Swedish intelligence services. He then handed Einseln the submarine fax.

The story has a postscript. Kriisa had fallen ill. One day, Einseln received a message on his answering machine. It was Kriisa, with a voice sounding like a man in the throes of death. "I have some very important information for you," Kriisa said with urgency. At the time, Einseln couldn't make it to Sweden. Kriisa passed away shortly after.

Later, Einseln spoke to Kriisa's family and asked if he could pick up whatever information it was that had been left for him. Einseln was invited to come to the house where all files were stored. But it turned out that Kriisa had deliberately burned all his files before he died.

Another attempt to explain the ferry sinking came from Swedish television. In the tradition of the Felix Report and the Submarine Fax, it bore some telltale signs of disinformation--lack of specifics and anonymity. Swedish TV ran an investigative program on the *Estonia* ferry disaster that included a Swedish Navy submariner who "claimed he was aboard a submarine ordered to tail the *Estonia* and that his vessel in turn was followed by a Russian submarine which fired on the ferry, causing her to sink."

"New bombshell as *Estonia* row goes on," *Lloyd's List*, December 16 2000 by Nick Savvides.

Aside from committing an act of war against Estonia, a Russian sub firing a torpedo would leave overwhelming technical evidence. A torpedo would have destroyed the hull. Confetti-like debris and oil slicks from the ferry would be floating for days. The sound of a torpedo explosion would've been picked up by an array of underwater acoustic equipment.

[22] Einseln was never shown the phone record. He also said he had been at his home in California when the ferry sank and first heard about the disaster on CNN.

[23] Einseln's televised statements came at the end of 1995, when the Estonian presidential election campaign was about to get underway. In the following weeks, Einseln was arrested on charges that he failed to adequately supervise officers under his command who had been convicted of smuggling handguns. Einseln believes the arrest was linked a circle surrounding Lennart Meri, who was running for president at the time. This group, Einseln believes, engineered the arrest because he himself had been courted as a presidential candidate. The group did not want a potential spoiler candidate to ruin Meri's chances.

Einseln's trial dragged on curiously long without any satisfactory explanation. In April 2003, he was acquitted of the charges and his arrest declared illegal by the court.

[24] The Estonian Security Police kept a list of all former agents and every applicant for Estonian citizenship was cross-checked. In adddition, in 1992, the Security Police purchased files on some 500 KGB agents. "Estonia Secretly bought KGB Files," RFE/RL, August 7, 1997, citing Postimees on August 6.

[25] Interview, Laar.

[26] Another *Estonia* detour concerns a reprint of a sonar photograph that appeared on an *Estonia* conference brochure in 2000. The image has caused confusion and lasting misunderstanding. Some have claimed that the sonar photograph shows the shape of an object resembling the bow visor sitting on top of the sunken ferry. This interpretation has led to theories that the bow visor was attached to the ferry when it sank and later blown off by a team of divers. However, in the tradition of disinformation, the reproduced sonar photograph has no date or source.

The bow visor was hoisted to the surface in November 1994 and brought to Finland, then moved to a Swedish island, where it rests today. The sonar photograph first appeared six years after the visor was already sitting on land. Whether the sonar photograph was intentionally introduced to sew discord or an innocent mistake is unclear.

STRATEGIC COMPASSION

[1] "Remains Identified Via DNA As Those of 2 9/11 Hijackers," Associated Press, February 28, 2003.

[2] "The 94 bodies were recovered in an arduous operation that began when the *Kursk* was raised from the sea floor in October [2001] and transferred to dry dock in Roslyakovo

near the northern port city of Murmansk. The unprecedented operation...[fulfilled] President Vladimir Putin's promise to grieving relatives that the lost crew would be buried on land." "All 94 Bodies Of *Kursk* Crew Identified," AFP, March 1, 2002.

NOTE: All recovered Kursk victims were positively identified, despite the destructive forces of the explosion on board.

The *USS Greeneville-Ehime Maru* collision occurred February 2001; Gujarat earthquake, January 2001; China Airlines crash, May 2002; Gulf Air crash, August 2000; Tanzania mine disaster, June 2002.

[3] Human remains from the *Titanic* could not be recovered in the early 20th century due to technical limitations of the time. The wreck lies in the extreme depth of 3800 meters (12,500 feet).

One exception, more recently, involved the U.S.S.R. In 1983, when a Soviet military fighter jet shot down commercial jet Korean Airlines flight 007, the Soviets took control of the crash site in the sea. Moscow refused to allow the entry of U.S. or Japanese search-and-rescue teams into its territorial waters and seriously harassed them, even when their ships were in international waters. The passengers' bodies were never recovered. The Kremlin refused to allow recovery in order to protect the sensitive military installations of the Soviet state. The KAL 007 shootdown had probably been the only contemporary incident in which victims of a civilian accident at sea were discarded as a matter of official policy--until the *Estonia* sank.

[4] "Psychological Responses to a marine disaster during a recoil phase: Experiences from the *Estonia* Shipwreck," *British Journal of Medical Psychology*; 1996 June, Vol 69(2), 147-153, Taiminen, Tero J., Tuominen, Taina.

[5] "Relatives March to Demand Raising of Sunken Ferry" Associated Press, November 17, 1994.

[6] Interview Calamnius.

[7] Interview Tidstrom.

NOTE: In Sweden, transport comes under the Ministry of Industry, Employment and Communications. In this book, "Ministry of Transport" is used as shorthand.

Mona Sahlin, head of Sweden's Ministry of Transport from 1998-2002, has categorically refused to discuss any aspect of the catastrophe with the media.

The Swedish government's attitude toward relatives who wanted the remains recovered is crisply summed up by Anders Iacobaeus, in 1996 head of legal affairs for the Swedish Ministry of Transport and Communications and a top aide to Transport Minister Ines Uusmann: "I understand the desire of people who wanted to recover bodies during the first months after the accident," said Iacobaeus. "But those who want to do it now--I find it, well, sick. You have to let bygones be bygones." "Relatives Recoil at Swedish Plan for Sunken Ferry," *Los Angeles Times*, May 5, 1996, by Dean E. Murphy.

[8] "Two attempts were made..." BNS, July 3, 1995.

"'morally atrocious'..." "Private Initiative to Retrieve Bodies in Baltic Sea Disaster" Associated Press, January 10, 1995, by Katarina Bjarvall.

[9] "Sweden Doubts *Estonia* Blast Conclusion," *Albuquerque Journal* (New Mexico) from their website ABQjournal.com, November 2, 2000, By Joseph Ditzler. NOTE: The forbidden square of water lies in the middle of a heavily-traveled fishing area and shipping route. An estimated 5000 ships per day sail on the Baltic Sea.

[10] Interview Tidstrom.

[11] "deliberately avoided blessing the site…" Interview, Archbishop Weman.
"bodies outside the wreck..." The ROV from the *One Eagle* dive filmed "roughly 8-10 remains of human bodies…[outside the wreck] scattered over and within the debris. The remains were in varying states: Some were skeletons, while others were still wearing clothing which was almost intact." "Report on the diving expedition in the Baltic Sea to the wreck of the passenger ferry ESTONIA from August 19th to August 31st 2000," By Gregg Bemis and Jutta Rabe, p. 3.

Bemis added in an interview: "I saw several of the 'remains' live at the time we were scanning the bottom with the ROV...Several others in the group also saw these remains and can corroborate the facts. We of course told the heads of the victim's committee, who were quite upset. We were very careful not to disturb these remains in any way."

Additionally, from Rabe, p.174-180: "--[T]here were about ten to fifteen bodies scattered on the seafloor amid all sorts of luggage and items from the ship. Most of the bodies were already skeletons. The ROV's camera showed us two skeletons lying close together, one of normal size, the other somewhat smaller. The breastbone on the larger one had caved in, a suitcase lying next to its lower leg…The ROV bumped into another body, a man, he was wearing ankle-high shoes, light-colored jeans and a white shirt, his arms folded over his chest in a protective gesture. The whole extent of this tragedy came flooding back into my consciousness anew…We saw another body through the ROV camera. Quite clearly recognizable as a man. He only had on a T-shirt and pants. His head was missing, his body gnawed by fish.

Moreover, human remains have washed ashore despite government promises in December 1994 that the Rockwater divers sealed the ferry after completion of their dive.

In 1995, a woman's body was found on the coast of the Sorve peninsula of Estonia's Saaremaa Island, believed to come from the *Estonia* ferry. A year later, near the Tammisaari archipelago in Finland, a boy found arm bones believed to belong to an Estonia victim. The bones of a woman found on the coast of the Estonian island of Gappa, near Paldiski, proved to belong to a Swedish victim.

See: "Corpse Washed Ashore in Estonia May be From Sunken Ferry," BNS, March 2, 1995; "Remains of Possible Ferry *Estonia* Victim Found in Finland," BNS, July 6, 1996; "Bones Found in Estonia Belong to *Estonia* Ferry Victim," BNS, May 15, 1996.

[12] Interview Bemis.

[13] Interview Tidstrom.

[14] "Return to the Western World: Cultural and Political Perspectives on the Estonian Post-Communist Transition," Tartu University Press, 1997, Chapter: "Contexts in Transition," Marju Lauristin and Peeter Vihalemm, eds.

[15] Interview Lauristin.

[16] "Even if it is technically possible ..." *Reuters*, October 20, 1998, by Vibeke Laroi.
"The sea from time to time..."   "Vanishing captain holds key to riddle of disaster," *The Independent* (London) October 2, 1994, by Andrew Higgins.

See also: "Estonia's Meri refuses to accept Swedish panel's stance on ferry victims," BNS, November 12, 1998; "Angry Haitians blame voodoo for ferry sinking," CNN website www.cnn.com, September 11, 1997.

NOTE: Two requests to Meri's spokesman to interview Meri for this book were declined.

[17] Interview Mearns.

[18] "Raise the *M/S Estonia!*" http://heiwaco.tripod.com/salvage.htm, website of Anders Björkman.

[19] "TWA recovery work exemplifies Navy's capabilities," *Navy News & Undersea Technology*, February 17, 1997.

NOTE: The wreckage of the 93-foot section of TWA Flight 800 has not only been salvaged but reassembled and now serves as a teaching tool for air crash investigators at the NTSB Academy in Virginia.

[20] Interview Alenius. Baltic Sea marine life on average is proportionally less than sea life in the world's oceans. In the area where the *Estonia* sits, at 50 meters depth, oxygen content is 8 milliliter per liter. At 80 meters, the figure is 1 milliliter per liter.

[21] Interview Downs. Downs stressed he was making a general comment and is not familiar with the specific condition of the human remains in the *Estonia* ferry.

[22] If no dental X-rays are available, forensic dentistry has developed new techniques that could contribute to the identification process. For example, a computer analysis of digital images of the recovered victim's teeth compared to a digitized photograph of the person smiling.

[23] Stolorow added: "Rapid progress has been made in the detection of DNA in highly degraded bone and tissue since the 9/11 disaster. Significant improvements have been made in conventional STR marker analysis, mtDNA analysis and the newest--the use of SNP markers to detect DNA in highly degraded samples. [Yet] in practice, nearly half of the samples from the World Trade Center still did not yield interpretable DNA profiles by any of the methods refined for the highly degraded WTC samples."

Stolorow also estimated DNA testing to cost $100 to $300 per sample range with mtDNA being the most expensive of the three DNA testing methods. Interview, Stolorow.

Advances in forensic identification are continually emerging. Improvements in DNA-extraction techniques have allowed extraction of DNA from 83 percent of bone samples that previously turned up nothing. See: "Tech May ID More 9/11 Victims," *Wired* online, December 20, 2005, by Randy Dotinga.

[24] "Ferry Salvage," Associated Press, October 5, 1994 by Matti Huuhtanen; "Sunken Ferry Must Be Surfaced, Estonian Minister Says," BNS, October 5, 1994.

[25] "Efter *Estonia*," Statens offentliga utredningar, 1996:189, Inrikesdepartementet, Rapport av Utredningen for vagledning efter Estoniakatastrofen, [summary in English] p. 196.

[26] Interviews Örn and Franson.

[27] "The Economics of Dealing with Despair," Lloyd's List, August 16, 1991.

[28] "Efter Estonia" p. 196.

[29] Interview, Coe.

[30] "Divers Tell of Retrieving Kursk Bodies," *Moscow Times*, November 15, 2000.

[31] "The Survivors," *The Daily Telegraph*, *Telegraph* Magazine, March 8, 1997.

[32] Interview Franson.

[33] Interview Örn. NOTE: The ethical board made no public comments on the unfairness of their unilateral judgments. Moreover, key questions were never subject to vigorous public debate: Why should efforts to recover human remains and forensically identify them be done in Europe and the U.S. and not in Scandinavia? Why indeed take up one set of remains from a plane that fell into the sea and not from a sunken ferry? Are ethical decisions based on the category of transport?

[34] "Swedish panel recommends to recover remains of *Estonia* victims," BNS, November 12, 1998.

[35] Ibid.

[36] Interviews, Paeorg and Andresson.

[37] Interviews Vare and Paeorg.

[38] "horror movie..." *Eesti Päevaleht*, November 13, 1998.
NOTE: Bodies submerged in water tend to bloat due to gases released from bacteria eating the flesh. Bacteria that normally live inside the large intestine feed on the decaying flesh and excrete gases--carbon dioxide and sulfur dioxide--which inflate some

body parts, mainly the face, abdomen and male genitals. But this happens in a relatively short time frame, 1-3 months after drowning. The Analysis Group was recommending recovery four years after the sinking. No one pointed out these facts. Daniel Vaarik, former press secretary to Estonian Prime Minister Siim Kallas, told the author that Estonians even thought raising the ship from 80 meters depth was technically impossible. This was among the gross misunderstandings that Sweden did not try to help clarify.

Interview Örn.

"Estonia's opposition puts Sweden in predicament," BNS, Wednesday January 27, 1999.

[39] "Government Decision on M.S. *Estonia*," Press release statement. Swedish Ministry of Industry, Employment and Communications (Naringsdepartementet), February 11, 1999.

[40] Interview Örn.

[41] Interview Weman. "The Church was arguing that the sea is a tomb. But we were paralyzed by different opinions of different groups...If the Church said yes or no, some groups would be offended...Those with a connection to the sea could more accept that the sea is a tomb. Those in Eastern Sweden do not believe it. They argued that [authorities] brought up bodies from the collapsed [Alexander L. Kielland] Norwegian oil platform [in 1980], why not in this case?"

[42] US Embassy correspondence, July 14, 2000, Classification: "Sensitive," From: American Embassy Stockholm "Olson," To: Secretary of State, Washington DC, Subject: "Objection to 'Estonia' shipwreck dive." The embassy had also received several faxes from groups representing relatives and survivors in support of the dive. In addition, apparently someone in the upper levels of government--either U.S. or Swedish--was curious as to what Sweden was hiding. A highly-placed official, whose name is still classified today, gave official blessing for the Bemis dive:
"--[P]ost also received a call from [NAME DELETED] He is generally supportive of an exploratory dive. We did not mention this conversation to the MFA [Swedish Ministry of Foreign Affairs] at the caller's request."

[43] "Efter *Estonia*," p. 194.

CONCLUSION: A WORK IN PROGRESS

[1] The NSA response letter is reproduced in Appendix V.

[2] The Finnish Navy has a sonar surveillance system that was deployed on the seabed of the south littoral of Finland. The technology used should be sufficient for good acoustic acquisition and a natural assumption is that the NSA receives the intelligence gleaned from this equipment. U.S. intelligence sources would not comment on the existence of SOSUS in the Baltic Sea or on SIGINT assistance from officially neutral countries.

[3] Submarine communication may have been completely unrelated to the *Estonia* catastrophe, but the region was already volatile, and revealing that a sub was simply in the area would fuel accusations.

According to "Russian Strategic Nuclear Forces," MIT Press, 2001, Pavel Podvis, ed., p.280, a sub rarely makes radio contact. At scheduled times the submarine may surface to periscope depth and deploy its antenna to receive information. In other instances, the commander may radio when he needs help to stop another sub from trailing his own, if a crewmember should die, or in the case of a major accident.

[4] Swedish forces may also have been jamming *One Eagle* communications. It could be that the NSA picked up the signal jamming, though there is still no compelling reason to formalize it by writing a report.

[5] Interview, Schmill.

[6] Interview, Angstrom.
See also: "Money! Guns! Corruption!" *Forbes*, July 7, 1997, by Pranay Gupte and Rahul Singh.
"Carl-Fredrik Algernon, director of Sweden's arms agency, a key figure in a Bofors inquiry that had been secretly initiated by the Swedish police, fell or was pushed to his death before an incoming subway train at Stockholm's Central Station. His death was ruled a suicide, a verdict that almost no one in Sweden accepts."

NOTE: Every country has scandals and Sweden probably has had fewer than other comparable countries. But Sweden has been highly efficient at hiding scandals. Others that were revealed more than four decades after they occurred include the 60,000 forced sterilizations of Swedish citizens from 1935 until 1976 and inhumane dental experiments from 1946 to 1951 conducted on hundreds of "mentally deficient" Swedes, who were made to let their teeth rot after being force-fed sticky toffee. See, for example, "Eugenics scandal rocks Scandinavia," *Manchester Guardian Weekly*, p. 1, August 31, 1997; "Inferior" Swedes force-fed candy in dental study 1946-1951," AFP, September 22, 1997.

[7] Interview, Heyman.. "We cannot just accept that an accident with nearly 900 dead is left without any reasonable explanation," Heyman added. During Heyman's presentation, a former advisor to Carl Bildt was present and he aggressively challenged all of Heyman's points. "Every statement I made, every fact I could present, was questioned." Heyman retired from parliament in 2002.

[8] The nuclear launch incident was mentioned in Chapter 5, Alternative Scenarios.
"Finnair confirms unexplained missile fly-by in 1994," *Helsinki Sanomat*, January 13, 2003.
The U.S. government also opposed Alexander Einseln's decision to head the Estonian armed forces due to--the familiar phrase alluding to Russia--"sensitivities in the region."

POSTSCRIPT A: THE STRUGGLE TO EXPLAIN THE SWIFT SINKING

[1] BNS, November 12, 1996.

[2] Interview, Schager.

[3] Final Report, 13.6, "Flooding of the accommodation and sinking of the vessel," pp. 181-183.

[4] According to the ship's blueprints, on Decks 4, 5 and 6 the *Estonia* had 160 cabin windows measuring 0.20cm x 0.40cm and 184 windows measuring 0.30cm x 0.80cm.

[5] Rockwater Survey Report, p. 8.

[6] Final Report, 13.6, "Flooding of the accommodation and sinking of the vessel," pp. 181-183.
The Independent Fact Group in Sweden has also pointed out the intentional vagueness of the broken window theory: "It is also remarkable that no doors or windows have been tested regarding strength to withstand waves. No other record of strength is shown, but still the commission states that this is how the water came in to the ship." http://est.jbn.nu/factgroup/est/reports.html

[7] A debris field can be likened to a crude sketch of the a ferry's final moments and could either bolster or diminish the JAIC's proposed chain of events. But for unexplained reasons, the debris field was left unexamined.

[8] Final Report, 13.6, "Flooding of the accommodation and sinking of the vessel," p. 183.

[9] Interview, Carlqvist: "If they were open and underwater and the inflow was unimpeded they could account for, say, not more than 10 tons/minute because of hydro-dynamic effects. The same problem you encounter when drinking from a beer bottle...So that inflow was marginal, indeed. More important is that those openings got underwater at a list > 37 degrees, probably around 40 degrees. That means the ship should capsize before those shafts came under water, as the critical list according to the Final Report was 37 degrees."
The ventilator theory has also been discredited by Hummel, head of the GGE, for similar reasons. In 2005, the Swedish government launched a new investigation into why the ship went under so quickly, presumably because the ventilator theory could not be possible in light of the facts.

[10] "Ferry sinking not caused by bomb, investigators say," AFP, September 24, 1999. "Uno Laur, chief of the international investigation commission, said the German shipyard continues to question the findings in order to escape responsibility for the construction faults of the ship. 'The shipyard has many versions, and it seems it will continue producing them,' Laur told *Postimees* daily. 'The only one missing is the UFO version,' he added."

[11] "Both lifts had only non-watertight doors to starboard...the sills of the sliding doors had a total height of 230 mm." GGE, 21.3.1, "Reports from Deck 1 - Passenger Area"
Norske Veritas Report on *Estonia* 22 November 1994, p. 29.

[12] Another argument is that if the ramp was yanked wide open like JAIC claims, then it should be moveable, especially in light of the ship's sinking motion. The *Estonia's* stern slid into the water first and the bow lifted into the sky. After a moment, the ferry fell forward into the water in a nearly upside down position. As it sank to the seafloor, a freely-swinging ramp would have been forced wide open by the falling motion. The principle is familiar to anyone who has extended his arm out a car window while driving. The ship settled onto the bottom of the Baltic Sea in its final position at 120 degrees starboard. The cardeck ramp would then lightly fall into place.
A wide-open ramp should be freely moveable. Given the extra buoyancy of water, even the pull of a diver's hand should move it. But in August 2000, when a diver from the *One Eagle* expedition tried to open the ramp, it wouldn't budge. He had to take off his side gas tank in order to pop his head into the cardeck, Bemis said.

[13] "The Mistakes by the Crew are Suppressed," *Dagens Nyheter*, December 3, 1997, by Bengt Schager, translated from Swedish. "The investigation after the accident shows that the vessel was loaded without conformity to the rules. The distance between vehicles was approximately 10cm instead of the required 60cm. Passage between cars for fire extinguishing would have been impossible."
See also: GGE, 17.1 "Loading."
See also: Testimonies in the GGE Report of crew members Margus Treu, Jaak Mullo and Valdur Matt. The crew descriptions of cardeck loading were backed up by truck drivers who survived.

[14] "The vessel's trim had changed since the departure from Tallinn from down by the stern to down by the bow because of the [water-filled] full visor, and the water having entered the cardeck via the damaged bow ramp and other openings..." GGE, "Summary Report."

[15] "*The Naval Architect*," September 1998, pp. 13-14.

[16] "Tysta Leken. Varfor sjonk ESTONIA?" ["Silent Game. Why did the ESTONIA Sink?"], Stockholm: (Fischer & Co), 2001, pp. 135-140, by Knut Carlqvist. Translated from Swedish.
Carlqvist added: "Five survivors saw the visor swing, hanging on the actuator [arm], from 01.05 (Mats Hillerström) to 01.30 (Pierre Thiger). They generally believed it to be a stabilizer fin, moving in and out. But they describe it moving laterally...and they all place it at the bow, while the fin was situated midships. It was white, 'like a big door.' It could only be the visor."
Late detachment scenario:
Carlqvist believes that if the ramp had been pulled open, it would follow the visor all the way down to the bottom. Wrenched open, the ramp would smash with violent force against the forepeak deck. "The impact would have blown the partly defect ramp

hinges to smithereens. [However] the ramp locks are undamaged.

"Most likely, the visor hung from the ramp, supported by the actuator, in phase 1, up to say 50 or 60 degrees list, then it must have slid off. The actuator became fully drawn out and bent in phase 2, when the visor fell off the ramp. When the support from the iceknife was lost, it was torn loose and sank straight down."

According to the German investigators, the ramp was misaligned well before the night of the accident because of a collapsed bearing on the port outer hinge. Due to this misalignment, the port lower securing bolt was unable to extend fully while the port upper bolt was just touching the inside of the ramp pocket. The result was that the crew had to secure the ramp shut in a makeshift way with ropes.

Carlqvist adds: "The ropes no doubt would stand the pulling a lot better than the locks, as you don't have the same problem with fatigue in ropes. They give way a bit instead of snapping. That explains why the ramp could be slightly open on the wreck."

Anders Björkman has proposed that the visor tore off as the ship lay on its side. The visor wasn't designed to absorb sideways wave hits: "--[W]hy did the visor fall off? When [the] *Estonia* heeled over, the flare angle between starboard bow plate and the water became almost zero, so when the pitching ship hit the water it headed straight into the waves with a sideways (transverse) impact load on the visor that tore it off. This sideways impact load was probably between six and 10 times bigger than the total transverse design load (assuming she was upright).

"Letter: Time to look at a new theory on 'Estonia'" by Anders Björkman, *Lloyd's List*, August 2, 1996.

The Independent Fact Group in Sweden proposed that the visor fell off and only damaged the forward ramp: "During the loss of the visor the ramp was bent forward and to starboard, leaving an opening in the top of the ramp of approximately 40 cm. The locking to the ramp was damaged and broke, but the ramp was held in place by the starboard side lower locking that still is in locked position. This together with the damages on the ramp that could only [have] been done if the ramp was closed when the visor fell off, is the strongest proof that the ramp was mainly closed during the sinking." http://est.jbn.nu/factgroup/fgframe_eng.html

[17] Apparently the JAIC initially believed that the ramp had indeed only partially opened, yet later the story was changed. According to "Ferry's bow door ripped off at sea," *Manchester Guardian Weekly*, October 9, 1994, by Greg McIvor and Rebecca Smithers: "The three-nation inquiry said the inner ramp behind the 60-ton visor door was exposed to the sea and was prised open about a meter, causing the influx of water. 'The water inflow through the partly dislodged forward ramp has been of a sufficient magnitude to result in a lack of stability and the capsizing of the ferry,' the investigation team said in a statement."

NOTE: The JAIC's computer-generated animation of the ferry's final minutes has no physics underpinning it. Frames from the animation are on p. 177 in the Final Report.

[18] GGE, 21.2.4, "Summary of testimonies by system engineer Henrik Sillaste."

Moreover, former JAIC member Bengt Schager, who interviewed crew members, also said that the crew had been briefed before their interviews with the JAIC. "We didn't

have the force to bend arms...They probably had more to tell than they really told. The interviews were done through a translator in Gothenburg [Sweden] airport. They flew in from Tallinn. Afterwards we learned they had been briefed by our Estonian counterparts before they came. They happened to say so. So we didn't really act as one commission because the Estonian part was really suspicious of the Finns and the Swedes. So it was like three teams. If you are one commission, there's no need for pre-briefing [of crew]. [During the crew interviews] was the only time when I saw [Estonian] Andi Meister [head of the JAIC], in full captain's uniform--when we interviewed the crew. He was their boss, the headmaster in Estonia."
Interview, Schager.

[19] The German Group has fortunately attached to their report copies of all the original statements they could obtain.

[20] Technically, eight passenger survivors from Deck 1 saw water if the statement by Yasmina Weidinger is included. She states that her cabin mate Daniel Svensson yelled about water in the corridor upon leaving the cabin. However, when Svensson gave his own statement, he did not speak about water on Deck 1.

[21] GGE, Section 21.3.1, entitled "Reports from Deck 1 - Passenger Area"
Reintamm, Enclosure 21.3.1.289
Övberg, Enclosure 12.4.2.151
Wachtmeister, Enclosure 17.2.232, also see addendum attached to his statement.
Juhanson, Enclosure 21.3.1.291
Arak Enclosure 21.3.1.290
Weidinger statement made on 29.09.94 - Enclosure 21.3.1.296; Second statement made on 04.10.94 - Enclosure 21.3.1.297. NOTE: As mentioned above, Svensson in his testimony did not talk about water on the first deck, though his cabin mate, Weidinger, said he had yelled about water in the corridor. Therefore Svensson is not counted in this listing. The GGE Report includes Svensson and they put the total number of first deck passengers who saw water before running upstairs at nine.
Stern Enclosure 21.3.1.286
Raba, Enclosures 21.3.1.292 / 21.3.1.293. NOTE: Taavi Raba's claim about water on Deck 1 is contested by Tuomo Karppinen. In 1999, Karppinen stated that he had contacted Raba, who then denied the "water wall" description made in his 1994 statement just after the disaster. "More thoughts on the *Estonia* Accident," *The Naval Architect*, July/August 1999, pp. 10, 12, by Tuomo Karppinen, Mikael Huss, Klaus Rahka.

However, incidents recollected years later have been influenced by discussions and by the media, and the singular effort by a former government commission member to contact Raba could result in an eagerness to comply.
But the main reason to suspect Raba's later denial of the curtain of water is that he was a crew member. As mentioned earlier, Estonian state officials had threatened crew members not to give independent accounts that could harm state interests.

[22] Final Report, p. 68.
GGE, Chapter 41, item 20: "The JAIC mentions that one passenger saw a 'thin

trickle of water' in the corridor. This was meant to be Carl-Erik Reintamm, who actually saw a lot of water under pressure rushing through the corridor. As the JAIC spoke to none of the 1st deck passenger survivors they cannot know better. No doubt, they should have gone deeper into the matter, because water on the 1st deck penetrating from the [zero]-deck [where the sauna compartment is], under pressure indicates one or more flooded compartments of the [zero]-deck."

[23] Final Report, "Summary of Testimonies by Survivors," 6.1 Introduction, p. 61.

[24] "*Estonia*: Hard Facts and Realities," *The Naval Architect*, September 1998, by Tuomo Karppinen, Mikael Huss, Klaus Rahka; *The Naval Architect*, July/August 1999.

[25] *The Naval Architect*, September 1998, p.17. NOTE: Karppinen writes that there were 20 survivors on Deck 1. There were 24 survivors, specifically 3 crew members and 21 passengers. See: GGE, Chapter 41, item 20.

[26] See also: "Testimonies of Survivors show that the Commission is wrong," in "Lies and Truths about the *M/V Estonia* Accident," Anders Björkman, Section 2.12, http://heiwaco.tripod.com/news.htm: "The Commission states in the Final Report...that water first flooded the car deck in the superstructure and that this water flowed down to deck no. 1 and alerted passengers. The water must then have flowed through locked and closed fire doors with 25 cms high sills..."

POSTSCRIPT B: HISTORICAL SPOTLIGHT

[1] The *Jan Heweliusz* was one-seventh the tonnage of the *Estonia*. The comparatively few windows and corridors should have resulted in the ferry filling up faster than larger and more complex *Estonia*. Nonetheless, the *Heweliusz* still floated because its hull was intact.

[2] Report: "*M/V Herald of Free Enterprise* Formal Investigation," Report of Court No. 8074, U.K. Department of Transport, September 1987, p. 7.

[3] Ibid, p. 68. "It was and is impossible to quantify the final sinking of the vessel. The temporary but quite considerable buoyancy of the deckhouses may have allowed the vessel to continue to move for some appreciable time while nearly upon her beam ends. We do not consider that a detailed explanation of this part of the sinking is material."

[4] A computer simulation concluded that a time of well over 60 seconds was required between the start of the *Herald's* capsize and the final resting at past 90 degrees. Other researchers put it at 3 minutes. In any case, the rotation was fast enough to suggest a continuous, natural turn to an upsidedown position was underway.

[5] *Express Samina* sinking: "Ferry Disaster: The Ferry - 'This was an accident waiting to happen,'" *The Independent*, September 28, 2000, by Terri Judd and Charles Arthur.

[6] Information about the *Nakhimov* sinking: Oberg, p. 92-93; an interview with St Petersburg author David Chapkis, who has written a book about the *Admiral Nakhimov*; "Maritime Casualties, 1963-1996," Hooke.

NOTE: Like the *Estonia*, the *Nakhimov* catastrophe happened so suddenly and the ship sank so quickly, many people didn't have time to make it out of their bottom deck cabins. And like the *Estonia*, the *Nakhimov* investigation reflected the Soviet government policy of secrecy. In the end, no one was blamed. Relatives of the victims and survivors were never given a complete explanation of the tragedy. Like the *Estonia*, the Soviet ship still lies on the bottom, several miles from port.

[7] The torpedo hits were in the bow, amidships and the engine room. "The Damned Don't Drown," Naval Institute Press, (Annapolis, Maryland), 1973, Bluejacket Books, by A.V. Sellwood.

CPSIA information can be obtained
at www.ICGtesting.com
Printed in the USA
LVHW052004071019
633444LV00012B/231/P

9 781492 778363